HARVARD HISTORICAL STUDIES

PUBLISHED UNDER THE DIRECTION
OF THE DEPARTMENT OF HISTORY

FROM THE INCOME OF
THE PAUL REVERE FROTHINGHAM BEQUEST

VOLUME LXVII
Oscar Handlin, Editor

Dr. Samuel Gridley Howe in His Early Thirties
From an oil portrait by Jane Stuart, daughter of Gilbert Stuart

Samuel Gridley Howe
Social Reformer

1801–1876

✺

Harold Schwartz

Harvard University Press   *Cambridge*   1956

To
Mr. and Mrs. Sam Jacobs
without whose love and encouragement
nothing would have been accomplished

Foreword

What meaning can the career of Samuel Gridley Howe have for a world racked by a sense of doom? He lived in an age of faith when science directed reason and showed the way to a better life for all. Progress was the watchword. Of its inevitability there was no doubt.

Mid-twentieth-century intellectuals regard such faith with a wearied air. Nothing is inevitable they say, as they write long essays to prove it. Progress? Instances of those who have taken one step forward only to fall two steps behind are all around us. We seem to spend most of our time just trying to keep what we have; who can think of progress? According to them, the doctrine of progress is a chimera. Things are getting worse all the time, and have been for centuries. And so they write their studies of history and their declines of civilization, leaving it to the younger men, generally eighteen and up, periodically to repair the damage their pessimism has generated. And so the world staggers on, faithless and rootless, getting worse, because everybody says it cannot get better.

How Howe would have raged! He knew how to make the world better, and he cries to us from Mount Auburn to let him show us that integrity and morality are the secret. Bolster them with firmness, and a refusal to compromise with evil, and you have it. That prescription may not meet our needs, but it worked for him.

Now that the work is completed, the author would like to thank the many librarians who assisted him, particularly those of the Houghton Library, the Perkins School for the Blind, the Massachusetts Historical Society, and the Boston Public Library. Without their suggestions he would have missed many valuable sources.

Mr. Arthur M. Schlesinger, Sr. comes in for special thanks. He has read the text, made many valuable suggestions as to style and organization, and encouraged the author over many of the rough spots a writer encounters doing his first book. At all times, he guided the author's attention to what seemed the unlikely goal of publication. The author is proud to have fulfilled his old professor's faith in him.

Kent, Ohio   Harold Schwartz
July 1956

Contents

Samuel Gridley Howe

Social Reformer

I

Early Years

The naïveté of nineteenth-century America is as touching as it is refreshing. How wonderful it would be if we could end our days convinced of the progress, goodness, and perfectibility of man. Samuel Gridley Howe was of that happy generation that did. He saw good triumphant over evil because he willed it so, and by his efforts helped bring it about. To him the doctrine of progress did not mean complacent acceptance of life as it was. Rather it spurred him to vigorous efforts. Progress comes through struggle, and man must fight for his rights if he is to deserve them. For half a century he answered almost every appeal for help from the helpless, and shared in almost every fight in their behalf, sometimes leading and at other times following. Only one thing mattered to him, contributing his "mite" to the cause, whatever it was at the moment.

I

Samuel Gridley Howe, the second son of Joseph Neals Howe and Patty Gridley, was born in the family home on Pleasant Street, Boston, November 10, 1801.[1] The Howes were an old Boston family claiming descent from Abraham Howe, who settled at Roxbury in 1636 or 1638.[2] Edward Compston Howe, Samuel's grand-

---

[1] Julia Ward Howe, *Memoir of Dr. Samuel Gridley Howe* (Boston, 1876), p. 2.
[2] Mary H. Graves to Laura E. Richards, Nov. 8, 1903, Howe Papers, Houghton Library, Harvard.

father, was, according to family legend, one of the "Indians" at the Boston Tea Party, and the boy's great-uncle, Richard Gridley, was the engineer who designed the Patriot fortifications on Bunker Hill.[3] Joseph Howe was a prosperous maker of ropes and cordage who had his ropewalk near the site of the present Public Gardens. He was a kindly man and indulged his children in their wants. As the house was well supplied with servants to do one's bidding, there was no need to learn habits of thrift and conservation, but this lush existence ended with the War of 1812. Father Howe sold cordage to the federal government for which he accepted payment in treasury notes, "hoping that the sacrifice he was obliged to make in disposing of them would be remembered by a 'grateful country'! & all that sort of nonsense," the son later explained.[4] His losses ruined the old man, and the family was in straitened circumstances for the remainder of Howe's minority.

Otherwise, Howe's boyhood was normal. He was mischievous and adventurous. The lure of Back Bay was irresistible, and he was more than once fished out, suffering from submersion and exposure. He played with firearms and bore scars of powder burns all his life. There was apparently nothing in his little world that he was not eager to investigate.

Even as a child, Howe showed the traits of character which became prominent in the man, namely, pugnacity and protection of the weak. He delighted to take the part of smaller children against the town bullies, and fought valiantly in their behalf, although, as he said later, "quite as much for the glory to myself, as the good to them."[5]

The Howes were in those days Jeffersonian Republicans in a city overwhelmingly Federalist, and the young boy, while still at the Latin School, learned early in life the penalty which bigoted societies exact of nonconformists. When Samuel insisted on clinging to

[3] Graves to Julia Ward Howe, Oct. 4, 1898; Graves to Richards, March 24, 1905, Howe Papers, Houghton.

[4] Howe to Horace Mann, 1857, pp. 4–5, Howe Papers, Houghton. This is a long autobiographical letter running to over twenty-five pages.

[5] Howe to Horace Mann, 1857, p. 3, Howe Papers, Houghton.

his father's politics, the Federalist boys kicked him down the stairs and out into School Street, while he fought back all the way.[6]

II

Unable to send more than one of his three sons to college, Joseph Howe, still smarting under his losses, decided which one would go by having them read from the Bible. Sam read best, and in September 1817 the fortunate youth took up residence in Providence, Rhode Island. Politics had even decided the college he would attend. As Harvard was too firmly under Federalist control, the boy was sent to Brown.[7]

When Howe entered it, Brown was a small provincial college flourishing under the kindly ministrations of Asa Messer. Its resources were meager, consisting of one building, a library of less than 5000 volumes, and a student body of about 150. Its endowment, supplied mostly by Nicholas Brown whose name the College of Rhode Island had adopted, was between $14,000 and $15,000, yielding an income of about $900 annually. The rest of its finances came from the students who paid $16 a year.[8] Its curriculum was the traditional classical course current at American colleges of the time: Latin and Greek, rhetoric, and moral and natural philosophy. There is reason to believe that French was also taught, but on an informal basis, since Howe was able to speak that tongue when he arrived in Greece.[9]

Unfortunately, Howe failed to get as much out of his studies as he might have. Colleges in those days were marked by rowdy undergraduate behavior, which probably stemmed from the youth of the students and the lack of satisfactory extracurricular activities to keep

[6] Howe to Horace Mann, 1857, pp. 5–6, Howe Papers, Houghton.

[7] Samuel G. Howe, *Journals and Letters*, Laura E. Richards, ed. (Boston, 1906), I, 15.

[8] Walter C. Bronson, *The History of Brown University, 1764–1914* (Providence, 1914), pp. 156–176.

[9] *The Laws of Rhode-Island College Enacted by the Fellows and Trustees* (Providence, 1803), pp. 5–6; contains the curriculum. My source for the teaching of French at Brown is Mr. H. B. Van Hoesen, the Librarian, who told me so in an interview, June 2, 1949.

them occupied. A student's manhood seemed to be proven by the number of scrapes he got into. In December 1817, the boys burned a building. Two years later they carried off the doors of the chapel and dining hall.[10] Discipline broke down in the classroom as well. In 1820, Horace Mann, then a young tutor in classical languages, was hissed out of recitation. It should be said that Howe does not appear to have been a member of that group.[11]

The outsider from Boston, and a Unitarian among Baptists, needed the approbation of his fellows. The only way he could gain their favor was by "excellence in roguish scrapes." Instead of offering advice and guidance, the tutors only threatened him. Thus challenged to do his worst, Howe became one of the rowdiest of the students.[12]

For pranks such as squirting ink through a tutor's keyhole, or leading the president's horse into the belfry and leaving him there overnight, Howe was several times "rusticated," that is, sent to live with a minister who would tutor him, and, it was hoped, exercise a steadying influence on him, but he returned from these rural sojourns worse than ever. The authorities came to accuse him of every student lapse, when, as he used to say ruefully, he was guilty of only a few. Such treatment impelled him to go on displaying his skill.[13] However, the charitable side of his personality was given some play as well as the self-indulgent. He was able to control his mischievous proclivities long enough on occasion to assist in the work of the Philendean Society, an association to aid poor students by lending books.[14]

Although Howe became the outstanding member of the class of 1821, he showed no such promise while he was a student. His standing in his class was, as a classmate put it, "not what it should have been in view of his abilities." [15] Fifteen of the forty-two boys who were graduated with him had commencement parts. Howe was not

[10] Bronson, *History of Brown*, p. 185.
[11] Howe to Elijah Hamlin, August 26, 1820, Howe Papers, Houghton.
[12] Howe to Mann, 1857, p. 6, Howe Papers, Houghton.
[13] Alexis Caswell, in Julia Ward Howe, *Memoir*, p. 86.
[14] Bronson, *History of Brown*, p. 182.
[15] Alexis Caswell to Julia Ward Howe, Feb. 21, 1876, Howe Papers, Houghton.

among them. Probably he stood somewhere in the middle third of his class, if not lower.

Yet these years were not completely barren intellectually. He had done some thinking and read some worthwhile books, although rather sporadically and without plan.[16] A letter written in his junior year indicates that not only had he been affected by recent religious developments and the subsequent rise of Unitarianism, but had been giving some attention to problems of society as well. Man, he wrote, gives implicit belief to certain principles of truth implanted in the human mind. By mingling errors with them, one could come to the principles on which the great religions of the world are built. But he was still not the champion of the oppressed. His love of humanity had not as yet pressed itself to the fore of his consciousness:

Knowledge, alone, can free men from error; and it is impossible that the diffusion of this should ever become so general, as to produce the effect; for the lower classes always have, and always must, continue in ignorance, and be the dupes of others. . . .[17]

Paternalism and condescension were always aspects of Howe's character.

III

Faced with the problem of choosing a career after receiving his degree in September 1821, Howe decided on medicine and entered the Harvard Medical School. He put his undergraduate outlook behind him, became very conscientious about his studies, and strove to make up for time lost in college. His earnestness paid off, for he developed into an expert dissector and a "pretty good" anatomist. Although he had checked his adventurous spirit, he allowed it free rein whenever it was necessary to find a body for dissection. One

[16] Ms. Ledger of books lent out, John Hay Library, Brown University Library. During his four years at Brown, Howe borrowed 21 times. Included among the books are Bartram's *Travels*, Scott's *Works*, Burke's *Works*, Plutarch's *Lives*, Cooke's *Voyages*, Franklin, *On Electricity*, Smith's *Wealth of Nations*, and Priestly on *Electricity*.

[17] Howe to Hamlin, Aug. 26, 1820, Howe Papers, Houghton.

evening he and some of his fellow students went to a low-lying damp cemetery to exhume the body of a newly buried convict. While at their ghoulish work, the nervous youths were alarmed and hurriedly scattered. But Howe lingered in the vicinity, and after midnight returned to complete the unearthing. Singlehandedly he dragged the body out of its grave, into a chaise, and carried it in triumph to his room.[18]

Howe finished his course without incident in 1824 and faced the world, ready to make his own way. The secure and respected life of a Boston physician seemed to lie ahead, but it was not to be. Adventure was tonic to his soul, and the smoke and flame of embattled Greece, with all its insecurity and danger, proved a stronger lure than anything his native city had to offer.

[18] Howe to Mann, 1857, p. 7, Howe Papers, Houghton.

II

First Years in Greece

Only a romantic cause could have enticed Howe away from the career for which he had prepared himself. He found that cause in the service of the Greek people and their revolution, a war that combined nobility and excitement. It was a glorious opportunity for a hot-blooded youth.

I

Waged with inconceivable savagery by both sides, the revolution captured the imagination of Western society as nothing had since 1789. It seemed the resurrection of a civilization that had given the Christian world its ideals of art and literature, the foundations of its philosophy, and the origins of its science. Nothing was more fitting than for the West to repay the debt owed ancient Greece by helping her great-grandchildren, as it were, to return to the traditions from which they had been for long centuries separated.

Christian Europe and America were subjected to a high-pressure propaganda campaign such as had never been known before. Philhellenes, as active partisans of the cause were called, preached a crusade against Turkish oppression. Committees sprang up all over Europe, and aid in the form of money, food, and ammunition began to flow toward the Peloponnesus. From the propaganda viewpoint, if not in actual achievement, the most significant of Philhellenes was Lord Byron, who arrived in 1823, resplendent in uniform and helmet, to live long enough to supervise the fortification of Missolonghi and lose his illusions about the people he had come to help.

Americans followed more slowly in Europe's footsteps. Having long fancied themselves the upholders of the traditions of popular democracy, dating from the city-states, they had their own reasons for sympathizing with the Greeks. Not only did they name their newer settlements after the ancient towns of Athens, Troy, Syracuse, Ithaca, and Utica, but modern heroes also provided inspiration. Ypsilanti, Michigan stands today as the tribute paid by backwoodsmen to the first of the revolutionary leaders to gain fame.[1]

Not much positive Philhellenic action took place in America until the autumn of 1823, when Byron's example provided the impetus needed to start aid moving across the ocean. Edward Everett acted as the catalytic agent. In the *North American Review* for October 1823, he published an article ostensibly reviewing a new edition of Aristotle's *Nichomachean Ethics,* but in reality summoning Americans to go to the aid of embattled Hellas. To this end he printed the text of the *Greek Appeal to America* of May 1821, and the new constitution. Proud that the revolutionists had turned to his country for aid, he called on his compatriots to contribute money, and even to join the military forces.[2] He implied that the Greeks were Christians of sorts, even if addicted to a most benighted variety of Christianity. Theirs was no mere revolution, but "a war of the crescent against the cross." [3] His readers could take their cue from that.

Everett, destined to be of great service to Howe many times in later years, was still in the early stages of his dazzling career which was to lead to high public office. Barely twenty-nine years old, he had already been a Unitarian minister in Boston's most fashionable church and a wandering student in Europe. Now for the moment he doubled as Harvard's first Eliot Professor of Greek, and editor

---

[1] Some scholars even say that the Greek Revolution had some effect on the Greek Revival in architecture. James Marston Fitch, *American Building* (Boston, 1948), p. 51.

[2] Article XX, *North American Review,* XVII (Oct. 1823), 417.

[3] *North American Review,* p. 420.

of the country's most distinguished periodical. Through his correspondence with Greek leaders both in Greece and in Paris with whom he was personally acquainted, he was of all Americans the best informed on the situation.

Committees for Greek aid appeared all over the United States. Mathew Carey was secretary of one in Philadelphia, and William Bayard was chairman of another in New York. The Boston committee was organized on December 19, 1823, with Everett as secretary and Thomas L. Winthrop as chairman. It issued an *Address* denouncing the Turks as barbarians, and praising the Greeks as upholders of civilization, with a natural affinity for progress.[4] Public meetings throughout the country took up the cause. The nation seemed to be sincerely concerned with the tribulations of those whom they thought to be simple, kindly, democratically inclined, Christian folk, victims of infidel barbarity.

Several Americans had already enlisted in the Greek forces. Of these George Jarvis was outstanding. He rose to be a lieutenant-general in the army after landing friendless and completely ignorant of the language.[5] Howe would have left his studies when the revolt broke out, but his recently widowed father would not consent.[6] Nevertheless, after Lord Byron's example, the fledgling physician was firmly resolved to go. He never claimed that he was inspired exclusively by the nobility of the cause or higher emotional stirrings, although they undoubtedly influenced him. In later years he said,

I think that I was impelled in early life to courses of conduct, such as going to Greece, rather by thoughtless indifference, perhaps ignorance of what course would have been profitable to me. Lacking prudence & calculation, I followed an adventurous spirit.[7]

[4] *Address of the Committee Appointed at a Public Meeting Held in Boston December 19, 1823, for the Relief of the Greeks to their Fellow Citizens* (n.p., n.d.), 18 pages. This is bound in with pamphlets by Edward Everett in Harvard Library. A useful article on the whole aid movement is Edward Mead Earle's "American Interest in the Greek Cause, 1821–1827," *AHR*, XXXIII, 1 (Oct. 1927), 44–63.

[5] Howe to Sampson, March 28, 1825, Howe Papers, Houghton.

[6] Howe to Mann, 1857, p. 7, Howe Papers, Houghton.

[7] Howe to Mann, 1857, p. 2, Howe Papers, Houghton.

A more decisive factor in forming his resolve was an affair with a girl whom he could not marry, probably because he could not afford to. He mentions her name vaguely, Sophia Hyatt.[8] Consequently, there may have been an aspect of boyish petulance about his decision. He would go to Greece to forget her.

During his last year in medical school, in the summer of 1824, he sought out Jonathan Peckham Miller, a Vermont soldier, who was in Boston preparatory to sailing for Greece. Miller was astonished when the callow youth confided his desire to join up. With soft hands, he "looked more like a doll than a soldier," wrote Miller, doubting that Howe could endure camp life.[9] But Howe would not be dissuaded by anyone's doubts. Instead he sought to convince Miller of his aptitude by demonstrating his fencing prowess when Miller visited his home.

The family was shocked when Samuel announced his decision. He spurned his sisters' tears and his father's pleas. Only his friend William S. Sampson proved sympathetic.[10] Realizing finally that he could not dissuade his adamant son, Joseph Howe capitulated and gave him some money. The Boston Greek aid committee contributed instruments and more money, while Everett gave him letters to his Greek friends.[11]

The latter-day crusader sailed from Boston in November 1824 and arrived in Malta in time to spend Christmas. He contemplated his future in a melancholy mood, feeling that he had received harsh treatment from the world. Nothing seemed to matter. If he were commissioned, he would remain, and if not, he would return, but it was immaterial since there were few persons in America he cared to see. He felt that there was nothing for him in Boston but the possibility of amassing a fortune, and to him the goal of gold was

[8] Journal I, July 13, 1825, Howe Papers, Houghton. He wrote in this entry that he had nothing to live for, the only person with whom he could be happy, torn from him by a cursed fortune. In his journal, March 28, 1829, he wrote that a Greek girl named Katingo "does look something like Sophia Hyatt."

[9] Jonathan P. Miller to Editor, *Boston Atlas,* Oct. 13, 1843, Howe Papers, Houghton.

[10] Howe to Sampson, Dec. 20, 1824, Howe Papers, Houghton.

[11] Myrtle Agnes Cline, *American Attitude toward the Greek War of Independence, 1821–1828* (Atlanta, Ga., 1930), p. 118.

ignoble.[12] After waiting a few days, he managed to board an Austrian vessel that was to stop at Monemvasia. There he landed, alone in a foreign country cut off from all that was familiar to him. Ignorant of modern Greek, he set out to find the provisional government.[13]

II

The land to which Howe had come was no longer the fabled home of culture about which he had studied in college. It had long since degenerated into one of Europe's most backward countries. The "glory that was Greece" was a completely alien concept to its ignorant people, for whom the only problems of any significance were those of day-to-day existence. The ancient cities, the homes of great splendor, had dwindled, and in their stead stood dreary towns of varying sizes and degrees of squalor. Athens, the pride of ancient Attica, had sunk to a secondary town, with possibly 10,000 inhabitants.[14] Nauplia, the largest city, had barely 20,000.[15]

Centuries of Turkish oppression had driven all compassion from the people, leaving them as depraved and brutalized as their masters. Amid scenes of fiendish butchery, the Christians exterminated the 20,000 Moslems living among them at the start of the war.[16] Massacres of helpless prisoners characterized the behavior of both sides. If Turks impaled their victims on upright posts, as Howe said they did,[17] Greeks could, amid festival atmosphere, slaughter hundreds of Turkish prisoners, as it is known they did at Hydra in June 1825.[18] Unable to deny Greek barbarity, Philhellenes claimed

---

[12] Howe to Sampson, Dec. 20, 1824, Howe Papers, Houghton.

[13] Howe to Mann, 1857, p. 8, Howe Papers, Houghton.

[14] George Finlay, *History of the Greek Revolution* (Edinburgh and London, 1861), I, 199.

[15] Howe, Journal III, August 11, 1827, Howe Papers, Houghton.

[16] Finlay, *History of the Greek Revolution*, I, 172.

[17] Samuel Gridley Howe, *An Historical Sketch of the Greek Revolution* (New York, 1828), first edition, p. 260.

[18] Journal I, July 2, 1825 — expresses his horror at the deed. He observed that all classes of the population approved of the slaughter of several hundred Turkish prisoners. Howe to Sampson, July 13, 1825, has a fuller account.

extenuating circumstances. Greeks acted on the spur of the moment, they said, contrary to the wishes of their leaders, but Turks committed their atrocities as part of a conscious policy derived from the Koran.[19]

While there was much heroism, daring, and self-sacrifice on the part of many, the Greek Revolution produced no man of real greatness, either from the military point of view or that of statesmanship. Nationalistic feelings were still weak, and not all Greeks shared the revolutionary ardor. Segments of the population made no sacrifices and carried on their occupations as well as they could all through the war.[20] The leaders who developed were generally unfit for the positions they occupied.[21] Uneducated for the most part, with but little conception of the broader issues at stake, they were, with few exceptions, unable to subordinate their own interests to the good of the nation.

In the period of optimism following the Turkish defeats in 1821, the Greeks had called a constitutional convention to set up a government. The so-called Constitution of Epidaurus was proclaimed on January 1, 1822, according to the Julian calendar. Showing Western influences in its phraseology, the document promised religious freedom to all Christians, equality before the law, and civil and political rights to all. Legislative power was vested in a senate, and executive power in a five-man council whose president was to be the president of Greece. American principles were incorporated in the plan of government as well. The executive was to have the veto over bills passed, and the senate was to ratify treaties.[22] This system was theoretically in effect when Howe arrived.

There was less in this constitution than met the eye. Designed as a blind to deceive western Europe, the constitution was not meant to be enforced. Its administrators were expected to override its provisions whenever they felt it convenient. They were to rely on their

[19] Howe, *Historical Sketch*, p. 160.
[20] Finlay, *Greek Revolution*, I, 10.
[21] Finlay, *Greek Revolution*, I, 178.
[22] Text printed in Everett's article, *North American Review* (Oct. 1823), pp. 405–412.

own talents. By no means is the Constitution of Epidaurus to be considered an organic law.[23]

In actual operation, the government was run by a corrupt and inefficient system of precariously balanced cliques. As first president of the new republic, Alexander Mavrocordatos, a Phanariot, was chosen. He was the most widely known Greek statesman and the obvious choice, since he had studied and traveled much in western Europe. Familiar with advanced political thought, he put his knowledge to good use by his service on the drafting committee of the constitution. While personally honest, he was totally unfit for his office. He was of great ambition but limited abilities, and he lacked firmness and hardihood necessary for leadership in a revolutionary struggle. Maintaining his influence, notwithstanding ups and downs in personal fortune, through skill in intrigue and political cunning, traits in which the Phanariots were outstanding, he lasted less than a year in office. His administration, typical of its successors, was replaced by a new cabal.[24] The later coalitions were even more tragic failures. During 1824 they squandered a sizable British loan, and left the country unprepared and defenseless for the vital campaign of the spring and summer of 1825. The government of Greece throughout the revolutionary period was a grotesque travesty on constitutional principles.

By 1823 the war against Turkey had sunk to secondary importance; civil war had taken its place. Armed bands of brigands called *klephts,* led by wild chieftains, terrorized the countryside and threatened the government. Earlier they had fought the Turks as part of the revolutionary forces, but as the military leadership of Demetrios Ypsilanti declined, they became more independent.

Klepht leaders could on occasion be brave and daring, but they were untrustworthy. Unable to distinguish right from wrong,[25] they were unable to keep faith even with their own men, but tried to cheat them out of their share of booty.[26]

[23] Finlay, *Greek Revolution,* I, 299.
[24] Finlay, *Greek Revolution,* I, 300–301; Howe, *Historical Sketch,* pp. 49–51.
[25] Finlay, *Greek Revolution,* I, 188.
[26] Finlay, *Greek Revolution,* I, 270.

When Howe arrived in mid-January 1825, things were relatively peaceful; internal bickerings had been momentarily silenced. Plans were being made for the future. The stormy petrels of Greek politics were out of harm's way. For having engaged in rebellions against the government, Theodore Kolokotrones, a chieftain, and his followers, and a number of primates languished in prison.

III

At Nauplia Howe met Miller and the other Americans. He roomed with the Hellenized General, George Jarvis, who eased the path of adjustment for him. The city gained its new doctor at a most opportune moment, an epidemic having swept off the regular physicians. In a short time Howe had a private practice large enough to support himself, despite the fact that he was inexperienced and had to speak French to his patients. It was well for them that he was there, since he used the latest scientific methods rather than the herb-woman cures the native practitioners employed. The fame of the stranger from far away spread after he cured several "hopeless" cases.

Howe was happy now, contributing his "mite to the cause of liberty and humanity." Besides, he was getting a more valuable and varied experience than he could have gained in Boston. The government eagerly accepted his proffered services, and promised him a high surgical commission.[27]

IV

But then disaster struck. Sultan Mahmud II finally took positive action to regain control of his recalcitrant provinces. Enlisting the assistance of his tributary, Mehemet Ali (sometimes called Mohammed Ali), of Egypt, he promised him any islands he might conquer, and the pashalik of the Morea for his son, Ibrahim, the commander of the expeditionary force. Ibrahim's arrival in the spring of 1825 proved disastrous for the revolutionists. For the first time the Greeks faced an adversary who knew how to fight and

[27] Howe to Sampson, March 28, 1825, Howe Papers, Houghton.

who would expose them for what they were, conceited, corrupt, and ignorant provincials. Ibrahim was a keen strategist who had studied European methods; he drilled his troops carefully, so that they marched and fought with precision.

Making an easy landing at Modon, he captured Navarino in May 1825. The news came as a terrible shock to the revolutionists who could not imagine that a Turkish army (they classified Egyptians with Turks) could defeat them. A few weeks later Ibrahim captured Tripolitza and in June he laid siege to Nauplia itself. A swath of charred towns and villages marked the brilliant Egyptian's line of march.[28] The government proved powerless. Its army was speedily broken and its leaders discredited. Mavrocordatos, now one of the secretaries of state, and the president, George Konduriottes, a Hydriote merchant, gained only the scorn of the people with their comic-opera attempts at playing soldier.[29] Popular pressures forced the release of the colorful but perfidious Kolokotrones to assume the post of general-in-chief.[30]

Howe went out as surgeon with the army in the spring of 1825. Although he did what he could to help the wounded, he found that without adequate instruments, bandages, and medicines, he could be of greater use as a soldier. If he were lucky, he would kill more Turks with his yataghan, than he would Greeks with his medical arts. On April 21, fifteen miles from the battle line, he heard cannon for the first time. Since he could not practice his profession, "why here goes life and soul for Greece & liberty." [31] While awaiting the beginning of battle a few days later, he described his feelings as "singular" but not those of fear. At this tense moment he admitted to himself an inordinate desire to be great, but he feared that his talents were only a little above mediocrity.[32]

In the weeks and months that followed, he grew hardened to

---

[28] Finlay, *Greek Revolution*, II, 73; Howe, *Historical Sketch*, pp. 236–249; Howe Journal I, April 20–June 29, 1825.

[29] Finlay, *Greek Revolution*, II, 63; Howe, *Historical Sketch*, 225–238.

[30] Finlay, *Greek Revolution*, II, 74.

[31] Howe to Mann, 1857, p. 8; Journal I, April 21, 1825.

[32] Journal I, April 25, 1825.

the life, and became the equal of any of his *pallikari* colleagues in endurance. He even developed a tolerance for lice on his body and fried insects as food.[33] Miller testified to his gallantry in battle as well as afterward when he tended the casualties:

I have known him [to] stand dressing the wounded until exhausted, then throwing himself down upon the ground & resting a few moments he would again resume his labour. He shared his crust with the famishing & would often times give all & fast himself, knowing that his chance[s] of getting relief were far better than theirs.[34]

Only one other tale of Howe's heroism has come down to us. Although an account appeared anonymously in the *New England Magazine,* Charles Sumner "wormed" the incident out of Howe and told it to John Greenleaf Whittier who wrote "The Hero" to commemorate it.[35] The deed took place at Kalamata during this 1825 campaign, when Howe, while fleeing with the troops in disorderly retreat eastward, noticed a wounded soldier lying at the side of the road. To stop for him meant losing valuable time, but Howe took that risk.[36] The rescued man, Francesco, proved to be an experienced *pallikari,* who, becoming his benefactor's orderly, introduced Howe to all the fine points of living off the country. Through his knowledge of the national character, he procured many meals and shelter for his master out of unwilling hosts who disliked the idea of quartering and feeding soldiers. Blustering his way into private homes, ignoring evidence of poverty and empty storerooms, Francesco pried food from the most secret hideouts. Howe always smoothed ruffled feelings, and gained the blessings of half the saints in the register, by producing a bag of money, once his servant had proven there was something to pay for.[37]

[33] Howe to Mann, 1857, pp. 9–11.

[34] Miller to Editor, *Boston Atlas,* Oct. 13, 1843, Howe Papers, Houghton.

[35] Howe to Mann, 1857, p. 14; John Greenleaf Whittier, *Poetical Works* (Boston, 1900), IV, 80–84.

[36] "From the Mss. [*sic*] of a Traveler in the East," *New England Magazine,* I (Sept. 1831), 242. This article is obviously by Howe. Much of what he says coincides with his journal. This incident, however, is not to be found there.

[37] *New England Magazine* (Oct. 1831), pp. 293–295.

V

Howe was all over the Morea during this crucial spring, from Coron in the southwest to Nauplia on the Gulf of Argolis. He saw more of the country and formed more definite ideas of its people and their army than would have been possible had he remained in the capital. In spite of what he wrote later about the gallantry of the Greeks, he was unfavorably impressed while he was among them. The people were ungrateful, and the native doctors, with whom he had some conflict, were conceited and ignorant.[38]

The army was especially incompetent, with no *esprit de corps* to speak of. The *klepht* band was the unit of organization; the men took their orders from their captain and deserted at will.[39] Not only would the *klephts* steal from the enemy, but they would even rob their leaders. Demetrios Ypsilanti once returned to camp after an unsuccessful foray to find his men had deserted, taking his property with them.[40] The soldiers, Howe complained, were without honor. They fought only for money, and could not understand why anyone else should join their forces.[41] He despaired of convincing them that he wished to serve them without regard to personal convenience.[42]

The disillusioned idealist was terribly disappointed with the nation as well. Like many of the foreigners whom he met, he had originally entertained the same "ridiculous and extravagant notions" of the Greeks that he now jeered at in them. They had thought of the Greeks as descendants of Leonidas and found them instead cautious, cunning, and common men.[43] In his disillusionment he went to the other extreme. The people he said were inhospitable, unfeeling,[44] ungrateful wretches who could not conceive of unselfish motives:

[38] For difficulties with Greek doctors, see Journal I, May 7, 17, 18, 28, 1825.
[39] Journal I, May 2, 1825.
[40] Howe to Sampson, Aug. 12, 1825, also Journal I, Aug. 8, 1825.
[41] Journal I, May 2, 1825.
[42] Journal I, May 6, 1825.
[43] "From the Mss. of a Traveler in the East," *N. E. Mag.* I, 291.
[44] S. G. Howe to Joseph N. Howe, Dec. 29, 1825, Howe Papers, Houghton.

They are one of the most disagreeable of all people in the world to have anything to do with; ignorant, selfish, & thievish; none can equal them in deceit, & cunning; none surpass them in treachery. In his religion the Greek is no better than an idolator; the Virgin Mary is his God, her image his idol.[45]

If he were in real need, he could not even expect a glass of water.[46] They tried to cheat him in every transaction, and were he not a physician able to earn his own livelihood, he feared he would have been a lost man.[47]

Howe's thoughts on the Greeks were still plastic; at the moment that he denounced them as scoundrels, he explained why they were so and mitigated his own scorn. He granted that their brutality and depravity came from their four centuries of oppression. Their redemption could not be effected in a moment, and he placed his hopes in the next generation.[48]

VI

Late in June, Howe suffered a slight injury during an enemy attack on the Mills across the bay from Nauplia, which the government, in a last ditch effort, repulsed. The capital was saved, and Egyptian pressure was eased for the rest of the summer. Ibrahim withdrew to Tripolitza to await reinforcements from his father.[49]

Shortly thereafter, Howe removed to the more congenial locale of Hydra where he spent the next two months tending wounded sailors and recouping his dwindled finances by private practice. He liked the Hydriotes, who impressed him as the noblest of the Greeks, fighting not so much for their own freedom as for that of the country. They had always been comparatively free, paying

[45] Journal I, Sept. 5, 1825.
[46] Journal I, Oct. 27, 1825.
[47] Journal I, Aug. 8, 1825. Thirty years later they had become romanticized. He wrote to Horace Mann in 1857, p. 13, "I had many friends in humble life, God bless them; & can say sincerely, that I found the Greeks kindly affectioned, trustful, grateful; & as for my intercourse with them went, honest people. They always treated me as well as I wished to be treated."
[48] Howe to Sampson, July 13, 1825.
[49] Journal I, June 27, 1825.

their tribute to the Porte in return for being let alone.[50] The naïve youth soon learned the true situation. Actually, the islanders were pirates, who under the guise of privateers, with letters of marque to attack Turkish vessels, roamed the Levant, preying on all shipping indiscriminately. The British, who suffered the most from these depredations, finally took stringent action that summer, and blockaded the port for several days. Aboard one of His Majesty's frigates, Howe cruised around observing the success of the disciplinary action. He returned on July 30 to find that the chastened Hydriotes, confusing the English-speaking peoples, gave increased respect to Americans also.[51]

Late in August he became surgeon to the fleet sent to aid the Candiotes (Cretans) who had at last joined the revolution.[52] With Miller as assistant, he arrived at Grabousi, an island fortress off the coast under command of General Callierges.[53] But the campaign went badly; the rebels were outfought in every skirmish. Howe stayed until the end of October caring for the wounded, quarreling with native doctors,[54] and confiding his low opinion of the people to his journal.[55] Nevertheless he gave the wretched patriots the last ounce of his strength. On at least one occasion, during the height of a battle, the number of wounded was so great that he was kept at work until after midnight. For a man planning to open a medical practice later, as he still intended, the experience was invaluable. He estimated that he had dressed more difficult wounds and performed more operations than he would have done in Boston in a lifetime. "I could not weary," he wrote. Inwardly, however, he raged at the selfishness of his patients who brazenly urged him to neglect others in order to come to their aid. He had seen them even refuse water to a dying comrade who lay too weak to brush flies away.[56]

[50] Howe to Sampson, June 24, 1825.
[51] Journal I, July 31, 1825.
[52] Journal I, Aug. 23, 1825.
[53] Journal I, Sept. 1, 1825.
[54] Journal I, Oct. 21, 1825.
[55] Journal I, Sept. 27 and 30, 1825.
[56] Journal I, Oct. 27, 1825.

On October 28, when his charges were either dead or out of danger, Howe was able to leave. After a leisurely sight-seeing cruise through the Cyclades, he reached Hydra on November 9. There he learned of the final fate of the venture. It had failed entirely. He felt especially annoyed, since he knew that the government had sent enough men and supplies to insure victory. Insubordination had ruined another excellent opportunity.[57]

VII

After a few months' inactivity, Ibrahim began to stir again. Newly reinforced, he was determined to conquer the Morea in as short a time as he could, and to set himself up as its ruler. In this second campaign he came within grasp of final victory. Roaming western Greece at will, he marched from his main base at Navarino to Patras without meeting organized opposition. In December he joined forces with the Turkish army under Reshid Pasha (called Kiutahi, or Kiutaye), who since July had been besieging Missolonghi.[58] Here Greeks proved that they were capable of heroism when given the inspiration and opportunity. The attention of the nation was focused on the 12,000 fisher-folk of the town as they repulsed Moslem attacks during four more months, though facing starvation and certain death. The combined army finally forced its entry on April 24. Amid scenes of unrestrained sadism they massacred the remainder of the population and looted their homes.[59] The Egyptians continued on for the rest of the fighting season repeating their successes of the year before. Formal Greek resistance ceased. Kolokotrones and other Greek commanders, hidden in the mountains, confined their gallantry to raids against the peasants for food. Greek fortunes were at their nadir. It looked as if the end were at hand. Certain areas of the Morea resubmitted to the Turks and acknowledged the Sultan as their master.

Howe watched this tragic change of fortune with dread apprehension. He did not go out in 1826 as he had the year before, since he

[57] Howe to Sampson, Dec. 19, 1825.
[58] Finlay, *Greek Revolution*, II, 99.
[59] Finlay, *Greek Revolution*, II, 110.

was now in charge of a hospital at Nauplia which he had taken over in December upon his return from a sight-seeing trip to Attica. Physically more comfortable than during the previous campaign, he was no less disturbed in mind. In the year he had been in Greece he had come to identify himself completely with the Greek cause, and would not think of leaving the country so long as he could be useful. Breathing defiance, he planned on joining a partisan band to pick off enemy stragglers in order to show the Greeks how to fight. If necessary, he felt he would die for them.[60]

During these months when the independence of Greece hung in the balance, Howe's financial position was very insecure. He had earned little money and had little prospect of earning more. He appealed to Edward Everett for aid. The erstwhile professor, now in Congress, heeded the young man's cry by promptly writing to Colonel Thomas H. Perkins, one of Boston's wealthiest merchants, to ask him to establish a credit of $100 at Smyrna for the doctor's use as passage money, if necessary. Everett nobly took responsibility for the sum, by offering to reimburse the noted philanthropist.[61]

In late October 1826, Howe gave up his secure post at Nauplia to become director of the medical department of the Fleet. Sailing on the *Karteria,* a steam vessel under Captain Frank Hastings, one of the most competent of the Philhellenes and certainly superior to any Greek captain, the new surgeon-general spent the next two months among the islands of the Greek archipelago in closer contact with the sailors than he had ever been before. His experiences with the army repeated themselves. Within two months, as scornful of Greek seamanship as he was of Greek soldiering, he pronounced the inhabitants of the nation's foremost maritime centers, Hydra, Ipsara, and Spetzia, avaricious, deceitful, mean, dishonest, and cowardly. The world was deceived in its ideas of them, he said. In six years of war, not even 200 men had been killed in battle.[62] The sailors would not stay at sea more than a month at a time. Neither they nor the middle class would sacrifice anything for the country.

[60] Howe to Sampson, June 8, 1826.
[61] Everett to Perkins, Dec. 27, 1826, Perkins Papers, MHS.
[62] Journal II, Jan. 1, 1827.

Hundreds had vast fortunes, but none contributed any of it to the cause.[63] Actually, Howe's career as *archichirurgos* was placid enough. He saw some action at the siege of Athens in February 1827, but on the whole he did little more than see the sights on the islands and muse on the national character.

VIII

In the spring of 1827 he and Miller took on another duty, as almoners of American Greek relief committees. In this task they had assistance from three newcomers, Dr. John D. Russ and John R. Stuyvesant of New York, and Dr. Edward Jarvis of Boston. The food situation was critical, since the populace had begun to suffer from Ibrahim's crop-burnings of the previous summer. Through a letter from Kolokotrones to Jarvis, July 1826, America first learned of the miserable conditions. Mathew Carey published it widely, and in January 1827, the first of a steady stream of relief ships left for Greece.[64] It was American sympathy, in the opinion of eyewitness Finlay, that sustained a large part of the population before the battle of Navarino.[65]

Unlike European committees that dealt with the government directly, American aid bypassed the authorities and went straight to the people, upon whom Howe felt it had a great moral effect. They could see their relief, not just hear about it. They knew that somewhere people cared for them.[66]

Howe and Miller divided up the cargoes and went to opposite parts of the country. Howe, with George Finlay to assist him, ranged from the mainland to the islands. He made his now familiar circuit of the Morea, observing the country and the changes wrought by the turn the war had taken. Military operations on both sides were suspended. Greece lay prostrate, and but for the intervention of the Western powers would have been forced to capitulate. Ibra-

---

[63] Journal III, July 6, 1827.
[64] Edward Everett, review article of Howe's *Historical Sketch of the Greek Revolution*, in the *North American Review*, XXIX (July 1829), 184.
[65] Finlay, *Greek Revolution*, II, 159.
[66] Howe to Henderson Tuckes, undated, Journal III.

him, blockaded by the combined fleets of the Great Powers, lay encamped at Navarino, cut off from reinforcements.

With Turkish pressure removed, civil war raged unrestrained. The *klephts,* unpaid and unsupplied, now surged forth from their mountainous refuges to complete the destruction the Turks and Egyptians had begun. Everything was fair game. They fell on the countryside with all the fury they should have reserved for the enemy. Soldiers from distant parts of Greece felt no qualms about taking and destroying the property of the strangers among whom they found themselves.[67]

Howe and Finlay had difficulty keeping their supplies from these bandits. Kolokotrones was on the loose again, fighting another chieftain named Grivas in the vicinity of Nauplia. Both made attempts to divert American aid to themselves and their men.[68] Only by prompt action in calling upon an American naval vessel for protection was Howe able to fulfill his mission.[69] Other attempts by brigands elsewhere were equally unsuccessful.[70]

The suffering in Greece that summer was frightful; the civil war was taking a horrible toll. At Nauplia in August, Howe estimated that 8000 out of 20,000 inhabitants needed assistance. This, the largest city in the land, was completely ruined. Only 1000 residents were huddled in its limits at one period during these months while it underwent shelling by Grivas. The remainder of the population had taken refuge in the huts and caves of the neighboring countryside. Every house had been broken into and ransacked.[71]

All Argos, Howe reported, was destroyed. Twenty miles of the plain were exposed to view. Crops and olive trees were smoldering ashes. The legal government, cowering in Aegina, was penniless, and unable to do anything.[72]

[67] Journal III, Aug. 20, 1827.
[68] Jonathan P. Miller, *The Condition of Greece in 1827 and 1828* (New York, 1828), p. 45.
[69] Miller, *The Condition of Greece,* p. 46.
[70] Journal III, July 18, 1827, at Astros.
[71] Journal III, Aug. 11, 1827.
[72] Journal III, Aug. 23, 1827.

Through this hellish country the small band of Americans went on their mission of mercy, along the coast, into the interior, even to the islands. Howe realized that emergency relief was insufficient. The people needed permanent institutions, such as hospitals of the type he had organized at Nauplia, to give continuing aid. He was able to start another hospital at Poros with the proceeds of part of a cargo.[73]

At long last, after a residence of two and a half years, his shock at seeing the people as they really were wore off. With the memory of ghastly scenes before him, sympathy and understanding tempered his scorn. He could finally admit: "The Greeks *are not a bad people* in fact all things considered it is strange they are so good; for without religion without the still stronger tie of a spirit of honor, what can be expected of a people?"[74]

The government had asked Howe to go to America in June to raise money, but he had delayed in order to complete his relief work.[75] On November 13 he and Stuyvesant embarked, taking four refugee children with them, and leaving Russ in charge of the hospital at Poros. Howe also had in his possession Lord Byron's helmet which he had picked up at an auction of the poet's effects.[76] He left with joy in his heart. Things were looking up. The battle of Navarino had been fought, Turkish power had been destroyed by Western force, and Greek freedom assured.[77] The rescued country awaited eagerly the arrival of the very flashy John Capodistrias to assume the presidency.

[73] Miller, Howe, and Russ to the Greek Committee of Boston, Nov. 1, 1827. Ms. Journal III, letter dated 1826, but obviously wrong. Brig *Statesman* arrived 1827.

[74] Ms. Journal III, Oct. 11, 1827.

[75] Howe to Joseph N. Howe, June 24, 1827, also undated letter to Henderson Tuckes, Journal III.

[76] Miller, *Condition of Greece*, p. 141. *Bower of Taste*, I, 12 (March 29, 1828), 189.

[77] Howe to Edward Everett, Nov. 2, 1827, Howe Papers, Houghton.

III

Later Years in Greece

Howe landed in New York on February 5, 1828, after an absence from his native land of over three years.[1] He had left it an unknown student, and returned to it a widely traveled young man whose opinions were respected by learned and influential men.[2] His views had been widely publicized through the friendly auspices of Everett, who, with family permission, had published a number of his letters.[3] These communications were highly regarded. One newspaper commented that Howe's letters from Greece were a more accurate source of information than any other.[4] Famous or not, the returned native had made little money. He was practically penniless and had to ask the Greek Committee of New York to pay his passage for him.[5]

Howe made it clear that his trip to America was on behalf of Greece; he still considered himself in that country's service, and was ready to return when he could best help out there.[6] Attending to first things first, he spent a few weeks in New York before

[1] Howe to Joseph N. Howe, Feb. 5, 1828, Howe Papers, Houghton.
[2] Howe to Everett, Feb. 6, 1828, Journal III; in this letter, for example, he told Everett of the situation in Greece and the British relationship to Turkey.
[3] Everett to Joseph N. Howe, Sept. 12, 1825, Everett Papers, LVI, 38, MHS. In this letter, Everett asked permission to publish Howe's letters.
[4] *Essex Register*, Nov. 14, 1825, reprinted from *Boston Courier* Howe's letter of Aug. 12.
[5] Howe to S. J. R. Stuyvesant, Feb. 1828, Journal III.
[6] Howe to ? (possibly a Greek Committee), Feb. 1828, Journal III.

returning home to discuss official matters with the committee. He promised to direct the hospital for one year at all hazards if he were given sufficient funds to maintain an institution of 200 beds in a manner creditable to Americans.[7]

When he finally did go to Boston, on the twenty-fifth, he found his reputation had preceded him. He was "somewhat of a lion," socially in such great demand that his time was not his own.[8] As he looked about him in his home town, he became dissatisfied with the state of relief activities. Finding the pulse of Philhellenism very low, he begged Everett to use his influence to breathe life into the movement. There was plenty of sympathy for the suffering Greeks, he wrote, only the impulse to action was wanting.[9] Without waiting for his patron to act, he asked others for names of benevolently inclined persons to whom he could appeal directly.[10]

Howe maintained an extensive correspondence with men all over the country, and learned that if Philhellenism was moribund in Boston, it was lively enough in other parts of the nation. Many communicated to him that they had raised large sums of money, and wished him to distribute it. From New York, for example, came welcome tidings that a group of women had made a sizable contribution.[11]

II

The idea of writing a book on the history of the Greek Revolution had long been in Howe's mind. In fact, he had been collecting material on it since the spring of 1826.[12] At home in Boston, he was at last able to begin. Throwing himself into the project, he worked rapidly, since he wished to state Greece's case as fully and as quickly as possible. He regretted the necessity of haste, but realized the urgency of the situation.[13]

---

[7] Howe to Executive Greek Committee, Feb. 8, 1828, Journal III.
[8] Howe to Sampson, Feb. 28, 1828, Howe Papers, Houghton.
[9] Howe to Everett, Feb. 23, 1828, Journal III.
[10] Howe to W. S. Stone, Feb. 29, 1828, Journal III.
[11] Howe to Theodore Dwight, March 3, 1828, Journal III.
[12] Howe to Sampson, July 8, 1826, Howe Papers, Houghton.
[13] Howe to Sampson, Feb. 28, 1828, Howe Papers, Houghton.

Circumstances prevented his working on the history without interruption. Everett suggested that he go on a fund-raising lecture tour.[14] Howe at first refused,[15] but in mid-March he began his circuit when he accepted an invitation to speak in New York. "I am enlisted . . . in the cause of Greece, & must not hesitate to do anything to serve her, even if disagreeable to myself," he explained to Sampson.[16]

The doctor traveled as far south as Philadelphia, where he discussed the matter of a publisher for his book with Mathew Carey, and as far west as Albany, covering the towns in the Hudson Valley as he passed.[17] He was not the only one raising money for Greece. Miller, who arrived in America at about this time, added his weight to the cause by also beginning work on a book, *The Condition of Greece in 1827,* which appeared during the summer. The periodicals aided in publicity as well. The *Bower of Taste,* a magazine for women, published extracts from Howe's Journal on the suffering in Nauplia the year before.[18] Meetings for Greek relief were held, even when Howe could not address them. Others read his speeches, and committees were set up to receive contributions.[19]

Joseph Howe disapproved of these activities, but no more so than his son, who found it disagreeable to be continually addressing meetings. The young man kept on, however, because he felt it was the best way to serve Greece. He had thrown himself completely into that country's service, and did not care about raising himself in the opinion of the "sensible part of the community." He felt that those who knew his motives would appreciate his services, and his reward would consist in having gained their respect.[20]

Howe's speeches were designed to arouse sympathy for the unfortunate Greeks. In impassioned rhetoric he spoke of the "descendants of that glorious race whose genius crowned them with im-

---

[14] Howe to Everett, Feb. 23, 1828, Journal III.
[15] Howe to W. S. Stone, Feb. 29, 1828, Journal III.
[16] Howe to Sampson, March 15, 1828, Howe Papers, Houghton.
[17] S. G. Howe to Joseph N. Howe, April 2, 1828, Howe Papers, Houghton.
[18] *Bower of Taste,* I, 12 (March 22, 1828), 184–185.
[19] *Bower of Taste,* p. 189.
[20] Howe to Joseph N. Howe, April 10, 1828, Howe Papers, Houghton.

mortality," fighting for their very existence against the brutish barbarity of the Turk. He excused the Greeks their ignorance, degradation, depravity, and dishonesty on the ground of four centuries of
shameful abuse. His rather bombastic peroration, in which he ignored his own earlier views, aimed at crushing the last bit of sales
resistance:

Shame on those who use such arguments to put down the spirit of
charity and who talk continually of the treachery of greek [sic] merchants & of the piracies of greek [sic] sailors — Turkish oppression
made those merchants resort to treachery as the only mode of getting
that livelihood which open honesty could not obtain. starvation [sic]
has driven the sailors to those piracies which the Government of the
country have never had means to put down. I found much to condemn
in the Greeks character — but much also to admire — that there is
spirit in the nation — the desperate struggle which they have kept up
for seven years will prove — that there is virtue & patriotism the names
of Botzaris, Miaulis and Canaris will show.[21]

Howe was quite pleased with the generosity of New York State,
which contributed a great quantity of dry goods and between
$50,000 and $60,000 in cash. He found that his name was known to
thousands, and accompanied by two Greek ladies he visited all
places of note, addressing many public meetings.[22]

During these weeks he worked sporadically on his book. A new
cause for haste had presented itself. He now had to forestall a
bookseller who had published a scissors-and-paste-pot concoction entitled *Howe's History of the Greek Revolution,* which reached the
market before the authentic work was ready.[23] Howe hurried so
much that he feared he would hurt his reputation as a writer, but

[21] Draft in Journal III, also similar speech in Miller, *Condition of Greece,* pp. 255 ff.
The three men Howe mentions were truly heroic, but I could not include them in
my brief sketch of the revolution.
    Somewhere during this period he produced a little pamphlet containing extracts
from his remarks, *A Voice from Greece in Appeal to the Sympathies and Charities
of America* (New York?, 1828?, according to the card in NYPL). In it he denounced America for not doing as much as certain parts of France and Switzerland.
[22] Howe to Sampson, May 30, 1828 (says raised $50,000), Howe to Benson
J. Lossing, Sept. 16, 1875, Misc. mss. NYHS, says $60,000.
[23] Edward Everett, Art. V, *North American Review,* XXIX (July 1829), 142.

he felt his book would sell. If its profits were large enough, he hoped to be able to spend two more years in Europe, visiting Italy, Germany, Switzerland, and France.[24]

His labors finished, the book appeared in August as *An Historical Sketch of the Greek Revolution,* rather than a full-fledged history, because he said he was unable to write one.[25] Howe graciously dedicated it to the two Philhellenes who had done the most for the cause in America, Mathew Carey and Edward Everett.

The *Sketch* met with favor, going into a second edition that year. As a historian Howe made a good journalist. His book was a highly colored, personal account of the war, not to be compared with the Scottish George Finlay's later *History of the Greek Revolution,* which appeared in 1861. The American author lacked judiciousness, being entirely too overwrought in his use of adjectives, though he tried to be fair, praising and damning the Greeks wherever he felt it necessary. Though accurate in most things he said, some of his interpretations were wide of the mark. He thought too highly of Mavrocordatos, for example, when available evidence indicated that statesman's inadequacy. Despite its author's prejudices and inaccuracies, the main value of the work is as an eyewitness piece of reporting. Howe saw many of the events he recounted, and knew personally many of the men of whom he spoke.[26]

III

Howe's mission was completed by July. He made his own financial agreements with the committees, who were to pay his passage and quarantine charges, and also his living costs in Greece so that

[24] Howe to Sampson, May 30, 1828, Howe Papers, Houghton.

[25] Preface.

[26] Edward Everett reviewed it in the *North American,* finding it a book of great value despite its carelessness and inaccuracies. He felt that Howe presented a more perfect and complete sketch of the revolution than anyone else. Independent in judgment, Howe had neither vilified nor panegyrized anyone, but praised when he could and denounced where he should. "Dr Howe," he continued, "is plainly the slave neither of enthusiasm nor of spleen. . . . We feel that we can trust Dr Howe, in his favorable anticipations, because we see they are those of a fair and impartial man." He did feel though, that Howe had been too harsh on Alexander Ypsilanti. *North American Review* (July 1829), pp. 143–144.

he could appear respectably and not have to sell any wheat or other supplies entrusted to him. The committees also promised to contribute to the upkeep of the hospital.[27] After a placid voyage, it was with great affection that Howe espied the mountains of his adopted homeland on November 5. No land he felt could look sweeter to him.[28] He reached Aegina a week later, and decided to make that city his headquarters.

Great changes had taken place since he had left Greece just one year earlier. With its independence assured by Great Power action, the republic had been reconstituted on a new, and it was hoped, firmer basis. The war was in its last six months.[29] The Morea was finally free of enemy troops; the greater part of the country was pacified, and what sporadic fighting continued was confined to the area above Athens. The northern boundary was still uncertain.[30]

The government had also changed completely in personnel. A new president, John Capodistrias, a Corfiote, had been optimistically elected by the Council of Troezene for a term of seven years, April 14, 1827. An experienced diplomat, who had spent years in the Tsar's service, he seemed the best qualified Greek to fill the highest office. Unfortunately, he failed to fulfill the promise he had shown. In the eleventh month of its three years' duration when Howe returned, his government had already replaced the old incompetents with equally inept puppets and relatives, whose inadequacies made efficient government well-nigh impossible.[31]

Howe, throwing himself into his work immediately on debarking, planned to adopt a new method of administering relief. Rather than dole out food and clothing, he would have his charges work for their aid, which they would receive as wages. He hoped thus to keep them out of idleness and do some vital public work. Howe also wished to set up a permanent relief agency, one that would continue under its own force after an initial push. His first idea was to get a grant of land from the government which would bring in suffi-

[27] Howe to Henderson Tuckes, July 19, 1828, Journal III.
[28] Journal IV, Nov. 5, 1828.
[29] Finlay, *Greek Revolution*, II, 207.
[30] Finlay, *Greek Revolution*, II, 223 ff.
[31] Finlay, *Greek Revolution*, II, 195; 245–246.

cient rent for the maintenance of a hospital, and build it with the labor of the poor.[32]

Howe and Finlay began an inspection trip of the Peloponnesus, going first to Poros to sound out Capodistrias. The sharp-eyed New Englander came away uncertain; Capodistrias had not impressed him favorably. He thought the suave diplomat vain and conceited, completely wanting in great talents, and leaning towards despotism if the opportunity offered.[33] While in the city, Howe learned that his hospital, which he had resolved to move to Aegina, was no longer in operation. Russ had agreed to maintain it for one year, but after running it for exactly that time, with great credit to himself and his native country, he despaired of ever seeing Howe again. Just a few days before Howe's arrival, he had closed the hospital and left for another city.[34]

Resuming their journey, the two friends saw evidence of the country's recovery, both physically and spiritually. The people were beginning to complain about conditions again. There was much dissatisfaction with the new administration, which in its brief tenure had alienated support by stocking the civil service with Corfiotes, a people who had neither joined the revolution nor shared in the suffering. To the nation's chagrin, these "slackers" were reaping the gains. The peasantry was especially displeased with Capodistrias' nepotism. The president had appointed his brothers to responsible positions far beyond their feeble abilities.[35]

Another sign of improvement was the resistance the peasants showed to the soldiers, who on their part were meeker in manner than they had been the year before. The farmers now stood up bravely and refused to quarter troops. Gone were the days when bands could stalk into a hut, eat up the food, destroy the furniture, force the quaking family to spend the night in the open while they slept inside, and then leave without making restitution.[36]

[32] Journal IV, Nov. 19, 1828.
[33] Journal IV, Nov. 24, 1828. Howe's intuition was correct. Finlay gives more evidence of that in his *Greek Revolution*, II, 198–199.
[34] Journal IV, Nov. 24, 1828.
[35] Journal IV, Nov. 22, 1828.
[36] Journal IV, Nov. 25, 1828.

Howe pushed on alone for another week after Finlay left him. He found that in some regions the government still had strong support. The people attributed to it gains that came with time, such as the beginnings of orderly administration and the ending of piracy. On the other hand, informed men gave the authorities little credit, and in the islands where the changes had not as yet been felt, Capodistrias was decidedly unpopular.[37]

While the physical scars of the war were healing, more serious ones lingered on and in an aggravated condition. The most disquieting development Howe observed was a general demoralization of the population which he attributed to the presence of the Philhellenes, who set the Greeks a bad example.[38] The women of Poros, he complained, were almost all "corrupted, or depraved."[39] Morals in Nauplia were bad too. Foreigners there saw in the misery of families an opportunity to take advantage of wives and daughters. Howe knew of only two foreigners who would not have done so. Religion suffered too. Whereas the people had earlier been known for their piety, he estimated that nine-tenths of the educated Greeks were now confirmed infidels.[40]

[37] Journal IV, Dec. 3, 1828.

[38] After thinking about them some months he wrote in his Journal IV, Feb. 9, 1829: "What a queer set! what an assemblage of romantic, adventurous, restless, crackbrained young men from the four corners of the world: how much courage & talent are to be found among them; but how much more of pompous vanity, of weak intellect, of mean selfishness, of utter depravity! Quixotism and egotism undoubtedly abound in the mass of queer materialism; but egotism swallows up all the others, and the Philhellene becomes a crackbrained and unprincipled being puffed up by vanity, while his coat is out at the elbows, cursing the Greeks as depraved while he himself is carrying on open & shameless debauchery; and crying out against their trickery and baseness, while he himself by every possible means honest or dishonest is trying to gorge down the fat of the land; and fill a purse which he brought empty from home. I must say however that as a body English Philhellenes are more respectable and disinterested than the French; who are too often thoughtless, vain or unprincipled adventurers who think of nothing but glory and enjoyment; and who curse the Greeks for not more appreciating a character which their own conduct sets forth as selfish and unprincipled. Little have Philhellenes done toward raising the reputation of Europeans here."

[39] Journal IV, Nov. 25, 1828.

[40] Journal IV, Nov. 30, 1828.

IV

By December 8 Howe was back in Aegina with a new plan in his mind. He deferred working in the Morea to assist the refugees clustered on the island, who were mostly Athenians, completely destitute. He conceived a public-work project made to order for their needs. In ancient times Aegina's harbor had been important, but now it was blocked with sediment and garbage, forcing ships to anchor far out. It was a health hazard as well, since from the polluted waters emanated an unhealthy odor. To repair the port required only that a mole, or solid wall, be built around the borders of the shore a little way into the water, and then filled up behind with stones and earth. In that way workmen could form a wharf that would render the port usable by enabling ships to come right up to the water's edge.

The physician-turned-food-administrator now added engineering to his accomplishments. As he planned the project, he estimated that he would need only twenty masons to build the mole and four or five hundred unskilled refugees to haul stones and do the filling.[41] The project did not pose any great technical problems. Howe had only to build a cofferdam across the inner side of the harbor, bail out the water, and build the wall. Conveniently for him, there was an ample supply of stone near at hand. Just outside the city lay the ruins of a temple of Venus buried under centuries of rubbish. Its foundation blocks were of hewn stone and of perfect regularity, from four to six feet long, three to four wide, and about eighteen inches to two feet thick, requiring only excavation to become immediately useful.[42]

When the news of work spread, the unemployed of Aegina flocked around Howe in such numbers that he had difficulty in making his selection. He finally chose 300 of the most destitute of both sexes, 100 men at a daily wage of three pounds of Indian meal, and 200 stout, rugged, married peasant women who could offer no temptation to foreigners, at two and a half pounds. He divided them

[41] Journal IV, Dec. 8, 1828.
[42] Howe to Mann, 1857, p. 18.

up into companies with a captain at the head of each. On December 19 they were ready to begin. After making the sign of the cross, they blessed him, "then spittling their hands, they struck their pickaxes in the ground, and went on with great glee." [43] The work progressed peacefully. Within a week he had a crew of 600, but the number needing aid had swelled beyond his expectation. They swarmed down from the hills to surround him, pleading for employment.[44] The benevolent-hearted relief worker had his hands full.

Unable to delegate any of his tasks, because there was no other to share the responsibility, Howe had to attend to every detail for himself. Despite the fact that his masons were supposed to be skilled laborers, he had to get down with them and show them how to bail water and build the cofferdam.[45] More serious was his trouble with the *Gerontia,* or Commission of Elders. When they saw how much the "rich American" was spending, they figured he might as well spend more and give them the best port in Greece. Howe offered to do it if they would pay the difference. They promised to pay in installments, but he distrusted their word.[46] He was so vexed that he felt inclined to cancel the project unless he received a petition from them begging him to go on. The thought of the misery he would bring to his dependents pained him, but he had his pride. His workers, upon learning of his difficulties, appointed a committee to tell the *Gerontia* how dependent they were on his bounty for their livelihood and to beg them to accede to his wishes. During that day the petition was made out on Howe's terms.[47]

Work resumed and continued without note until the mole was finished on March 22, 1829.[48] It was a creation of great utility. All Aegina admired it; even Count Viarro Capodistrias, one of the

[43] Journal IV, Dec. 19, 1828.
[44] Journal IV, Dec. 24, 1828. He also aided those too weak to work in the open. He hired old women to work in their homes cutting Greek *fustinellas* on a piecework basis. Dec. 26.
[45] Journal IV, Dec. 30, 1828.
[46] Journal IV, Dec. 24, 1828.
[47] Journal IV, Dec. 26, 1828.
[48] Journal IV, March 22, 1829.

president's inept office-holding brothers, approved.[49] The "American Mole," as it was called, was in use for many years; Howe himself was to land there in 1867 when he returned to Greece on another errand of mercy. His achievement had manifold significance; he had restored Aegina's harbor to usefulness, he had kept several hundred persons alive, and as a by-product, he had done some valuable archaeological work by uncovering an ancient temple of some historic significance.

While most of the individuals with whom he dealt acted in good faith, there had been attempts to take advantage of his generosity. He suspected some dishonesty among the poor begging for assistance. One day a beggar came who, Howe felt, had purposely left off his clothes. He was fat, and his body skin was white, while his hands and head were tanned. The doctor did not tell him how he discovered his trick, but peremptorily sent him off.[50]

V

As the Mole approached completion, Howe began thinking of other projects he might undertake to keep his dependents from starving. They were exiles from Athens, and were likely to be so for quite a while longer, since conditions there were still unsettled. The idea of an agricultural colony appealed to him, and he resolved to ask the government to appropriate a bit of national land for the purpose, for which he would supply the seeds and means of cultivation.[51] He explained his plans to Capodistrias, who after a long delay promised to second any schemes laid before him fully.[52]

Howe chose Hexamilia, at the narrowest part of the Gulf of Corinth, as his site. The soil was good, with sufficient water to commence activity. He expected it would lie along the course of a canal if one should be cut, and certainly on the route of a railroad if one should be put through. He decided to ask the authorities for

---

[49] Typescript Journal, April 5, 1829. There is a slight overlapping of the typescript and manuscript journal. All references to the typescript will be clearly labeled.

[50] Journal IV, Dec. 20, 1828.

[51] Journal IV, Feb. 9, 1829.

[52] Journal IV, Feb. 20, 1829. There are two entries of this date. This reference is to the second.

5000 stremmata, about 2000 acres.[53] Applying on his return, he waited so long without a response that he was ready to abandon the plan, since his pride did not let him press it,[54] but he received authorization at the last possible moment. Just as he was about to leave for a vacation trip with Finlay, Russ, and Stuyvesant, during which they planned to visit Thermopylae and climb Helicon, a government secretary brought official letters of approval. Howe canceled his trip and set to work.[55]

He had been granted the tract he had requested in a section known as Apano-Hexamilia, with an exemption from taxation for five years. Capodistrias promised the assistance of his government.[56] Howe, as the agent of the American Greek relief committees, undertook to furnish seed and cattle for four months, and to leave all the produce for his colonists except for a reserve of equitable proportion to be devoted to some charitable purpose.[57]

During the next few weeks he divided his time between his colony site, which he decided to call Colombia[58] (sometimes he used the term "Washingtonia"), and Aegina, getting supplies and choosing colonists. Howe was in his element. In later years he said this venture was perhaps the happiest part of his life.[59] He had carte blanche, the administration was of no assistance to him, and there was none to dispute with him.

In company for some months with the Englishman, David Urquhart, later an M.P., whom he considered as his only "civilized companion," he traveled around Rumelia buying cattle and whatever implements were available.[60] Wherever he could, he hired skilled craftsmen. By the beginning of May, with his colony nicely

---

[53] Journal IV, March 13, 1829. He also examined the area carefully and sent Benjamin Silliman of Yale an archaeological account of the region—Boston Recorder, XV, 33 (Aug. 18, 1830), 132.

[54] Journal IV, March 25, 1829.

[55] Journal IV, March 25, 1829.

[56] Capodistrias to Howe (in French), March 12/24, 1829, Howe Papers, Houghton.

[57] Howe to a Greek Government secretary, undated, Howe Papers, Houghton.

[58] Typescript Journal, March 8, 1829.

[59] Howe to Mann, 1857, p. 21.

[60] Howe to Mann, p. 21.

established, he began to think of the higher life for his people and later that month he opened a Lancastrian school under a trained schoolmaster.[61]

During these weeks Howe strained his physical endurance. Besides practicing medicine all over the area, he had much administrative detail to attend to.[62] "I laboured here day & night in season & out; & was governor, legislator, clerk, constable, & everything but patriarch," he wrote.[63] It was too much to expect that he could keep up the pace. In July he suffered a severe attack of malaria, which kept him from his work until August.[64] The rest of his stay was marred by recurrent seizures.

Internal order at Colombia was good. With the colonists peaceful and hard-working, the only threats to peace came from outside, from bands of soldiers who roamed and pillaged the countryside. They attacked the village many times, and Howe himself had several narrow escapes. Urquhart showed daring in one of these forays when he disarmed and captured two robbers.[65]

The harried minor potentate managed to get away from his colony for several weeks during the fall when he appears to have gone to Smyrna. Upon his return he learned of illness and discouragement at Hexamilia.[66] Howe blamed all the difficulties on Capodistrias, who never kept his promises.[67] The enraged American had several stormy sessions with the wily Corfiote, until finally, in December, Howe came to realize that he had been deceived.[68] Testily he entered in his Journal that Capodistrias was a confounded and willful liar. He regretted that he had started his colony without having first made sure of the government's good faith in granting him the land, and the privileges he demanded, without which more than half the projected good would be null. Howe very con-

[61] Typescript Journal, May 21, 1829.
[62] Ms. Journal entry for June 24 does not agree with typescript of same date.
[63] Howe to Mann, 1857, p. 21.
[64] Typescript Journal, Aug. 4, 1829.
[65] Howe to Mann, 1857, p. 22.
[66] Typescript Journal, Oct. 29, 1829.
[67] Typescript Journal, Nov. 7, 1829.
[68] Typescript Journal, Dec. 1.

sciously noble-minded felt his conscience was clear; his intentions had been the best, and they still remained so.[69]

Sometime after January 1830, the veteran Philhellene left Greece, nursing his bitterness towards Capodistrias who, he said, wished to rid Greece of every foreigner of principle and independence who refused to be his humble servant.[70] Greece was not to be so devoid of gratitude as he thought. Once the situation there became stabilized, after the establishment of a monarchy, the king created him a Chevalier of the Order of St. Savior.[71] He was ever after to be known as "Chev" to those closest to him, especially to his wife, Julia Ward, and Theodore Parker, the noted clergyman.

VI

Howe spent the next year touring Europe as he had planned. He traveled through Italy, Switzerland, and Germany before settling in Paris to study surgery.[72] Reaching the French capital in time to witness the July Revolution, he enjoyed the sight of the final overthrow of the Bourbons. To him, it was the people's movement, and joining their side he served as one of a band who escorted the Marquis de Lafayette, the idol of a generation of American youth, to the Hôtel de Ville.[73] The turbulence was tonic to his jaded mind.

[69] Typescript Journal, Dec. 21. Howe was unfavorable to the whole family. A few months earlier he had written: ". . . sure am I that if Count Capo D'Istria, and his two brothers had been born and bred with those six hundred labourers who are at work for me, I should never have discovered enough intelligence in them to have made them overseers, possibly Capo, might have merited the place of overseer of twenty-five; for though by no means a man of talent or original thought he has a clear head, and good judgement [sic]: he is rather a made man however; and his fort [sic] is labour in the detail of a cabinet: he would make a fine secretary of State under an able President: there is no end to his patience in labour and writing." Ms. Journal IV, Jan. 19, 1829. Finlay in his *History* agrees fully.

[70] Howe to Sampson, dated from "Washingtonia," Jan. 30, 1830, Howe Papers, Houghton.

[71] Howe to Rizo, Secy. of State, Sept. 26, 1835, Howe Papers, Houghton. Acknowledges receipt of award. I am indebted to Father Joseph R. Frese, S.J., for deciphering this letter.

[72] Howe to Sampson, July 1, 1830, Howe Papers, gives an account of his passage to Switzerland; Howe to George C. Shattuck, July 31, 1830, Shattuck Papers, MHS, gives an interesting and unfavorable view of Heidelberg students.

[73] Howe to Sampson, Aug. 8, 1830, Howe Papers, Houghton; Howe to Mann, 1857, p. 23.

His faith in democracy was restored. For the next months he lived the life familiar to students of all ages, namely, cheap rooms and cheap meals, with long hours of work. The city's noted charms could not attract him. He went to the hospital at six every morning all winter, and was much too busy to fritter his time away on frivolities, he told his father.[74] He spent ten weeks in England, returning to Boston on April 16, 1831, over six years after his first departure.[75] Now a battered veteran of twenty-nine, with his soldiering behind him, Howe was ready to take up a new career, although uncertain as to his future course.

VII

Howe's character had broadened and deepened during his *Wanderjahre*. His long stay abroad had left its impression on him. The thrill-seeking youth who dashed off to war to forget a love affair had widened his field of activity from dealing merely with physical ills to handling social ills as well. He could not bear to see suffering or injustice without making some effort to mitigate them. This fiery passion to right social wrongs, which became the leading characteristic of his later years, was untempered by mellowness. He lacked the quality of indulgence of personal failings in others that increasing age and understanding can give.

Above all, he lacked humility. For years he had given orders to persons several times his age, who bowed to his will. He had seen his knowledge vindicate his views in differences of opinions concerning medical methods and general policies. It is not at all surprising, under the circumstances, that he should have developed an inordinate pride and on occasion an uncontrollable temper, as is shown by his dealings with the *Gerontia,* and his relationship with Capodistrias. He was thin-skinned and quick to take offense at the slightest ridicule. These qualities of character were never to disappear.

[74] Howe to Joseph N. Howe, Aug. 28, 1830, Howe Papers, Houghton; and F. B. Sanborn to Laura E. Richards, Jan. 2, 1905, Howe Papers, Houghton.
[75] Howe to Sampson, April 19, 1831, Howe Papers, Houghton.

IV

Choosing a Profession

As frequently happens with military men returning to civil life, Samuel Gridley Howe faced the future with uncertainty. He knew only that he did not wish to practice medicine, yet his past career and experiences had not prepared him for anything else. During the years when other men of his age had begun to find their niche in society, he had been leading a picturesque existence which led nowhere. But the final choice of a career, the decision he had avoided for almost a decade, could no longer be delayed. While still in the Morea, he had begun to think seriously about the matter and decided that he preferred to remain in Greece at an American consular post. He appealed to Everett, who had never failed him in his hours of need, but for once the golden-tongued politician was unsuccessful.[1] President Jackson turned a deaf ear to the patronage plea of a Clay partisan.

I

A few days after arriving home, Howe received an unexpected offer from a Philadelphia friend, named Howard, to manage a Whig paper. Joyously accepting, he went to the Quaker City to make arrangements. Matters at first proceeded smoothly, and the backers, who were closely associated with Nicholas Biddle, issued a

[1] Edward Everett to Pres. Andrew Jackson, April 22, 1830, Everett Papers, letter book 12 (LXVI), p. 24, MHS.

prospectus.[2] Everett appears to better advantage in this enterprise, doing what he could to smooth the path of the tyro journalist by his usual stream of florid letters to influential friends;[3] but in a short time the possibility of a journalistic career in Pennsylvania faded for Howe. Fearing that he lacked "enough of moral courage or brass perhaps for an editor," he withdrew, recommending a friend for the job, and returning to Boston discouraged.[4]

The task of finding a permanent position was hard indeed; a combination of idealism, the urge to lead a useful life, and lingering immaturity kept him in a sea of indecision. Disinclined to practice his profession, he spoke of a

desire to attack the Powers that be, Powers [which] I think from my soul have disgraced the country; desire for the excitement of an active life; hope of rendering myself of use to the country and known to its best and most powerful citizens, and some idea that it may facilitate my ulterior plans on Greece, For there I wish to go and spend my days; there I am sure I can be of great use, fill a wide field of some kind, probably a professor of anatomy live respected and die remembered. This country is too well supplied with men of talent and experience and ambition for those of my moderate pretentions [sic] and mediocratic [sic] talents, to hope to make much of a figure or do much good.[5]

At home for the next several weeks, and after failing to secure the directorship of a colony in Liberia, he "lay on [his] oars," doing a little writing for periodicals such as the *New England Magazine* which, under the aegis of Joseph T. Buckingham and his son Edwin, began its brief but brilliant career in July 1831. In his enforced leisure during that summer he listlessly pondered his future. Expecting to settle down within the next couple of years, anywhere

[2] Typescript Journal, May 16, 1831. Where he might have developed Whig sympathies it is impossible to say. He had been out of touch with American developments for years.

[3] For example — Everett to John A. Sergeant, May 21, 1831, Everett Papers, 12 (LXVI), 53–55, MHS.

[4] Howe to Sampson, July 24, 1831, Howe Papers, Houghton.

[5] Typescript Journal, May 16, 1831. A quarter-century later, he gave a different reason. Writing to Horace Mann in 1857, page 23, he said, ". . . I did not like to enter on the practice of my profession. I had then a good deal of nonsense about me, & did not like the notion of charging money for medical services."

from Athens to the Oregon Country, he felt no joy at the prospect. He brooded over his lost opportunities, and looking about him, he realized he was falling behind. His schoolboy friends were now men of affairs, and the girls he had known had bloomed into matronly maturity. He alone was rootless. Though marriage was prominent in his thoughts, he saw no possibility for matrimony in the foreseeable future. He could not afford to marry a poor girl, nor would he wed a rich one, preferring to starve an old bachelor than live off someone he should support. These ruminations made him feel old. Still a few months under thirty, he already felt that the greater part of his active career was spent, that there was little ahead.[6]

The change in his fortunes and possibly his mood came rather suddenly. One day he visited a college friend, Dr. John D. Fisher, the leading spirit in a committee that had incorporated the New England Asylum for the Blind in 1829, which was seeking a director. When Fisher asked the unemployed social worker to take the job, he accepted. At once Howe was galvanized into action. Within a few days he had completed his arrangements to return to Europe to study methods of teaching the blind and engage teachers.[7] Supplied with letters of introduction from the ever-obliging Everett,[8] the destined world-foremost educator of the blind sailed at the beginning of September 1831. His appointment had met with approval; commented the *Boston Advertiser*: "The selection argues well for the success of the work. We doubt not that under his auspices the benevolent intentions of those who have engaged in it will be carried into full effect."[9]

---

[6] Howe to Sampson, July 24, 1831.

[7] Franklin B. Sanborn to Laura E. Richards, Jan. 2, 1905, Howe Papers, Houghton. For some reason, Laura Richards does not use this account in her biography of her father, *Samuel Gridley Howe* (New York, 1936), even though it was available to her when she edited his papers, *Letters and Journals* (Boston, 1906), 2 vols., and seems more probable than the one she gives, I, 389. As she tells it, three members of the committee met Howe on Boylston Street. "Here is Howe!" Fisher said to his companions, "the very man we have been looking for all this time."

[8] Everett to Francis Jeffrey, Lord Advocate of Scotland, Aug. 19, 1831, Everett Papers, 12 (LXVI), 85, MHS.

[9] *Boston Advertiser,* Aug. 30, 1831.

II

Howe was a student again as he returned to his former haunts on the Continent, but this time he was determined to learn all that the Old World had to teach him of the mystic art of teaching the blind. He threw himself into his labors in Paris, but he was unable to ignore new cries of agony from an old source of pain.[10]

A revolution in Poland the summer before had been speedily crushed by the Russian government. Many of the insurgents had fled to East Prussia, and now the advent of winter made their situation serious. As news of their plight crossed the Atlantic, the pattern of American charity had reasserted itself: committees sprang up and contributions were raised. Since it was too late to send aid to the scene of conflict, a large proportion of the funds were directed to the Marquis de Lafayette, occasionally with the stipulation that Dr. Howe be the agent in their disbursal. At the venerable hero's urging, the Americans in Paris formed a committee, with Howe as chairman, since he was most experienced in such matters. Their Wednesday night meetings in James Fenimore Cooper's home were enlivened by the presence of the Marquis. All were surprised at his appearance of vivacity and youth. Though he was over seventy-five, age had not dimmed his powers in the least. Marshaling the urbanity and charm of a highly literate citizen of the world, he entranced his audiences with his wit and tales of his experiences.[11]

The chairman took his Polish relief work seriously. As his roommate reported years later, he maintained open house for all who came,

many of them to my knowledge getting no food elsewhere, and among others, Lelewel, the distinguished poet and patriot, coming in one morn-

---

[10] Howe to Sampson, Nov. 14, 1831, Howe Papers, Houghton, gives an account of his life during these weeks.

[11] "Lafayette in 1832. Scenes in Europe," *New England Magazine*, VIII (May 1835), 337–339. The article was published anonymously. Offhand I would have ascribed it to Howe, but a penciled notation in Charles Sumner's copy in the Harvard Library gives the credit to Henry Cleveland. At any rate, the author was a member of the Polish relief committee and spoke from personal observation.

ing to ask a breakfast, as I well recollect, after having slept out a winter's night in the street.[12]

In January 1832, Howe left for Prussia, taking with him the Committee's funds to the site of need. He thus innocently embarked on an adventure more harrowing than any he had yet undergone, one that was to leave marks on his character for the remainder of his days. After inspecting the Berlin school for the blind, he left the city in mid-February to seek out the fugitives in their camps. Though scenes of misery were familiar to him, what he encountered in East Prussia seemed as unprecedented to him as if he were on his first job. His heart went out to the refugees suffering physically and mentally, many of whom he saw wandering around in the middle of winter with bare feet swollen and bleeding from the cold. They had no money, and no means of gaining any, yet they preferred to die in exile rather than return to their homeland and oppression. Theoretically the Russian government was paying Prussia for their support, but he saw no reason to believe that St. Petersburg's claims of benevolence had much basis.

Howe presented himself to the commandant of the area, a certain General Schmidt, and gained from him a grudging consent to distribute relief. Before he could do much, however, the permission was rescinded, and the unwelcome snooper was ordered out of the region.[13] Disappointed, he returned to Berlin, arriving there at the end of the month. The authorities, however, had watched his movements very carefully, and late on the evening of his arrival a company of gendarmes came to arrest him. Taken aback by their appearance, Howe asked the officer to allow him to spend the night in his room, and promised to go with them peaceably in the morning. Ignorant of what he might have done, but fearing the worst, he worked feverishly that night hiding what he considered incriminating papers in the hollow head of a bust of the Prussian king and tearing up some unimportant ones which he left in the

---

[12] *The New Mirror* (Oct. 14, 1843), p. 30; available in Howe clippings at the Perkins School for the Blind, Watertown.
[13] Howe, Letter from Berlin Prison, Ford Collection, NYPL.

sink.[14] At dawn he was escorted to the Ministry of Police, and later that day after an intensive examination was imprisoned. At no time had his captors told him the charge against him, nor was he allowed to communicate with anyone.

Howe lay *au secret* in a dungeon eight feet wide, seeing no one but his interrogators who from time to time questioned him. Their method reminded him of what he had read about the Spanish Inquisition:

the solemn scribe who was ushered into my cell the first day sat for hours scribbling away the history of my life, . . . and scratching down the words as fast as I could speak them without ever lifting up his eyes from his paper. . . .[15]

He addressed a petition to the Prussian King in French plaintively maintaining innocence of any crimes and begging him to intercede, but there is no reason to think that His Majesty concerned himself about the anti-monarchical American who succored revolutionists.[16] The distraught prisoner, next trying bluster, wrote the Minister of Police (again in French) demanding to see the accusation against him, to communicate with friends, and the termination of his case with as little delay as possible. He even brought the Christianity of the realm into question, but all to no avail.[17]

His imprisonment might have lasted longer than it did, had it not been for the fact that the only other American in the city knew that he was supposed to be there. Albert Brisbane, the famous socialist, at this time a follower of St. Simon, had traveled into Berlin with Howe, and decided to pay him a courtesy call the first afternoon after their arrival. His suspicions were aroused when the clerk at Howe's pension claimed to know nothing about a recently arrived American who had given that address. Brisbane, realizing

[14] This same roommate in the same article says that Howe wrote to a friend six months later who took the secreted letters from the hollow bust, but his daughter says they were there until 1843, when Horace Mann recovered them.

[15] Howe, Letter from Berlin Prison, March 1832, Ford Collection, NYPL.

[16] Howe to the King of Prussia, undated, Howe Papers, Houghton.

[17] Howe to Monsieur le Ministre, March 5, 1832, Howe Papers, Houghton.

what had happened, went to the Minister of Justice, who was uncompromising and greatly irritated at this interference with the workings of Prussian justice. Without wasting more time, the worried Brisbane wrote the American Minister at Paris (the United States had no representative in Prussia), William C. Rives, who learned the news March 13, and who hurriedly notified the members of the Polish relief committee which held a meeting three days later.[18]

Howe in the meantime was completely ignorant of any efforts being made on his behalf, although he suspected that the presence of a countryman in the city would probably save him from foul play.[19] Throughout his first week in prison he was questioned repeatedly about his activities at the home of the French consul in Danzig, and where he had met certain persons with whom he had been seen. They seemed especially interested in his connection with Brisbane and why the latter went to Berlin. Howe told them that he knew nothing of St. Simonian teaching. He knew only that his traveling companion had preached weird doctrines and seemed deranged.[20]

After March 10, they left the prisoner completely alone to meditate his sins in solitary confinement. Suffering terribly under this treatment, he managed to gain the good will of the turnkey, who smuggled to him some coarse paper and a stubby pencil. Howe spent the next few days pouring out his soul to an unnamed friend, in a letter that shows to what depths of despair he had sunk. He knew he had been imprudent with his captors, but republicanism was rooted in his bones; he admitted he had been uncourtly and answered them too boldly as well. He suspected them of laying traps for him, but he was sure that since he was a Yankee, they would meet their match. In desperation he pleaded:

Do what you choose with this information . . . but if by the next packet you should not hear of my liberation, then for God's sake do what you can for me to get an intercession from [the] Government. I

[18] *Boston Recorder,* XVII, 19 (May 9, 1832), 75.
[19] Letter from Berlin Prison, March 1832, Ford Collection, NYPL.
[20] Memoir (in French) of imprisonment, March 9, 1832, Howe Papers, Houghton.

keep up a bold face & look careless but I own my heart sinks at the thoughts of wasting away my strength in this miserable cell.[21]

Apparently deciding after three weeks of imprisonment that the game of cat and mouse had gone on with him long enough, that he was really innocent of any serious crime, and that they had given him a good fright, his captors allowed him to write Rives on March 21. Howe stated his case fully. Now knowing that the turn in his fortunes had come he boasted, "I have gone unscathed through hands of Turk & Tartar; & trust in time to be delivered from this people, who though a bit suspicious, are neertheless [sic] Christian & civilized." [22]

Rives all along had been doing what little he could. He communicated with the Prussian Minister in Paris.[23] Whether the diplomatic negotiations succeeded in getting the prisoner out any more quickly is highly problematical. At any rate, Howe was suddenly released. As he was leaving the prison, the Minister of Police finally informed him that he had been held for persuading the Polish soldiers to disobey the orders of the Prussian government about returning home. For that crime alone he could have been brought to trial, but His Majesty "in his indulgence" had merely ordered him to be taken to France. Howe, in high dudgeon, protested against this summary treatment. He insisted on a trial, and, failing that, to be sent at least to Saxony which was next on his itinerary. It was to no avail. His guards were ordered to rush him to the frontier with all possible haste. They were to travel night and day, to avoid large cities, and under no circumstances to suffer their charge to speak to anyone, or be allowed to rest. He was to be imprisoned if he made the slightest attempt to escape. The 600-mile journey to France lasted six days, during which time Howe, weakened by his incarceration, suffered physical agony so great that even the guards took pity and did allow him some rest.

With his dignity ruffled by this cavalier treatment, he was dumped across the border near Metz. Though glad to be out of Prussian

[21] Letter from Berlin Prison, March 1832, Ford Collection, NYPL.
[22] Howe to Rives, March 21, 1832, Howe Papers, Houghton.
[23] Rives to Howe, April 24, 1832, Howe Papers, Houghton.

clutches, he was so enraged at his mistreatment that he demanded
Rives gain redress for him.[24] Rives quietly suggested that he take
his case to Washington.[25] It does not appear that anything further
was done.

Howe was now free to resume his mission in Europe. He returned to America in July 1832, prepared to breathe life into the
New England Asylum for the Blind.[26]

In conclusion, it should be mentioned that Lafayette and the
American Committee in Paris issued statements in the fall of 1832
which paid tribute to Howe's honorable service in the cause of the
Poles.[27] Howe retained his interest in the Polish refugees for several
years more. From June 1834 until June 1835, he served as secretary
of a Boston committee which handled large sums for their relief.
His group lasted much longer than its New York counterpart which
Albert Gallatin headed.[28] Both groups agitated for the establishment
of a colony for Poles that Congress approved in June 1834.[29] Nothing came of the act.

[24] Howe to Rives, April 6, 1832, Howe Papers, Houghton.
[25] Rives to Howe, April 24, 1832, Howe Papers, Houghton.
[26] Boston Weekly Messenger and Massachusetts Journal, Aug. 21, 1832. Most
readily available in Howe Clippings, Perkins School.
[27] Laura E. Richards, ed., Letters and Journals of Samuel Gridley Howe (Boston,
1906), I, 411–415.
[28] Howe-Gallatin Correspondence, NYHS.
[29] Register of Debates in Congress, 23 Cong. 1st session, X, 2127.

V

The Early Years of the Perkins Institution

The movement for the education of the blind received its impetus from Valentin Haüy (1745–1822), a French educator who founded schools in Paris, Berlin, and St. Petersburg, and inspired the creation of many more on the Continent. With few precedents to guide him, he taught several generations of children to read, write, do calculations, the manual arts, and music. So impressive were his achievements that for forty years his methods and his ideas dominated the schools of Europe.[1] None equaled him in achievements until the advent of Samuel Gridley Howe.

Howe's years of indecision were over. He had found his place in society. Henceforth his destiny was to bring those deprived of sight, and in some cases hearing as well, into closer relationship with society. Under Howe's direction the Perkins Institution and Massachusetts School for the Blind, as it was called during most of his lifetime, quickly surpassed all schools in existence to become the foremost educational agency of its type in the world, and he the foremost educator. Pioneering in the development of new techniques of instruction and in the improvement of old, he demonstrated that a learned blind man need not be considered an extraordinary

[1] Ishbel Ross, *Journey Into Light* (New York, 1951), pp. 96–115.

phenomenon, and that a common-school education was within the grasp of all so handicapped.

I

Howe was determined to fulfill in his school the hopes of those who had founded it three years before.[2] Designed to meet American needs, it would be organized on a plan entirely different from any he had seen. European schools he regarded as "beacons to warn rather than lights to guide."[3] In his opinion, they had made little progress since the days of Haüy. Typically Yankee, the apprentice had seen how to improve on his masters immediately on setting up his own shop.

While granting that all existing institutions were of benevolent intent, he declared their chief error lay in neglecting the individual needs of the students, since they failed to maintain a proper balance between the intellectual and mechanical curricula. In Paris the children learned flashy intellectual stunts in order to wheedle appropriations from the authorities, but no attention was paid to their ultimate destiny in life. Though from all sides he heard the school in the French capital praised as the best in the world, he was forced to disagree.[4] He had found it pervaded with a spirit of illiberality amounting almost to charlatanism. A cold and jealous secretiveness had greeted his attempts at inspection there.[5]

[2] *Laws of Massachusetts,* XI, chap. cxiii, March 2, 1829. The charter provided for a board of twelve trustees, eight chosen by the corporation, and four publicly appointed. The state agreed to meet the expenses there of thirty pupils annually without regard to age, in addition to which the school could receive as many private paying pupils as it could accommodate. Among the petitioners were Thomas H. Perkins, Robert Rantoul, Theodore Sedgwick, Stephen C. Phillips, William Appleton, Samuel A. Eliot, Amos Lawrence, Abbott Lawrence, William H. Prescott, John D. Fisher, and John Lowell, Jr. An account of events leading up to the incorporation is to be found in Justin Winsor, ed., *Memorial History of Boston* (Boston, 1881), IV, 271.

[3] "Education of the Blind," *North American Review,* XXXVII (July 1833), 34. A penciled notation in the Lamont Library's copy ascribes the article to Howe.

[4] *Address of the Trustees of the New England Institution for the Education of the Blind to the Public* (Boston, 1833), p. 7. This will henceforth be referred to as the *First Report,* and the subsequent reports will be given their brief title.

[5] *North American Review* (July 1833), p. 45.

The remaining schools in Europe were deficient in other respects. Dresden treated its pupils very kindly, but failed to teach reading.[6] London and Edinburgh went to the opposite extreme from Paris, both doing excellent work in preparing children for trades, but neglecting academic studies. The mats and mattresses that came from the Scottish school were the best in its vicinity, but he found no books there.[7]

Though Howe desired to establish the balanced curriculum that no school had, he did not lay down a general rule to be observed towards all pupils: they would learn what they were best fitted for. He decided that those who manifested no talent for academic work would learn handicrafts only. The majority however would get a combination of some mechanical art and a basic store of intellectual knowledge. Even those with obvious intellectual capacities would get some manual instruction in order to round out their course.[8]

Howe foresaw no difficulty in teaching reading. All would read from raised letters. He proposed to publish books for the blind as cheaply as printed ones, and to provide whole libraries in that form as soon as possible. Among early projects would be an edition of the evangelists and, later on, the entire New Testament.[9] In his opinion this venture was as desirable as sending Bibles to savages, and could be done at less cost.[10]

The doctor indicated that in Boston the children would learn self-reliance. His observations on his tour had convinced him that the greatest obstacle to the proper education of the blind was that their previous treatment hampered the development of their remaining senses. Too often they had been prevented from groping their way around freely by overattentive mothers who pulled obstacles from their path instead of allowing them to fall over them and in that way learning the arrangement of things. Eventually, he warned, such treatment would lead to their injuring themselves much more severely. Cautioning against the use of expressions of

[6] *First Report* (1833), p. 8.
[7] *First Report*, pp. 9–11.
[8] *First Report*, p. 15.
[9] *First Report*, p. 11.
[10] *First Report*, p. 10.

pity which led to the blind child's feeling more helpless and never becoming inclined to put forth his own energies, he called on people to stop reminding the blind of their infirmities and pressing their inferiority upon them.[11] He had seen blind men who moved in normal society and refused assistance. To achieve a similar result, others in their condition needed only the same opportunity to look after themselves.

II

The New England Institution for the Education of the Blind (its name had been changed from Asylum to Institution during the interim) finally began operations in its director's home at 140 Pleasant Street, Boston, in August 1832, with a staff of three, consisting of Howe and two blind teachers he had hired in Europe, a Frenchman, Edouard Trenchéri, who taught the academic subjects, and an Edinburgh mechanic. The student body numbered seven and ranged in age from six to twenty.[12] Howe had done everything himself from planning the curriculum to rounding up the students, even traveling around the state for pupils. One day, having heard of a family in Andover with eligible children, he drove out with John D. Fisher. At the toll house he saw two pretty little girls, one about six and the other eight standing hand in hand, both blind, who had come from home to hear the gossip of the neighborhood. It seemed to Howe as if they had been brought "providentially to meet messengers sent of God, to deliver them out of darkness." [13] Their mother was overjoyed at the opportunity, and so were enrolled Abby and Sophia Carter, the first pupils of the first American school for the blind. They later became teachers and supported themselves and their parents.

Howe threw himself into his job with characteristic energy. Owing to the newness of the work, none of the customary aids to teaching were available; all had to be made by hand. This was a

[11] *First Report,* pp. 16–18.

[12] *First Report,* p. 19. Though it was the first institution of its type to be chartered, it was not the first to begin operations. The State of New York had beaten Massachusetts by opening its school in the spring.

[13] *43d Report,* Oct. 1874 (Boston, 1875), p. 74.

minor problem. A man who could supervise the construction of a wharf and set up an agricultural village was not to be stopped by a lack of maps and textbooks. Elizabeth Palmer Peabody has left a touching description of how she saw him at work during these early months in the house on Pleasant Street where Horace Mann, one of the trustees, had taken her and her sister Mary, his future wife.

> [There] . . . in the simplest surroundings we found Dr. Howe with the half dozen first pupils. . . . He had then been about six months at work, and had invented & laboriously *executed* some books with raised letters, to teach them to read; & some geographical maps — and the geometrical diagrams for mathematics. He had gummed *twine*, I think — an enormous labour — upon cardboard forming the printed letters!
> I shall not in all time & eternity, forget the impression made on me, by seeing the hero of the Greek Revolution . . . wholly absorbed & applying all the energies of his genius to this —. . . and doing it — as Christ did — without money & without price. . . .[14]

The students showed great promise from the start. After six months Howe proudly exhibited them before the Massachusetts legislature in the hope of getting more money, since he had exhausted his appropriation. His plan was successful. The General Court voted an annual $6,000 for the maintenance of twenty students, aged six to twenty-four.[15] Connecticut, New Hampshire, and Vermont also fell before his onslaught, voting to send students to Boston.[16]

Private citizens equaled the liberality of the states. So impressed was Colonel Thomas H. Perkins by the children's performance before the General Court that in April 1833 he donated a mansion on Pearl Street on condition that sufficient funds be raised to ensure the perpetuity of the institution. Both Boston and Salem held fairs to raise the required sum. Salem's citizens produced over $2000, while Boston's elaborate May Fair proved to be the social event of

[14] Elizabeth Palmer Peabody to Julia Ward Howe, Feb. 9, 1876, Howe Papers, Houghton.
[15] *Mass. Acts & Resolves,* chap. XXVIII, Feb. 16, 1833.
[16] *Second Report* (1834), p. 6.

the season. Mrs. Harrison Gray Otis, the city's undisputed society leader, headed the committee on arrangements. Faneuil Hall was transformed into a garden with branches, flowers, garlands, and potted trees decorating every available space. "Yorick" Howe's *nom de plume* when he wrote it up) estimated that half of the "respectable" females of the city had been engaged directly or indirectly in preparing articles for the fair. For weeks it was the only topic of conversation.[17] Even children assisted; little Edward Everett Hale, a lad of ten, spent hours cutting hearts out of gum copal with his jackknife for his mother to string on a golden thread.[18] Not to be outdone by women and children, three of Boston's younger poets, Park Benjamin, Oliver Wendell Holmes, and John O. Sargent, put their heads together and produced an anthology of their works, *The Harbinger; A May Gift.* In it were to be found such verse destined for fame as the "Last Leaf," "The Ballad of the Oysterman," and "My Aunt." [19] The fair raised over $11,000.[20] Within a month, $50,000 had been contributed, and in the fall of 1833, alterations having been completed, the children began to study in their new quarters.[21]

During 1833, the institution received $61,279.43 from various sources, and from having started $2000 in debt, it ended the year with $33,000 to its credit, truly a remarkable showing for a school of as yet more promise than fulfillment.[22]

III

The regimen at the school was firm but kind. Just as Howe had promised, there was no pampering of the children. In winter they were up at 5:30 A.M.; roll call was at six. Work began a half hour

---

[17] "Yorick" "The May Fair," *New England Magazine,* IV (June 1833), 504–506.
[18] *Proceedings at the Celebration of the One Hundredth Anniversary of the Birth of Dr. Samuel Gridley Howe, Nov. 11, 1901* (Boston, 1902), p. 11. There is a catalogue of articles sold at the fair in the Houghton Library.
[19] *The Harbinger; A May Gift* (Boston, 1833), pp. 34, 36, 44, respectively.
[20] *Second Report* (1834), p. 15.
[21] *Second Report,* p. 6.
[22] *Second Report,* p. 15.

later and continued throughout the day with breaks for meals and rest until six in the evening. During the leisure hour from seven to eight, they listened to reading, and by ten even the eldest were in bed.[23] Religious services, which Howe led every morning, consisted of Scripture reading without comment. On Sunday all were required to attend church. The children could go to whichever church they wished, but the majority during the years on Pearl Street went to the Park Street Congregational Church.[24]

Howe never lost sight of the fact that his students' physical health was also his responsibility. He insisted that they exercise in the air, and during the 1830's they took a warm bath once a week.[25] Later on, after the school transferred to South Boston, he added ocean bathing.

The curriculum followed that of the common schools as closely as possible, but with certain variations. There was more emphasis on handicrafts and music than in ordinary schools. Some studied no academic subjects, but all took instruction in music. A great believer in the theory that music offered to the blind one of the fairest opportunities for competition with the seeing, Howe felt that he should train as many as possible to be church organists. He encouraged the growth of a large music department, and spurred it into becoming one of the institution's major divisions, which it has ever since remained. Always on the lookout for the best music teachers, he hired, as his first one, Lowell Mason, who later became one of the outstanding figures in the cause of music education in the common schools. Mason, who taught both voice and piano,[26] was on the faculty for about two years, and the training he imparted was so successful that Howe became even more convinced that music should be a feature of the curriculum.[27]

The students organized a band, and demonstrated their prowess at concerts which the public paid to hear. They earned $205 during

[23] Second Report, pp. 9–10.
[24] Second Report, p. 10.
[25] Second Report, pp. 10–11.
[26] Second Report, pp. 8–9.
[27] Third Report (1835), p. 7.

1835, while one boy earned $32 teaching piano to some young ladies.[28] In 1837 there were thirteen pianos in the building plus an organ on which some of the students had begun to play. The director hoped that within a year they would be sufficiently trained to officiate as church organists. By 1839 the study of music as a science occupied a large portion of the time of most pupils. Of the sixty students doing school work, forty-five played the piano and eighteen performed on the organ.[29]

The more academic subjects were not neglected either. Indeed, Howe found that more time was spent on intellectual studies than he had originally expected. The children seemed to like them.[30] They learned their letters by feeling plaster models, and were taught two systems of writing, regular paper and pencil communication with normal people, and pricked letters for the blind. Howe improved on the method used abroad where the schools employed racks with horizontal metal bands which served as guide lines, the letters filling the space between the lines, by developing a grooved paper which was much easier to handle.[31]

Howe was also proud of his method of teaching arithmetic. His arithmetic board had fewer types than the Parisian, while the types themselves were more easily distinguishable than those of Edinburgh. He was sure that all would soon come around to his way of teaching the subject.[32]

Geography was given a spur by his development of maps embossed on paper. Hitherto the only maps for the blind had been produced by gluing strings to ordinary charts and pasting other maps over them. There was no lettering, nor were subdivisions finely drawn. Howe produced a map of New England on which names, state borders, rivers, and other interior features appeared plainly. Chief cities were identified by dots, and mountains by hatched lines, all in relief and tangible for fingers. The trustees

---

[28] *Fourth Report* (1836), p. 5.
[29] *Seventh Report* (1839), pp. 5–6.
[30] *Third Report* (1835), p. 6.
[31] S. G. Howe, "Education of the Blind," *Literary & Theological Review*, III (June 1836), 273.
[32] *North American Review*, XXXVIII (July 1833), 39.

claimed that a chart of similar size and quality would have cost five dollars if manufactured under the old method. Theirs had come to less than five cents.[33] If the Boston teacher could produce his other works as cheaply, the savings would be tremendous, and a vast opportunity would be opened in the field of providing the customary visual aids of the common schools adapted for the use of the blind. A prize acquisition was a globe in relief on which coastlines, islands, and valleys were clearly distinguishable.[34]

By 1836 some of the students had progressed sufficiently to begin the study of French, higher mathematics, and natural philosophy.[35] Howe had no objections to their studying such subjects. His guiding principle was that the gaining of knowledge should be pleasurable in itself, and he was satisfied so long as the children studied what they could understand. In a period when corporal punishment was still resorted to in the common schools of the state, he wrote that so long as schools worked on the principle he set down, there was no need of corporal punishment, prizes, precedence, or degradation.[36]

IV

The mechanical crafts were always a major part of the curriculum. All realized that they offered the largest number of the blind their best opportunity to earn a livelihood. Nevertheless, Howe disapproved of teaching sightless students to do intricate mechanical work, since only after great expenditure of time and labor could they hope to compete with normal workmen in such skills. He felt that it was better that they stick to mats, baskets, and mattresses, crafts that persons of moderate ability could master. The blind had to learn to do satisfactory work. In the beginning their products would be a novelty, but eventually customers would refuse to give

[33] *First Report* (1833), p. 19. The map was included in the report.
[34] James M. Barnard to Howe, Jan. 28, 1843, Howe Papers, Perkins, mentions it as being under construction in Berlin. The globe has been in use over a century, and stands at present in the entrance lobby of the institution in Watertown.
[35] *Fourth Report* (1836), p. 4.
[36] *Seventh Report* (1839), p. 4.

charity.[37] As soon as possible, the school organized a sales department to market student-made articles. A sales office was opened at 152 Washington Street; it was later moved to 20–22 Bromfield Street, where for over twenty-five years Howe had an office conveniently located for his outside activities.

In 1840, it was found necessary to open a separate work department to employ graduates unable to gain employment outside. The workers could earn as much as they cared to over and above the cost of their board. The department was to exist solely for their benefit, but it was not to be a disguised alms-giving. Howe promised that those who did not earn their board would be dismissed.[38]

The doctor wished to carry even further the idea of providing safe places of employment for the blind. He was aware of the possibility of their becoming mountebanks or objects of charity and indulgence on leaving the institution, particularly if forced to compete alone against normal persons. To avoid this danger as well as to provide steady and honorable employment, he urged the creation of an establishment where the blind could work together and secure the advantages of large-scale production. He hoped to see in every large city such a place to help raise skilled workmen, though blind, "above the crushing sense of dependence upon charity" to self-support.[39]

V

Howe's fostering of raised-letter printing is among the most significant of his accomplishments. His achievement in preparing reading matter more cheaply and in greater quantity than ever before is an example not only of his own imagination but of his skill in adapting and improving on the work of others. Haüy had developed a system of printing in raised letters that was so expensive that only a few books had been produced.[40] Other methods were

[37] *Sixth Report* (1838), p. 6.
[38] *Ninth Report* (1841), pp. 14–17.
[39] *Eleventh Report* (1843), pp. 16–17.
[40] In thirty years fewer than 100 volumes had been printed in French and less than a tenth of that number in English. With materials so scarce, most schools did not teach reading. Howe to Lathrop, Oct. 27, 1835, Howe Clippings, Perkins.

equally impractical. Edinburgh used a stenographic alphabet but the characters were not distinctive enough, while Glasgow's plan of transforming words into knots on a string rolled into a ball he considered the "clumsiest and most uncouth system" ever devised.[41] Howe was not familiar with a new development going on in Paris at this time, the work of the lone genius, Louis Braille, who developed during the thirties and forties a system of raised points that eventually became the standard and to which he gave his name.[42] Howe was faced with the choice of designing a new phonetic alphabet, employing a series of stenographic symbols, or using the common alphabet as Haüy had done. He adopted the last, although he felt that a new system would eventually replace it.

Not only cost, but their awkward size had kept Haüy's volumes from a larger public. Howe through much experimentation managed to make books smaller and cheaper by using thinner paper and a smaller type face. He decreased the area of each letter to a minimum sufficient for the blind to feel, and cut off all ornamental flourishes, in addition to shortening interlinear spaces by carrying up such letters as "g" and "p," and straightening the bottom of the lines. This face became known as the "Boston" or "Howe type." [43]

Determined to set up his own press, Howe conducted a fundraising drive in Nantucket and New Bedford which produced $15,000, a sum sufficient to buy what he believed to be the best equipment in the world. One of his first publications, once he got under way, was the *Acts of the Apostles*. Printed in Boston type, it embodied all the economies he had suggested. Each page contained nearly twice as much text as in French books and there were three times as many pages in the same bulk. In fifty-six square inches

---

[41] *North American Review*, XXXVIII (July 1833), 41–42. Glasgow struck back in a stinging article in the *North British Advertiser* (April 10, 1841), which stirred Howe to a response as soon as he learned of it. In a pamphlet *To the Editor of the North British Advertiser* (Boston, July 16, 1841), he disclaimed any desire to depreciate the achievements of other schools, but still, he smugly claimed, he had been more successful, and his alphabet was easier to learn.

[42] Ishbel Ross, *Journey Into Light* (New York, 1951), pp. 121–132.

[43] *Seventh Report* (1839), p. 20.

Paris could put 408 letters and Edinburgh 590, but Howe squeezed in 787.[44]

During 1835 various Bible societies contributed over $3000 toward an edition of the entire New Testament.[45] Work on it proceeded all through the next year and it appeared in September 1836.[46] As the books approached distribution, Howe's joy mounted at the thought of the pleasure they would bring readers whose souls thirsted for learning. He took special pride in having produced such an elaborate work in only four years, while England, which was years in advance of America in undertaking publishing for the blind, had printed only the Four Gospels. Looking to the future, he hoped for a greater flood of works.[47]

A few years later the printing office issued an eight-volume Old Testament at $20 a set, as against the nineteen-volume work at $40 being done in Europe. The Bible Society gave free copies to the indigent blind.[48]

Closely allied to his printing activities was Howe's work as an author of textbooks, among which were a grammar, a speller, an atlas, and a geography. Howe claimed that his texts were as complete as any printed in ink. Supplying a great need, the press published other classroom books in quick succession: an outline of history and a series of readers, all of his preparation, plus an edition of the *Viri Romae* done at the commission of a New Orleans father whose daughter had become blind.[49] The books were also used in other schools for the blind. The New York Institution for the Blind bought many texts and received gratuitously copies of others; possibly it may have shared the cost of publication.[50]

[44] *Third Report* (1835), p. 15. These claims were a bit extreme. Europe lowered the gap so that by 1840 he was getting a fifth more to the page. *Eighth Report* (1840), p. 14.

[45] *Fourth Report* (1836), p. 6.

[46] *Fifth Report* (1837), p. 14. *The Christian Watchman* (Sept. 30, 1836) has a notice of its publication.

[47] Howe to (?), undated, Howe Clippings, Perkins.

[48] *Eleventh Report* (1843), p. 17.

[49] *Eighth Report* (1840), p. 14.

[50] Howe-Theodore Dwight, Jr., Correspondence of the 1830's. Dwight Papers, NYPL, discusses these transactions.

Howe's ambitions as a writer fed on the encouragement he received. He hoped to invade the field of ink print, but Horace Mann, by this time Secretary of the Massachusetts Board of Education, dissuaded him.[51] As Howe got deeper into publishing, he conceived a grandiose scheme of a national library for the blind, but Congress failed to provide funds.[52] Howe then proposed that each of the New England states appropriate a small sum on the condition that every sightless person in the area receive a copy of each work printed, but this plan also failed.[53]

Despite this promising beginning, Howe had much trouble in carrying out his publishing program, since in the absence of a state appropriation, all his funds had to come from private sources. He continued printing by fits and starts, mostly on commission of various religious establishments for such devotional works as the *Book of Common Prayer* and *Psalms*. Fearing he would be forced to close down operations, he appealed repeatedly for contributions, but money was not always forthcoming, and much of the time his press was idle. Yet with all these difficulties he managed to print more books for the use of the blind than any other school in the English-speaking world.[54]

VI

From its earliest years the New England Institution for the Education of the Blind thrived, its student body increasing as news of its attainments spread. In addition to the four states already mentioned as sending students, a spot check of the lists of resident pupils shows that almost from the start it attracted paying students from distant regions. The trustees followed a liberal admissions policy, admitting all applicants who in their opinion would benefit by its program without regard to the legislative grant. At the begin-

[51] Mann to Howe, July 21, 1839, Mann Papers, MHS; for a press comment of his books, see *American Annals of Education and Instruction* (July 1835), most readily available in the Howe Clippings, Perkins.
[52] *Fifth Report* (1837), p. 13.
[53] *Eighth Report* (1840), pp. 15–16.
[54] He hoped that the press of the Philadelphia school would be able to carry on if his were shut down.

ning of 1835, when there were forty-two students, the trustees complained that the building on Pearl Street was too small.[55] Though they enlarged it during the summer of that year, Howe serving as architect for the extension, it was soon apparent that the institution would need even larger quarters to realize its full potentialities.[56] There were also other factors that made a move desirable. The surrounding neighborhood had become too congested for the children to walk safely about, and land values had risen too high to permit necessary expansion.

Howe, looking about for a more suitable site, found it in South Boston. Learning of the availability of a hotel known as the Mount Washington House, he exchanged his hard-pressed city lot for a more remote and spacious enclosure of 55,000 square feet, which included buildings and an additional 20,000 square feet on the opposite side of Broadway. There would be ample space to house the students and keep the sexes apart. In addition, the air was better, the streets were safer, and proximity of the ocean enabled Howe to add salt-water bathing to the children's pleasures. The trustees approved unanimously, but before anything could be done, they needed Colonel Perkins' consent, which he readily gave, since without it the Pearl Street estate would have reverted to him on ceasing to be a school. In return, the trustees voted to change the name of the school to the Perkins Institution and Massachusetts Asylum for the Blind.[57] The shift was made in May 1839, and Perkins, as it was now familiarly to be known, remained in South Boston until 1912.

VII

One of the most significant aspects of Howe's work in these years was his missionary activity for adequate educational facilities for the blind, a task that he more or less performed to his dying day. He felt the zeal of an apostle of old spreading the true faith as he persevered from city to city throughout the eastern half of the United States. He, and the children he took with him, ignored

---

[55] *Third Report* (1835), pp. 4–5.
[56] Howe to Sampson, July 27, 1835, Howe Papers, Houghton.
[57] *Eighth Report* (1840), pp. 3–5.

physical discomforts only too familiar to travelers in America during the thirties and forties of the last century. Like any impresario of an itinerant opera company, he had his circuit to make, and whether great coastal city or rural state capital, he had to be there on time with his performers. He was gone for weeks at a time almost every year, putting his students through their paces for state legislatures and the general public. He did these things willingly, determined that, "It shall not be my fault if any blind child remains uninstructed through ignorance on the part of his parents & friends of the existence of means." [58]

During 1836 he made two trips besides his annual circuit of New England's capitals, a successful one to Ohio with three pupils, and a fruitless one to Congress to seek funds for printing a library for the blind.[59] In all, he visited seventeen states during the first decade of his directorship at Perkins.

Late in 1841 he undertook an extensive tour that lasted well into the next year to prod the South and the West into action. Charles Sumner enlisted the aid of Francis Lieber, then a professor in South Carolina, for handling publicity and placing notices in the papers about the doctor's great achievements.[60] Howe left Boston on December 1, taking with him Abby and Sophia Carter, his star pupils. His trip down the coast was a great success. After an exhibition of the girls' accomplishments in Richmond, he pushed on southward. South Carolina proved so impressed that every year until the mid-fifties it appropriated a sum sufficient to keep several students at Perkins. As winter conditions prevented him from crossing the mountains into Tennessee, Howe returned home early in January.[61]

Later that month, he set out once more, this time to the West, sailing down the Ohio to Kentucky where he met the greatest triumph of his tour. *"Io Paean!* my dear Sumner," he exulted after

---

[58] Howe to Mann, June 20, 185?, #1187 (catalogued under 1857), Howe Papers, Houghton. Although this letter is from a later period, it expresses his feeling during these years.

[59] *Fifth Report* (1837), pp. 12–13.

[60] Sumner to Lieber, Nov. 30, 1841, Sumner Papers, Houghton.

[61] Howe to Mann, postmarked Dec. 28, 1841, Howe Papers, Houghton; *Boston Recorder*, Jan. 7, 1842.

his appearance before the legislature, "we have met the enemy and they are ours body soul & purse." He had induced the lawmakers to appropriate $10,000 for the establishment of the Kentucky Institution for the Education of the Blind.

Many members [he continued] who were violently opposed to the bill last year today declared they would vote duoble [sic] the sum asked if it were needed. . . .

A dozen members fought hard each to have the accouchement of the Institution take place in his own town; but every one before he sat down exclaimed Mr. Speaker I wish the Institution to be located in such a place but understand me sir — locate it where you will I will hold up both hands & vote & pray for it.

The people were so enthusiastic that Howe was "afraid some Mammas will put their children[']s eyes out." [62] The populace took up a subscription for the school with the utmost readiness and zeal. Frankfort lay at the feet of the great teacher, the obedient servant of his will.

As for poor me [he wrote Mann], never was a poor mortal so inundated with soft soap as I was. I was continually looking around for small holes to crawl into; especially when one venerable Judge after putting it on with a trowel, before an immense audience, turned solemnly to me & said, — "yes fellow citizens, I would rather be that man, than — than — than the Tzar of all the Russias, and — *Siberia to boot!*" [63]

Only one blemish marred his triumph. The Massachusetts and Ohio institutions had originally been scheduled to hold a joint exhibition before the Kentucky legislature, but at the last moment the directors quarreled and each school performed separately. It is impossible to say who was at fault, but there is no denying that Howe had an arbitrary streak in his character that made it difficult for some to work with him. The prima donna complex of his Greek years persisted and he could brook no rivalry. He would not share the leadership of the movement; he had to do all or nothing.[64]

[62] Howe to Sumner, Feb. 1, 1842, Howe Papers, Houghton.
[63] Howe to Mann, Feb. 17, 1842, Howe Papers, Houghton.
[64] Howe to Sumner, Feb. 1, 1842, Howe Papers, Houghton.

From Kentucky he went down the Mississippi as far as New Orleans, prodding the states along the way to make some provision for their blind. He was gratified with the results:

It is pleasant to plant trees that will live when we are dead; and especially if they are to adorn or benefit a barren & benighted land. I want to see these Institutions multiplied & magnified, not for the blind alone, but for the influence they have upon the community by furnishing occasions for the *exercise* of the benevolent affections.[65]

VIII

By 1843 Perkins was world-famous. In the ten years of its operation it had become an established part of the common-school system of New England. The Joint Committee on Public Charitable Institutions of the Massachusetts legislature declared in 1840 that it was no longer a doubtful experiment. "Humanity, justice, policy and honor alike forbid that this service should be permitted to languish for want of adequate support." [66] Its future was apparently assured. Its students had entered into many fields of endeavor with success; some were in colleges, others were teachers;[67] at least one was a promising lecturer,[68] and one was director of the Kentucky school.[69]

As Perkins became better known, visitors flocked to its weekly exhibition days. It became one of the sights of the city, especially after Laura Bridgman came.[70] People were amazed at what they saw. Horace Mann once showed a "female friend" (probably one of the Peabodys) through the old Pearl Street quarters and

was delighted at her delight. Indeed, who can witness the natural privation of sight, & think of all its lamentable train of consequences, & then behold those successful acts of skills & benevolence by which that privation has been supplied without deep & abiding gratification.[71]

[65] Howe to Mann, March 27, 1842, Howe Papers, Houghton.

[66] *Senate Document* 43 (March 1840), p. 7.

[67] *Ninth Report* (1841), p. 12. One student was in Harvard.

[68] *Boston Advertiser,* Feb. 20, 1843, favorable review of a lecture this person had given in New York.

[69] Howe to Mann, Feb. 17, 1842, Howe Papers, Houghton, says that a Perkins alumnus was to be appointed.

[70] See the next chapter.

[71] Mann's Journal, May 12, 1837, Mann Papers, MHS.

The school received much favorable publicity in such periodicals as the *North American Review* and the *New England Magazine*. Articles, some of which Howe may have written, were profuse in their praise. As early as 1835 an anonymous reviewer in the latter publication wrote, "The mere consideration, that it fits for the business of life a class of persons who have hitherto spent their days in inactivity, and in a precarious state of dependence, should be sufficient to impress on every mind its vast importance." [72]

During his first decade at Perkins, Howe fostered the creation of schools in three states, Ohio, Virginia, and Kentucky, while Maine, Vermont, New Hampshire, Connecticut, New Jersey, Maryland, South Carolina, and Louisiana made provision for sending their blind children to other states.[73]

Hence, by 1843, Howe's success was assured. He could take a year's leave of absence to tour Europe on his wedding trip, and accept the homage the Old World chose to heap upon him.

[72] *New England Magazine,* VIII (April 1835), p. 321, literary notice of *Third Report*.

[73] *Tenth Report* (1842), p. 25.

VI

The Education of the Deaf-Blind

Famous as Howe was for his work with the blind, even greater renown came to him for his work with the deaf-blind. It is given to few men to play Providence, to take an amorphous mass of being and mold it into individuality. Yet Howe was called upon twice to perform this role in the education of two afflicted children, Laura Bridgman and Oliver Caswell. Their achievement in gaining a common-school education made them symbols of optimism incarnate for a generation that believed in the doctrine of progress, and the proof, if any was needed, of the power of mankind to reach greater perfectibility, provided the effort was made.[1]

I

Shortly after beginning his work with the blind, Howe began to consider the possibilities of educating the deaf-blind. No such person had ever been successfully taught; in fact, all available evidence pointed to the impossibility of the task. Sir William Blackstone, the noted British jurist, whose opinions were of great influence in America, had stated flatly that the deaf-blind were in a class with idiots since he supposed them "incapable of any understanding, as wanting all those senses which furnish the human mind with

---

[1] See the *Common School Journal*, II, 6 (March 16, 1840), 91.

ideas." [2] Contemporary cases of double deprivation of sense had been declared helpless. Leading British teachers who examined James Mitchell in Scotland believed nothing could be done for him.[3] In America, Julia Brace, an inmate of the American Asylum for the Deaf in Hartford, had become noted for her condition. She was a fully grown woman at this time, but attempts at making contact, beyond simple signs, had failed. Howe remained unconvinced that such individuals had to be written off as hopeless, even though he had himself seen Julia. He resolved to teach the next deaf-blind person that came to his attention. His opportunity came in the spring of 1837, when he learned of Laura Bridgman.

An article in a country paper by a Dr. Muzzey, of the Dartmouth faculty, told of a little girl seven years old, totally deaf and blind, who resided near Hanover, New Hampshire. Here was the chance for Howe to try out his theories, since she was eligible to attend his school. He left as soon as he could to investigate the matter further. On his arrival at the comfortable farm home of the Bridgman family he saw the little girl who might have been pretty, had it not been for the deadness around her eyes.[4] She was to be his most famous student.

Laura Dewey Bridgman was born December 21, 1829, the third daughter of Daniel and Harmony Bridgman. Her father was a prosperous farmer, a prominent citizen of the region who had held a number of elective offices. As an infant, Laura had all her faculties. She was able to see and hear and was otherwise normal. At the age of a year and a half she suffered an attack of scarlet fever during an epidemic in which her two older sisters and brother died. As she convalesced, her parents were horrified to realize that her sight and hearing had been totally destroyed, and her senses of taste and smell seriously impaired.[5] She seemed doomed to live

---

[2] Sir William Blackstone, *Commentaries on the Laws of England* (Phil., 1771), I, book I, chap. 8, 304.

[3] *74th Report of the Trustees of the Perkins Institution* (1906), p. 84.

[4] Interesting details of the trip may be found in Maud Howe Elliott and Florence Howe Hall, *Laura Bridgman, Dr. Howe's Famous Pupil and What He Taught Her* (Boston, 1903), pp. 38–39.

[5] *Sixth Report* (1838), p. 18.

walled up in utter loneliness and abysmal ignorance, a sub-human. There appeared to be nothing anyone could do for her. It was even difficult to express love. The stricken girl could only play by herself, sometimes holding a boot as normal girls hold dolls. Occasionally she would torture the household cat or imitate her mother's movements as she performed her household duties, knitting, darning, and cleaning.

Laura needed constant attention, but her preoccupied parents could not give it to her, nor would the hired girl who, unable to bear the presence of the child underfoot in the kitchen, occasionally struck her. There came to the rescue of the distracted family Asa Tenny, a semiliterate old man with an addled brain and a way with the girl, who took her under his wing. He, of all the region, offered her the companionship and affection no one else could, and saved her from the hideous solitude that would otherwise have been her fate. With the Bridgmans' blessing she went with him willingly all over the countryside. Laura developed a warmth of feeling for Tenny that never diminished, even when she had become in adolescence a world celebrity. She felt closer to him than to her father. They developed their own signs so that they could commune. In his own way, following the natural method of dealing with a frightened child by gaining its confidence, the senile handyman paved the way for the eventual return of Laura Bridgman to society. Without his groundwork, Howe's task would have been a great deal more difficult.

As she grew older it became apparent that a stronger hand was needed. Laura became mischievous and difficult to control. By the time she was seven only her father could sway her. (When it was time for her to go to bed, he stamped very hard on the floor.) It was just at this period that Laura was brought into the parlor to meet a strange man. In her fear she shrank back, rejecting the little gift he presented her.[6] Howe discussed his proposition with the parents, who consented to his attempting to teach her. Four months later, over old Tenny's protests, they brought her to the building on

---

[6] These details are taken from E. C. Sanford, *The Writings of Laura Bridgman*, reprinted from the *Overland Monthly* (San Francisco, 1887), pp. 8–18.

Pearl Street, in time for the beginning of the fall term. On October 4, 1837, Laura Bridgman entered the New England Institution, in whose precincts she was to live for the rest of her life.[7] The great experiment in education now began.

Howe gave Laura some time to get adjusted to her new surroundings before beginning his work. During these early weeks her plight was pathetic. She knew she was in a strange place, yet no one could tell her why. The best and most moving account of her experience is to be found in her *Autobiography*.

I dreaded leaving home so much that it made me shed an abundance of tears from my eyes many long days. . . . I kept clinging on my dear parents, so as to not let them escape from me, but did not succeed in detaining them. I was removed from them; they attempted to avoid me as quickly as possible. at [sic] the very moment that I lost them I burst in[to] bitterest tears. Miss J[enette] Howe, one of Dr.'s Sisters, was with me then. She tried to pacify and sooth [sic] me, but my heart was too full of sorrow and trouble. . . . I believe that I was drawn along toward my trunk, and I put my hands in for something to taste of, which my Mother put in my trunk. I had a very sad and pleasant time with Miss J.[8]

During the months of waiting, the doctor had mulled over which teaching method to use with her. The choice lay between allowing Laura to use natural signs to express her wants, teaching her the deaf and dumb system of arbitrary symbols, or the vernacular language in a form adaptable for her. The only precedent for him to follow was Julia Brace at Hartford, who used only the most primitive signs and had remained in a primitive state. Howe decided in favor of language, since, if he succeeded, Laura would be able to communicate with a great many more persons, gain a common-school education, and possibly learn abstract concepts.

After about two weeks, when he estimated that Laura's original bewilderment had worn off, Howe decided to begin her formal instruction. He told Miss Drew, a young member of the staff who had been spending time with Laura, to bring her to the nursery.

---

[7] *Ninth Report* (1841), p. 25.
[8] Sanford, *Writings of Laura Bridgman*, p. 19.

The doctor was at a table awaiting them, eager to start the first lesson. Before him lay common articles, which he had labeled in raised letters. He asked Laura to feel each one carefully.[9] With "knife" for instance, he had her feel the label separately, then the utensil with the same marks on it, in the hope that she would understand the relationship. With Miss Drew's assistance, he did the same with the other articles. The session lasted three-quarters of an hour, and was repeated that afternoon and twice each day following.[10] Within several days Laura was able mechanically, without understanding, to match up each label to its object. As Howe put it, his success with her at this stage was like teaching a knowing dog tricks. After a while, she gained insight into the process; the truth flashed upon her. By making a sign for what she wanted, she could express her ideas. Howe was there at the time and noticed that

at once her countenance lighted up with a human expression: it was no longer a dog, or parrot, — it was an immortal spirit, eagerly seizing upon a new link of union with other spirits! I could almost fix upon the moment when this truth dawned upon her mind, and spread its light to her countenance. I saw that the great obstacle was overcome, and that henceforward nothing but patient and persevering, though plain and straightforward efforts were to be used.[11]

Howe had succeeded in proving that the deaf-blind were not necessarily idiots and ought not to be considered as such. He had demonstrated that they needed only an education to be brought into the circle of society. This moment was the high point of his career. No success he achieved in later years can compare in significance to what he had accomplished at the instant Laura Bridgman understood that by learning the strange symbols before her she could gain contact with humanity. A new world was opened to her and to the similarly afflicted of a later generation.

The great hurdle was passed over, but even greater ones lay

[9] *Sixth Report* (1838), p. 11.

[10] Mary Swift Lamson, *The Life and Education of Laura Dewey Bridgman* (Boston, 1899), pp. 5–6.

[11] *Ninth Report* (1841), p. 26. Howe gives another account in his *43d Report* (1875), pp. 83 and following, but I used this earlier account since it is closer to the period, when his memory was presumably fresher.

ahead. The immediate problem facing her teachers was the imparting of cumulative knowledge. This was to be a long, slow, tedious process, testing the mettle of all who dealt with her. Without any competent guidance, Howe, barely launched on his career, had to feel his way carefully.

In the early days of her instruction a system of natural signs, dropped as quickly as possible, was resorted to. The doctor patted her head when she was right, and knocked at her elbow when wrong. He stroked her hand when she was dirty or shabby, and patted her cheeks to express love and affection. The severest punishment he could inflict upon her was to put her in a closet or shake her, but this caused her to weep so pitifully that he would always forgive her for the disobedience. Laura was trained like a household pet to obey her master's will.[12]

With Laura's intellect miraculously awakened, as it seemed, she eagerly pursued her studies, astonishing her teachers with her rapid progress. Howe had his press man, S. P. Ruggles, make a set of metal types with separate letters on their ends for Laura's use in forming words on a frame. After she had learned a basic vocabulary, Miss Drew taught her the order of the alphabet.[13]

She was next taught the manual alphabet used by deaf-mutes. Laura learned this with extraordinary rapidity; within a year she spelled out words and sentences so fast that only experts could follow her.[14] It was all poor, tired Miss Drew could do to keep up with her questions.

I shall never forget the first meal taken after she appreciated the use of the finger alphabet. Every article that she touched must have a name; and I was obliged to call some one [sic] to help me wait upon the other children, while she kept me busy in spelling the new words. Dr. Howe had been absent for some time, and on his return was much delighted with the progress she had made, and at once learned the manual alphabet himself.[15]

---

[12] Sanford, *Writings of Laura Bridgman*, p. 19.
[13] *Sixth Report* (1838), p. 11.
[14] *Seventh Report* (1839), p. 15.
[15] Lamson, *Laura Bridgman*, pp. 7–8.

Miss Drew followed a set routine in teaching Laura new words. She began by giving her pupil a new object to examine, following this, she spelled out its letters with her fingers, while Laura grasped her teacher's hands and studied their movements. Immediately after, the child held up her fingers and spelled back the word. To conclude the lesson, she arranged the letters in types, and triumphantly placed them in contact with the object.[16]

After having mastered the manual alphabet and learned nouns (to spell the names of everything within reach), she was taught the other parts of speech. How slow the process was is demonstrated by the fact that it took Laura, a child of superior intellect, four years to learn all the parts of speech.[17] As was to be expected, she was far behind other children of her age in the use of language. At the age of nine she had the vocabulary of a baby of three. This gap was narrowed as she studied further, but she remained behind in her knowledge for many years. Her teachers had no difficulty in imparting concrete facts, but words expressive of them had to be communicated by a circuitous, and tedious, method.[18] For example, Laura had trouble in learning words of positive qualities, such as hard and soft when used in their abstract sense. Something that she could feel had to be hard or soft, but she did not grasp the thought alone without great difficulty.[19]

Laura's mind became ever more alert, and the longer she studied, the more inquisitive she became. She would learn fewer things by rote, insisting regularly on explanations. Her questions kept Miss Drew on her toes, and when printed in Howe's reports created international ripples of laughter. Once she refused to believe that a long metal object with a sharp point on its end was a nail, because her nail was on her finger, and she knew what nails were. Owing to her deafness, some questions could never be explained to her satisfaction. When she learned how to spell cat, she wondered why it could not as easily be spelled "tac." Laura had imagination as well.

[16] *Sixth Report* (1838), p. 12.
[17] *Tenth Report* (1842), p. 29.
[18] *Seventh Report* (1839), p. 16.
[19] *Eighth Report* (1840), p. 20.

She made up words as she needed them. Shortly after having learned the word "alone" she said that she would go "al two" (that is, together) with someone.[20]

Within a year of the beginning of her instruction, she learned to write on grooved paper, as did the other students. When she realized what advantages lay in a mastery of this new subject, mainly that she could write her mother, her delight was unbounded. In a few months she had progressed sufficiently to write home.[21]

Laura's personality was always a source of wonder to her teachers. They were amazed that she should be so happy. After her homesickness wore off, and she adjusted to the routine of Perkins, she seemed at ease. She was affectionate, playful, and constantly active. Desiring approbation, nothing pleased her more than to have her "Doc" pat her head in approval.[22] When left alone, she seemed happy, knitting or sewing busily for hours, and practicing her lessons. If she spelled a word wrong, she struck her guilty hand with the other, and if right, she patted herself on the head. She would playfully misspell a word with her left hand, look roguish for a moment, laugh, and then strike the stupid fingers.[23]

She soon came to know that her home was in the school and that she belonged there. At the end of six months her mother came to visit her. They had an affectionate meeting, Laura clinging to Mrs. Bridgman all during their time together. They walked to the threshold locked in their embrace, but the loving daughter made no attempt to cross. She hesitated for a while, then let go of her mother, to take the hand of the matron who stood alongside.[24] Mrs. Bridgman walked out alone.

Howe made no attempt to wean Laura from her family. She returned every year to spend a few weeks in Hanover at her old home. During these periods she renewed her friendship with Asa Tenny who had never forgotten her. When she learned to write, he sent her long letters in his own peculiar sub-literate style that

[20] *Eighth Report* (1840), pp. 21–22.
[21] *Eighth Report*, p. 9.
[22] *Sixth Report* (1838), pp. 9–10.
[23] *Seventh Report* (1839), p. 14.
[24] *Ninth Report* (1841), pp. 28–29.

roused laughter among those who read them, but were nevertheless as sincere as the polished missives she had begun to receive from the celebrities of Boston.

For everyone at South Boston, she developed deep affection, especially for Howe and her teachers. Miss Drew, the first of the series of talented young women who cultivated her mind and instilled social graces, was with her constantly, even sleeping in the same room with her.

> I had such a very pleasant time with her for 4 years or longer [wrote Laura]. I felt in my own heart as if she was my real Mother. she [sic] always loved to caress and pacify me very much indeed. I never liked to have her leave me alone for a second.[25]

Howe came to feel toward her as if she were his daughter.[26] She lived in his quarters, ate with him, and played with him every day, returning his affection in equal measure. When he had to leave on his tours, she missed him terribly; and on his return, she was overcome. On one occasion, Howe's return from South Carolina, she was so excited that she lost control of her fingers and could say nothing for a few minutes.[27] There grew up an attachment between them that never weakened; not even the six Howe children who were eventually born of his marriage to Julia Ward could diminish the warmth of his feeling for her.

Laura provided an ideal subject for Howe's inquiring mind. He submitted her to all sorts of examinations in order to determine the extent of her senses of smell and taste. Disagreeable as these probings were to her, she submitted to them with as good grace as she could. It is from his findings that we know as much as we do of her character and personality. He discovered that she liked to use her voice, even though she could not hear it. She grunted, snorted, screeched, and howled. Within a short period she developed characteristic noises for her friends, which she uttered upon encountering them. She had one for the doctor, one for Miss Drew, and so on.[28]

---

[25] Sanford, *Writings of Laura Bridgman,* p. 20.
[26] Howe to Mann, July 16, 1841, Howe Papers, Houghton.
[27] Sumner to Lieber, Jan. 11, 1842, Sumner Papers, Houghton.
[28] *Tenth Report* (1842), p. 30.

So impressed was Howe at her vocalization, that he even thought it was possible to teach her to speak, but he never made the attempt.[29] Howe also had her taste foods of various kinds to see if she could differentiate them. He had her smell flowers as well. Nothing daunted, the rampaging investigator even sent electric charges through the hapless child, applying one electrode to her nose and the other to her tongue in the hope of eliciting a taste sensation.[30] Laura was undoubtedly the most fully experimented upon child of her time. Very few things she did went unnoted either in her teachers' journals or in the official reports of the Perkins Institution.

As a consequence of his extensive investigations, Howe came to see philosophical implications in the development of Laura, beyond the mere pedagogical. In his opinion her example disproved Locke's theory that moral qualities and faculties are limited in proportion to the limitation of the senses, since Laura had shown herself to be morally very acute. This was proof to him that moral dispositions were innate too.[31]

II

Laura was merely the most sensational of deaf-blind pupils at Perkins, of whom there were three others for varying lengths of time: Lucy Reed, Oliver Caswell, and Julia Brace. These later cases are possibly of greater significance in the education of the deaf-blind, since their minds were of a more normal type. Laura was evidently of a superior intellect, to which cause can be traced much of Howe's success. If he could have shown that his method was suitable for one of average intelligence, he would have established beyond question the reliability of his technique.

The longed-for second student, Lucy Reed of Danby, Vermont, came to Perkins in February 1841. She was older than Laura, having been born in October 1827. Deafened by scrofula in her third year, and blinded by its lingering effects in her eighth, her parents

---

[29] Articulation is discussed in Chapter XVII.
[30] *Tenth Report* (1842), p. 35. He even published a phrenological analysis.
[31] *Ninth Report* (1841), pp. 41–42.

finally allowed attempts at her instruction to be made when she was
thirteen. Her arrival shocked the school. Laura was at first afraid
of her.[32] Howe described the unfortunate creature as having been
in a lower stage of humanity than any other person he had ever
seen except for some mental defectives. Evidently sensitive about
her condition, since she wore a kerchief over her head, she seemed
unmanageable. Her parents had seen her face only once in two
years. It was apparent that Lucy would present problems for which
experience with Laura would furnish no precedent.

After the customary period of adjustment, in this case several
weeks, during which a younger sister to whom she was greatly attached had stayed on, the day came when Howe deemed it desirable
to begin Lucy's education. With the sister to reassure her, she was
led into the schoolroom and seated. Lucy, willful and unrestrained
as an untamed colt, was frightened by these strange developments,
and sprang up. Dazed by this response, the doctor lost his own control, and acting impulsively, used force to keep her down. Calling
upon all her strength, Lucy squirmed out of the chair, and with
Howe still grasping her, dragged herself across the room. The
savage girl struggled with her tormentor for two hours, attempting
to bite, scratch, and claw her way loose. After the first minutes of
battle had drawn the kindly teacher's blood, causing him to release
her temporarily, he returned to the fray protected with fencing mask
and thick gloves, this time to fight on valiantly until he had brought
about the submission of the exhausted child. These frightful proceedings had not discouraged Howe. Lucy's plan of attack had
shown him that she could reason, and could consequently be taught.
Twice within the next twenty-four hours, she renewed her struggle,
but at last surrendered entirely. Like any horse that has been tamed
by having had its will violently broken, she would obey no one but
the one who had mastered her. Whenever she attempted resistance,
he bound her hands behind her with leather handcuffs. Lucy became so fearful of them that she obeyed at their touch. Howe regretted later that he had had to use force. He came to realize that
it would have been better to have lost months in trying to gain her

[32] Laura Bridgman's Ms. Journal, July 1841, Bridgman Papers, Perkins.

confidence than to have followed his precipitate course. He apologized publicly in his annual report to the Trustees, claiming only that "I acted according to my best judgment."

Once Lucy submitted to the incomprehensible efforts of those assigned to her, the leavening atmosphere at Perkins began to work a miracle. Totally transformed within a few weeks, docile and obedient, coming to desire company, she became humanized. A month after her battle in the schoolroom she took off her covering to expose a face completely "etiolated" and inexpressive. In the place of the kerchief, she donned eye shades as did the rest of the students. Her shyness was still very great, and she sat with her face turned to the wall. In a few days even her shyness wore off; she began to smile.[33]

For two months her teachers, Miss Drew and Mary Swift, with aid from Laura, who felt occasional pangs of jealousy, tried without success to teach her the letters of the alphabet.[34] She would repeat the signs with her fingers, but it was apparent that these acts had no meaning for her. In the face of discouragement, Howe was determined to persevere for six months before writing off the case as hopeless. Fortunately, well within that deadline, Lucy's rusty mind gained the insight necessary for learning.[35]

On April 14, Miss Drew got her to spell "fig" properly, an indication that her interest was mounting.[36] She started to gain an inkling of understanding. Early in June she felt the ring on Miss Swift's finger, implying that she wanted to be taught the name of the round object.[37] The teacher showed her with pleasure, but the confused girl got the letters in the wrong order. Laura asked one day to be allowed to teach Lucy the word "not," but after struggling for a while, gravely declared that Lucy was a "very dull scholar." [38]

By mid-June, Lucy was really trying hard to learn, and made steady progress for the remainder of that month. Her instructor had

[33] *Tenth Report* (1842), pp. 52–53.
[34] Mary Swift, Ms. School Journal, June 8, 1841, Bridgman Papers, Perkins.
[35] *Tenth Report* (1842), p. 54.
[36] Lamson, *Laura Bridgman*, p. 48.
[37] Swift's Journal, June 8, 1841.
[38] Swift's Journal, June 11, 1841.

no trouble with her from a want of interest.[39] In July she began to express her wants at the table. She spelled out "cake" to indicate her desire for some.[40] This was what the staff had been waiting for. Although it had taken them as many months to reach the stage of insight with Lucy that Laura had attained in weeks, they had shown that some instruction could be imparted to a deaf-blind individual of subnormal intelligence as Lucy probably was, although Howe did not indicate her mental level.

It was at this moment of rejoicing for the director and his staff, that Lucy's mother took her home. Mrs. Reed had visited the school in June to see how her daughter was being taught. She had some idea that her retarded offspring would soon be equal to the quick-witted Laura. Miss Swift tried vainly to explain to the fatuous woman the extreme slowness with which they proceeded in the education of one so handicapped.[41] A few weeks later Lucy's father and sister arrived. Apologetically the Vermont farmer explained that his wife insisted on Lucy's return, although he was in favor of letting her stay. The object of this maternal solicitude greeted her family coldly. It was quite apparent that she did not wish to go with them, and gave signs of distress at being forced to return home. Poignantly she gestured to the teachers, who stood helplessly by, to accompany her. There was nothing anyone could do. With all prospects of a bright future blighted, the unfortunate creature was sentenced to the dreariness of her rural home, to sink back into the degradation from which she had barely begun to arise. Her departure saddened everyone. Howe, while regretting the action, took "a quiet satisfaction to think we broke through the crust, & got at the living spring within. . . ."[42]

There were repercussions among the students as well. Many of them took this occasion to vent their jealousy of Laura, who was by

[39] Swift's Journal, June 18, 1841.
[40] Swift's Journal, July 12, 1841.
[41] Swift's Journal, June 19, 1841.
[42] Howe to Mann, July 16, 1841, Howe Papers, Houghton; Miss Drew's Ms. Journal, July 12, 1841, Perkins. "Lucy lived to be seventy-seven and sewed, did patchwork and covered boxes quite peacefully in her later years," Ishbel Ross, *Journey Into Light* (New York, 1951), p. 237.

now the school's most noted student. Their universal opinion was that Laura had been much better treated than Lucy.[43] This spirit of sullen rebellion lasted a few days, then quietly expired.

III

About a week after Lucy Reed's departure, Dr. Howe told Laura that there was to be a new deaf-blind student in a few weeks, a little boy. The news pleased her. Miss Swift noted in her journal that Laura expressed eagerness to talk with him when he should have learned enough to use the finger alphabet, although she declared she would not kiss him.[44] The much anticipated Oliver Caswell arrived September 30, 1841 to take Lucy's place as the second deaf-blind student at the institution. His career there was to be as pleasant for him as Laura's was for her, and he was to take a place slightly below hers in the public's heart.

Oliver was born November 1, 1829, in Newport, Rhode Island. Scarlet fever destroyed his sight and hearing when he was three years old. After this, his development at home followed the pattern of the other deaf-blind. As he grew older he too became a disciplinary problem, much given to tantrums. Having seen him three years before, Howe had tried all that time to have his parents enroll him at Perkins. While they waited, probably to see how Laura would turn out, Oliver had grown into a twelve-year-old lad, short, thickset, with light hair, a fair complexion, and pleasant expression, quite different from Laura, who at eight had been like a little animal.[45] Understanding apparently that he had come to a place where he would be helped, the new boy showed great promise from the start, and had no difficulty adjusting. His new surroundings fascinated him. Miss Swift reported that, "He employed every moment till he went to bed, in examining persons and things about him." [46]

Howe wasted no time in getting to work on Oliver. He began

---

[43] Swift's Journal, July 13, 1841.
[44] Swift's Journal, July 20, 1841.
[45] *Tenth Report* (1842), pp. 45–46.
[46] Swift's Journal, Sept. 30, 1841.

lessons the next day, aided by Miss Swift and Laura who had made friends with him on arrival. Using short cuts gained from experience, the doctor commenced immediately with finger language rather than natural signs.[47] Oliver was happy and gay throughout the session, laughing heartily whenever he succeeded in duplicating his teacher's mystic finger manipulations. Howe has left a touching account of that morning:

Laura was by, interested even to agitation, and the two presented a singular sight; her face was flushed and anxious, and her fingers twined in among ours so closely as to follow every motion, but so lightly as not to embarrass them; while Oliver stood attentive, his head a little aside, his face turned up, his left hand grasping mine, and his right held out; at every motion of my fingers his countenance betokened keen attention . . . then a smile came stealing out as he thought he could do so, and spread into a joyous laugh the moment he succeeded, and felt me pat his head, and Laura clap him heartily upon the back, and jump up and down in her joy.[48]

The Rhode Island youth perceived the relationship between the words and their objects fairly quickly, but without the "radiant flash of intelligence" that flowed over Laura when she had reached that stage. Otherwise, the method of instruction was the same as that used earlier. Oliver was clever, although lower in intelligence than Laura, and he learned rapidly. He showed a violent temper once, but Howe, drawing on his Lucy Reed fiasco, had earlier had the boy's nails cut. Oliver was quickly brought under control, and never caused trouble again. On the whole Howe was pleased with his new pupil. He was really very affectionate and amiable, and Howe was certain that he would grow into intelligent manhood.[49] Laura for her part was very much taken by the presence of Oliver. Her whole conversation the first day was about him and that after all she had kissed him.[50] Falling into the pattern that Laura had been the first to follow, Oliver developed a great attraction for

[47] *Tenth Report*, p. 46.
[48] *Tenth Report*, p. 47.
[49] *Tenth Report*, pp. 48–50.
[50] Swift's Journal, Oct. 1, 1841.

Howe, and missed him also when he left on his tours, but it should be added that he quickly recovered from his despondency.[51]

Laura and Oliver were henceforth educated together. They were in each other's company a good deal and became the focus of interest of the institution. Despite their apparent similarity, the children were actually quite different. Oliver had nowhere near Laura's quickness. He was willing enough to learn and did well, but those who taught both children, as Miss Swift did, were struck by the contrast. She reported that he asked few questions, and, never inquiring further, seemed perfectly satisfied with what she told him.[52] However, Oliver was much more affectionate and sympathetic than Laura. She was very refined in her manners and sought companionship, too, but she was never as truly sympathetic.[53] She was quite demanding in her companions. When she sensed that some were inferior to her mentally, she precipitately dropped them.

IV

Nothing could more strikingly show the power of education to redeem the deaf-blind for humanity than the meeting between Laura and Julia Brace which took place at the American Asylum in Hartford during November 1841. Laura was radiant in her interest. She had to learn the name of everything, go everywhere, and talk to as many as she could. Julia, on the other hand, was without animation and expression. Her keepers, introducing them to each other, tried to show her that this friendly being was like her. Laura grasped her affectionately, but the other was uninterested, and, withdrawing, left the puzzled girl to wonder, "Why does she push me — why does she not love me?"[54]

The contrast between the twelve-year-old child and the thirty-five-year-old woman was so marked that the authorities at the Asylum

[51] Swift's Journal, Dec. 1, 1841.
[52] Swift's Journal, Feb. 21, 1845.
[53] *43d Report* (1876), p. 96.
[54] Undated clipping cut from *N. Y. Commercial Advertiser,* but apparently about the beginning of Dec. 1841: to be found in the first of two scrapbooks containing Laura's press notices at the Perkins School.

decided to send Julia to Boston, in the hope that there under Howe's proven teaching method she might improve. She arrived April 6, 1842,[55] seeming to understand why she had come, and anxious to learn. But Howe had misgivings. His new charge was far beyond the age for learning. She had been so long neglected that he feared she could not be aroused.[56]

The familiar course of instruction began now for the fourth time. Julia's instructors tried to teach her to make the letters of the alphabet with her fingers, but she preferred the old signs she had been using for years. Her education had not been completely neglected, nor were her senses entirely dulled. Miss Swift was surprised that Julia knew so many arbitrary signs. She had one for "friend," another for "today," and one for "yesterday."[57] Though a slow student, she did learn to use metallic types and eventually could spell many words which she used at table. Miss Eliza Rogers, who was assigned to her, could always get her to bring things by spelling them out to her, but there was no way of getting her to utilize her vocabulary on her own initiative. The great difficulty was in rousing her from apathy.[58]

On occasion she could become excited. Once in September she and Oliver were given figures of animals to examine. The alert boy was, of course, instantly interested, while Julia "exhibited all the pleasure that a child of two years might be expected to."[59] A month later Miss Rogers noted that she knew seventy words.[60]

Howe was satisfied that Julia had the capacity to learn.[61] However, after being at Perkins for a year, her guardian had her returned to Hartford. The South Boston school was left with its two deaf-blind students, whose education proceeded satisfactorily.

[55] According to Miss Swift's journal of that date. Howe in his *Tenth Report* (1842), p. 59 gives the date as April 9, but this is probably a typographical error.
[56] *Tenth Report* (1842), p. 60.
[57] Swift's Journal, April 7, 1842.
[58] Rogers Ms. Journal, Aug. 12, 1842, Perkins.
[59] Rogers Journal, Sept. 8, 1842.
[60] Rogers Journal, Oct. 8, 1842.
[61] *Eleventh Report* (1843), p. 46. Laura was properly saddened at Julia's departure, and wrote to Mrs. White, Julia's matron, regretting that "no one can not teach her. . . ." Swift's Journal, April 14, 1843.

V

Laura had by this time reached the stage in her development where, along with her more advanced lessons in the ordinary school subjects, Howe felt that he might begin to teach her immaterial concepts, leading eventually to religious instruction. For a number of reasons he had delayed teaching her religion. He feared that a premature effort would give her "ideas of God which would be alike unworthy of His character, and fatal to her peace." [62] Also, he refused to act without definite permission of the parents. When he judged that Laura could understand religious instruction, he wrote them to know their wishes. The Bridgmans left the matter to him.[63] With their *carte blanche* thus secured, he was free to proceed as he wished.

Howe preferred to wait until Laura's understanding of natural phenomena would lead her to a realization of the existence of a supernatural power. As he probed her mind seeking for indications of its bent, he found only an innate intellectual and moral disposition that promised a fertile field for the inculcation of piety.[64] He began by teaching her magnetism and the process of plant growth. Extreme caution was necessary since he wished her to learn the basic facts of religion without becoming a slave to sectarianism. He did not want her to learn any concepts her reason would later repudiate, causing her to become suspicious of the entire subject.[65] Nor would he force the development. What he taught her about God during the next year came mostly from her own questions, which he felt were inspired by carelessness on the part of others.[66]

To all urgings that he instruct her in a revealed religion, Howe demurred. While he realized that he could press on her any doctrinal system he wished, which she could learn to parrot like any other child, he did not wish to do so. First Laura had to be able to

---

[62] *Ninth Report* (1841), p. 40.
[63] *Fifteenth Report* (1847), pp. 28–29.
[64] *Ninth Report* (1841), p. 40.
[65] *Thirteenth Report* (1845), p. 32.
[66] *Eleventh Report* (1843), p. 37.

understand before he would instill any faith. He stated his problem
succinctly:

Unaided by any precedent for this case, one can look only to the
book of nature; and that seems to teach that we should prepare the
soul for loving and worshipping God, by developing its powers, and
making it acquainted with his wonderful and benevolent works, before
we lay down rules of blind obedience.[67]

Laura, quite interested in her subject, found Howe's cautious
policy too slow for her. She took matters in her own hands by seeking information elsewhere, namely from Miss Swift. But the staff
had received its orders; religion was the doctor's preserve. All the
eager girl's questions had to be directed to him.[68] At this juncture,
in the spring of 1843, Howe married and went to Europe for a
year, leaving Laura in the charge of Miss Swift.[69] The young
teacher tried to follow her instructions not to give the child ideas
she should not have, but after a few months, with Howe's restrain-
ing hand removed, she took advantage of the situation to instill
certain doctrinal views Howe had specifically forbidden. The defenseless girl, subjected to concepts she could not understand, became steadily more upset. In her confusion, she turned again to her
"Doc":

Is God ever ashamed? I think of God very often to love him. Why
did you say that I must think of God? . . . When will he let us to go
to see him in Heaven? . . . Why is He our Father? . . . . Why can
not he let wrong people to go to live with him & be happy — Why
should he not like to have us ask him to send us good thoughts if we
are not very sad for doing wrong —[70]

In far-off Rome Howe sensed that she was becoming fearful and
unhappy. He tried to restore the God of Love and disperse any dark

[67] *Eleventh Report,* p. 38.
[68] Swift's Journal, Feb. 9, 1842.
[69] Miss Drew had married in 1841 and left Perkins.
[70] Laura Bridgman to Howe, Jan. 28, 1844, copied in Miss Swift's Journal, Feb. 4,
1844.

thoughts that might have crept into her consciousness by the use of simple terms. Urging her to be patient and not afraid, he wrote,

> Mrs Howe has a sweet little baby. . . . You love her too. . . . But you never felt of her, and she never kissed you, and how can you love her? It is not your . . . body . . . which loves her, and loves me, but your soul. If your hand were to be cut off, you would love me the same. . . . Nobody knows what the soul is, but we know it is not the body . . . and cannot die. . . . When I say there is a spirit of love in the world, I mean that good people love each other; but you cannot feel the spirit of love with your fingers, it has no shape, nor body; it is not in one place more than in another, yet wherever there are good people there is a spirit of love. . . . All this world, . . . and all things, were made by God. . . . I cannot see Him, nor feel Him . . . but I know that He has the spirit of love, because he too provided every thing to make all the people happy. God wants every body to be happy all the time, every day, Sundays and all, and to love one another; and if they love one another they will be happy; and when their bodies die, their souls will live on, and be happy, and then they will know more about God. . . .[71]

It was all to no avail; Howe came back to find Laura chattering about the Atonement, the Lamb of God, and other "very mystical points of mere speculative doctrine." [72] He was furious at this breach of his command. Years later Miss Swift, or Mrs. Lamson since she was by this time married, admitted that she had violated instructions, but justified her course on the ground that Howe had delayed too long before opening the subject with Laura. She claimed that the benighted girl had never known the name of Christ until the last month she was with her, as if to hint that Laura might never have learned of him at all had it not been for her courageous stand in refusing to follow her superior in his error.[73]

Howe set about to remedy the damage Miss Swift and her friends had ill-advisedly caused. He resumed his conversations with Laura,

---

[71] *Thirteenth Report* (1845), p. 34.

[72] *Thirteenth Report*, pp. 32–33. Laura could not understand the metaphorical language used in her instruction, and wondered why the Lamb of God did not grow into a sheep.

[73] Lamson, *Laura Bridgman*, p. 277.

speaking of a benevolent God, kind not only to humans, but to animals without souls as well.[74] No mention was made about diverse sects.[75]

So long as Howe stuck to elementary education, he met nothing but praise, but when his reports on the religious training of Laura were published, he aroused a storm of controversy. Many orthodox believers shook their heads at his labors. The *Christian Observatory,* disapproving of his *Fifteenth Report,* suddenly awakened to the fact that Perkins was a sectarian institution propagating Pelagianism, the controverted doctrine that man is by nature holy, that children are as pure as Eve was before the Fall, and that temptation alone makes man evil. Howe's critics denounced him for being illiberally sectarian, since he denounced anyone who taught a faith different from his own. Under the guise of disinterestedness, they said, he was attempting to make converts to Unitarianism, and that Laura, who was to be a refutation of Calvinism, had shown at the age of seven that she needed restraint, since she had already gone into ways of transgression. They believed Howe was endangering the souls of Laura and Oliver and that he would have to answer to God for his sin.[76]

Howe immediately wrote a firm defense of his stand, taking complete responsibility for Laura's training. He sought to teach only the basic points of belief all Christians held in common, he said. The choice of which church Laura would join, if any, belonged to her family.[77] The Bridgmans were Baptists, and it was into that faith that Laura was baptized by immersion in July 1852 at Hanover.[78] She remained a devout believer for the rest of her life.

[74] *Thirteenth Report* (1845), pp. 35–36.
[75] Sarah Wight's Ms. Journal, May 1, 1846, Perkins. Not until 1846 did Howe take over her entire religious training, even to reading the Bible, which she had been doing with her teachers. He told her that as she studied the holy book, she should bear in mind that it was full of errors. Laura, for her part, could not understand why Miss Wight should think differently from the doctor in matters of religion.
[76] *Christian Observatory,* I, 3 (March 1847), 138–139.
[77] *Christian Observatory,* I, 5 (May 1847), 236.
[78] *Telegraphy and Pioneer* (Chelsea, Mass.), July 26, 1852; found most conveniently in Bridgman Clippings, Perkins.

VI

The impact of Laura Bridgman on her time was dynamic. Through her, the world became aware of a class critically in need of assistance. The child made her first appearance in Howe's *Sixth Report,* 1838, and was henceforth in the public domain. Amazement and incredulity were Boston's original reactions to its first news of her but soon all over the Western World, people were eagerly devouring every bit of information and marveling at her progress.

Howe's reports furnished the basis of hundreds of articles in newspapers and magazines all over the United States and Europe. In England, France, and Germany there was a steady reading public for his writings in the original language and translation. George Sumner, Charles's dilettante younger brother, wrote from Paris that copies were passed from hand to hand, "exciting the admiration of many enlightened Frenchmen." Both the Academy of Medicine and the Academy of Moral and Political Sciences of the Institute listened to papers about Laura, which were later published.[79]

In America, the most distinguished savant to write on Laura was Francis Lieber, then professor in South Carolina. Each year, the German expatriate came to Boston to observe Laura's development at close hand. He published an article on her for the Smithsonian Institution.[80]

Wherever Laura went, crowds gathered. She was the chief attraction of the Perkins Institution. The citizenry flocked there on exhibition days to stand behind a barrier to watch her at work, she unaware of their attentions.[81] Among the visitors, more than once, was the charming Miss Julia Ward of New York, soon to be the doctor's wife.[82] Charles Dickens, the most popular writer of the

[79] George Sumner to Howe, Aug. 2, 1845, Howe Papers, Houghton.

[80] "On the Vocal Sounds of Laura Bridgman," *Smithsonian Contributions to Knowledge* (Washington, 1850), II. He also wrote a book on her in 1841 for which Howe and Sumner acted as agents in a fruitless quest of a publisher.

[81] Howe feared a growth of vanity in Laura, if she became aware of the attention being heaped on her. Oliver was safe, since much less "untoward attention" was exerted on him, *Thirteenth Report* (1845), pp. 49–50.

[82] Julia Ward to her sisters, undated, 1842, Howe Papers, Houghton.

time, saw Laura on January 29, 1842. The Englishman marveled at what he saw of both Laura and Oliver. Miss Swift noted that "He could hardly believe the evidence of his senses, and was much more surprised than people generally are. . . ." [83] His rapturous account, which he published in his *American Notes* during the next year, brought Howe and his pupils to the attention of many more people than the American educator could have reached by his own writings.

Thomas Carlyle, without crossing the sea, followed the progress of the children. After reading the *Ninth Report,* he wrote Howe a note glowing with his spiritual uplifting:

> The good little girl: one loves her to the very heart. No Goethe's Mignon, in most poetic fiction, comes closer to one than this poor Laura in prose reality and fact. . . . That little question of hers, "Do horses sit up late?" stirs us to laughter, to tears — when one thinks of the good little creature, — and probably to as kind a mood as human speech alone can awaken in a human heart. [84]

Laura melted the heart even of the King of Prussia, and caused him to forget his antipathy to Howe long enough to award the distinguished teacher a gold medal for "scientific merit." The medal according to newspaper accounts was quite splendid. On one side was Apollo in his chariot drawn by four horses, with the signs of the zodiac at his feet, and on the other, the head of Frederick William IV. [85]

Laura became a legend while she lived. Unfounded tales of her achievements circulated widely, for example, that she performed at the piano and could sing, although a little reflection would show anyone she could do neither. [86] Hers was a story that parents loved to tell their children, sometimes getting strange reactions. Certain

---

[83] Swift's Journal, Jan. 29, 1842.

[84] Carlyle to Howe, typescript, Oct. 23, 1842, Howe Papers, Houghton.

[85] *Christian Advocate,* Jan. 21, 1846. Howe Clippings, Perkins. Family legend has it that when Howe received it, he weighed it, and found that the gold was worth exactly what he had been charged for his board in prison in 1832. Laura E. Richards, *Samuel Gridley Howe* (New York, 1935), p. 69.

[86] Mrs. H. L. Wellington, "Laura Bridgman," *The Watchman,* Aug. 11, 1881.

little girls were so moved on hearing of her for the first time that they pushed out the eyes of their favorite dolls, and named them "Laura." [87] For others made of sterner stuff, she became a bogy, and the *bête noire* of at least one strong-willed child. Whenever "Nellie Bly," eventually a famous Pulitzer journalist, rebelled at learning the alphabet, she invariably heard a tale of a girl who could neither see nor hear, but who learned her letters. Laura ended up in Nellie's mind alongside other disciplinary aids like the bears who ate children for calling an old man "bald head." [88]

The lives of Laura and Oliver affected Howe greatly. His veneration for God was increased. His faith in divine goodness was reaffirmed. Each day the children lived proclaimed to the world the benevolence of the Lord. He thought of Laura as a force that could regenerate society.

Everything which brings out the hidden virtue of humanity; everything which puts aside for a moment the selfishness & egotism that obscures its native qualities of love & sympathy, & shows the heart of man beating in unison with the joys & woes of his fellows, every such thing I consider a compliment to me as one of the race.

The case of Laura Bridgman has done this . . . and . . . it has been better for her generation that she lived in it.[89]

The fame of Laura Bridgman established that of Samuel Gridley Howe as a humanitarian more firmly in the minds of Americans. His later prominence in campaigns for social reform stemmed from the reputation he gained at Perkins.

[87] E. Addie Heath, "Laura Bridgman," *The Woman's Magazine*, VIII, 8, p. 238, Bridgman Clippings.
[88] *New York World*, Feb. 17, 1889.
[89] Howe to Mrs. Howitt, July 31, 1847, Howe Clippings, Perkins.

VII

Fads and Reforms

Samuel Gridley Howe was in the full vigor of his manhood during the fourth decade of the nineteenth century, with seemingly boundless stores of energy. His manifold duties at Perkins, far from exhausting his powers, left room in his mind for other intellectual activities and space in his heart for other reform interests. During the thirties and forties, besides serving as a magazine editor, he lectured and wrote on a variety of subjects, followed intellectual fads that for the moment were fashionable, and played a significant part in several constructive reform movements. More than most persons, he was robustly involved in the currents of his time.

I

Howe gave vent to his love of journalism by frequent contributions to the more respectable periodicals and occasional letters to newspapers.[1] His most important writing appeared in the *New England Magazine.* Founded by Edwin Buckingham, the promising and talented son of Joseph T. Buckingham, editor of the *Boston Courier,* the *New England Magazine* was the most significant monthly published in Boston before the advent of the *Atlantic* in 1855. It was one of the first to break away from the review type of article in favor of general contributions, and it was the vehicle for the earliest works of such authors as Nathaniel Haw-

[1] He wrote political letters to the *Boston Courier* on his second trip to Europe. Howe to Sampson, Nov. 14, 1831, Howe Papers, Houghton.

thorne, Park Benjamin, and Oliver Wendell Holmes, whose "Autocrat of the Breakfast Table" appeared in the first volume.[2]

Howe, showing interest in the venture, wrote a series of five articles drawn from his Greek experiences, "From the Mss. [*sic*] of a Traveler in the East," which started with the first issue of the magazine in July 1831.[3] His many later contributions ranged widely: "The Education of the Blind" (March 1833), "The May Fair" (June 1833), "Letter on Slavery" (August 1833), "Thoughts on National Character, Illustrated by the History of Greece" (April 1834), "Atheism in New England" (December 1834 and January 1835), and "The Polish Exiles" (January 1835).[4]

Howe's ambition for journalistic distinction led him to take over the editorship when the opportunity offered. In 1834, following the death of the younger Buckingham. Howe formed a partnership with John O. Sargent for the purchase of the magazine.[5] The first issue under their direction appeared in December 1834. Filled with great hopes for their publication, the new proprietors proposed to conduct it on the plan of the most popular English magazines, without however, reprinting from them. Theirs would be a journal to meet American needs.[6]

Howe, throwing himself into his new job with his customary vigor, wrote the lead article, "Atheism in New England," for the December issue. He scouted around for outside contributions, and solicited from his friends and acquaintances, to whom he offered one dollar a page for prose, and double that for poetry.[7]

The partners edited only three numbers, the last, of 1834, and

[2] Frank Luther Mott, *History of American Magazines* (Cambridge, 1939), I, 599–602; George Willis Cooke, "First *New England Magazine*," *New England Magazine*, N.S., XVI, 1 (March 1897), 103–117.

[3] July–Nov. 1831.

[4] The collection of Howe clippings at Perkins is useful in tracking down the titles of Howe's articles.

[5] Sargent was one of the collaborators of the *Harbinger*. He went to New York later, where he practiced law, journalism, and politics.

[6] Howe to George C. Shattuck, Dec. 1, 1834, Shattuck Papers, MHS. Prospectus enclosed.

[7] Howe to Albert G. Greene, Nov. 9, 1834, Greene Papers, Brown University Library; and Howe to B. B. Thatcher, Jan. 19, 1835, Misc. Mss. Columbia University, offer examples of his solicitations.

the first two of 1835. Unable to continue, possibly because the task was too laborious for men burdened with other activities, they sold out to Park Benjamin, a New York poet and journalist.[8] Evidence indicates that Sargent wished to retire and persuaded Howe to give up the venture also.[9] Nevertheless Howe's interest in journalism remained strong throughout the succeeding years, to blossom forth in the fifties in the columns of the *Commonwealth,* a Free-Soil daily that he edited for a time.[10]

II

Howe was deeply affected by intellectual fads of the time, such as hydropathy (the "water-cure") and phrenology. The latter in particular attracted him. This pseudo-science, an early form of psychology, was propagated by two Viennese physicians, Franz Joseph Gall and John Gaspar Spurzheim. It was based on the principle that the shape of the head determined character, and won adherents among such scientific leaders as John C. Warren of the Harvard Medical School and Benjamin Silliman of Yale. Finding in it the answer to the vexing problem of the relationship of the material to the immaterial in the human being, Howe became one of Spurzheim's most devoted disciples, and served as corresponding secretary of the Boston Phrenological Society. He wrote and lectured extensively; he even prepared a handbook for the use of his students. After Spurzheim's death, Howe became equally attached to the work of the leading Scottish phrenologist, George Combe. Indeed, there arose between them a warm friendship.

Though phrenology quickly lost its respectability when its defects as a science became apparent, Howe retained his faith in the great principle he drew from its teachings, that the mind and body are inseparably joined, and that a proper educational system aims at the full development of both. This was his object at Perkins, later at the Idiot School, and in his work in the common schools.[11]

[8] Merle M. Hoover, *Park Benjamin, Poet & Editor* (New York, 1948), p. 52.
[9] Howe to Sargent, Jan. 30, 1835, Sargent Papers, MHS.
[10] Discussed in Chapter XII.
[11] For a fuller discussion of this topic, see, Harold Schwartz, "Samuel Gridley Howe as Phrenologist," *American Historical Review,* LVII, 3 (April 1952), 644–651.

III

Besides fads, Howe advocated serious reforms, such as the improvement of public education. A literate society was part of the Jeffersonian ideal; no democracy could exist without it. The work Howe did in furthering this ideal is one of his proudest accomplishments, even though he was not the leading figure in the movement, but the first lieutenant of Horace Mann who was, from 1837 to 1848, the Secretary of the Massachusetts Board of Education. Howe's admiration for Mann's ability, intellect, and integrity transcended the feelings one bears a friend. The two were more than friends; blood brothers in reform is an apter description. Howe drew inspiration from Mann's nobility and selflessness. Considering him as one who was "hitting harder knocks on Satans [*sic*] cranium than any other person living," Howe felt Mann the only one able to stimulate him constantly to act up to the highest motives.[12]

Truly [he wrote on one occasion] to me you are becoming . . . the sun to my sincipital region; & under the genial influence of your presence I feel the better parts of my nature struggling up through the reeds & thorns of the propensities. Would you had arisen with healing in your beams upon my moral horizon years ago — or would I could secure the continuance of your influence for years to come.[13]

Mann reciprocated this feeling as warmly. The enjoyment of Howe's friendship was always one of his greatest satisfactions.[14] He liked Howe's uncompromising driving energy, and thought of him as one of the greatest men of the time. "I should rather have built up the Blind Asylum than to have written Hamlet," Mann wrote him, "& when human vitality gets up into the coronal region every body will think so." [15]

[12] Howe to Mann, March 27, 1842; June 6, 1841, Howe Papers, Houghton.
[13] Howe to Mann, May 17, 1841, Howe Papers, Houghton.
[14] Mary Mann, *Life of Horace Mann*, p. 44.
[15] Mann to Howe, May 20, 1841, Mann Papers, MHS. He wrote this when trying to dissuade Howe from going to Spain, and the sentiment may be somewhat inflated, but considering how many times he expressed something similar, there was not much exaggeration.

But then Mann was one of the those dedicated souls who considered the improvement of society the most worthwhile occupation for a man. Born into a home devoutly Calvinist, he early repudiated the harsh doctrines which had terrorized him during his childhood in favor of the God of love and benevolence. Unable however to overcome Puritanism's moral injunctions, his life was a ceaseless struggle against evil wherever he could seek it out. In chronic ill-health, his weak body housed an iron will mystically certain that Divine Providence led him along paths whose righteousness he never doubted. Trained in the law following a tutorship in Classics at Brown, where he may have known Howe, and from which he had graduated brilliantly at the head of his class in 1820, he entered the Massachusetts legislature where he eventually rose to be Senate President.[16] But the main interest in the back of his mind was public education, and when in 1837 a movement led by George B. Emerson culminated in the establishment of a state Board of Education, he resigned his legislative post to become its first Secretary.[17] Reading for months in order to qualify, he longed for the job so intensely that he sacrificed his $3000 salary to earn half that, in order to be in the place where he felt he could do the most good.[18] Throughout his career, Mann never sought more than just enough money to live on.

Howe was a rock in the hours of Mann's travail which began immediately on his assumption of office. A minority in the various organized churches sought to reinject the religious issue in the public schools, a matter which for a decade had lain dormant.[19] Mingling charges of the Prussianization of the schools through the agency of an all-powerful dictator who must perforce be unacquainted with local conditions, they prophesied "godlessness"

---

[16] Mary Mann, *Life of Horace Mann*, pp. 9–58.

[17] *Laws of the State of Massachusetts, 1837*, chap. ccxli.

[18] Mann to Parker, Jan. 17, 1848, transcript, Letterbook 11, p. 82, Parker Papers, MHS.

[19] Mann's Journal, Oct. 27, 1838, Mann Papers, MHS; Raymond B. Culver, *Horace Mann and Religion in the Massachusetts Public Schools* (New Haven, 1929), pp. 1–180. Excellent summary. The law of 1827 had set up a nonsectarian school system. *Laws of the State of Massachusetts* (1827), chap. cxliii.

triumphant if the Secretary's program were not restrained.[20] Undeterred by these latter-day Cassandras, Mann proceeded steadily with the program he had outlined: the creation of normal schools for the training of teachers, the preparation of cheap editions of classics and new works for school libraries, and the publication of the *Common School Journal,* a financially unprofitable biweekly which served as his organ of expression.

At the 1840 legislative session, the opposition came out in the open on the floor of the House in a motion to close the normal schools, those seed beds of "free thought," and abolish the Board through repeal of the Act of 1837. So powerful were the forces of reaction that the House Committee on Education reported the motion favorably.[21] The Board seemed doomed, but Mann, marshaling his supporters, fathered the minority report which four days later put to shame the charges against him.[22] When the vote came, repeal was beaten down, and the continued existence of the Board seemed assured for a while at any rate.

During all this time Howe encouraged Mann, writing and speaking on his behalf, and gathering information. Wherever he went he examined the local school systems and sent back reports on students, the abilities of the teachers, their salaries, and the conditions of the buildings.[23] In practical matters, such as lighting and seating arrangements, hours of study, and rest periods, Howe's views were significant since he drew on his own experience as an educator.[24] Though overlaid with much nonsense because of his belief in phrenology, his advice was sound in the main. He stated that school work should be planned so as not to fatigue the brain of the young. Too much study was bad, even in the case of children who pre-

---

[20] See for example the anonymous review article on Mann's *Second Report,* in the *Boston Quarterly Review,* II, 4 (Oct. 1839), 393–434, Orestes Brownson, editor. He denounced the Board on the grounds of its being un-American, Godless, and Whig.

[21] *House Documents,* No. 49 (March 7, 1840).

[22] *House Documents,* No. 53 (March 11, 1840). The draft of the report in the Mann Papers is in his handwriting.

[23] Howe to Mann, July 30, 1840, Howe Papers, Houghton, contains his views on the common school system of New York State.

[24] *Common School Journal,* I, 19 (Oct. 1, 1839), 299–301, contains an extract of a letter from Howe to Mann on this subject.

ferred study to play. Precocious prodigies would eventually sink below the level of their contemporaries and remain for life weak and inefficient. Children under eight should not be confined in one position or study any subject longer than half an hour at a time. If they were given long recesses in the open air, he felt they might study four hours daily. Older children could work longer periods at a stretch. The best hours were from eight until noon in summer, nine to noon in winter, and three to six in the afternoon. A single session from nine until two was bad. Furthermore, no vacation longer than two or three days was necessary in a well-regulated school. Vacations of six weeks and longer were destructive of regular study habits and mental discipline. Mental powers should not be allowed to lie idle for long periods. Where schools were concerned, Howe had only one guiding principle, the best arrangements possible were the only acceptable, "cost what it may." [25]

Howe considered the normal schools of the most vital significance, and did what he could to aid in their creation and defense. As a school director he had come to realize that the greatest obstacle to a good national educational system was the lack of competent and well-trained teachers. "I have felt it in my own case, I have witnessed it in scores of others," he wrote Mann, while their creation was still under discussion. He continued further,

I would give duoble [sic] wages to a teacher of twenty years old, who had served as usher two years under a good master, than to one of four & twenty who brought an A.M. & M.D. or any diplomas & certificates whatever, of mere acquirements.[26]

When the Lexington Normal School, the first of the teacher training institutes established, was under attack, he spoke frequently in its behalf. It was regrettable, Howe told one of his audiences, that in such an enlightened region as nineteenth-century Massachusetts, a question should arise as to whether a man should be specifically trained for his profession.[27] Lexington Normal was the best institu-

[25] *Common School Journal*, III, 24 (Dec. 15, 1841), 383–384.
[26] Howe to Mann, March 19, 1838, Howe Papers, Houghton.
[27] *Common School Journal*, III, 21 (Nov. 1, 1841), 328.

tion of its type he had ever seen, so good that he drew his faculty from there, except for music teachers who were still men.[28]

During these years when it seemed as if all Mann had striven for was in danger of being swept away, the support Howe gave him was his greatest source of strength.

How can I thank you enough for the interest you take in me. . . . [Mann wrote in 1841], I have tried many times but I choke, I feel that, if I have [had] any success, I have been mainly indebted to you for it. Without your aid, I do not believe the cause would have survived to this time. . . . If I love the cause then, how must I feel towards one to whom it is so much indebted?[29]

At last, the legislature appropriated an adequate sum for school libraries. Mann rejoiced. "Take your fill then of drink," he wrote Howe, "for you smote the rock out of which the living waters have gushed. . . . Never give up. . . . Massachusetts may yet be a spectacle for men & angels. . . ."[30]

They had won a great victory. But there was still energy enough in the opposition for one more fight, the last of a dying cause, one in which Mann and Howe were to win a greater victory and share the glory together.

IV

At the same time that Howe aided Mann's reforms, he also rendered great service in behalf of the insane, serving as the chief aide to Dorothea Lynde Dix. A strange woman, one of those in whom the New England conscience was the guiding force, she differed from most of her contemporaries in that she pursued the same project for life, proper care for lunatics. Perhaps it is this concentration that explains her success, since she never dissipated her efforts. Her most striking characteristic was her willfulness. She could never be swerved from her decisions. Even as a child she showed determination when at the age of twelve she made her

[28] *Common School Journal*, II, 15 (Aug. 1, 1840), 238–239; *ibid.*, IV, 17 (Sept. 1, 1842), 272.
[29] Mann to Howe, Aug. 1841, Mann Papers, MHS.
[30] Mann to Howe, March 17, 1842, Mann Papers, MHS.

way alone from her drunken father's home in Hampden, Maine to the Boston mansion of her wealthy grandmother, under whose carping surveillance she spent the rest of her minority. Insecure, devoid of parental affection, she early thought of self-support, and opened her first school at the age of fourteen, so as to earn money to bring her younger brothers to live with her. Following an unhappy love affair, the auburn-haired beauty put aside thoughts of domestic felicity. She took up the practice of her profession in earnest as head of a private school in Boston.   *101122*

Relieved from financial concern at the age of thirty-nine through a bequest from her grandmother, she was free to devote herself to a mission in life. The call to service came through the request of a young theology student that she conduct a Sunday school class at the East Cambridge jail. Miss Dix consented to teach the prisoners. At the jail on March 28, 1841, she was horrified by the sight of insane inmates lying huddled in cramped unheated cells. (The state asylum at Worcester, whose creation Horace Mann had fostered in 1830, was much too small to hold all the state's mentally deranged.)[31] Miss Dix decided at that moment to begin a campaign for their benefit. She would remove them from the degrading influences of the prisons into hospitals where they would get the attention of trained keepers.[32]

An unknown maiden lady working alone could accomplish nothing. Needing the assistance of one who could command a respectful hearing, she turned to one long known for his humanitarian achievements, Samuel Gridley Howe. She told him of her shocking discovery and of her plan to travel around the state to investigate all prisons and almshouses, the publicly designated depositaries of the insane, to see if they were as inadequate as the Middlesex County House of Correction. Howe cautioned her against undertaking this arduous project, since she had only recently recovered from a serious illness and might overtax her strength again.[33] But the inflexible

---

[31] *Massachusetts Acts and Resolves* (1830), chap. lxxxiii.

[32] Biographical data culled from Francis Tiffany, *Life of Dorothea Dix* (Boston, 1890), pp. 1–74; and Helen Marshall, *Dorothea Dix, Forgotten Samaritan* (Chapel Hill, 1937), pp. 1–85.

[33] Marshall, *Dorothea Dix*, p. 86.

woman had made up her mind; she saw her duty, and was unconcerned for her own welfare.

Howe conducted his own inspection of East Cambridge in the summer of 1841, apparently just to check up on Miss Dix. Over a year later, on August 6, 1842, the *Boston Courier* published an exposé of conditions at the jail which led Howe to add his corroborating evidence on September 8 in the *Advertiser*. Charging that animals in a menagerie were better treated, he described the "horrors of that demoniac den." Filth was merely the most apparent condition, not the most serious. The air,

foul as it is, is pure compared to the moral atmosphere loaded so often with blasphemies and imprecations; the raving maniac and the drivelling idiot are in close contact; and the curses of the one and the gibberings of the other, serve to put out the little light of reason which may be feebly flickering in the mind of the partially insane.[34]

A joint special committee of the legislature was appointed two days later to report on the state of the East Cambridge jail. Discovering the disquieting fact that the newspapers for once had printed the truth without overstatement, the lawmakers recommended a bill to permit all counties to build separate insane quarters without delay, wherever it would suit the convenience of the authorities.[35] No such law was ever enacted.[36]

Miss Dix completed her inspection tour of the state in the fall of 1842. Her disclosures to Howe of what she had seen convinced him of the need to force public action. Appointing himself her spokesman, he determined to lead the fight by entering the Massachusetts House of Representatives. Late in October his nomination as Whig candidate was announced, and two weeks later he was elected.[37]

He began his agitation even before taking office. In a steady stream of newspaper and magazine articles he discussed the possibility of enlarging the Worcester State Hospital and building

[34] *Boston Advertiser*, Sept. 8, 1842.

[35] *House Doc.* 47 (1842), 5.

[36] A bill passed the House of Representatives, but went no further. *Boston Courier*, Sept. 16, 1842.

[37] *Boston Advertiser*, Oct. 25 and Nov. 16, 1842.

others. Lunatics, he insisted, must be cared for at state expense.[38] There could be no doubt that when he took his seat in the House, there would be action.

After introducing Miss Dix's petition with her attached *Memorial,* January 19, 1843, the freshman legislator, as chairman of the Committee on Public Charitable Institutions, began work on a bill to meet her demands.[39] The *Memorial* was a simple statement of what its author had seen of the care of "the miserable, the desolate, the outcast." [40] She told of the almost universal use of cages, and even of chains, in some towns, of the woman maniac who tore off her own skin, and of others "wallowing in dirty straw, in a place yet more dirty, and without clothing, without fire. Worse cared for than the brutes, and wholly lost to consciousness of decency!" [41] Certain that with proper care some of the unfortunates might be cured and the condition of others improved, she urged that special institutions be created for the insane.[42]

The public response was favorable. Horace Mann thanked the lone woman for the work she was doing in aid of those who could not requite her.[43] The *Newburyport Herald* hoped that her appeal would not be in vain. The inaccuracies in her report did not lessen its value.[44] There were of course complaints from those who felt they had been unjustly dealt with, such as Anson Hooker, physician at the East Cambridge jail.[45] Also, the Overseers of the Poor in Danvers and Shelburne protested Miss Dix's statement of conditions in their towns.[46] These countercharges caused some persons to

[38] Howe to Jarvis, Nov. 29, 1842, Washburn Papers, XI, 58, MHS. S. G. Howe, "Insanity in Massachusetts," *North American Review,* LVI (Jan. 1843), 171–191. Reprinted as separate pamphlet.

[39] *Boston Advertiser,* Jan. 20, 1843.

[40] Dorothea Lynde Dix, *Memorial to the Legislature of Massachusetts* (Boston, 1843), p. 4.

[41] Dix, *Memorial,* pp. 6–7.

[42] Dix, *Memorial,* pp. 25–30.

[43] Mann to Dix, Jan. 27, 1843, Dix Papers, Houghton.

[44] *Newburyport Herald,* Feb. 6, 1843. Newspaper comments can be most conveniently found tied together in a bundle in the second box of clippings in the Dix Papers.

[45] Hooker to Dix, Jan. 24, 1843, Dix Papers.

[46] John M. Proctor to Dix, Feb. 14, 1843, Dix Papers; *Salem Gazette,* Jan. 27, 1843; *Greenfield Democrat,* Feb. 9, 1843. Danvers Overseers of the Poor, *Memorial to the Legislature* (Salem, 1843).

reconsider their earlier approval. The *Courier,* hitherto well-dis-posed, decided that it was best to accept her statements "at a discount of about fifty per cent." [47] However her defenders remained firm. The *Mercantile Journal* said she should be congratulated for her work instead of censured, while Charles Sumner took the back-sliding paper to task.[48]

At length Howe's resolves relating to the lunatic asylum came up for debate on February 25. His committee reported a bill authoriz-ing the trustees to enlarge the Worcester Hospital for the accom-modation of 200 more insane patients.[49] Howe, addressing the House, urged its passage. Others spoke too, successfully beating down the few opponents, and the measure passed to its third read-ing that day.[50] John Gorham Palfrey, the Harvard theologian, a member for Middlesex County, glowed over his colleague's skillful leadership of the debate. He had "managed the business admirably; — to say, like an old stager, would be doing him injustice; — like a man of humanity, energy; & abundant resources, as he is." [51]

On March 20, when the bill came up to be engrossed, the Speaker of the House left his chair to make an eloquent appeal. The final vote was overwhelmingly favorable.[52] Howe exulted to Sumner over the victory:

Glory — glory & good tidings for all sane & insane. We have carried the measure through its final stage in the House 25,000 $ [*sic*] and all by 151–80.

I'm off like a rocket, shall be sneaking back like a stick on Wednes-day.[53]

Early on the morning of the twenty-fifth, the last day of the ses-sion, the Senate approved the proposal, which Governor Marcus Morton signed shortly afterward.[54]

[47] *Boston Courier,* Feb. 22, 1843.
[48] *Boston Evening Mercantile Journal,* Feb. 21, 1843; for Sumner's comment, see *Boston Courier,* Feb. 25, 1843.
[49] *Mass. House Doc.* 38 (1843), 12–13.
[50] *Boston Advertiser,* Feb. 27, 1843.
[51] Palfrey to Dix, Feb. 25, 1843, Dix Papers.
[52] *Boston Advertiser,* March 21, 1843.
[53] Howe to Sumner, March 20, 1843, Howe Papers, Houghton.
[54] *Boston Advertiser,* March 27, 1843; *Mass. Acts and Resolves* (1843), chap. 73 (March 24, 1843), 83–84.

VIII

Bachelorhood and Marriage

It was Laura Bridgman's fame that brought Howe and Julia Ward together in the summer of 1841. The vivacious New York belle was spending the season at a cottage near Boston with her two sisters when one day Henry Wadsworth Longfellow and Charles Sumner, friends of her brother Sam, came to call. After hearing about the miracle child, they decided to ride over to South Boston to see her in person. Sumner did the honors as host that afternoon, showing them Laura and Lucy Reed together. Just as the company were about to return home, Sumner noticed Howe arriving on horseback, and called their attention to him.

I looked out also [Julia tells us], and beheld a noble rider on a noble steed. The doctor dismounted, and presently came to make our acquaintance. . . . He made upon us an impression of unusual force and reserve! Only when I was seated beside Longfellow for the homeward drive, he mischievously remarked "Longfellow, I see that your horse has been down," at which the poet seemed a little discomfited.[1]

Howe had finally met the woman whom he would marry, and the emptiness of his life ceased. How wrong he had been when in 1831 he wrote his friend Sampson that since he had not married by the time he was thirty, he would die a bachelor.[2] At the age of forty, love came to him at last. What had kept him from it for so

---

[1] Julia Ward Howe, *Reminiscences, 1819–1899* (Boston, 1900), p. 82.
[2] Howe to Sampson, Nov. 14, 1831, Howe Papers, Houghton.

many years one cannot say. Certainly he had not been unaware of the existence of pretty girls during his years abroad, but after his return to America his letters are completely devoid of any references to women. Perhaps his heart still cherished its old affection for Sophia Hyatt, but if so, he never spoke of her to anyone.[3]

I

Howe was probably considered quite a marital catch in his circle. Internationally known as a humanitarian, much more experienced and sophisticated than most of his associates, he was among the most polished of Bostonians. When relaxing among friends in the drawing room after dinner, he could be very charming and witty (one gathers this from the free and easy colloquialism of his personal letters), not at all the thundering, censorious, choleric, hagridden keeper of the New England conscience he sometimes appeared in public. Physically he was very attractive. Just under six feet, with a wealth of brown hair that showed no signs of thinning, and never did, he was strikingly handsome.[4] A painting of him in Greek dress in Brown University and a photograph in the late 1850's attest to his good looks.

Besides filling in his conscious moments with complete devotion to his work, he had tempered his loneliness by drawing around him some of the most stimulating young men in the Boston area. There developed the pattern of friendships that lasted him the rest of his life. Besides Horace Mann, whom he may have known as far back as his undergraduate days, his closest companions came from his membership in the "Five of Clubs," the so-called "Mutual Admiration Society," which met for dinner and whenever else they felt like it. Two members of the Harvard faculty, Henry Wadsworth Longfellow, and Cornelius Conway Felton, and two Harvard-trained lawyers, Charles Sumner, and his partner George Stillman Hillard, besides Howe, comprised the group.[5]

[3] Elizabeth Peabody tells us though, that Howe was engaged briefly to a certain Mary Ann Marshall, a Boston belle, during the summer of 1834, but the Howe Papers have no mention of this. "Cuba Journal," Nov. 29, 1834, Berg Collection, NYPL. I am indebted to Mrs. Louise Hall Tharp for this note.

[4] Description in Passport, dated March 9, 1867, Misc. Mss. Houghton.

[5] Howe replaced Henry R. Cleveland.

These four provided the warmth Howe needed to carry him along. He could not help liking them. None could be immune to Longfellow, the lonely roomer in the Vassall House, whose stature belied his name.[6] His childlike simplicity, his unquestioning optimism, shown by his faith in the supremacy of good,[7] and the gay-colored clothing he affected, indicative of an essential joviality,[8] were irresistible magnets to one of Howe's warmth. After a hard day's struggle with Harvard's undergraduates, during which he tried (generally with indifferent success) to get them to see the beauties of some recondite German, French, or Italian work, "Longo" liked nothing better than a good dinner, a choice wine to add bouquet to the meal, and a lively conversation that would last, with luck, far into the night. Genteel to a fault, the poet never publicly showed his disapproval of anything or anybody. Retiring, mild, and shy, he was fiercely proud of his work. Every criticism wounded him deeply. Still, for years Longfellow, occupying Ticknor's chair as Smith Professor of Modern Languages, lived and worked in a vacuum. Deeply embedded in his soul was a profound and abiding sadness that few could fathom. He had known great sorrow through the death of his young wife, and this had given him a tenderness and compassion rare in one so young.[9]

Successor to Everett as Eliot Professor, was "Corny" Felton, "heartiest of Greek professors." [10] Among the most entertaining of men, he was in addition an outstanding scholar. In a long series of carefully edited texts that did much to improve the teaching of classical literature in America, he early fulfilled the brilliant promise he showed in his youth. Tall, broad, and stooping slightly, as if his encyclopedic knowledge of Hellenic culture were too much for him, he was beloved by all because of his "sweetness" and "purity." [11]

---

[6] Florence Howe Hall, *Memories Grave and Gay* (New York, 1918), p. 24, recalls that the poet's sons used to say their father should have been called "Mr. Shortfellow."

[7] Samuel Longfellow, *Henry Wadsworth Longfellow* (Boston, 1891), I, 14.

[8] Hall, *Memories,* pp. 24–26, testifies to the fun at his children's parties.

[9] His journal gives many insights into his sadness and loneliness between 1837 and 1843 when he remarried.

[10] Hall, *Memories,* p. 60.

[11] George S. Hillard, "Remarks on Felton's Death," Mass. Hist. Soc., *Proceedings,* V (March 1862), 451.

The two lawyers in the group fitted in well with the professors, since they were as much literary men as attorneys. George Stillman Hillard had entered law by default, having lacked the financial means to pursue literature, his first and greatest love. Producing an edition of Spenser's *Works* in 1839, he refused to give in completely to his profession, and fought a rear-guard action for years against the call of the courts on his exclusive services. Though not as robust as the others, a "physical weakness" gave him an "odd walk," he had a sharp mind that did not cringe at telling the truth, even to his friends.[12] He liked Howe, and was as aware of his good points as the rest, yet upon recognizing some of his personality defects, he told him bluntly that people liked him more for what he could do for them than for what he was.[13]

Hillard's partner, Charles Sumner, was the exact opposite. Well over six feet tall, athletic, and incredibly thin (he weighed a little over 120 pounds when he graduated from Harvard in 1830), with a great shock of hair, two rows of pearly white teeth that smiled readily in those days, and eyes bloodshot from too much reading, he was passionately dedicated to the law.[14] Though he maintained an active interest in literature, it was commonly assumed, even in the earliest days of his practice, that he was more deeply read in his profession than any other lawyer of his years.[15] While still a student he had attracted the attention of his two professors, Judge Story and Simon Greenleaf, who thought so well of him that shortly after graduating he returned to Harvard to lecture during their absences.[16]

Sumner and Hillard had too many irons in the fire to be able to give all their attention to the day-to-day activities of the bar; they were too busy editing, lecturing, and writing to bother with the grubby work of the law. At their offices in the lawyers' building,

[12] Francis W. Palfrey, "Memoir of the Hon. George Stillman Hillard," Mass. Hist. Soc., *Proceedings*, XIX (June 1882), 339–345.

[13] Howe to Sumner, April 21, 1848, Howe Papers, Houghton. This was the sort of thing Howe was always doing to others, but Hillard was probably the only other person besides Mrs. Howe who did that to him.

[14] Edward L. Pierce, *Memoir and Letters of Charles Sumner* (Boston, 1877), I, 92.

[15] Pierce, *Memoir and Letters of Charles Sumner,* I, 146.

[16] Pierce, *Memoir and Letters of Charles Sumner,* I, 149–150.

4 Court Street, an intellectual atmosphere prevailed; one was as likely to find literary figures there as lawyers.[17]

Howe enjoyed them all, and wished he were worthy of the favor they showed him by inviting him into their company.[18] But of all this lively crew, he was most intimate with Sumner. Their friendship, after their initial meeting during a riot in June 1837, grew closer each year. They found something in each other that caused them to open their inmost thoughts to each other as they would to no one else. They shared their lonely hours together, dining, talking, riding, and vacationing, the attorney making the long trip out to South Boston several times a week.[19]

Sumner, who was ten years Howe's junior, was most impressed by the elder man's burning devotion to humanity's betterment. Of his liking for Howe, he wrote Lieber:

He is the soul of disinterestedness. He has purged his character from all considerations of *self,* so far as mortal may do this; & his sympathies embrace all creatures. To this highest feature of goodness add intelligence & experience of no common order, all elevated & refined by a chivalrous sense of honor & a mind without fear.[20]

Howe, for his part, saw in the callow counselor what few others did, namely warmth and tenderness. Only to Sumner could he confide his most intimate secrets, such as his disagreement with the director of the Ohio school for the blind before their exhibition in Kentucky. "You, you dog," Howe wrote telling of it, "are, *malgré moi* my *alter ego!*"[21]

Sumner's charms, however, were pretty well hidden. Felton, who had known him for a longer period, called him "anthracite,"[22] while Laura could not understand what her "Doctor" liked in him.

[17] William Wetmore Story has left a verse account of their quarters. Mass. Hist. Soc., *Proceedings,* XIX (June 1882), 346–348.

[18] Howe to Sumner, May 4, 1843, Howe Papers, Houghton.

[19] Sumner to Lieber, June 3, 1841; Sumner to Lieber, June 27, 1842, Sumner Papers, Houghton.

[20] Sumner to Lieber, June 3, 1841, Sumner Papers, Houghton.

[21] Howe to Sumner, Feb. 1, 1842, Howe Papers, Houghton. Imagine the use of such familiar language to the passionate Senator during President Johnson's impeachment trial.

[22] Howe to Sumner, Feb. 2, 1844, Howe Papers, Houghton.

"Sumner is not gentle like Dr.," she complained to Miss Swift.
"Why does Dr[.] want Sumner to come here if he is not gentle.
. . . I do not love or like Sumner. . . ." [23]

The one great blind spot in Sumner's social development was the
cultivation of the opposite sex. The Five of Clubs all worried about
him; Felton and Hillard (with tongue in cheek) constituted themselves a "committee" upon his domestic relations,[24] while Howe
constantly urged upon him that he was all love.[25] Sumner was
aware of this lack in his life, and discussing it freely, would go to
Howe's quarters on one Sunday "to bewail his celibacy . . . and on
the next to Longfellow to do the same." [26]

Apparently the solitary scholar in his shyness[27] had even as a
young man built up a wall of reserve that few could level. The heat
and passion that other men expended in more enjoyable ways, he
released in his work, the relentless intensity of which is startling. He
had insulated himself so well that, like a good thermos bottle, he
presented only a cold exterior to the world without any indication
of his interior temperature.

II

Despite the attractions of the Five of Clubs Howe wanted more
than male companionship. In his unhappiness he wished to leave
Boston for a foreign field. Upon learning that the secretaryship of
the American Embassy at Madrid was vacant, he determined to
apply and felt that his chances were good, since the appointment
was to be made on recommendation of William H. Prescott, who,
besides being the historian of Spain's golden age, was also trustee
of the Perkins Institution.[28] As he told Horace Mann,

I think I could do all the duties of the office — & have much time &
favourable opportunity for the only work in which I can ever engage

[23] Swift's Journal, Jan. 9, 1843, Perkins.
[24] Felton to Howe, May 24, 1843, Howe Papers, Houghton.
[25] Howe to Sumner, Feb. 2, 1844, Howe Papers, Houghton.
[26] Hillard to Howe, undated, 1843, Howe Papers, Houghton.
[27] All accounts lead me to this view.
[28] Daniel Webster, the Secretary of State, wished to oblige Prescott by sending
someone who would further his historical researches.

with interest — the endeavour to elevate humanity. All other ambition is dead within me, — & I am sure the future would be to me the most cheerless blanks — did it hold out only the prospect of wealth, & rank, & reputation.[29]

His attempt failed, and Howe seemed doomed to continue at tasks that no longer had charm for him.

III

He remained sunk in gloom for the rest of that spring until his meeting with Julia Ward. She changed everything for him, even inspiring him with the joy of living as no mere man could do, no matter how attuned in temperament he might have been. Eighteen years younger than the doctor, plump, with round face, and hair parted in the center, she may not have been a dazzling beauty,[30] but she had a sparkling personality to accompany a mind of extraordinary quickness. Her father, the wealthy Samuel Ward of the Wall Street banking firm of Prime, Ward, and King, had given her, as he had his five other motherless children, the best education he could afford. His three sons went to the Round Hill School, presided over by George Bancroft, and to Columbia College, while Sam, the eldest, went on to Europe to study at Göttingen where he met Longfellow.

Julia, too, followed her own tastes, concentrating on music, dancing, literature, and modern languages. The best teachers available directed her training. For instance, none other than Lorenzo da

[29] Howe to Mann, May 17, 1841, Howe Papers, Houghton. Horace Mann's interpretation of Howe's motives differs from this author's. Mann cautioned him against the move telling him he was doing more good than any other man in Boston. Spain had nothing to offer, and one might as well go live among the Black Feet. "I can explain this sudden impulse only on the ground of its falling in with your predominant spirit of enterprize & adventure. Had you lived before Columbus you would have anticipated him in his discovery, or got the start of Peter, in the Crusades. The nineteenth century is too late for your military knight-errantry, tho' bent on ever so noble or generous a deed." Mann to Howe, May 20, 1841, Mann Papers, MHS.

[30] The reproductions of portraits of her in her daughters' biography of her (Maude Howe Elliott, and Laura E. Richards, *Julia Ward Howe* [Boston, 1916], 2 v.), lead me to this conclusion despite what they say of her beauty.

Ponte, in his youth Mozart's librettist, but in penurious old age a part-time professor at Columbia, taught her Italian. Early in adolescence she showed a decided talent for versifying, and constantly wrote poems and doggerel. Throughout her youth visions of presenting a great work to the world danced before her; she meant to write the "novel or play of the age." [31] When one of her compositions actually did see print, all her old-fashioned bachelor uncle John could say was, "I wish that she knew more about housekeeping." [32] But why should Julia need to bother with the scullery and linen closet when there were plenty of servants around? She devoted herself to the more exalted study of learning to be a lady of fashion and an ornament to a gentleman's home.

Culture and gentility reigned supreme in the spacious Ward mansion at the corner of Bond Street and Broadway in lower Manhattan. There was a library built specially to hold Sam's books, and a picture gallery for Julia's instruction and amusement. After their mother's death, however, father Ward took refuge in Low Church Episcopalianism saturated with Calvinism. Exercising a loving but firm oversight on his children, he clipped their wings, and none more severely than those of his eldest daughter when he "early recognized in me a temperament and imagination over-sensitive to impressions from without, . . . his wish [being] to guard me from exciting influences until I should appear to him fully able to guard and guide myself." [33]

In the later years of girlhood she fancied herself "a young damsel of olden time, shut up within an enchanted castle," while her father appeared to her as the jailer.[34] The deaths of the senior Ward and her favorite brother Henry, occurring within a year of each other, caused her to stay locked in her castle more firmly than ever, while she underwent the usual period of mourning, from which she did not emerge until her knight-errant on a black horse came to rescue her, in 1841.

[31] Julia Ward Howe, *Reminiscences*, p. 57.
[32] Julia Ward Howe, *Reminiscences*, p. 20.
[33] J. W. Howe, *Reminiscences*, p. 53.
[34] J. W. Howe, *Reminiscences*, p. 49.

IV

All through that summer and on into the next year Howe paid active court to Julia and almost as much to her two sisters, Louisa and Annie. These charming girls formed the "three graces of Bond Street." Sumner, with him on many of his excursions, watched the love light in his friend's eye grow brighter. Nothing could keep the doctor down, not even a horse's kick. Though it was difficult for him to walk, yet, as Sumner wrote Lieber, "If the trinity of Bond St were visible, he would limp with me to Gotham or any where else." [35]

Sumner could read the handwriting on the wall. In June 1842 he suspected that Howe would probably soon be married, and wondered, "What then will become of me? — It is a dreary world to travel in alone." [36] He was right. The doctor had fixed his affections, and sometime in February 1843 Julia accepted his proposal of marriage. Although she did not believe it, she reported that later the same evening Sumner found him dancing on his head.[37]

The Five of Clubs congratulated their fellow member on his new joy. Longfellow, who lost a bet he had made with Howe over who would be engaged first, sent him a note in his customary charming style.

The great riddle of Life is no longer a riddle to you, the great mystery is solved. . . . You walk above in the pure air, while Sumner and I, like the poor spirits in Faust, who were struggling far down in the cracks and fissures of the rocks, cry out to you, "O take us with you." [38]

Poor Sumner, while he rejoiced with the others, suffered fleeting fears that he was about to lose a dear friend until he realized that Howe's nature was large enough for his wife and his friends. "Him I shall not lose, then," he wrote Sam Ward, "& have I not gained a friend in Julia? I trust she will let me be the friend to her, that Howe will say I have been to him." [39]

[35] Sumner to Lieber, Sept. 22, 1842, Sumner Papers, Houghton.
[36] Sumner to Lieber, June 27, 1842, Sumner Papers, Houghton.
[37] Julia Ward to sister, undated, 1843, Howe Papers, Houghton.
[38] Henry Wadsworth Longfellow to Howe, Feb. 26, 1843, Howe Papers, Houghton.
[39] Sumner to Sam Ward, Feb. 21, 1843, Howe Papers, Houghton.

Julia was at last tamed as nothing else could tame her. She hurriedly brushed aside the few qualms she felt about the step she had taken, for she knew the "Chevalier is an angel of light — so all will be well." [40] Howe had last-minute misgivings too; as frequently happens to men in love, he felt himself unworthy of his fiancée.[41] There were other difficulties in the way. Julia was wealthy, having what for those days was a comfortable income in her own right. Hence he wanted it clearly understood that he was not interested in her fortune, since from his salary and investments he could count on $3000 a year.[42] His pride even forbade his allowing her to pay for their wedding trip to Europe. It took all of "Bro Sam's" tact to soothe him. He urged the nervous groom not to be "angry with the old bird for having some *$2000s* a year of her own, because such circumstances help to eke out amazingly." [43]

There was also the matter of Julia's literary proclivities, which Howe disliked in a woman. Howe needed eloquent proof, in which Sam was not deficient, before he was reassured that nothing blocked a happy life with his chosen one, who loved him dearly.[44] At last all rough edges were smoothed over, and with Annie and Louisa making all the arrangements, since the bride "could not be brought down from the clouds sufficiently to give them much attention" (she even had difficulty choosing her wedding dress),[45] the ceremony took place April 23, 1843 at her brother's house in New York.[46]

The proud groom, with all fears forgotten, rejoiced in his happiness. Julia was at last his, and he found her a pure, noble, gifted creature, "gushing over with tenderness & love." He reassured Longfellow hovering on the brink of engagement (it was announced later that spring) that he would find matrimony "none the less sweet that it will be to you Paradise regained." [47]

[40] Julia to sisters, 1843, Howe Papers, Houghton.
[41] Sumner to Ward, Feb. 21, 1843, Howe Papers, Houghton.
[42] Howe to Ward, Feb. 3, 1843, Howe Papers, Houghton. The month should be March, but Howe was so upset that he got the date wrong.
[43] Ward to Howe, March 4, 1843, Howe Papers, Houghton.
[44] Ward to Howe, April 4, 1843, Howe Papers, Houghton.
[45] Richards and Elliott, *Julia Ward Howe*, I, 78.
[46] Julia Ward Howe, *Reminiscences*, p. 88.
[47] Howe to Longfellow, April, n.d., 1843, Howe Papers, Houghton.

Julia paid tribute to her husband's love, all kindness and devotion. To her he was "Chev," never anything else. Yet her surrender had not been complete. At the behest of her family, in whose desires she concurred, she retained her maiden name, preferring to be known as "Mrs. Julia Ward Howe," and not "Mrs. S. G. Howe." [48] Julia had always been independent; she would remain so.

V

With Sumner assigned to see that everything went well at the institution, and farewells taken of Laura Bridgman and Oliver Caswell at the ship, where they were brought (and had a fine time running all over it), the happy couple sailed for Europe, taking with them sister Annie.[49] Chev was determined to show *Diva,* his pet name for Julia because of her musical accomplishments, everything there was to see. After an ocean voyage during which he hurt his leg so severely that he was unable to walk, they reached London in mid-May.[50] There he found that his fame had preceded him, and all doors were open to the trio from America. The little New Hampshire girl had gained entry for them into the highest level of London society.

Edward Everett, now American Minister to Britain, and Dickens had been instrumental in preparing the way for this cordial reception, the former having distributed Howe's reports into strategic hands, while the latter through his *American Notes* had reached a class of people who never could have been touched by the original writings. "None of our Countrymen, since I have been here," wrote the diplomat, "have excited greater interest, — received more attention, — or left a better impression than the Howes — " [51]

---

[48] Julia Ward Howe to Eliza Ward Francis, undated, 1843, Howe Papers, Houghton.

[49] Howe to Sumner, undated, Howe Papers, Houghton; Swift's Journal, April 29, 1843, Perkins.

[50] They sailed on the same ship as Horace Mann who was going to Europe on a combined wedding professional trip with his second wife, whom he had just married.

[51] Everett to Sumner, Aug. 11, 1843, Everett Papers (vol. 46, pp. 514–516), MHS. The witty Rev. Sydney Smith was one of the first to call. He presented the lame Howe with his crutches (much too low), so that as he "beaued" Julia about, he could quip, when speaking of the money he had lost on American bonds, that now an American doctor had deprived him of his last means of support. J. W. Howe, *Reminiscences,* pp. 91–92.

Julia was dazed at the adulation heaped on Chev. She wrote her aunt, who apparently had grumbled somewhat about the marriage,

If you saw what people here think of my husband, you would think him more than good enough for me. Every body comes to see him, and to talk about Laura Bridgman. . . . London has rung with my husband's praises, while William Wadsworth [sic] has been left in inglorious obscurity.[52]

Howe felt humbled by receiving such a large degree of what he considered unearned kindness. In telling Sumner of his experiences, he confessed as to no other, "I have had a reception which would be indeed gratifying & flattering had I felt I deserved it." Leaving the *beau monde* to the girls, Howe, following Dickens' lead, prowled into the dregs of the city. What he saw confirmed his provincialism, convincing him that his native city was a superior place to live. With all its features,

London never never could hold in my heart or my mind so high a place as does Boston; because measured by God's scale it is not so high. I have not been so dazzled by the head & the front of the mountain as to overlook or forget that it has a tail which draggles along in the foulest slough through which humanity ever wallowed. I have seen the tail of the beast, as well as the head; & in the *cloaca* of London have seen welling up from the dark scum of humanity those streams of vice & crime which fill the prisons to overflowing, & waft their victims . . . to distant quarters of the Globe.

With the British capital as his example, he realized that English institutions gained their glory by elevating the few at the expense of the many far more than anything in the United States.[53]

After several weeks the gay family group went to Ireland, where they visited Maria Edgeworth, a popular novelist of the time, who wanted to hear all about Laura Bridgman.[54] They also attended a meeting for the repeal of the Corn Laws addressed by Daniel O'Connell, the famous Irish leader. The sons of Erin did not impress

---

[52] Julia Ward Howe to Eliza Ward Francis, June 13, 1843, Howe Papers, Houghton.
[53] Howe to Sumner, June 18, 1843, Howe Papers, Houghton.
[54] Julia Ward Howe, Combined Diary and Scrapbook, undated, 1843, Howe Papers, Houghton.

Howe. Unfamiliar with the economic and social situation, he blamed O'Connell for the depressed state of the nation. He was shocked by the vast numbers of beggars on the streets, when there were 120 "fine large, clean, well administered workhouses, judiciously located over the Island," that stood only partially filled. Beggary, it seemed to him, was resorted to only by those "who prefer it to the quiet, orderly, temperate life of a well regulated work house." [55]

In midsummer they visited the Continent. Howe had hoped to take Julia and Annie through Prussia, but was chagrined to learn that "my old & very dear friend the King of Prussia or my former host the Minister of Police insist upon it I shall not enter the Prussian territories!" [56] Ordering Everett to cease all further efforts to get him a visa, he haughtily refused to solicit their favor any longer. [57]

VI

In October they reached Italy, where Chev left Julia in Milan while he went to Paris to have his teeth looked after. This was the first time he had been away from his wife since their marriage; he realized now how much he loved her. [58] On his return he found her knitting baby frocks while she read George Combe's *On Infancy*. His fondest hopes were realized, he was beside himself with joy as he experienced a love more deep than ever he had conceived. Together the happy parents-to-be planned the future of their unborn babe, their souls riveted together forever by the new life they were bringing into being. A richer understanding pervaded him as he announced the news to his "brother":

Oh Sumner, it is no burden to bear ones child; & so much do I love ours, that, God knows how gladly I would myself — (could such a

[55] Howe to Sumner, July 15, 1843, Howe Papers, Houghton.
[56] Howe to Sumner, Aug. 2, 1843, Howe Papers, Houghton.
[57] Howe to Everett, Aug. 3, 1843, Howe Papers, Houghton. Boston decided that Howe had reached no mean eminence if he was forbidden entry into Prussia. Sumner told him that he was also on Naples' blacklist (untrue), and hinted facetiously that his marriage might be set aside when Julia realized half of Europe was cut off — Sumner to Howe, Aug. 31, 1843, Sumner Papers, Houghton.
[58] Howe to Sumner, Oct. 29, 1843, Howe Papers, Houghton.

thing be) nourish it within my bosom, & suffer the pangs of martyrdom for its dear sake. . . . I am happy. The first great want of my nature — an object to love, is supplied; henceforth I feel that I am better fitted to discharge every other duty of life.[59]

Feeling it best that Julia be in a warm climate during this delicate period, they took an apartment in Rome for the winter, whither the third Ward sister, Louisa, came to complete the family.[60] Howe postponed his trip to Athens for several months.[61]

There was quite an Anglo-American colony in the Eternal City. Thomas Crawford, the sculptor, was there, and came often to visit them, but really to pay court to Louisa, whom he eventually married. Old George Combe was also in residence that year, which happy coincidence enabled him and Howe to renew their warm friendship. They had a grand time touring the art galleries, viewing the exhibits in the light of phrenology. Julia on one occasion accompanied these demon art critics as they wandered through the sculpture hall of the Vatican, and has left an amusing account of their debating whether the contours and features of a Zeus satisfied phrenological criteria.[62] They came in for a great deal of scoffing because of their belief in the discredited science, but stuck to their guns, and finally scored a triumph. One day as they watched a sculptor at work on the head of a British nobleman, Combe noticed that the head failed to match the character of the man as shown by the mouth. Upon inquiring of the family, it was learned that Combe was indeed correct; the subject's mouth indicated his character. Hurriedly retouching his work, the artist filled in the space behind the ears to fulfill Combe's analysis.[63]

Among the other Americans in Rome who made life bearable for

---

[59] Howe to Sumner, Nov. 8, 1843, Howe Papers, Houghton.

[60] Howe to Sumner, Dec., n.d., 1843, Howe Papers, Houghton.

[61] Howe to Sumner, Dec. 28, 1843, Howe Papers, Houghton.

[62] Julia Ward Howe, *Reminiscences,* p. 132.

[63] Howe to Sumner, Feb. 18, 1844, Howe Papers, Houghton. The head was that of Sir Frederick Adam, and he had been given a combative mouth. Combe insisted that to match the mouth, the sculptor should give the model a certain amount of fullness behind the ears. The family reported that while the world thought Sir Frederick bland, he was in reality combative. There does not appear to have been any inquiry as to whether the deceased's head was full behind the ears.

the prospective father during his anxious period of waiting was the Reverend Theodore Parker of West Roxbury. Their meeting marked the beginning of an intimacy that ended only with the clergyman's death in 1860.[64] They found much in common; both shared a relentless zeal in the extirpation of suffering and injustice that led them to coöperate in the reform movements of later years. There was also a personal compatibility that could arouse out of each the unburdening of souls.[65]

Parker was undoubtedly the most brilliant of Howe's circle of friends. Like the others, he had a veneer of modernity over an old Puritan foundation that gave a distinctive New England flavor to his thought and action. In understanding, however, he far transcended them, going to the fringes of Unitarian orthodoxy, while in his own time many placed him beyond. Parker suffered for his questioning of the truth as his neighbors conceived it. He was ostracized from the fold; no minister would exchange with him, but he was not to be swerved. Glorying (as Sumner did later) in a feeling of martyrdom which grew stronger as time passed, he was willing to face an outward life of gloomy separation for the sake of an inner life of "profound peace," for he knew that "the Father is with me." [66]

VII

Marooned in Rome while awaiting the birth of his first child, Howe was bored. A year away from work was too much for him. To pass the time away he thought up a plan for organizing a school for the blind, but he found no official encouragement.[67] The longer he stayed in the depressed city of faded grandeur, the more unfavorably he felt towards it. As a favor to Mann, now home in Boston defending himself against the Boston schoolmasters, he un-

---

[64] Julia Ward Howe, *Reminiscences*, p. 161.

[65] At least one biographer considers Howe to have been Parker's closest friend. John White Chadwick, *Theodore Parker* (Boston, 1900), p. 308.

[66] Parker to Chandler Robbins, Jan. 27, 1843, Letterbook 4, p. 166, Parker Papers, MHS. All references to Parker's letterbooks are to transcripts.

[67] Howe to Sumner, Jan. 30, 1844, #958 (catalogued under 1846), Howe Papers, Houghton.

dertook an inspection of the schools of the city. His mission took him to all parts of town. It occurred to him that the Papal government was interested only in preserving the *status quo*. It fostered no institutions that might enlighten the people and inaugurated no public works. Foreigners were tolerated only because they brought money in, with the policy of the administration being to divert the minds of the populace from political matters, even by encouraging them in the national vice of gambling.[68] Though the Pope received him and listened attentively as Howe spoke to him about Laura Bridgman, there was no softening of the jaundiced view Howe took of the Pontiff's rule of the city.[69]

At length Julia's confinement came, and she was delivered of a girl, the first of six children, March 12, 1844. Parker christened her Julia Romana.[70]

The proud father was at last free to go to Greece to see what changes fourteen years had brought. On the whole he was disappointed with what he saw. The nation had been consistently misgoverned since the days of Capodistrias. It pained him to see that much of the hope he had entertained for a progressive Greece had been frustrated. But there were some bright spots of his tour. As he rode through the site of his colony at Hexamilia, some of the residents recognized him and pulled him, along with his traveling companions, from their horses. They had a grand impromptu banquet, from which only with great difficulty Howe could tear himself away. Pushing on, he eventually reached Athens, where he was formally presented to the King. While going through the round of official cordiality he realized that the years had taken their toll. As a young man he felt that he had been a much more pleasant and familiar person than he was now. Perhaps, he ruefully admitted, Hillard was correct after all.[71]

---

[68] Howe to Sumner, Jan. 17, 1844, Howe Papers, Houghton.

[69] Julia Ward Howe, *Reminiscences*, p. 126.

[70] Howe to Sumner, March 24, 1844, Howe Papers, Houghton. There was a family joke that a son born at home would be named "Samuel South Boston."

[71] Howe to Sumner, April 21, 1844, Howe Papers, Houghton.

VIII

On Chev's return to Rome, the happy family turned northward for the move to America. All through France, the Low Countries, and England, Howe made side trips at every stop to inspect all types of schools for the handicapped.[72] He paid special attention to methods of teaching articulation to deaf-mutes.[73] In August, just before sailing from England, he hunted up cases of deaf-blind in order to show the English how they could improve that class of suffering souls. He demonstrated his technique on one case, and worked a marvelous change in three lessons.[74] Late that month the Howes embarked for home, arriving in September to set up housekeeping in the director's wing of the Perkins Institution.

During his year abroad Howe's nature took on a mellowness that had hitherto been lacking. The love of a woman and the birth of a daughter had transfigured him. He understood at last what a full life was. As this awareness spread over him, his thoughts turned to Sumner. Howe felt his joy was not complete, so long as Sumner was still a bachelor. He felt as if he had entered paradise and left his best friend outside. Julia good-humoredly put up with her husband's attachment, remarking often that Sumner should have been a woman so that he could have married her.[75]

Finally, the suffering Howe had witnessed had aroused in him a compassion for society that he could no longer resist. He confessed to Sumner, "Every year I live brings closer home the conviction that we must work for others & not for our own happiness (God will take care of that). . . ."[76] Anyone who had that outlook would not want for activity in the America of the forties and fifties.

[72] Sumner to Howe, June 30, 1844, Howe Papers, Houghton. Mann requested him to look at some schools for him too.
[73] Howe to Sumner, June 12, 1844, Howe Papers, Houghton.
[74] Howe to Sumner, Aug. 2, 1844, Howe Papers, Houghton. Howe, *Thirteenth Report* (1845), pp. 60–77, discusses his observations at greater length.
[75] Howe to Sumner, Sept. 11, 1844, Howe Papers, Houghton.
[76] Howe to Sumner, June 30, 1844, Howe Papers, Houghton.

IX

The Common School Controversy

Howe returned home to find Horace Mann in trouble again, this time with the Boston schoolmasters. There was nothing to do but rally to his aid, and this Howe did with all the energy he could muster. The two friends saw the new controversy as a phase of the struggle that had been going on since 1837, the cause of enlightened education against bigotry and reaction. With their consciences directing them, as always, they refused to compromise, and fought to the end.

I

Mann started it by throwing down the gauntlet in his *Seventh Report,* published in January 1844. He had seen schools in Europe superior to any in America and felt it was his duty to tell his countrymen the truth even though he knew it would hurt. While few European schools could compare physically with even a second-rate district schoolhouse in America, and certainly no school for the blind was superior to Perkins, let alone its equal, the plain fact was that European teachers knew their trade better than their American counterparts, and did much better work.[1]

[1] *Seventh Annual Report of the Board of Education; together with the Seventh Annual Report of the Secretary of the Board* (Boston, 1844), pp. 47, 24. This will be referred to briefly as Mann, *Seventh Report.*

The Prussian educational system impressed Mann so favorably that he called it the best in the world, although he spoke highly of the Scottish as well.[2] In all parts of the German kingdom he found a conscientious vibrant quality in the teachers' work, which was marked by an absence of "higgling pedantry." Their success in teaching reading by beginning with words first, and then imparting the alphabet, was very gratifying to Mann, who for years had favored this system. It was universal in Prussia.[3] The teaching of grammar was another subject in which the Germans excelled. There was

very little of the ding-dong and recitative of gender, number and case, — of government and agreement, which make so great a portion of the grammatical exercises in our schools; and which the pupils are often required to repeat until they really lose all sense of the original meaning of the terms they use. Of what service is it for children to reiterate and reassert, fifty times in a single recitation, the gender and number of nouns, about which they never made a mistake even before a grammar book was put into their hands? . . .

The Prussian teachers, by their constant habit of conversing with the pupils; by requiring a complete answer to be given to every question; by never allowing a mistake in termination or in the collocation of words or clauses to pass uncorrected, nor the sentence, as corrected to pass unrepeated; by requiring the poetry of the reading lessons to be changed into oral or written prose, and the prose to be paraphrased, or expressed in different words; and by exacting a general account or summary of the reading lessons, are — as we may almost literally say, — constantly teaching grammar. . . .[4]

A great deal of this success was attributable to the government's "intelligent" program of teacher-training. To the Prussians, pedagogy was an honorable profession whose members were respected citizens, not incompetents driven from other fields. The prospective teachers spent three years in seminaries where they were inculcated

---

[2] Mann, *Seventh Report,* pp. 60–68, contains his description of the Scottish schools whose method of teaching reading impressed him the most.

[3] Mann, *Seventh Report,* p. 91. "I am satisfied," he wrote, "that our greatest error in teaching children to read, lies in beginning with the alphabet."

[4] Mann, *Seventh Report,* pp. 105–106.

with the nobility of their calling. Upon graduating they began their work glowing with enthusiasm, determined to fulfill their responsibilities.[5] Painstakingly they prepared for their meetings with their classes; the dynamic atmosphere they created seemed capable of charging the students to the point of explosion.[6]

With few exceptions Mann never saw a master leading a lesson with book in hand, nor sitting during a recitation, nor did he see any corporal punishment, not even the threat of it.[7] There was no occasion for the rod since there were no "idle, mischievous, whispering children" who needed it.[8] In Prussia, as well as in Saxony and Scotland, the *sine qua non* of the teacher was his power to command and retain the attention of a class. Those who could not were ordered out of the profession.[9]

However Mann was no blind admirer of everything he saw abroad. In Prussia children left school at far too early an age. Furthermore, the absence of district libraries resulted in a serious lack of adequate reading matter.[10] But the gravest defect, because practically universal, was that Prussian schools, despite their efficiency, failed to prepare for intelligent citizenship. Adults had little use for the faculties that had been developed or for knowledge acquired.[11]

II

The report met with a favorable response in most quarters. The old-guard opponents of nonsectarian public education rushed into the attack, but they were quickly silenced.[12] Agitation might have died down at this point but for the entry into the fray of the

[5] Mann, *Seventh Report*, pp. 129–132.
[6] Mann, *Seventh Report*, pp. 124, 135.
[7] Mann, *Seventh Report*, p. 133.
[8] Mann, *Seventh Report*, p. 135.
[9] Mann, *Seventh Report*, p. 136.
[10] Mann, *Seventh Report*, p. 155.
[11] Mann, *Seventh Report*, p. 156.
[12] See for example: *Christian Witness*, X, 1 (Feb. 23, 1844), 3. The March 8 issue contains the editor's comments. A further letter was published May 17, 1844, pp. 49 and 51.

Orestes Brownson was an especially caustic critic. That "Proteus of doctrine" (as Mann called him [Mann to Howe, July 21, 1839, Mann Papers, MHS]) had never been favorable to Mann. Earlier he had criticized him on political grounds. In 1844,

masters of the Boston grammar and writing schools, the "Thirty-one" as they came to be called, who, feeling that Mann had singled them out for ridicule, sought to vindicate themselves before public opinion. The basis of their discontent was the Secretary's war against corporal punishment, their chief prop in the maintenance of discipline.[13]

In September 1844, after several months of intense labor, a committee of the Association of Masters of the Boston Public Schools, under the lead of Barnum Field, grammar master of the Franklin School, issued *Remarks on the Seventh Annual Report of the Hon. Horace Mann.* Apparently working on the assumption that the best defense is offense, they attacked everything for which Mann fought. Mann, they charged, had needlessly shaken the confidence of the population in the school system, and had caused the people to lose respect for the teachers.[14] They claimed that he was ignorant of the true condition of the city's schools; that he never visited them, and never took the masters into his confidence.[15] His recommendations were all wrong, in their estimation, and they felt that the proper way to hear recitations was with textbook in hand.[16] As for the normal schools, they were run according to "hot bed theories, in which the projectors have disregarded experience and observation." They said it was impossible to learn practical teaching in them.[17] In their opinion, the views of Mann's friends, in particular those of Dr. Howe, need not be taken at face value, since their mutual admiration was well known.[18]

---

after living in many mansions and having at last found rest and certitude in the bosom of Rome, he belatedly denounced Mann with all the ardor of the convert, as being ignorant not only of the philosophy of education, but of human nature, and of Christian morals and theology. If the teachers followed his program, they would rear up a generation of infidels. *Brownson's Quarterly Review*, I, 4 (Oct. 1844), 547.

[18] Mann had only scorn for them. He jeered at their association as a *"Club, for eating and drinking and telling bawdy stories."* Mann to Parker, Jan. 17, 1848, Letterbook 11, 87, Parker Papers, MHS.

[14] *Remarks on the Seventh Annual Report of the Hon. Horace Mann* (Boston, 1844), p. 10.

[15] *Remarks on the Seventh Annual Report of the Hon. Horace Mann,* p. 23.

[16] *Remarks on the Seventh Report of Horace Mann,* p. 53.

[17] *Remarks on the Seventh Report of Horace Mann,* p. 8.

[18] *Remarks on the Seventh Report of Horace Mann,* p. 19.

But the crux of their complaint was Mann's attack on corporal punishment. Mann had threatened their supremacy and questioned their competence by showing that there were teachers who maintained order through skill and personality. The Thirty-one insisted that they were justified both by precedent and principle in striking unruly children. "The community have a right to expect that the pupils of the public schools shall be really taught and governed within them," they said, and they intended to fulfill their obligations to the taxpayers.[19]

Mann was unimpressed. The *Remarks,* he wrote, had been

begotten, conceived, *gestated,* born, nurtured in disappointed, rabid self-esteem. It was because I would not throw a sop to them, that the masters have flung a fire-brand at me. You may judge what the spirit that manages the Boston schools is from the source of that spirit as exhibited in the pamphlet.[20]

He decided to take counsel with his supporters before answering them.

At this point, Howe returned from Europe. For a while he remained in the background, leaving it to others who had been in the country all through the dispute to carry on the fight. However he did attend the conference which Mann called to discuss strategy. The group decided to fight the Thirty-one in kind. They too would publish pamphlets and articles. Howe began writing an article for the *North American Review;* Theodore Parker offered his virile pen in the cause.[21] George B. Emerson, the founder of the American Institute of Instruction, the director of an outstanding school for girls, and one of the leaders in the movement for the creation of the Board of Education, produced his *Observations,* a scathing attack on the masters' position.[22]

---

[19] *Remarks on the Seventh Report of Horace Mann,* p. 112.

[20] Mann to Parker, Sept. 18, 1844, Parker Letterbook 11, p. 80, MHS.

[21] Parker to Mann, Sept. 17, 1844, Mann Papers, MHS.

[22] George B. Emerson, *Observations on a Pamphlet, entitled "Remarks on the Seventh Annual Report of the Hon. Horace Mann, Secretary of the Massachusetts Board of Education"* (n.p., n.d.); for a biographical account of Emerson, see R. C. Waterston, "Memoir of George Barrell Emerson," MHS, *Proceedings,* XX (May 1883), 237–238.

All these articles, letters, and pamphlets were merely preliminaries for Mann's own statement, eagerly awaited by his friends. Late in September he informed Howe that he had "cleared ship for action, & shall bear down upon the piratical craft soon." The foe might think that the Board was dead, but he would show them who was Mordecai and who was Haman. "Thirty one of them hung on the same shaft would look like a string of onions," he gleefully anticipated. All he wished from Howe was advice as to whether he should be gentle or sardonic, "just to keep folks from yawning over my reply." [23] Evidently the doctor, as skilled a polemicist as could be found, advised vigor, for after weeks of threshing out its points with Mann, who would not retract or modify his stand in the slightest, even when Howe insisted that some of his claims were wrong, there was published November 18, the withering *Reply to the "Remarks,"* a restatement of the *Seventh Report* with none of its punches pulled.[24]

This time there could be no doubt as to Mann's opinion of the Boston schools. Scornful toward the Thirty-one, all he said of them was that if they treated their pupils with "a tithe of the superciliousness and injustice" with which they treated him, it was no wonder that, "in order to preserve their ascendancy in school, they are obliged to put in practice the inexorable doctrines respecting 'School Discipline'" they defended so earnestly in their *Remarks.*[25]

The *Reply* caused a sensation. The initiative had now passed to the reformers. Howe dashed off a note during the first week of its publication informing Mann of its reception:

You ask what is going on: I can tell you what is going off — that is the reputations of the Boston School masters. Oh! Horace! You have a

[23] Mann to Howe, Sept. 25, 1844, Mann Papers, MHS.

[24] Howe told him he was wrong in some of his statements about the teaching of articulation to the deaf [this subject will be discussed later], Howe to Mann, Oct. 9, 1844, Howe Papers, Houghton. Mann told Howe that everything he said on that matter was based on competent authority or his personal observations, Mann to Howe, Oct. (n.d.), 1844, Mann Papers, MHS.

[25] Horace Mann, *Reply to the "Remarks" of Thirty-one Boston Schoolmasters on the Seventh Annual Report of the Secretary of the Massachusetts Board of Education* (Boston, 1844), p. 113.

heavy debt to pay in good deeds for the gratification you have given to all the sons & daughters of Cain by your public flagellation of their old tyrant. I thought you disapproved of public executions, & never supposed you would turn hangman. Even cold Buckingham [editor of the *Courier*] *"rises with enthusiasm"* from the perusal of your pamplet [*sic*]; & every one strives to find some new & strong expression of his gratified destructiveness. . . . It is in fact the town talk: last night at a large party at the Abbot Lawrences [*sic*] there was laid out a large pile of them for distribution.[26]

Under the counterblasts of Mann's forces, one of the Thirty-one, William J. Adams, "acknowledged and proclaimed" his regret at having signed the *Remarks,* although he still clung fast to his belief in the error of much of the *Seventh Report.*[27] A new attack on the masters came from the Primary School Board, an unexpected source, which, incensed by charges that the city's children did not learn to read properly, charged in their turn that the secondary teachers knew nothing about the elementary schools. In the preceding six years not one of their graduates had been rejected in the grammar schools for faults that could be blamed on the system.[28]

Mann's friends decided to press every point in their favor. In the fall of 1844, a committee under the leadership of Charles Sumner, numbering among its members such men as Josiah Quincy, George B. Emerson, John D. Fisher, and Edward Greeley Loring, began action further to bolster the normal schools, showing thereby where the leaders of progress in Massachusetts stood. Memorializing the legislature when it met in January, they asked the state to appropriate $5000 on condition that an equal sum be contributed by the public for the creation of new normal schools.[29] Following favorable action by the legislature, Governor George N. Briggs, on March

[26] Howe to Mann, Nov. 26, 1844, Howe Papers, Houghton.
[27] *Boston Advertiser,* Nov. 21, 1844. The letter was dated the 18th, the same day as the appearance of the *Reply,* and presumably was written earlier. Consequently it is dangerous to say that Mann's statement forced his disavowal, but Adams probably knew what was coming.
[28] *Report of the Special Committee of the Primary School Board on a Portion of the Remarks of the Grammar Masters* (Boston, 1844), pp. 7–8.
[29] *Senate Document,* No. 24 (Jan. 1845). The manuscript of this is in Sumner's handwriting, and is to be found in the Mann Papers, MHS.

20, 1845, signed into law a bill authorizing new teacher-training schools to be built and designating those in existence along with the new ones, "State Normal Schools."[30] Thus were the masters' views, on at least one subject of the controversy, rejected.

III

All through the autumn of 1844, Howe champed at the bit for a more prominent part in the fight. Since his return in September, he had worked behind the scenes, encouraging and advising Mann, supplying him with information on teaching methods, and acting as his chief confidant. His attempts at writing articles were unsuccessful. One lukewarm letter in the *Mercantile Journal* was all that appeared during these months.[31] The article he prepared for the *North American Review* was rejected on the grounds of its extremism. Editor Francis Bowen explained himself to Sumner:

> The cause will do well enough, and Mr. Mann will long enjoy his triumph, if his more ardent and uncompromising friends will not insist on his stooping his head, shutting his eyes, and running a tilt like a mad bull, against the Boston schools and the prejudices of two thirds of the population of the city. He has too many enemies already; I would lessen their number, not increase it.[32]

Howe's opportunity came early in October when Mann broached the idea of a maneuver to outflank the Thirty-one by having his friends seek election to the School Committee that fall. Once in office, they would have the whip hand over the masters and could put through a "purgation" of the personnel of one school, replacing

[30] *House Document*, No. 17 (Feb. 1845); *Acts and Resolves of Massachusetts* (1845), chap. 100, p. 623.

[31] Howe to Mann, undated typescript, Howe Papers, Houghton. (It is listed in the accession sheets as no. 931.) Just which letter he was referring to, it is difficult to say, since there are several such in the *Journal* during October that speak favorably of Mann.

[32] Francis Bowen to Sumner, Dec. 14, 1844, Sumner Papers, Houghton. Bowen wrote the article reviewing the *Seventh Report* himself. It appeared in Jan. 1845 (pp. 224–246) and was highly favorable, even though it took Mann to task for the harshness of his *Reply*. Bowen predicted the victory of Mann, and foresaw the complete prostration and crushing of the masters if they persisted in their blind opposition.

them by progressives who could then run it as a model that would effect a revolution in education.[33] Howe agreed completely with this plan. Immediately on receiving the suggestion he began drawing up a list of possible candidates. "I feel," he answered Mann, "that now is the time for your friends to come to your aid, and I for one will do what little I can . . . heretofore I have cheered you only in words; now if you will show me how to work I will do it." [34] Mann was much relieved. Now pinning his hopes on his lieutenant's success, he foresaw an early triumph if they should win the election, but should they fail he feared that even "an arch angel can't help us. . . ." [35]

At the Whig convention Howe played the leading part in the proceedings. A hostile observer claimed later that the doctor had "packed" the hall. "Though the meeting was unusually large, but little interest appeared to be felt in the nomination of candidates to any of the offices except that of School Committee; — after that was made, a large portion of the persons present left the room." Without difficulty, Howe received the nomination from Ward 12 in South Boston; but a great fight arose over the designation of Charles Sumner from Ward 4, which included East Boston. After having rammed the dutiful attorney's name down the throats of a rebellious representation from across the harbor, a number of that region's angry delegates met later, determined to counter the doctor's dictation with a candidate of their own.[36] With a multiplicity of candidates splitting the vote in Ward 4, Sumner was beaten, in this, his first try for public office. Howe joined the School Committee without the aid of his right-hand man. In other parts of the city such men favorable to reform as Theophilus Parsons, better known at this time for his classical scholarship, though later a prominent Harvard Law professor, the Baptist Reverend Rollin H. Neale, William Brigham, a lawyer, the Reverend Harris C. Graves, editor of the *Christian Reflector,* and the Unitarian Reverend James I. T.

[33] Mann to Howe, Oct. 8, 1844, Mann Papers, MHS.
[34] Howe to Mann, Oct. 9, 1844, Howe Papers, Houghton.
[35] Mann to Howe, Oct. 19, 1844, Mann Papers, MHS.
[36] *Boston Times,* Sept. 1, 1845.

Coolidge were also chosen. The Mann forces did not gain a majority, but there were enough men to insure fireworks.[37]

Howe's course of action was determined by the poor organization of the Boston common-school system. Nominally under the control of the School Committee, an unpaid board of twenty-four lay members elected annually, the system actually had no effective head. In the absence of a full-time superintendent of schools, coördination among the schools was poor. The primary schools did not fit their curricula to match the needs of the secondary schools, which in their turn were inefficiently organized, most of them having two masters equal in authority, one in charge of the writing school, and the other of the grammar school. If anyone ran the system, it was the thirty-one grammar and writing masters to whom the School Committee frequently looked for guidance. Faced with such a condition, Howe vowed to bring some order out of chaos, and thrash the masters roundly in the process.

On May 6, 1845, the main work of the School Committee began when Howe, Parsons, and Neale were appointed to make the annual examination of the first class of the grammar schools (three other men took care of the writing schools), and report in August.[38] For the next three months, the trio was busily engaged in conducting a probe, the results of which were known in advance, but striking in the originality of the method employed. Hitherto the yearly investigation had been conducted orally, but this year the reformers instituted written tests. The masters were to know nothing of the questions.

Howe had by this time taken over the tactical command of the field forces from Mann's somewhat conciliatory hands. From his retreat in Concord, where he was preparing a new blast, Mann urged Howe to moderate his course, openly admitting that he could not feel "so wrathy with bad folks . . . because I am not so good." [39]

---

[37] *Boston Advertiser,* Dec. 12, 1844.

[38] "Reports of the Annual Visiting Committees of the Public Schools of the City of Boston," *City Doc.* 26 (1845), 5.

[39] Mann to Howe, May 7, 1845, Mann Papers, MHS. While the examination was in progress, Mann was busily preparing his *Answer* to the Masters' *Rejoinder* to his *Reply* to their *Remarks* to his *Report.* It appeared in July.

Mann's efforts were futile. Howe was out for blood. Although Howe chuckled as he told of the masters' attempts to keep the reformers off the examining committees ("screwing machines" they called them), he became steely hard as he solemnly told Mann,

> I will promise nothing, but I have made a resolution, as deep as my nature allows, that I will falter not until I have effected an entire reformation in our system. I have been making what friends I could. I have brought over some to the necessity of a superintendent.[40]

He did not rest all that summer, nor did his two co-workers. Starting at 8 A.M., with each one taking a different area, they swooped down on the schools without notice, distributed papers that had been privately prepared and printed, examined the pupils, and within the hour rushed off to repeat the whirlwind process elsewhere. To prevent the children of one school having an advantage over those of another, all were tested in the same subject on the same day.[41] There were nineteen public grammar schools in the city, thus, in the course of a day, one took seven schools and the other two had six each.

Over Mann's disapproval the masters were also asked to fill out questionnaires. It seemed to him that this procedure made his antagonists' opinions worth something, while in reality their value was *"minus* squared and cubed a thousand times." If they had to answer questions he would have preferred straight factual inquiries, such as how frequently they resorted to corporal punishment, how well they got along with each other, and whether they ever met with the parents.[42]

On the whole the investigation went quietly, once the children became used to writing their answers. Howe and Parsons carried on alone for some weeks during the summer, while Dr. Neale traveled to other cities such as Roxbury, Hartford, and New York to administer the same examinations. At the end of his second day's work Howe reported to Mann that the pupils were doing better than he had expected, although some answers taxed his self-control.

---

[40] Howe to Mann, May 8, 1845, Howe Papers, Houghton.
[41] "Reports of the Visiting Committees," p. 7.
[42] Mann to Howe, June 20, 1845, Mann Papers, MHS.

The "good masters" were unafraid, while the "poor" ones cried out about a trap. What chagrin he must have felt when Barnum Field's school did the best of the seven he examined that day in Natural Philosophy! [43]

The report was read before the full School Committee on August 7.[44] As might have been expected, it was a sweeping three-hour indictment of the secondary-school system and its personnel. The investigators found that the method of teaching in most schools forced the students to rely too much on their memories, and enabled the masters to lean on the textbook exclusively. The children were not being taught to think, or to handle their information in any way that might develop their thought processes.[45] In looking over their returns the subcommittee's first professed reaction was one of incredulity. They were shocked at the great number of wrong answers and the frequency of errors in grammar and punctuation.[46] For instance, in geography the highest percentage of correct answers in a Boston school was 46 per cent while in the Dudley School in Roxbury, which was their control institution, it was 55 per cent.[47] (Undoubtedly this institution was the best of all the out-of-town schools Neale visited. It was charged later that he told his colleagues privately that the Boston schools were better than those in New York.[48] This allegation was neither confirmed nor denied.)

The Boston children could always answer when questioned on their texts, but they were lost when taken out of the common routine of questions.[49] Again they were perfect in parsing poetry, but they failed to understand its meaning. "Such is the power of drilling!" groaned the "Report." "Such is the effect of close attention to the mere osteology of language; to the bones and articulations,

[43] Howe to Mann, undated, #949 (catalogued under Sept. 1845), Howe Papers, Houghton.
[44] *Boston Atlas*, Aug. 9 ,1845.
[45] "Report," p. 24.
[46] "Report," p. 9.
[47] "Report," p. 11.
[48] "Scholiast" (M. A. De Wolfe Howe), *Review of the Reports of the Annual Visiting Committees of the Public Schools of the City of Boston, for 1845* (Boston, 1846), p. 39.
[49] "Report," p. 11.

in forgetfulness of the substance that covers, and the spirit that animates them." [50]

The report recommended the appointment of a salaried full-time superintendent of schools, which would leave the School Committee as an overall supervisory body of citizens. It also urged the adoption of the single-master system, so that each school would have at its head one who might direct its fortunes with undivided authority.[51] Turning finally to classroom practice, besides calling for the availability of cheaper texts, it insisted strongly on the abolition of corporal punishment. This was the point of agitation, around which everything else revolved. The object of the schools, they said, was to teach children to be men, which high function could not be done by relying exclusively on flogging. It was known that when youth was mischievous, it was mainly because there was little else to do, a state of affairs for which the masters were responsible.[52] There was abundant evidence to show that in other areas, with a student body just as difficult to manage, there was no resort to the switch.[53]

The reaction to these disclosures was as might have been expected. The reformers were of course cheered by this vindication of their views. The *Boston Atlas* called the document "masterly." [54] Mann's gratitude to Howe was touching. As he wished him the greatest success in the great impending battle with the Thirty-one, he wrote,

I feel as if my own life were nothing in comparison with the value of this enterprise, & if it fails in your hands, we shall have to wait another great Julian epoch for another opportunity. There is no man but yourself, who can carry it thro', *at this time,* but another year, if not now.[55]

[50] "Report," p. 16. Some of the questions were: Geography: 1. "Name the principal lakes of North America"; 12. "What is the cause of the rivers [in the four contiguous states of North and South Carolina, Kentucky, and Tennessee] running in opposite direction"; and 31. "Draw an outline map of Italy." *Ibid.,* p. 66. In History they asked: 1. "What is History?" 12. "Can you mention the names of the Roman Emperors?" 26. "What do you understand by an embargo?" *Ibid.,* p. 56.

[51] "Report," pp. 30–34.

[52] "Report," pp. 44–45.

[53] "Report," p. 48.

[54] *Boston Atlas,* Aug. 11, 1845.

[55] Mann to Howe, Aug. 18, 1845, Mann Papers, MHS.

Quick to respond, the masters and their supporters charged unfairness. To the *Boston Times,* the report was a "libel on our schools by its errors and mis-statements." [56]

Centered over Howe's head, the conflict quickly became resolved into a discussion of his behavior during his examination of the Lyman School in East Boston, while the real issue, the determination of the true condition of the city's schools, disappeared from sight. Howe was so convinced that the children failed to learn anything in school that when the pupils at Lyman did remarkably well in definitions, he was sure they had been coached, and prepared another test for them. Later it appeared that the headmaster had briefed his charges in only four words, and that even excluding them from the final results, the school was unexcelled.[57]

On the evenings of August 18 and 21, the parents of the pupils in the first division met to discuss the accusations leveled against the neighborhood teacher. The scholars involved signed a statement that they had learned all their words from their reading, with the exception of "kirk," "panegyric," "Thanatopsis," and "zoomonia" (zoomania?). In some way Headmaster Albert Bowker had learned of them, and had crammed them into his students just before Neale arrived to administer the examination. Subsequently Howe tested the children in other words. They accused him of deliberately trying to frighten them, for besides having accused them of talking when they were not, his manner was unlike that of anyone else they had ever encountered. He seemed unnecessarily severe and issued orders at variance to Neale's. Many parents reported that their children came home much excited. Bowker insisted that Howe knew nothing of his school, and was motivated by hostility to him because he had defeated Sumner's efforts to get on the School Committee. The story of Howe's part at the nominating conventions now came out.[58]

As these charges came thundering about Howe, Mann urged him to answer his accusers, to write articles to show that since the

---

[56] *Boston Times,* Sept. 1, 1845. The *Times* was Democratic.
[57] *Boston Times,* Aug. 14, 1845.
[58] *Boston Times,* Sept. 1, 1845.

children had been able to answer questions of fact better than those involving principle, the merit lay with them rather than the masters. Furthermore, the great differences between the schools was proof that the pupils could learn when properly instructed. "You have told me to have courage," he reassured the weary champion. "I now tell you the same. You will hereafter be hailed as the regenerator of the Boston Schools." [59]

In an attempt to wind up its affairs by early September, its customary adjournment date, the School Committee met throughout August. Affairs reached their climax on the thirtieth when balloting for the reappointment of masters was scheduled to begin. The hostile *Times* reported that

Instead of attending to this business, however, the Board got into one of those silly, unprofitable and unbusiness-like discussions which have disgraced themselves and done injury to the cause of education which they seek to benefit. If such be the course of our intellectual leaders and of our educational guardians, what will be the course of those who graduate from institutions over which they preside.[60]

Howe added to the turmoil with his protests against the treatment he had received, and denied that he had ever tried to foist anyone on East Boston. So convinced was he of his own rectitude that he introduced a resolution to have the mayor appoint a committee to inquire into the examination of the Lyman School and the part he had taken. After violent debate, this was adopted.[61] The committee was appointed the next day, but it does not appear to have held any hearings or to have reported publicly.[62]

Somewhat slowed up in its schedule by the South Boston member's battle with East Boston, the school board was now at last able to turn to its main job, the re-designation of the masters, and in this the reformers were partially defeated. During the balloting on August 30 and September 1, Howe kept the proceedings in an uproar with his acerbic comments on the individual teachers as their names came up. He wished with all his heart to have Barnum

[59] Mann to Howe, Aug. 29, 1845, Mann Papers, MHS.
[60] *Boston Times*, Sept. 1, 1845.
[61] *Boston Times*, Sept. 1, 1845.
[62] *Boston Times*, Sept. 2, 1845.

Field, the instigator and chief driving force of the Thirty-one, removed from the system, but all the committee did was transfer him from the Franklin School for girls to the Adams School for boys. So far as Howe was concerned, they had allowed an "ungentlemanly, coarse, & violent creature," declared unfit to run a girl's school, to preside over one for boys. Before the session ended, Howe had to leave because his wife had become ill, but he was sure that had he been able to remain he would have modified the vote, "for I saw two or three winced under the thrust which I made in search of consciences." [63]

Eventually, Field, after an intensive examination, was reinstated in his old position.[64] He remained there without scandal for the rest of his life, one of the most capable members of the Boston teaching profession.[65] There can be no doubt about it, Howe had overstated his case against that master at least. Even Parsons, who had always coöperated closely before, voted against dismissal.

The conclusion of his service on the School Committee left Howe in a complete state of physical collapse which he might have borne with better grace had he been more successful, but most of the masters had been re-designated, and there was still no superintendent of schools. Outwardly conditions appeared just as they had always been. Dourly he wrote Mann that at the last moment his supporters had weakened and taken compassion on the masters. They had "thought it best to let the children suffer. . . ." Howe knew that he had exaggerated and made so many errors that he would not be reëlected, but at least he had taught the masters not to meddle in matters outside their field. Still he hoped to go before the people with his proposed reforms.[66]

He was never to have the chance. In pre-convention agreements, Howe and many of the other reformers were dropped from the slates offered to the delegates, and they did not run for election in December.[67]

---

[63] Howe to Mann, Sept. 3, 1845, Howe Papers, Houghton.
[64] *Boston Atlas*, Sept. 19, 1845.
[65] "The Report of the Annual Examination of the Public Schools of the City of Boston," *City Doc.* 52 (1851), 6.
[66] Howe to Mann, Sept. 3, 1845, Howe Papers, Houghton.
[67] *Boston Atlas*, Dec. 8, 1845.

IV

With the old guard taking over its former position, the *status quo ante* 1844 seemed restored, but this reaction was deceptive, for Howe's efforts had borne fruit. Though only four masters had been removed, at least a dozen others had been shaken. Corporal punishment, the underlying cause of the disturbance and the source of "19/20" of the system's evils, was removed. During the next year one of the masters proved to another subcommittee of the school board that he had not struck a single pupil since the controversy, in addition to which, there had been a steady and perceptible improvement in discipline. Although still legal, in less than six months after the end of Howe's term on the School Committee, corporal punishment existed only in name.[68]

Howe's other recommendations were also adopted within a short period. A superintendent of schools was appointed in 1851 when the post was established by law.[69] By that time, too, the system of dual headmasterships had been ended. Each school had only one man in authority with a number of assistants under him,[70] while written tests became the standard method of examination, not only in Boston but in the state as well.[71]

Thus within five years, most of the goals Howe and Mann had striven for in their work on the Boston schools were attained, but they had accomplished their work in the worst way, having created by their tactics a vast reservoir of ill-will they could not overcome. Years later, when Mann had become President of Antioch College, Howe reported that he had been unable to get many contributions for him. "They'll never forgive your assailing their Fetish — showing him to be a Fetish," wrote the doctor to the sorely straitened educator.[72]

[68] William B. Fowle, *The Scholiast Schooled* (Cambridge, 1846), pp. 10–12.
[69] "First Semi-Annual Report of the Superintendent of Public Schools of the City of Boston," *City Doc.* 73 (1851), 3.
[70] *Second Annual Report* (1852), pp. 52–56.
[71] Mann to Howe, June 21, 1846, Mann Papers, MHS. The reports of the School Committee of Boston show that they used this method for several years.
[72] Howe to Mann, June 20, 185?, #1187 (catalogued under 1857), Howe Papers, Houghton.

X

The Education of the Feeble-Minded

In his own special field, the education of the handicapped, Howe continued to do significant work, adding the feeble-minded to his accomplishments. After proving that they could benefit from schooling, he led a movement that resulted in the organization of the Massachusetts School for Idiotic and Feeble-Minded Youth. It is now known as the Walter E. Fernald School and is as prominent in its respective field as Perkins.

I

For years Howe had been interested in the problem of the feeble-minded, ever since 1839 when an idiotic child, also infirm in body, was brought to him for instruction. The baffled teacher, not knowing how to proceed, and ignorant of what had been done elsewhere, improvised a program, the limited success of which indicated to him that even mental defectives were "not beyond the saving reach of the divine laws which promise improvement as the sure return of every kind of cultivation."[1] Sooner or later something would have to be done about them, he wrote in 1840. In the meantime, Perkins could not receive those mentally below normal since they

[1] "Twenty-Eighth Annual Report of the Trustees of the Massachusetts School for Idiotic and Feeble-Minded Youth," *Mass. Pub. Doc.* 28 (1875), 27.

had an adverse effect on the children around them. He recommended that an asylum for the feeble-minded be constructed on Perkins' grounds in South Boston.[2]

For some years the movement lay dormant, starting up again in mid-decade. Dr. Samuel Bayard Woodward, the Superintendent of the Worcester State Hospital, pleaded in a letter to the *Advertiser* for the creation of a school for mental defectives that would rescue them from the hideous mental and moral decay that faced them otherwise.[3] His appeal, published while Howe was in Europe, does not appear to have aroused much immediate attention, but it shows that there was ferment in the minds of educational leaders. During the turmoil brought on by the Common-School Controversy, when many educational schemes were discussed, Howe turned once more to the thought of providing education for the feeble-minded. In February 1845, Woodward convinced him that the time had come for action. European experience had shown that the feeble-minded, and even the congenitally insane, could be taught.[4]

With this encouragement, Howe published a series of four letters in the *Advertiser* on the desirability of a hospital or training school for insane and idiotic children.[5] Appealing to his readers' nobler sentiments, he reminded them that

humanity demands that every creature in human shape should command our respect; we should recognise as a brother every being upon whom God has stamped the human impress; no one can say with justifiable pride *homo sum!* unless he can add too, *nihil humani alienum a me puto!*

Christianity demands that in the great march of civilization, the rear rank should not be left too far behind; that none should be allowed to perish in their helplessness; but that the strong should help the weak, so that the whole should advance as a band of brethren.[6]

He urged the legislature to take up the matter.[7]

[2] *Eighth Report* (1840), pp. 12–13.
[3] *Boston Advertiser*, Feb. 28, 1844.
[4] Samuel Bayard Woodward to Howe, Feb. 16, 1845, Howe Papers, Houghton.
[5] The letters ran from Feb. 24 to March 5, 1845.
[6] *Boston Advertiser*, March 4, 1845.
[7] *Boston Advertiser*, March 5, 1845.

Upon conclusion of his work in the School Committee, Howe was free to turn his attention more fully to the training school. Throughout the fall of 1845 he discussed the problem with friends. At the next session of the General Court, on January 22, 1846, Judge Horatio Byington, of Stockbridge, introduced a motion into the House to appoint a committee to consider the expediency of appointing a commission to examine the condition of the feeble-minded in the commonwealth, to ascertain their number, and whether anything might be done for their relief.[8] In April, following a favorable recommendation, the legislature authorized the Governor to appoint three commissioners to inquire into idiocy in Massachusetts and to report the next year.[9] Naturally Howe was chosen to head the group and did most of the work. He sent out circulars to every town clerk and traveled to as many places as possible for a first-hand view of the state's assorted imbeciles and morons.

At the end of the period, April 1847, he made his preliminary report to the lawmakers. Available information, he wrote, although tentative and incomplete, indicated that those among the feeble-minded who did some sort of work were happier and of cleaner habits than those who did nothing. These latter, wasting out their lives in slothfulness, were given over to degrading habits and presented "the sad and demoralizing spectacle of men, made in God's image, whom neither their own reason, nor the reason of others, lifted up above the level of the brutes." The inference was obvious.[10] The achievements of the Paris school proved that there was nothing either visionary or impracticable in the attempt to teach the feeble-minded.[11]

The account pleased the legislators who extended the life of the commission for another year.[12] Howe applied himself to his task even more assiduously in 1847, giving up his summer vacation so that he might personally examine hundreds of feeble-minded. The

---

[8] *House Doc.* 72 (March, 1846).

[9] *Mass. Acts and Resolves* (1846), chap. 117, p. 239.

[10] S. G. Howe, *Idiots. Report in Part* (Boston, 1847), p. 4. Also printed as *House Doc.* 152 (1847).

[11] Howe, *Idiots. Report,* p. 17.

[12] *Mass. Acts and Resolves* (1847), chap. 75, p. 532.

resultant document, one of the most widely acclaimed he ever produced, remained the authoritative statement on the causes and prevention of idiocy for a quarter-century.

While demonstrating to modern readers, for whom it can have only historic interest, the state of medical knowledge that could acclaim such a paper as of first-rank significance, it also shows that Howe continued to cling to the teachings of George Combe, and his peculiar combination of science and religion, which made him see even in the impersonal workings of biology, the morality of divine law. To Howe, mental weakness was a manifestation of the principle of the sins of the fathers being visited upon the children unto the third and fourth generation. Shocked by the frequency of idiocy, he was firmly convinced that it did not result from natural processes, but was rather a diseased excrescence of society, the outward sign of an inward weakness.

It was hard to believe it to be in the order of Providence that the earth should always be cumbered with so many creatures in the human shape, but without the light of human reason. It seemed impious to attribute to the creator any such glaring imperfection in his handiwork. It appeared to us certain that the existence of so many idiots in every generation *must* be the consequence of some violation of the *natural laws,* — that where there was so much suffering, there must have been sin.[13]

He drew an analogy between the relationship of the body to mental health, and the individual's relationship to society. He said that owing to man's double nature and double interest, both as a social being and as a person, he cannot sin with impunity against one nature, any more than he can against the other. And that the suffering, ignorance, and depravity of one class affect others "in spite of all the barriers of pride and selfishness which they may erect around themselves." [14] The morals of one man, he claimed, influence those of his neighbor, whether for good or ill in spite of

[13] S. G. Howe, *Report made to the Legislature of Massachusetts, upon Idiocy* (Boston, Oct. 1848), pp. 3–4. This appeared originally in Feb. 1848, as *Senate Doc.* 51.

[14] Howe, *Report upon Idiocy,* p. 56.

themselves, so that the interest and duty of society are common and inseparable. The moral to draw from the existence of the mentally defective, in his opinion, was that either they or their parents had violated natural laws, thus marring the "beautiful organism of the body" until it had become unfit "for the manifestation of the powers of the soul." He believed idiocy could result only from this. To suppose it a dispensation of Providence "is an insult to the Majesty of Heaven." [15]

The most prominent and prolific cause of idiocy he found was "intemperance," which "lymphatized" the body and "diminished" the proportion of the "fibrous part." Investigation had shown that children of such parents were apt to be scrofulous, feeble in body and weak in mind.[16] Other causes were self-abuse, and the marriage of those closely related.[17]

Questionable as were Howe's conclusions about the causes of idiocy, when he spoke of the care of the feeble-minded he was on much stronger ground. His advice is not yet outmoded. Unmitigated kindness, he said, was harmful, and in this unintentional wrong Massachusetts was a serious offender, the committee having found no instance of willfully unkind treatment of idiots.[18] If anything, keepers were too indulgent, giving them too much food and not enough exercise, with the result that they became filthy, gluttonous, lazy, and given up to abominations of every kind. Not only did they not improve, but they sank deeper and deeper into bodily depravity and mental degradation.[19] Howe called attention to the necessity of cleanliness, mentioning in passing its desirability for all.[20]

---

[15] Howe, *Report upon Idiocy*, pp. 56–57.

[16] Howe, *Report upon Idiocy*, p. 83.

[17] Howe, *Report upon Idiocy*, pp. 87–90. Howe was following theories held by leading authorities; see Robert E. Riegel, *Young America 1830–1840* (Norman, Okla., 1949), pp. 280–281, for a discussion of the causes of insanity as they were thought to be in those days.

[18] Howe, *Report upon Idiocy*, p. 24.

[19] Howe, *Report upon Idiocy*, pp. 31–32.

[20] Howe, *Report upon Idiocy*, p. 27. On the subject of cleanliness, he wrote that too many persons went on "the doctrine that those parts only which are exposed need be clean; in which they are practically sustained by thousands of refined

Unwilling to accept a condition of ignorance when it was possible to save a class of people from sin and disgrace, he pleaded with his fellow citizens for the establishment of a school. The experiences of France, Switzerland, and Prussia proved that mental defectives could be taught, the Parisian institution in particular being a "beautiful example of practical Christianity; a temple in which acceptable service is done to God. . . ."[21] There were also economic reasons for the founding of a school for the feeble-minded. As a class, they were public charges, but with training they could be taught to care for themselves, perhaps even to earn something. The moral evil they presented was worse than the physical, since all men were injured by them. "Shall we, who can transmute granite and ice into gold and silver, and think it pleasant work," he asked, " — shall we shrink from the higher task of transforming brutish men back into human shape?"[22]

Howe's latest production proved a sensation. From all sides only approval was heard. Within a month the Senate Committee on Public Charitable Institutions asked him to draft a bill to implement his report.[23] This was promptly done, and on May 8 the Governor signed a measure which appropriated $2500 for three years to be used for the training and teaching of ten feeble-minded children at one of the state's charitable institutions to be chosen later.[24]

Perkins was naturally designated as the site of the experimental school. Swiftly Howe made preparations, hiring as teacher James B. Richards who went to Europe to study instructional techniques, as Howe had done sixteen years earlier. In August, Howe informed Governor Briggs that he was ready to begin operations. A wing of the large, rambling building in South Boston was set aside, and on October 1, 1848, the first publicly supported school for the instruc-

---

people, who, if they should break an ankle in a brilliant ballroom, and require to have their stocking drawn off before the company, would be more pained by the exposure of the state of the foot and toes, than by the accident itself; or, at least, they ought to be."

[21] Howe, *Report upon Idiocy*, p. 46.
[22] Howe, *Report upon Idiocy*, p. 53.
[23] Thomas Bradly to Howe, March 29, 1848, Howe Papers, Houghton.
[24] *Mass. Acts and Resolves* (1848), chap. 65, pp. 835–836.

tion of idiotic and feeble-minded youth in the United States began operation on an experimental basis, with ten beneficiaries and three private pupils.[25] The first school in the nation had been founded some months earlier in Barre, Massachusetts, by Hervey Backus Wilbur, who had been inspired through a study of the works of Edward Séguin, the leading French authority.[26]

His new scholars, Howe discovered, were not very promising. Some were so weak-minded that either they did not know how, or lacked the muscular energy, to bite their food when it was placed between their jaws; they could only suck.[27] The doctor understood that people might consider his efforts a failure, owing to the slow rate of progress the unfortunates would make, even if he himself should feel that he had succeeded.[28] He knew that he could not raise them to the level of ordinary persons, but he would try to strengthen their mental powers. In common with the rest of mankind they possessed "the feeble germs of those intellectual faculties, moral sentiments, and social affections which in man are superadded to his animal nature, and which make the crowning glory of humanity." [29]

Unable to get away from phrenology, Howe worried about the shapes of their brains, which he considered disproportioned. By working on the old assumption that as a faculty is exercised, that part of the brain controlling it enlarges, he sought ways of having them exercise neglected portions so as to forestall atrophy. Evidently he believed in some early doctrine of evolution, since he felt that organ peculiarities, instincts, habits, and appearances of idiots give some clue to the process of the development of the race of man. Mental defectives to him represented an earlier stage of man, more

[25] "28th Report of the Idiot School" (1875), p. 32. Some of his blind pupils at Perkins disliked the idea of having mental defectives in their quarters. Even Laura Bridgman, who should have understood the necessity of treating the handicapped, disapproved of the arrangement. Laura Bridgman's Journal, Sept. 14, 1848, Perkins.

[26] Wilbur to Howe, Feb. 26, 1850, Howe Papers, Houghton.

[27] S. G. Howe, Second Report, being the First Annual Report on the Experimental School for Teaching and Training Idiotic Children (Boston, 1850), p. 31. Also published as Senate Doc. 38 (1850).

[28] Howe, First Report on the Experimental School, p. 22.

[29] Howe, First Report on the Experimental School, p. 26.

like a monkey than the average Homo sapiens. He considered the physical likeness to animals most marked in those with the smallest brains, hence he was led to believe that not only can feeble-mindedness be caused by the diminutive size of the brain, but that there has also been a progressive enlargement of that organ during the centuries.[30]

With these concepts as the basis, he began his pioneer effort in the teaching of the feeble-minded. During his first year his primary aim was the improvement of the children's physical condition by a program of training, in order to increase their muscular strength and activity, to give them a more perfect and readier command over their bodily motions, as well as to quicken their senses.[31]

Closely related to this was the development of their social affections and moral sense, which he considered his main duty to develop. Though it was a difficult task, he was sure that with patience it could be done.[32] At the end of the year he was gratified to see that the process of deterioration among the pupils had been entirely stopped, and that the condition of many had improved.[33] Some progress was even made in the teaching of at least one academic subject, reading. All had learned within a few months to select words printed on slips of paper. To attain this result, Richards had adopted Howe's precedent with Laura Bridgman of teaching words before letters, and of repeating the lesson until it was understood.[34] Richards had to make one thirteen-year-old boy repeat three words 640 times before he was sure that the youth had gotten them correctly.[35]

The experimental school was a complete success; applause and thanks from parents and public guardians of the feeble-minded were heaped on Howe and Richards. The overjoyed father of Daniel Peatfield of Ipswich wrote of the improvement in his son, "Daniel[']s understanding in regard to fetching and carrying things

[30] Howe, *First Report on the Experimental School*, p. 56.
[31] Howe, *First Report on the Experimental School*, p. 44.
[32] Howe, *First Report on the Experimental School*, p. 66.
[33] Howe, *First Report on the Experimental School*, p. 72.
[34] Howe, *First Report on the Experimental School*, pp. 65-66.
[35] Howe, *First Report on the Experimental School*, p. 60.

. . . was more bright and cheerful than formerly betraying less the look of an Idiot than they used to do[.]"[36] So pleased were the Shrewsbury Overseers of the Poor with the appearance of their charge, James Smith, after having been at the school five months, that they allowed him to stay on.[37]

One of the few sour notes came from a wealthy father who objected to Howe's classless education. He protested against his twenty-one-year-old son's performing menial duties as "unbecoming his position as a gentleman." Naturally he "understood" the difficulties of the youth's position, but he hoped that there might be some other means of teaching him.[38]

Such protests were unavailing. Howe went on along his chosen path. After two years of experimentation the legislature put the school on a permanent basis, at double its original appropriation. Thus was created the Massachusetts School for Idiotic and Feeble-Minded Youth of which Howe, now having under his supervision two institutions, became the General Superintendent.[39]

His new enterprise went on for the next few years in its temporary quarters, gaining fame as it blazed a trail in this new field of education. In 1856 it left its corner of Perkins, to the relief of Laura Bridgman, to enter its own quarters, which remained near by so that its Superintendent could visit it without difficulty.[40]

The successful operation of the "Idiot School," as it came to be called familiarly, impelled other states to action. New York was the first. Following an impressive exhibition of ten pupils before the Legislature in Albany and an address by Howe, the New York State Asylum was chartered. Christopher Morgan, Secretary of State, later told the doctor that it was to his efforts, more than all other causes, that the Empire State owed its school.[41] As the fame

[36] Joseph Peatfield to James B. Richards, Jan. 2, 1850, Howe Papers, Houghton.

[37] Overseers of the Poor of Shrewsbury to Richards, Dec. 24, 1849, Howe Papers, Houghton.

[38] Benjamin Ogle Tayloe to Howe, Nov. 7, 1849, Howe Papers, Houghton.

[39] "28th Report of Idiot School" (1875), p. 35.

[40] "28th Report of Idiot School," p. 38.

[41] "28th Report of Idiot School," p. 35. Hervey Backus Wilbur became its director, moving from Barre to Syracuse. The State of Ohio was interested too. William Bushnell, chairman of the Committee on Benevolent Institutions of the House of

of Howe's new venture spread over the nation he received letters of inquiry from anxious parents seeking information as to the enrollment of their afflicted offspring.[42]

As at Perkins, he exercised general supervision over the establishment, leaving the actual work to the best teachers he could find. When Richards left after three years' service, he was replaced by the foremost teacher of the feeble-minded in the world, Edward Séguin, whom Howe employed in 1852.[43] However, their personalities clashed. The Frenchman, feeling himself at least as great in his field as the American tyro, followed his own ideas. Before the end of March, after less than three months' service, he left.[44]

It did not take Howe long to reach the stage of thinking that he knew more about the education of the feeble-minded than the more experienced Europeans. Writing Parker from Edinburgh during a trip to Europe in the summer of 1850, he said,

I have found out that in the matter of idiocy they do not know so much in England as they do in France, & in France not half so much as they & the world think they do. The French are a little given to charlatanism, it must be said, & the idiot school of Paris does allow the world to think that the wonderful things done [in] it, are wonderful only upon the supposition that the forward pupils are idiots which they are not.[45]

Whether the doctor was justified in his conceit is beside the point, for he was devoted to the cause of education for the feeble-minded, and labored with as much energy as he could spare from his manifold activities to have the new school established in public favor. He besieged public officials to assure adequate appropriations, and to have them speak publicly in its favor.[46] For twenty-five years he

---

Representatives, asked him for reports and any other information he had available. Bushnell to Howe, Jan. 25, 1851, Howe Papers, Houghton.

[42] There are dozens of letters in the Howe Papers, Houghton, usually beginning that the writer had seen a notice in a newspaper. For example, Lydia P. Mott of Cuyahoga Falls, Ohio, in a letter to Howe postmarked Feb. 19, 1850.

[43] Howe to Sumner, March 15, 1852, Howe Papers, Houghton.

[44] Howe to Sumner, March 25, 1852, Howe Papers, Houghton.

[45] Howe to Parker, Aug. 2, 1850, Howe Papers, Houghton.

[46] Howe to Sumner, March 21, 1851, Howe Papers; mentions the many efforts he was making.

managed the Idiot School with firm hand, impressing the force of his personality as distinctively there as at Perkins. He examined all children for admission, hired the staff, and even prescribed the diet. "I spared no efforts to have the institution included within the circle of state charities," he wrote upon his retirement from its direction.[47] With Howe's indomitable will pushing it on, the school shortly took its place in the front ranks of the state's charitable institutions, another monument to the philanthropic spirit of Samuel Gridley Howe.

II

Some mention should be made of Howe's activity in the Boston Prison Discipline Society, not for the intrinsic value of his achievements, which are questionable, but for the evidence it gives of his character development. American penitentiaries had early in the century gained such fame for their progressive practices that Europeans, of whom Alexis de Tocqueville and Gustave de Beaumont were only the two most famous, deemed it necessary to make the long ocean voyage to study them. Two rival systems contended for public favor, the solitary system as practiced at the Eastern State Penitentiary in Philadelphia, wherein the prisoner lived alone in his cell, seeing no one but his keepers, and the silent or congregate system, in effect at the Auburn State Prison in New York, where the convicts worked together but were forbidden to speak.

The Boston Prison Discipline Society favored the latter principle, while Howe, Sumner, and Mann, who had joined the Society early in the forties, favored the former. To their way of thinking, the only valid method of reform was to keep the prisoners apart. They reasoned that, since the criminals had originally been led astray by bad company, they should not be allowed to consort with the same type in jail as well. The remainder of the Society, failing to see things in this light, insisted that the separate system led to higher death rates, greater frequency of insanity, and was more expensive.

[47] "28th Report of the Idiot School" (1875), p. 45.

On the other hand, prisons following the Auburn plan not only had fewer such cases, but also fewer recommitments.[48]

For several years the dispute smoldered. As a consequence of the 1845 meeting, Howe, Sumner, and Mann were appointed to a committee to examine the rival systems. Naturally Howe bore the burden of preparing the inevitable report, in this case an unwonted minority opinion, which was read at the society's 1846 meeting. It was a withering diatribe against the adherents of the Auburn system, which the Society refused to print, and which had to be published privately.[49]

The climax of the dispute was reached in 1847. At the May meeting, Sumner spoke for one-and-a-half hours, shocking his audiences with his vituperative powers.[50] Equally vitriolic, Howe's comments were no better received. The *Boston Post,* terming his remarks a burlesque, mused on hearing him, "is *this* Dr. Howe . . . the man who holds so high a reputation at home and abroad as a gentleman of active philanthropic labors, and no contemptible place as a writer and thinker?"[51] On June 16, Howe spoke again, drawing tears from many eyes with his story of the month he had spent in the Berlin Prison and of how he would have gone insane had he been forced to consort with the inmates.[52]

Julia, loyal wife that she was, attended the debates assiduously to cheer her husband's side on to victory. Everything that side did, in her eyes, was wonderful; even Sumner's long polemic of the eighteenth was to her a "masterly" performance. "I never listened to any thing with more intense interest — " she wrote her sister, "he held the audience breathless for two hours and a half."[53]

To the general relief of the city, these acrimonious meetings, which had degenerated into personal recrimination, ended late in

[48] *Twenty-first and Twenty-second Annual Reports of the Board of Managers of the Prison Discipline Society, Boston (May 1846-7)* (Boston, 1848), pp. 129–146.

[49] S. G. Howe, *An Essay on Separate and Congregate Systems of Prison Discipline* (Boston, 1846), 90 pages.

[50] *Boston Post,* June 2, 1847.

[51] *Boston Post,* June 4, 1847.

[52] *Boston Semi-Weekly Courier,* June 24, 1847.

[53] Julia Ward Howe to Annie Mailliard, June 19, 1847, Howe Papers, Houghton.

June.[54] Howe and Sumner suffered a complete defeat. They gained no luster by their frenetic remarks. Beyond showing to what extremes men of good will can go when they lose control of themselves, the only interest the unpleasant dispute can have for us now is the opportunity it affords us to gain new insights into the development of both Howe and Sumner. Here, for the first time, they both appear in their complete maturity, patronizing when agreed with, but wild with rage, contemptuous, and vituperative when opposed. Howe had shown these characteristics earlier, most particularly against the Boston schoolmasters. Now Sumner too breaks forth as he is remembered by a later generation, a ranting demagogue who stopped at no oratorical device to gain his point. His speeches before the society were dry-runs for his *Crime Against Kansas* nine years later.

The hysterical nature of their behavior during this campaign causes one to wonder what ailed Howe and Sumner. Everyone who disagreed with them, and this included men like Samuel A. Eliot and Walter Channing, they characterized as maliciously inspired, and incapable of ever acting in good faith on any matter. They showed a stiff-neckedness that foreshadowed disaster when in a vital matter they faced men of like temperament. They were groping for a reform worthy of their best efforts, such as they were beginning to find in abolition, the culminating movement of their lives, for which they sacrificed all their other interests.

[54] *Boston Advertiser,* June 26, 1847.

XI

Free-Soil Days

It was inevitable that a man as deeply concerned about social welfare as Howe should eventually join the antislavery movement. He could not forever ignore the existence of a condition that every day made a mockery of the Declaration of Independence and the Constitution. Still for years he took no active part in abolition. On the contrary, he was bitterly attacked in the *Liberator* for alleged slights to Negroes.[1] Only as awareness grew upon him that the South's "peculiar institution," instead of withering away, was more flourishing than ever, and was planning to expand, did he overcome his long-standing reticence, and throw himself into a movement that eventually absorbed most of his time for over a decade.

I

Though mute, Howe had never been blind. As far back as 1833 he had published a "Letter on Slavery" in the *New England Maga-*

[1] In 1833 he refused to admit a four-year-old Negro child to Perkins because he was under age. He did promise to reconsider when the child should have reached the minimum age, six. The mother went away apparently satisfied. Howe never saw her again. He suspected she was a plant. In October of that year the trustees issued a formal statement on the matter of Negroes by voting to admit all applicants of proper age and qualifications. In May 1834, the New England Anti-Slavery Convention resurrected the issue at its convention. Garrison printed an account in the *Liberator* and despite Howe's denials, repeated the charges as late as May 23, 1845. Howe to Mann, April 16, 1853, Howe Papers, Houghton; Mann to Elizabeth Peabody, Aug. 24, 1833, Mann Papers, MHS; *Proceedings of the New England Anti-Slavery Convention* (Boston, 1834), p. 14; *Liberator,* V, 29 (July 18, 1835); and, XV, 21 (May 23, 1845).

zine in the hope that his views would be a "testimony of liberal and conciliatory feeling towards our southern brethren." [2] At that early date he recognized that slavery was becoming a problem "on the solution of which the future fate of the Union must hinge. It is in vain to put far off the evil day . . . it becomes the patriot to grapple with it . . . and to see if no means can be found to conduct harmless to the earth the bolts with which it is charged." [3] So discredited were the opinions and methods of William Lloyd Garrison and his followers that Howe, disclaiming any connection or sympathy for them, classed Garrisonians with fanatics clinging to false doctrine. Their efforts he said were mad, and anyone who advocated immediate emancipation was "the greatest enemy of blacks and whites." [4]

Nevertheless he abhorred slavery as a system which violated both natural and divine law. Were the slaves to rise in rebellion, and were he forced to choose sides, he knew he would join the insurgents, "and strike with them for the rights of man. . . ." [5] Though he looked on Negro servitude as the cause of the difference in the prosperity of the two sections, and though he sympathized with the plight of the masters caught in toils not of their own making, he claimed he had no right to interfere. He was convinced the slaveowners would take action themselves when they awakened to a realization of their condition. [6] He appeared to favor compensated emancipation, with deportation of the freedmen.

Howe's views were typical of members of his class, men who are ordinarily thought of as having had deep social consciences. The weird blend of mysticism, fanaticism, and impracticality of the Garrisonians repelled many who eventually threw in their lot with antislavery. So long as freedom was assured north of the line of the Missouri Compromise, so long were abolitionists considered disreputable agitators whose success would ruin the nation.

Sumner, though a subscriber to the *Liberator* after 1835, never approved its doctrine on the Union and Constitution; it seemed to

[2] Letter to the Editor, *New England Magazine*, V (Sept. 1833), 269.
[3] "Letter on Slavery," *New England Magazine* (Aug.), p. 122.
[4] Letter to the Editor, p. 270.
[5] "Letter on Slavery," p. 124.
[6] "Letter on Slavery," p. 125.

him "vindictive, bitter & unchristian." [7] Julia felt similarly. In her early years she had always supposed abolitionists to be "men and women of rather coarse fibre, abounding in cheap and easy denunciation, and seeking to lay rash hands on the complex machinery of government and of society." [8] Garrison was the particular object of her dislike. Of his malignity of disposition she entertained not the smallest doubt, until one evening at Theodore Parker's she shared the same hymnbook with him, much to her husband's amusement.[9] Even as late as 1842, Theodore Parker, soon to become one of the most prominent antislavery workers, refused to coöperate with abolitionists. He declined to read a petition in his church, as they had requested him to do.[10]

II

During the years, as Howe's first-hand knowledge of the slave system become more extensive, his hatred for it intensified. On his trip to the South and West, during the winter of 1841–1842, he had an excellent chance to see for himself conditions as they were. Even apart from the injustice to the slaves, he was struck by the evil effects of slavery on the whites. He noticed that everything below the Mason-Dixon line was in an unkempt state. Train schedules were undependable. One could leave almost two hours early to make a train connection twenty-two miles away, and still miss it. Describing his impressions to Sumner, he wrote:

Let a man be dropped from a balloon upon the surface of the earth, & he could tell in three minutes whether he were in a Slave State, or not: The very first sights, the very first sounds, the very first odours would attest the fact: the whites stand with their hands in their breeches pockets & and the blacks are "helping them do nothing": fences are down, doors are ajar, filth is in the streets, foul odours in the air, con-

[7] Sumner to Felton, April 9, 1850, Sumner Papers, Houghton.

[8] J. W. Howe, *Reminiscences*, p. 152.

[9] *Reminiscences*, p. 153. Wendell Phillips occupied a similar place until sometime in the fifties she heard that he had bought a volume of her poems at a bazaar, with the remark, "She doesn't like me, but I like her poetry." A personal meeting in Parker's living room cured her of this antipathy as well. *Ibid.*, p. 154.

[10] Parker to George Adams, Dec. 5, 1842, Parker Letterbook 7, pp. 34–35, MHS.

fusion and neglect are every where. Go into a house late at night —
they are all lounging about, too lazy to go to bed; go in in the morning,
they are all yawning in bed, too lazy to get up; no one has his prescribed duties — the master scolds & drives, the slave dawdles & shirks;
& if any thing *must* be done, it takes one white longer to hunt up two
negroes & force them to do it, than it would take one uncorrupted
Saxon to finish it alone.[11]

His visit to Georgia a few weeks later convinced him that the
evils and disadvantages of slavery fell more heavily on the whites
than on the Negroes. He admitted that Southern claims were true
in one respect, the physical condition of the slaves in the Carolinas
and Georgia was better than that of free Negroes or poor whites in
the North. In fact, almost the only systematic attention to physical
education he ever saw in the United States, apart from Perkins,
was among the slaves. He marveled at how their owners could be
such kind-hearted men while administering a system cruel enough
to "make Turks of them." He believed that the overseer who told
him that the slaves were happier there than elsewhere spoke the
truth, "but in this he speaks his own condemnation, & the brutal-
ising effects of a system which can make a human being content in
such utter degradation." [12]
The sight of a cultivated free Negro being refused service in the
men's cabin of the Ohio River steamboat which he took to Kentucky upset him so that he would have eaten with the humiliated
passenger at the side table had he not known that he would thus
have defeated his plan of creating a school for the blind at his
destination.[13] Ten days in New Orleans spent in examining public
institutions showed him that, in the administration of the penal
code, "there are abominations which should bring down the fate of
Sodom upon the city." In the Negro section of the prison he saw
"much which made me blush that I was a white man, and which

[11] Howe to Sumner, postmarked Dec. 6, 1841, Howe Papers, Houghton. In the
house of a Richmond friend, he noticed the door always came off its latch during
dinner, and that his host always ordered it repaired. Four years later when he returned, the master was still ordering it to be fixed.
[12] Howe to Mann, postmarked Dec. 28, 1841, Howe Papers, Houghton.
[13] Howe to Sumner, Jan. 30, 1842, Howe Papers, Houghton.

for a moment stirred up an evil spirit in my animal nature." For the first time in his life he felt his hair stiffen at its roots as he watched a young slave girl being whipped on order of her master, while the slaves in the cells facing on the court took no notice. Chilled to the marrow of his bones, he saw once more how low "can man, created in God's image, be sunk in brutality." [14] It was with relief that he returned from the "rowdyism, bullyism, and depravity" of the Southwest to the "cold but comparatively honest & moral NEast," which was to him "as Paradise to Purgatory." [15]

Despite his experiences, he still remained unconnected with any abolition movement, though convinced that slavery's disappearance was inevitable. He hoped it could be accomplished peacefully, though his New England morality was repelled at the thought that the "injustice may be exempt from the sorrow & suffering, by which atonement only can be made." [16]

III

The controversy over the admission of Texas in 1844–1845 stimulated Howe and his friends into a changed attitude toward active abolition. They, like many others throughout the North, were shocked into an awareness that, as the territory of the nation had been enlarged, slavery had also been extended. It seemed to them that the Southern aristocracy, the hated "Slavocracy," aided by their Northern minions, the wretched "doughfaces," held the freedom-loving people of the North in their power.[17] The time had come to resist further Southern encroachments on human dignity, not through the American Anti-Slavery Society's futile resolutions and editorial agitation, but through vigorous political action. The little Liberty Party, which for years had been struggling vainly, was now seen to have been on the right path.[18]

---

[14] Howe to Sumner, quoted in Harriet Beecher Stowe, *A Key to Uncle Tom's Cabin* (Boston, 1853), p. 35.

[15] Howe to Mann, March 27, 1842, Howe Papers, Houghton.

[16] Howe to Mann, postmarked Dec. 28, 1841, Howe Papers, Houghton.

[17] There is a clear statement of that view in Henry Wilson, *History of the Rise and Fall of the Slave Power in America* (Boston, 1872–77), II, 115.

[18] These later men never joined Garrison's organization, which did not believe in

The leaders of the anti-Texas movement, among whom were Sumner and Howe, conferred on strategy throughout the spring and summer of 1845. Meetings were held in all parts of the state to protest the annexation which had taken place months before.[19] Howe belonged to the Massachusetts Committee to Prevent the Admission of Texas as a Slave State, which at a "non-partisan" meeting in Cambridge, October 21, 1845, voted to organize a large state-wide body to procure as general an expression of the voice of the people as possible in remonstrance against the coup. Those present declared that resistance to slavery was to be made paramount to every other consideration of politics. True, they had lost on Texas, and had seen the Constitution "trampled under foot," but there were other places left where the institution was to be fought until either North or South was victorious.[20]

As a consequence of annexation, United States relations with Mexico worsened throughout the winter of 1845–1846. War impended. Antislavery men girded their loins to struggle for the right in a nation that to them had lost its regard for justice. Howe, not yet the fire-eater he was eventually to become, was still restrained in his views. His main interests continued to be his work at Perkins, to which he was beginning to add mental defectives, and prison discipline. He felt that dispassionate counsel between the sections was still possible. To Dr. Henry Ingersoll Bowditch, a prominent Boston physician, the son of Nathaniel Bowditch the famed mathematician, Howe wrote that he favored any measures except "such as directly tend to cut us off from the parent stock, for that I hold would diminish our usefulness & the slave's hope. If the slaveholder

---

the efficacy of political action, even though the term "abolitionist" was applied indiscriminately to Garrisonians and non-Garrisonians. Howe and his group continued subject to further occasional attacks from Garrison. See the *Commonwealth* (Boston's Free-Soil daily), March 18, 1853, for a scathing denunciation of the "ultra-abolitionists." Mann to Parker, April 15, 1853, Parker Letterbook II, pp. 107–108, discusses an argument between Wendell Phillips and Horace Mann.

[19] The other members of the group were Charles Francis Adams, Stephen C. Phillips of Salem, John Gorham Palfrey, Henry Wilson, Richard Henry Dana, Jr., Charles Allen, and Samuel and E. Rockwood Hoar.

[20] *Report of the Massachusetts Committee to Prevent the Admission of Texas as a Slave State* (n.p., n.d.).

listens to us his brethren & friends with so much impatience, how would he treat us if we became aliens & enemies." He still cherished the illusion that it was possible to maintain relationships with their Southern friends, and that freedom-lovers must continue to do so at all costs. "It is not enmity & force but love & reason that are to be used in the coming strife," he naïvely hoped.[21]

Theodore Parker, much more volatile, was already converted to the strenuous life. In an address to the convention of the New England Anti-Slavery Society, he was merciless in denouncing the nation's clergy for not taking a stronger stand on slavery. He also excoriated the North's commercial classes as unprincipled for accepting the *status quo* in order to gain profits. The trinitarian creed had become "I believe in the golden eagle; I believe in the silver dollar; I believe in the copper cent." Similarly the administration was at the disposal of the Slavocracy. In matters where the planters were unconcerned, Washington was wont to temporize as in the Oregon dispute, he alleged, but it had been unusually firm with Mexico.[22]

Sumner had long ere this become one of the inner council at party deliberations. He was one of the leaders in a faction called the "Young Whigs" (the term "Conscience Whig" had not as yet come into vogue), who scornfully referred to the regulars as "Cotton Whigs" since they disavowed the demands of conscience to bend the knee before the Slavocracy for the sake of trade.[23] The Howe circle was leaving its benign way of life of pleasantries and simple joys for a field of passion and pain; but the times demanded it.

IV

During the next few months Howe took his stand alongside his friends. By fall he was fully committed to their program. Events had forced him to it. The coming of the war in the spring proved to the Young Whigs' satisfaction the Slavocracy's iniquitous control

---

[21] Howe to Bowditch, Feb. 3, 1846, Howe Papers, Houghton.

[22] *Boston Courier*, May 29, 1846.

[23] Origin of "Cotton Whig" to be found in Wilson's *Rise and Fall of the Slave Power*, II, 117–118.

not only over the nation as a whole, but over their party as well. Robert C. Winthrop, the brilliant descendant of the first governor of the Bay Colony, and their representative in Congress, supported the Army appropriation bill.[24] A horror of revulsion passed through antislavery men. Of all persons to do so, the idol of Boston's intellectuals had betrayed them. It did not matter that he was on record in opposition to a war forced on the country by the administration, and had voted for the appropriation only because he was a *"National Defence* man" and "all wars involve an element of self-defence, after they have once commenced." [25] Honor seemed dead. Truth was every day being scorned and spat upon. Cotton thread, spun on the banks of the Merrimack from fiber raised by slaves, bound free Massachusetts the prisoner of Southern imperialism. Men of conscience writhed in shame and despair.

Winthrop had betrayed freedom; his sin could not go unpunished. It was hard to go against Boston's favorite, Webster's heir apparent. Stately in appearance and bearing, a man of unquestioned intellectual capacities and ability, he fulfilled the idealist's conception of the aristocrat in politics. There can be no doubt of his burning hatred for slavery and its abominations; there can also be no question of his sincerity and devotion to principle, but in the eyes of the reformers he had compromised with his conscience for mere expediency. As his father before him, who during the War of 1812 had supported national interests above the regional and opposed the Hartford Convention, his great crime had been to insist that for the sake of the Union, New England must accept the annexation of Texas. At the official city banquet July 4, 1845, following Sumner's sensational pacifist address "The True Grandeur of Nations," he had delivered his famous toast for which he was never to gain pardon:

OUR COUNTRY, — Whether bounded by the St. John's and the Sabine, or however otherwise bounded or described, and be the measurement

---

[24] *Acts and Resolutions Passed at the First Session of the Twenty-Ninth Congress of the United States* (Washington, 1846), chap. 16.

[25] Winthrop to Sumner, Jan. 4 and Feb. 2, 1846, Sumner Papers, Houghton.

more or less, — still our country, to be cherished in all our hearts, to be defended by all our hands! [26]

To the Young Whigs, this patriotic utterance, meretricious in its chauvinism, betrayed the guile of a patron of sin.[27]

Tempers reached the boiling point during the summer of 1846, with the final break coming in July when Sumner mercilessly flayed the Congressman, anonymously of course, in the *Courier* and *Whig*. The United States had drawn the sword with a lie on its lips. The doctrine of "Our country, right, or wrong, or *howsoever bounded,* is a sentiment of heathen vulgarity and impiety," he concluded, to be trod under foot as a serpent. Winthrop's duty was to shield his country from bloodshed. Mexico was America's blameless neighbor until a lying Congress made it an enemy.[28]

Winthrop recognized the style immediately. Sumner's explanation only made matters worse. There are things a gentleman does not say. Sumner was no gentleman.[29] Accusing his calumniator of having been deaf to everything but the admiration of his fanatical friends, Winthrop forgave him the injury done his honor, but refused to maintain his social relationship with him.[30] Brought into the open at last was the fast developing break in Boston society, on a microcosmic scale a manifestation of the illness at the root of the American body politic.

The Sumner-Winthrop rupture presaged the splitting of Whiggery into two factions. Still the radicals refused to recognize realities. Pertinaciously hoping to make it the agency of political antislavery, they hesitated to leave the party. At the state convention, which met in September at Faneuil Hall, Sumner still felt able to say that his was the party of liberty, justice, freedom, right, and humanity. But events proved otherwise. Stephen C. Phillips' resolutions denouncing the war and calling the slave power the "most formidable antagonist" to the Whigs were beaten.[31]

[26] R. C. Winthrop, Jr., *Memoir of Robert C. Winthrop* (Boston, 1897), pp. 44–45.
[27] The author uses these high-flown terms merely to recreate the spirit of the times. They are not necessarily his own views.
[28] *Boston Courier,* July 31, 1846.
[29] Winthrop to Sumner, Aug. 7, 1846, Winthrop Papers, XXXIV, 116, MHS.
[30] Winthrop to Sumner, Aug. 17, 1846, Sumner Papers, Houghton.
[31] *Boston Advertiser,* Sept. 24, 1846. The full text appeared on the 28th.

If any further evidence were needed that the Conscience Whigs could no longer work within their party, it came with the renomination of Winthrop in mid-October.[32] Though he had earlier wished to retire from public life, events had determined him to seek public approval of his acts.[33] The disgruntled insurgents, deciding upon independent action, announced a rally at Tremont Temple, on October 29.[34] Sumner as usual led the van, loosing in the columns of the *Whig* the most vitriolic attack he had as yet produced. Not only was everyone in uniform responsible for the war, but culpability reached "far back and incardines the Halls of Congress," in addition to staining the constituents of those who voted for it. The American Army should have been allowed to perish "like the legions of Varus. Their bleached bones, in the distant valleys where they were waging an unjust war, would not tell such a tale of ignominy to posterity, as this lying Act of Congress." [35]

Such was the background when in the fall of 1846 Howe, unable merely to observe without acting, publicly took his stand.

V

New proof of the Slavocracy's power over free Massachusetts came in September with the return of a fugitive slave. A Negro known only as "Joe" escaped from a ship in the bay and reached land before some of the crewmen captured him and returned him to bondage. This constituted a kidnaping so far as Howe and the others were concerned. They called a protest meeting at Faneuil Hall for the night of September 24. An enraged populace packed the auditorium. Feeble John Quincy Adams, making one of his last public appearances, graced the speakers' platform. In a weak voice he addressed the audience. But Howe delivered the major speech of the evening, his first as an abolitionist.

The time had come, he said, for action,

we have tried the "let alone system" long enough. . . . [Slavery] which has so long been brooding over this country like an incubus, has at last

[32] *Boston Advertiser*, Oct. 13, 1846.
[33] Winthrop, *R. C. Winthrop*, p. 56.
[34] *Boston Advertiser*, Oct. 27, 1846.
[35] *Boston Whig*, Oct. 27, 1846.

spread abroad her murky wings, and has covered us with her benumbing shadow. It has silenced the pulpit; it has muffled the press; its influence is everywhere.[36]

There was nothing they could do about Joe; he was beyond rescue. Nevertheless it was within the power of the people to prevent similar outrages in the future. The throng voted to appoint a vigilance committee to handle fugitive slave cases that might henceforth arise. Howe was elected chairman. Others on the committee, which numbered over eighty, were Parker, Sumner, Ellis Gray Loring, Richard Hildreth, Wendell Phillips, and James Freeman Clarke. On September 30, a week later, the members held their first meeting, and voted to raise a fund of one thousand dollars.[37] Apart from this, the committee does not appear to have done much, and shortly faded from sight, to be resurrected in more vigorous form a few years later.

Howe was henceforth in the councils of the Conscience Whigs, never to flag in his devotion to the cause.

At the "independent" meeting held on October 29, he spoke again, this time likening his group to the Pilgrims who, ignorant of where they were going, knew what they were escaping. While it might be difficult for the Conscience Whigs to tell where they were heading, they too knew from whence they came. Following this, John Albion Andrew, a young lawyer already marked for prominence, read the resolutions which placed Sumner, the obvious choice, in nomination for representative.[38] But Sumner declined to run. He had been out of town, in Bangor, at the time of the action. On his return, he issued a firm declination. He did not desire public office of any kind. "My tastes are alien to official life; and I have long been accustomed to look to other fields of usefulness." [39]

The attempted draft set at naught, the Young Whigs were in a quandary as to their next step. Howe, "very mad!" (but not at

---

[36] *Address of the Committee Appointed by a Public Meeting, Held at Faneuil Hall, September 24, 1846* (Boston, 1846), Appendix, pp. 4–5.

[37] *Address at Faneuil Hall*, p. 40.

[38] *Boston Advertiser*, Oct. 30, 1846.

[39] *Boston Advertiser*, Nov. 2, 1846.

Sumner), worked feverishly to discover a substitute. "I feel as though I had swallowed a peppercorn when I think that no one *dares* to be made a martyr of in the cause of humanity," he wrote the cringing orator. Still, Howe hoped to be able to find someone "who will have the courage to do what, as yet, *you & I* have not dared to do." [40] But there was no one else. Out of a sense of duty, albeit sadly, he consented to fill in. "You want a man to stand and be shot at —" he wrote the nominating committee, "to fall in a ditch that others may march over it. Well, if no better man can be found, you may make use of Your friend S. G. Howe." [41]

The reluctant candidate was placed in a cruel position. He had been planning to return to the School Committee in order to finish what he had started the year before. Had not the congressional election interfered, he was certain he would have been nominated and carried in "with a rush." Now he had to sacrifice the certainty of doing good to the certainty of going down to defeat.[42]

Howe never reproached Sumner for refusing his party's call. He understood that a scholar's entry into politics must necessarily bring with it developments the cloistered soul could hardly have expected. The political arena did not have the charm of Longfellow's drawing room on Sunday afternoon, or the dignity of a Harvard lecture hall. Sumner would need time to realize fully that he was now a prominent figure, whose words and acts were the business of all. He would learn this slowly and change accordingly. In the meantime, his closest confidant, even more of a novice in politics, looked indulgently on Sumner's bashfulness which required others to perform his duty for him. Howe understood that for principle (and what crimes were being committed in its name) Sumner was sacrificing what was

dearer than life, or fortune, or fame, — the social regard of those whom you so love as friends. Our fathers pledged their lives fortunes & honour in support of their cause, — you are doing more than they did in the way of sacrifice. . . .

[40] Howe to Sumner, Nov. (n.d.) 1846, Howe Papers, Houghton.
[41] *Boston Advertiser,* Nov. 5, 1846.
[42] Howe to Sumner, Nov. 3, 1846, Howe Papers, Houghton.

I should have thought you a braver man had you stood to the nomination that was forced upon you, but I had not the heart to urge you to do so because I saw you suffering torture. During your whole course in this matter I have watched you closely & have learned to respect & admire you even more than before. It has never been my lot to know a man so perfectly loyal to truth, right & humanity than you have been. Your efforts & sacrifices cannot be lost, for if no other good come out of them this will come that your example will kindle & keep alive high purposes in the souls of hundreds of whom I am one. You are my junior by many years, but to you I owe many of the public aspirations which I feel for progress upward & onward in my spiritual nature.[43]

The great *Sumnerius,* as Longfellow called him, could do no wrong.

The Native Americans, a short-lived nativist excrescence, also chose the insurgents' standard-bearer, in the belief that "the principles of our party have since their first promulgation met your cordial approbation. . . ."[44] Howe accepted the designation, with the simple remark that, "The rights of Petition and the purity of the ballot box should ever be held sacred, and no efforts of mine shall ever be wanting to keep them so."[45] Upon learning of this added support, he instructed Sumner, who appears to have been his campaign manager, to distribute copies of the *Whig* containing some favorable remarks he had made about Catholics.[46] He apparently understood enough about politics to know that a candidate should not alienate voters if he can help it.

The brief campaign was extremely bitter. The two Whig factions unrestrainedly hurled imprecations at each other, while completely ignoring the Democrats and a fourth group. The *Advertiser,* with unconcealed asperity, told its readers that Howe had joined the fight to do mischief, although it knew that "if he is doing evil it is with the expectation that through evil good may come." It had

---

[43] Howe to Sumner, Nov. 7, 1846, Howe Papers, Houghton.

[44] Committee of Native Americans to Howe, undated, Howe Papers, MHS.

[45] *Boston Advertiser,* Nov. 6, 1846.

[46] Howe to Sumner, Nov. 6, 1846, Howe Papers, Houghton. Howe does not appear to have favored nativism. There is nothing in his letters of the forties about it, but those after 1854 are scathing in their disapproval. See "Ferment of Abolition," section II.

thought him above that.[47] On the other hand, Elizur Wright's incendiary *Chronotype,* a small struggling independent abolitionist sheet, considered him the once-in-a-century candidate of the friends of peace, truth, and justice, whom "surely not a man will hesitate to follow." [48] Even Garrison, opposed as he was to ballot boxes, looked with pleasure on what he called a sign of progress. It proved there was some conscience left and "some willingness to apply the rules of private morality to public life." It was clear that he had no faith in the new party, but he would watch its progress with interest, if not with hope.[49]

Sumner, relieved at his narrow escape, contributed his forensic powers to the cause. In speeches throughout the district he characterized his beloved friend with the conciseness possible only to one thoroughly familiar with another. This was the Howe he knew:

> He is firm, ever true, honest, determined, a lover of the Right. With a courage that charms opposition, he would not fear to stand alone against a fervid majority. Knowing war by fearful familiarity, he is an earnest defender of peace. With a singular experience of life in other countries, he now brings the stores he has garnered up, and his noble spirit, to the service of his fellow-citizens.[50]

Election day was November 9. Howe ran third in a field of four. Winthrop received an absolute majority of the votes.[51] The *Advertiser* was relieved. All attempts at reviving the moribund Liberty and nativist parties had failed, it said, and the effort to divide the Whigs defeated. The returns proved that Winthrop possessed to a remarkable degree the confidence of his constituents.[52] To the *Chronotype* there was no longer any doubt that Boston was pretty "thoroughly steeped to the lips in pro-slavery or a correlative wickedness." [53] Garrison was of course encouraged. Now, perhaps, anti-

---

[47] *Boston Advertiser,* Nov. 5, 1846.

[48] *Chronotype,* Nov. 5, 1846.

[49] *The Liberator,* XVI, 45 (Nov. 6, 1846).

[50] Charles Sumner, *Works* (Boston, 1870), I, 335.

[51] *The Advertiser,* Nov. 11, and the *Whig,* Nov. 13, give different figures, but the results were the same.

[52] *Boston Advertiser,* Nov. 10, 1846.

[53] *Chronotype,* Nov. 11, 1846.

slavery men, having done their best by ballot, would learn its futility, and "devote their energies to the destruction of the overshadowing tyranny of the nation and not to an attempt to direct it." [54]

Regular Whigs all over the nation had followed the Boston election with keenest interest. Shocked by the schism, they could not trust the good faith of the dissidents whose general tone and behavior repelled them. Former Governor Levi Lincoln had neither sympathy for the scruples of the Conscience Whigs, respect for their character, nor charity for their motives. It seemed to him that by raising false issues on all occasions, thus fomenting artificial and unnecessary excitement, they created divisions through which they hoped to rise to greater importance. [55]

John Pendleton Kennedy, the noted novelist and the victor's closest friend, spoke of the opposition in the most contemptuous terms, finding it

impossible not to doubt the sincerity of men who prate so much of their consciences, and who so perversely endeavor to cripple the only party who can advance the country a single step towards the consummation they affect to desire. . . . Howe, I saw, came out *to fill a ditch* that others might walk over it. It is some consolation to find that he has been gratified, and that unlike those patriots who die in the last ditch he and his whole host have perished in *the first*. [56]

The beaten candidate had gone to New York before the election. Learning the outcome there, he preserved a stoic exterior. He had not really expected to win. Rather, his object was to show that there was a sizable number of persons who behaved without regard to personal convenience. Many of his oldest acquaintances had told him that he would be misunderstood by all except a few of his closest friends, but he was not to be deterred. Peace of mind and "entire self-approval" were all he desired, come what may. He began to pay the price for these elusive pleasures immediately. The Five of Clubs, that source of much personal delight, subjected to intense strains of political pressures, had begun to show signs of

[54] *The Liberator,* XVI, 46 (Nov. 13, 1846).
[55] Lincoln to Winthrop, Nov. 9, 1846, Winthrop Papers, XXXIV, 124.
[56] Kennedy to Winthrop, Nov. 15, 1846, Winthrop Papers, XXXIV, 125.

dissolution. Hillard was drawing away from the others. However, one renegade did not matter. There was still Sumner whom Howe longed to see so that he could comfort him, "for I know you are sorely stricken [by the bitterness of the campaign], & that you have not such means of defence as I have; you are thinner skinned, & you have not a wife & babies, more shame to you!" [57]

VI

During 1847 the Conscience Whigs remained with the main body, in the forlorn hope of bringing the others to their way of thinking. But the gulf grew wider. Howe became more impatient than ever with the mealy-mouthed sentiments of timid clergymen and others who preached submission to evil laws merely because of their existence.

Render to Caesar the things that are Caesars! [he snorted to Sumner], Aye, had I been a Jew I would have done so, — & rendered him defiance! opposition & *war,* — war to the knife, while a roman eagle floated over my country. "Government must be regarded as a divine institution"! — aye, & so must right & justice be regarded as divine Institutions; older, more sacred, more imperative; and when they clash — let the first be as the potsherd against the granite! [58]

To him there could be no further compromising with expediency. He felt that one must cease to look for precedents for rules of action, and turn to a heart cleansed of evil passions for guidance. With the arrival of 1848, a presidential year, he cried out in an agony of despair for a man who feared neither God, man, nor devil, but loved and trusted the first so much as to fear only what hid Truth. [59]

The others of the circle also stepped up their activities. In the spring of that year Mann joined Howe and Sumner in political antislavery when, upon the death of John Quincy Adams, he ran for the vacant congressional seat. The benevolent educator hated to leave his post; his work was still unfinished, but there was a

[57] Howe to Sumner, Nov. 9, 1846, Howe Papers, Houghton.
[58] Howe to Sumner, March, n.d., 1847, Howe Papers, Houghton.
[59] Howe to Mann, undated, 1848, Howe Papers, Houghton.

greater and more urgent need whose demands he could no longer ignore. One by one the reformers were being forced to curtail their interests in order to concentrate on one movement. Such was the tragic course of abolition.

Throughout that spring both major parties were in the throes of disorganization, the Democrats no less than the Whigs. The Barnburner faction among the Democrats stumped for the selection of former President Van Buren, who had been cheated out of the nomination four years before, they held, while the Whigs were being railroaded into naming Zachary Taylor, the slaveholding non-voting hero of the recent war. Howe, lost in the maze of intrigue, was unable to follow all that went on, but what he did understand dismayed him. He knew only that the Whigs were being sold out. Still, try as the politicians might, he was sure that "the great cause of humanity must make progress." [60] Optimism dies hard when it becomes the warp and woof of one's intellectual makeup.

That insufferable voice of conscience, the *Whig,* whose editorials bore the burns of Sumner's acid pen, called for the reconstruction of parties, since the Slave Power ruled the old ones:

It is time that the lines be now distinctly drawn all over the United States. We care not how soon the banner of Liberty be widely and proudly thrown to the winds, and on it shall be inscribed in letters of living light the words, "No compromise with the Slave power!" We care not how soon, the different sections of the people of the Free States, who are striving for a common object, be called together under one common fold. Democrat, Whig, Liberty man, native or foreign American, names are to us as nothing. — The issue *shall* be Freedom or Slavery. There is a will in God's providence which no human power can resist. Let it come. Let it come. — For our own part, humble as may be our agency in the business, one thing is certain,

IN THIS CAUSE, WE KNOW NOT THE WORD, SURRENDER.[61]

The Philadelphia convention was the last act in the tragedy. In the opportunistic selection of Taylor, the Conscience Whigs would

[60] Howe to Mann, June 9, 1848, Howe Papers, Houghton.
[61] *Boston Whig,* June 6, 1848.

not acquiesce. The effort of the regular party leaders to gain their support, by offering Abbott Lawrence the second position, failed. Charles Allen, of Worcester, speaking for his group, rejected the compromise.

> You have put one ounce too much upon the strong back of Northern endurance [he told the throng]. You have even presumed that the State, which led on the first revolution for liberty, will now desert that cause for the miserable boon of the Vice Presidency. Sir, MASSACHUSETTS WILL SPURN THE BRIBE.[62]

With these words, he led his delegation out of the hall. To Whig antislavery men, the fraud was consummated; their old party was no longer in existence. "No bale of goods was ever more palpably sold," cried out the *Whig* in disgust. The Conscience Whigs, seceding, issued a call for an independent convention to be held in Worcester later that month.[63]

Moral fervor was the only guiding force of the rebels. Relieved that they had at last taken the plunge and broken their old connection, the *Whig* expressed their feelings when it proclaimed, "We now sail on an open sea. 'Free Soil, Free Labor, Free Speech,' shall be the motto on our flag, and free and honest men shall be our companions. . . ."[64] Taking their name from this slogan which was being quoted throughout the North, antislavery men were now becoming known as Free-Soilers.[65]

Howe, of course, went along with all these developments, as did most of his friends, except for Horace Mann, who for a while kept his old affiliation. Orthodox, bigoted, illiberal elements were now in possession of the Whigs, Howe wrote. He was through with them. They had sold out the North, were false to high principle,

---

[62] *Boston Whig,* June 13, 1848.

[63] *Boston Whig,* June 10, 1848.

[64] *Boston Whig,* June 17, 1848. The slogan quoted was from the Herkimer Platform, October 1847: "Free Trade, Free Labor, Free Soil, Free Speech, and Free Men." Quoted in Arthur M. Schlesinger, Jr., *The Age of Jackson* (Boston, 1945), p. 461.

[65] The author regrets not having been able to discover where the term was first used.

and had betrayed humanity. It was futile to trust them any longer.[66]

Old Whiggery belittled the Free-Soilers. This was not the first time that that faction had tried to overthrow a regular nomination, the *Advertiser* said, but their machinations would have little effect.[67]

The Democrats, in the meantime, had alienated the Barnburners by again riding roughshod over Van Buren to choose Lewis Cass, a flat, colorless politician of undistinguished record and no promise. Both organizations were now ruptured. A process of new partisan alignments, the greatest shakeup in American political history, not to end until 1860, was in its preliminary stages.

Howe served as one of the vice-presidents of the independent convention which met on June 28. In tempestuous sessions the nominations of both major parties were denounced. Allen and Wilson delivered fiery orations, while Sumner read a letter from the absent Palfrey. In the afternoon, Joshua R. Giddings, the extremist Ohio Congressman, addressed the assemblage.[68] After concurring in the resolves of an Ohio body to hold a general meeting at Buffalo on August 9 to nominate a national ticket, they appointed a state committee and adjourned.[69] The *Advertiser* was relieved. At first it had feared (it said) that the conclave presaged a real threat, but now it saw it was merely a gathering of the same old "malcontents of all classes." [70]

Not a delegate himself to the Buffalo convention, Howe learned everything from Sumner who attended as an observer. Martin Van Buren was nominated for President, and Charles Francis Adams as his running mate on a platform of freedom. The Free-Soil party, an amalgam of Locofoco Democrats and antislavery Whigs, now stood forth as a challenger to the two old "corrupt" parties of "temporizing and compromise." The campaign was on in earnest. The Whig Free-Soilers, swallowing their ancient dislike for Van Buren, threw themselves passionately into the fight. Garrison nat-

---

[66] Howe to Mann, June 23, 1848, *New England Quarterly*, XVI, 3 (Sept. 1943), 481.

[67] *Boston Advertiser*, June 20, 1848.

[68] *Boston Whig*, June 29, 1848.

[69] *Boston Whig*, June 30, July 1, 1848.

[70] *Boston Advertiser*, June 30, 1848.

urally took some of the credit for the creation of the new movement. Hailing the rebellion with joy, he offered to do what he could to help the movement, while contradicting himself, he refused to work with the members. He could not acknowledge them as in the van of abolitionism, since they sought only to prevent the expansion of an evil, not its extinction.[71]

The outcome was never in doubt. The entry of a third party had guaranteed Whig success, since the Democrats lost more from the defections. But the Free-Soilers carried on as if they had a chance. Howe and Sumner were in the thick of the contest. On August 22 Howe was again one of many vice-presidents at a Faneuil Hall rally at which Sumner presided.[72] They also served as delegates to the state convention in September. Howe in addition was active in ward and district councils.[73] In October he delivered a fighting address while serving as chairman of a meeting. America was going against the trend of the world, he remarked. During the first half of the century slavery had been declining while human freedom progressed everywhere else. Only at home was human servitude growing stronger.[74]

The doctor also headed the committee which nominated Sumner for Congress, and this time the slowly maturing politician, though still timorous, consented. A "political crisis has come," he pontificated, "which calls upon every man to forego his personal wishes, without regard to resolutions formed under circumstances totally different." [75] It had taken him two years to learn that he should cease his prating of duty to others and begin to meet its obligations himself. There was nothing for him to lose since he had no chance of winning anyhow.

Running second in Massachusetts, the Free-Soilers made a remarkable showing for a new party in its first campaign.[76] Their vote

[71] *The Liberator,* XVIII, 32 (Aug. 11, 1848).

[72] *Boston Daily Republican* (the *Whig* had changed its name since it was no longer a Whig organ), Aug. 23, 1848.

[73] *Boston Daily Republican,* Aug. 31, Sept. 13 and 19, 1848.

[74] *Boston Daily Republican,* Oct. 9, 1848. The *Chronotype* of the same date has further extracts.

[75] *Boston Daily Republican,* Oct. 26, Oct. 28, 1848.

[76] *Boston Advertiser,* Nov. 9, and 16, 1848.

combined with that of the Democrats was a majority of the ballots cast. Though its leaders were primarily former Whigs, by no means was it a dissident wing, but a balanced party that had drawn almost equally from the two older ones. William Gleason Bean, who has investigated the matter closely, estimates that 48 per cent of the Free-Soil vote came from the Democrats.[77]

VII

Dissension was rife among Free-Soilers as events forced them into coalition with the Democrats. One faction, led by Charles Francis Adams, John Gorham Palfrey, Stephen C. Phillips, and Richard Henry Dana, Jr., repelled by the Locofoco program of anti-monopoly and anti-corporation, refused to consider such a move. A larger segment, headed by Wilson, Allen, and Francis W. Bird, was willing to coöperate with such Democrats as George S. Boutwell and Robert Rantoul, Jr., for the sake of fusing a new antislavery alignment. During 1849, the parties drew closer together.

The passage of the Compromise of 1850 was just the fillip needed to complete the process. After a violent intra-party struggle, Wilson seized control from Adams. Shortly thereafter he reached a working agreement with the Democrats, the details of which were kept secret for some months.[78]

Howe, just returned from a summer in Europe, viewed these developments with misgivings. His home was the frequent scene of party meetings, and he was at first in the defeated faction.[79] He doubted the morality of the move. Although he realized the ends were desirable, he had misgivings about the means being taken to achieve them.[80] To him, the coalition was a correspondence with the Devil, "a bad thing done that a good thing might come out of it. . . ."[81] Howe always showed an obtuseness in political maneu-

---

[77] William Gleason Bean, "Party Transformation in Massachusetts with Special Reference to the Antecedents of Republicanism, 1848–1860" (Ms. thesis in Harvard University Library, 1922), p. 32.

[78] Bean, "Party Transformation in Massachusetts," pp. 34–37; 56.

[79] Howe to Sumner, Jan. (n.d.) 1850, Howe Papers, Houghton.

[80] Howe to Sumner, no date but undoubtedly late 1850, Howe Papers, Houghton.

[81] Howe to Mann, Dec. 29, 1850, Howe Papers, Houghton.

vering which proved conclusively that he should never have entered upon such activities. He had no understanding of the practical requirements of politicians, nor of the need for compromise and coöperation. Of course he was not alone. Others refused to hide their disgust also. A number of Middlesex County Free-Soilers, among them Samuel Hoar, and Dana, published a blistering statement in the *Advertiser*.[82] Sumner, with a greater awareness of the exigencies of politics, favored the coalition, but then he stood to gain more than anyone else from it.

A Senate seat fell vacant in 1850 when Daniel Webster became Secretary of State in Fillmore's cabinet.[83] Winthrop was appointed to fill out the remainder of the term, much to the Free-Soilers' disgust.[84] Had this happened earlier, Winthrop would easily have secured election in his own right at the next meeting of the legislature as required by law, and the full term following, but conditions had changed. Though he had borne himself well, having served as Speaker of the House in the Thirtieth Congress, the erstwhile Conscience Whigs of 1846 hated him more violently than ever, and were prepared to do anything to block his accession to a six-year term.

The coalition furnished just such an opportunity. At the fall elections it gained a majority in the legislature which was to make the selection. In caucuses held before the General Court convened, the two parties agreed to divide the offices between them, the Democrats to have the Governorship, the Speakership, a majority of

---

[82] *Boston Advertiser*, Oct. 12, 1850.

[83] Massachusetts antislavery men had always hoped that Webster would lead their movement, but in each instance he had flouted them by aligning himself with the Whigs. It was not until his Seventh of March speech, favoring compromise, that they turned against him irrevocably. Whittier of course wrote "Ichabod," but even Longfellow was bitter towards him, blaming him for having wrecked the Whig party, and for all the defeats it suffered thereafter. [Samuel Longfellow, *Henry Wadsworth Longfellow*, II, 194.] To Howe, Webster was never anything but an "immoral, drunken, debauchee." [Howe to Mann, Dec. 29, 1850, Howe Papers, Houghton.] Nourishing his hatred until his dying day over a quarter of a century later, Howe even resented it when in 1865 at the unveiling of a statue to Horace Mann, Governor Andrew eulogized Webster who stood in effigy across the path. [Howe to Andrew, Sept. n.d., 1865, Andrew Papers, MHS.]

[84] Sumner to Howe, July 30, 1850, Sumner Papers, Houghton.

the Council, and the remainder of Webster's term until the expiration of the lame-duck Congress in March (Rantoul took this), while the Free-Soilers were to take the Presidency of the Senate and the long term. It was an ill-kept secret that Sumner was designated for the latter post.

Howe had finally been brought around to a grudging consent of the deal by the efforts of Sumner and others who took him to task. Now that he understood the necessity of carrying Free-Soil principles into local affairs, they had to repeat their lessons with him, "to *unconvince* me," he wrote, "& to prove . . . that it is not necessary to have a free soil Governor or to vote for one." He was dazed by it all. Confused or not, he supported the candidacy because it was Sumner. Still, as he told Mann, "my love for Sumner makes me wish that he could be exalted by something better than a Coalition which I regard as rather iniquitous." [85]

The legislature met in January, with the election of Senator as its major task. The two houses were to vote separately. Anti-coalition Free-Soilers, of whom Palfrey was the leader, tried to undermine the arrangement.[86] But it was from the Democrats that effective opposition came. The fight centered in the House following the Senate's election of Sumner on January 22.[87] Under the leadership of Caleb Cushing of Essex County (later Franklin Pierce's Attorney General), a skilled parliamentarian, a small clique which came to be called the "indomitables" frustrated all attempts at naming Sumner. From mid-January until late April, through twenty-five ballots, they jeopardized his chances.

Howe took the election to heart. Never had he felt so venomous towards any opposition as he did now. "Park St. & Beacon are sweating blood," he wrote Mann, "grant they may sweat to death." [88] His own perspiration was flowing as profusely in his Bromfield

---

[85] Howe to Mann, Dec. 29, 1850, Howe Papers, Houghton.

[86] *Boston Advertiser,* Jan. 6, 1851, published Palfrey's public memorandum. This was later printed separately as *To the Free Soil Members of the General Court of Massachusetts for the Year 1851* (Boston, Jan. 17, 1851).

[87] *Boston Advertiser,* Jan. 23, 1851. Had the chambers voted jointly, Sumner would have been chosen on the first ballot.

[88] Howe to Mann, Jan. 23, 1851, Howe Papers, Houghton.

Street office, a few minutes from the State House. There he spent most of his time during these weeks, planning strategy with other party leaders, and writing fiery articles for the *Commonwealth,* the new Free-Soil journal.[89]

Howe could only marvel at Sumner, who all through the campaign made a fetish of appearing unconcerned as he went about his daily affairs. Let his managers probe deeply, the candidate wrote, "they would see that other & keener sensibilities" moved him.[90] Nor would he sacrifice "any of his high principles," wrote Howe. "He is a rare & noble spirit; too good for the political *ring,*" Howe concluded.[91]

Nevertheless, Sumner had to be elected. All the Free-Soilers needed was five indefatigable workers to carry him through.[92] Howe became one of them. Overcoming his repugnance for electioneering, he put in an appearance at the State House. Yet he could never forget the arrangement that had brought about the situation, and the fact that he had to collaborate with pro-slavery men. What a disreputable crew he found them, faithless and insincere. Now that George S. Boutwell had become Governor, Howe doubted not that he was trying to worm his way out of the agreement, but the Free-Soilers would force him to keep his word. "We are manufacturing that pressure, & by the Jingoes we'll squeeze him tight but he shall do it," Howe swore.[93]

Both sides resorted to desperate measures to maintain their vote. Sumner's men tried unsuccessfully to bring an insane member, committed to Worcester, to his seat.[94] Winthrop's supporters were equally unethical. Fearful that the Free-Soil candidate would

---

[89] Howe to Sumner, March 1851, Howe Papers, Houghton, mentions some articles he had written for it.

[90] Sumner to Howe, Feb. 5, 1851, Sumner Papers, Houghton. His letters to Mann, e.g., Feb. 10, 1851, show how closely and objectively he tried to follow developments, even going so far as to speak of himself in the third person as the Free-Soil candidate.

[91] Howe to Mann, Dec. 29, 1850, Howe Papers, Houghton.

[92] Howe to Mann, Jan. 23, 1851, Howe Papers, Houghton.

[93] Howe to Mann, Feb. 6, 1851, Howe Papers, Houghton.

[94] Amos A. Lawrence to Samuel A. Eliot, Feb. 10, 1851, A. A. Lawrence Papers, I, 262, MHS.

probably be elected by default if too many Whigs returned home to attend to their own affairs during the prolonged session, Amos A. Lawrence proposed a fund to guarantee their business losses up to $3000.[95] As he made his contribution of $200, he piously insisted that the money was not to be used "for influencing any member in an improper manner." [96] Whether used improperly or not, this slush fund did yeoman duty for the remainder of the campaign, and undoubtedly added to its length. At critical moments, money flowed freely to keep Whig battle lines in order.[97]

As the deadlock continued, and new names were proposed, Sumner suggested that his name be removed.[98] Howe grew steadily more disturbed as he learned of new plots. Certain that by working alone the Free-Soilers could have captured the state within five years, he railed against the coalition. "[Y]et I have come to wish & pray that Sumner may be elected to the Senate," he wrote Mann, "because no man now eligible here can so well represent the anti-slavery *sentiment* of the North as he." [99] Number 20 Bromfield Street was like a "smoke-filled room" of a later day. All had done what they could, and so far to no avail.

Yet, victory lay closer than Howe thought. The last great push got under way on April 21, when polls of the House were scheduled daily. The opposition showed signs of weakening, as, through strategic absences (probably purposeful), Sumner's vote approached a majority.[100] There was temporary excitement on the twenty-third when rumors of a definite election were spread, but a careful recount showed one vote lacking. That day the House stayed in session eleven hours.[101]

[95] Lawrence to William Appleton, Feb. 10, 1851, A. A. Lawrence Papers, I, 261.

[96] Lawrence to Ezra Lincoln, Feb. 10, 1851, A. A. Lawrence Papers, I, 263.

[97] Memorandum of money to pay for the expense of sending for members to vote against Sumner's election, March 14, 1851, A. A. Lawrence Papers, I, 296–297; Ezra Lincoln to Lawrence, April 24, 1851, A. A. Lawrence Papers, IX, 25, speaks of the need for another $300.

[98] Sumner to Wilson, Feb. 22, 1851, printed in the *Commonwealth,* April 26, 1851. Wilson strategically withheld this letter until after the election.

[99] Howe to Mann, April (n.d.) 1851, Howe Papers, Houghton.

[100] Everett to Mrs. H. A. Wise, April 24, 1851, Everett Papers, MHS.

[101] *Boston Advertiser,* April 24, 1851.

The atmosphere was tense on the twenty-fourth as the clerks began the twenty-fifth ballot. This time Sumner was two votes short. At 12:40 P.M., the legislators began voting again. At 2:14, the Speaker announced the results. Of 384 votes cast, and with 193 needed for election, the Free-Soil candidate had received exactly that number. The battle was over. The packed galleries heard the news with mixed feelings. Those who attempted applause and cheers were quickly suppressed.[102]

While Whigs and "indomitables" mourned the shame that had befallen the commonwealth,[103] the Free-Soilers rejoiced at their success. Parker expressed Howe's feelings too, as he congratulated the new Senator. He recalled that Sumner had once claimed to be in *"Morals* not in Politics. Now I hope you will show that you are still in Morals *although* in Politics. I hope you will be *the Senator with a Conscience."* [104] The clergyman's satisfaction would have been infinitely enhanced could he have known how fully his hopes were to be met.

As the convening date of Congress drew near, the thought of Sumner's departure weighed heavily on Howe. Already he had begun to feel lonely. He knew it meant the divergence of their paths, and the ending of their old relationship:

[I]t makes me sad to think I shall no longer have the *power* when I have the will, to get *near* you for comfort & sympathy when I am sad. It is most true that we find comfort & pleasure in mere personal propinquity to those we love, whether there are any words of sympathy exchanged or not.

I can hardly *realise* that you are to go next week. . . .[105]

Sumner sensed it too. Late in November the reluctant statesman wept uncontrollably, "like a child," as he parted from his mother and sister, Longfellow, and Howe. He could not guess what lay ahead,

---

[102] *Boston Advertiser,* April 25, 1851.

[103] See the editorials in the *Courier* and the *Post* for April 25, 1851, as well as Winthrop's letter to Everett, May 21, 1851, Everett Papers, MHS.

[104] Parker to Sumner, April 26, 1851, Parker Letterbook 6, p. 233, MHS. There are no Howe letters available on this point.

[105] Howe to Sumner, Nov. (n.d.) 1851, Howe Papers, Houghton.

but I know that I now move away from those who have been more than brothers to me & I feel pained by the thought that we may never more meet each other as in times past. My soul is wrong, & my eyes are now bleared with tears. God bless you ever & ever, my noble, well-tried, & eternally dear friend. Be happy, & think kindly of me.[106]

With that, Sumner stepped on to the national stage, to begin one of the most distinguished, as well as controversial, careers in the history of the Senate. The retiring scholar, whom certain persons had found warm, kind, and lovable, had become a pushing, ranting monolith, possessed by the demon of one idea. At home, Howe waited anxiously for news of his reception in Washington, certain that "it will be kind at first; I know it will be hereafter, for you will win over the hardest devil of them all at last." [107] How little Howe understood the passions of his time, and what they could do to the souls of men!

[106] Sumner to Howe, Nov. 26, 1851, Sumner Papers, Houghton.
[107] Howe to Sumner, Dec. 3, 1851, Howe Papers, Houghton.

XII

The Ferment of Abolition

As the pace of abolition accelerated, Howe spent an increasing proportion of his time on antislavery activity. Though all was decaying, and few things were certain, he kept on unwaveringly in his devotion to the cause in whose name he could refuse no demands.

I

The demise of the *Republican* as a daily in 1849, though its semi-weekly edition remained, left the Free-Soilers without an organ to fight the battles that loomed ahead.[1] In the fall of 1850, with the coalition a fact and the hard-fought campaign to elect Sumner impending, the need for a party paper became more pressing. Acting quickly, the party raised a fund which was turned over to a four-man board of trustees, headed by Howe.[2] A new journal, tentatively called the *Compass* (no doubt since it was to point constantly toward the truth), quickly took shape. Howe worked feverishly, neglecting even his sleep. In his letters he speaks as if it took only four days to arrange everything, but this sounds fantastic.[3]

Within a short period the trustees bought up the *Emancipator and Republican*, the *Semi-Weekly Republican*, and the *Chronotype*,

[1] The Boston *Directory* for 1850 lists the *Republican* as a daily, but no library according to Gregory's *Union List of Newspapers* has it after 1849, only the semi-weekly.

[2] The others were William Jackson, Francis W. Bird, and John P. Jewett.

[3] Howe to Mann, Feb. 6, 1851, Howe Papers, Houghton.

Elizur Wright's struggling independent sheet, Wright agreeing to go along as subeditor. Original plans called for Palfrey to serve as editor-in-chief, but on December 28, just three days before publication began, he ruined his chances by issuing his circular against the coalition.

In the name of the trustees, Howe wrote the prospectus of the new paper. Although designed to set forth Free-Soil views, it would not be the "bond-servant of any cause, or party, except that of Freedom, Truth, and Humanity. THE POLE STAR toward which it will ever point will be THE RIGHT; but the right of ALL." There was to be at least one journal that would "recognize the obligation of Law, the necessity of Order, and the duty of Peace and Good Will to men." [4] This was a brave program, but Howe meant every word of it. With a sufficient financial reserve to maintain the new venture until it was self-supporting (it was hoped), and the promise of assistance from such talented pen wielders as Wright, Adams, Palfrey, and Richard Hildreth, but still editorless, the paper, now rechristened the *Commonwealth* ("a name proud in English liberty"), boldly appeared with the New Year to carry on in the cause of freedom. [5]

From its first issue it left no doubt as to its course. In a lead editorial (which to this author bears unmistakably the imprint of Howe's forceful style) it recounted the Slave Power's subversion of the Constitution "to purposes hostile to the freedom of the citizen, to the fair fame of the nation, and the rights of man. . . ." However the author (or authors) was an optimist, for he was sure that, try as the South might, human progress, the "law of society" could not be forever restricted. "Liberty is never in extreme peril, so long as its friends are true." The *Commonwealth* intended to restore the Union to the true theory of government and assert the claim of truth and righteousness in public affairs. [6]

Boston's journalistic circles greeted their new colleague with ill-humor. The *Advertiser,* noting its editorial, spoke balefully of the

---

[4] The *Commonwealth,* Jan. 1, 1851.
[5] Howe to Mann, Dec. 29, 1850, Howe Papers, Houghton, has all the background material on the organization.
[6] The *Commonwealth,* Jan. 1, 1851.

prospects of any paper that began "with such a perversion of the truth of history."[7] The question of the *Commonwealth*'s management was an intriguing problem. The *Advertiser* told its readers that Palfrey and Wright were connected with it, while the *Atlas* stated flatly that Palfrey had been in charge for the first two days before giving up, "probably from disgust."[8]

Though the awkwardness of the situation required a definite solution, the trustees remained in complete charge until late in March, when a regular publisher took over the business management, and Wright and Francis W. Bird the editorial side.[9] In April they began the publication of an evening edition.[10] A new shakeup in June brought in a different publisher, while Palfrey's name went on the masthead as contributing editor.[11] During its first two years there was a monotonous turnover in the management. Some of the changes were carried through with bitterness as in May 1852, when Elizur Wright was finally eased out and Charles List, an abolitionist lawyer, hitherto an assistant editor, succeeded.[12]

In December of that year the trustees installed J. D. Baldwin (his full name was never printed) as publisher, business manager, and part-time editor.[13] Howe, returning to his old love, journalism, as political editor, took over the task of keeping the paper stiffly on the antislavery track.[14] To him the *Commonwealth* was a sacred property. "Of one thing be sure," he told Sumner, "it shall not if I can help it be made the instrument of wire pullers & office hunters. If it must go down it shall be with the antislavery flag nailed to the mast."[15] Julia aided her husband in the business.

[7] *Boston Advertiser*, Jan. 3, 1851.

[8] *Boston Advertiser*, Jan. 2; *Boston Atlas*, Jan. 6, 1851.

[9] The *Commonwealth*, March 25, 1851. Wright served as general editor, and Bird as political.

[10] The *Commonwealth*, April 8, 1851.

[11] The *Commonwealth*, June 16, 1851.

[12] The *Commonwealth*, May 24, 1852. Two days later List said Wright's salary and his bad business habits constituted a serious drain on the paper's resources. Howe never liked his work either, Howe to Mann, Feb. 18, 1851, Howe Papers, Houghton.

[13] The *Commonwealth*, Dec. 20, 1852.

[14] Howe to Sumner, Jan. 1, 1853, Howe Papers, Houghton.

[15] Howe to Sumner, Dec. 24 (year missing, probably 1852, although it is catalogued as 1851), Howe Papers, Houghton.

We began our work together every morning [she wrote in her *Reminiscences*], — he supervising and supplying the political department of the paper, I doing what I could in the way of social and literary criticism. Among my contributions to the work were a series of notices of Dr. Holmes's Lowell lectures on the English poets, and a paper on Mrs. Stowe and George Sand.[16]

For a salary of $500, Howe contributed "The Spirit of the Press," a compilation of excerpts from Boston's morning journals.[17] He undertook his new chore with some personal misgivings, he said, since he had so many other tasks, but when he reflected upon the purity of his motives, to "appeal to & strengthen what [is] good & high" in his readers, he decided that he could add it. Howe was in one of his sanctimonious moods. He loved the work. For almost twenty years, since the old days on the *New England Magazine,* he had "hankered" for another try at journalism; this was it, and he made the most of the opportunity. It was no imposition. He fitted the article into his schedule with no difficulty. By ten each morning, he sent it off, and had the rest of the day free to attend to his students and other things.

Since few persons thought of the saintly Dr. Howe as the editor of an extremist newspaper, they expressed themselves freely about his work. Much to his surprise, he found that he was giving more satisfaction than he had any idea of. Again grandiose views began to fill his head as he thought of himself the proprietor of a full-fledged daily, the colleague of Buckingham of the *Courier,* and Nathan Hale of the *Advertiser.* He even proposed to buy nine-sixteenths of the paper.[18]

These deals fell through, and sometime in the spring he dropped his editorial work.[19] After April 21, 1853, the "Spirit of the Press" ceased to appear regularly, although it continued sporadically for

---

[16] J. W. Howe, *Reminiscences,* p. 253.

[17] J. W. Howe to Annie Mailliard, Feb. 25, 1853, Howe Papers, Houghton. A column of this title had been appearing at odd intervals since early 1851. Although anonymously prepared, it is conceivable that he had been doing it all along.

[18] Howe to Sumner, Jan. 16 and Feb. 14, 1853, Howe Papers, Houghton.

[19] Late in March Sumner commented on Howe's work on the *Commonwealth,* consequently this author assumes Howe did it until it ceased its daily appearance. Sumner to Parker, March 28, 1853, Parker Letterbook 10, p. 264, MHS.

several months. Under Howe's hand, it was a rather lively column, much more than an unconnected summary of newspaper opinion as one might be led to think from the description given here. It occasionally took on the character of a commentary on current affairs. Howe in these moments wrote on an elevated plane.[20] But in most cases he made short shrift of the "Hunker" press, usually with a snide remark for each one. Witness his devastating characterization of the *Journal*, "the ancient cold water and moral gruel paper." [21]

During most of its existence the *Commonwealth* was in precarious financial straits, although during its first summer Elizur Wright reported it as meeting its expenses.[22] This was a rare situation. The paper was not ordinarily self-supporting. In October 1852 it complained that it did not get as many advertisements as its rivals.[23] Since it had a smaller page, only six columns to the *Advertiser*'s seven, it could hardly have had the same revenue, though to this author it looks as if the same proportion of its space was devoted to commercial notices as in the others. On November 1 it switched to a smaller type face for its ads, so as to squeeze more of them in. Things looked up slightly during Howe's editorship when he reported that in addition to a circulation of 5000, there was actually a balance of $1000 to its account.[24] Conditions took a turn for the worse in 1854, when it began losing steadily at the rate of $50 a week. The trustees, taking over again, feared they might have to cease publication. In a last desperate effort they set out to raise $1500 which they hoped would tide them over until January.[25] Whether they raised the sum or not is impossible to say, but whatever they did obtain was insufficient to keep the poor "feeble lamp" alive beyond September. Much to Howe's grief, the *Commonwealth*

---

[20] See, for example, the *Commonwealth*, Jan. 17, 1853. A fuller discussion of his views on politics appears in the next section.

[21] The *Commonwealth*, March 5, 1853. Howe used the term "Hunker" frequently in his letters of these years apparently to mean everyone with whose politics he did not agree, Whigs and Democrats both. Originally it was a faction of the Democratic party in New York opposed to the Barnburners.

[22] Wright to brothers and sisters, July 23, 1851, Wright Papers, BPL.

[23] The *Commonwealth*, Oct. 28, 1852.

[24] Howe to Sumner, Feb. 14, 1851, Howe Papers, Houghton.

[25] Howe to Sumner, July 24, 1854, Howe Papers, Houghton.

printed its last edition on the twenty-first, having been sold to Williams, Morse and Company who merged it with a new evening offering, the *Telegraph*.[26]

So died the last Free-Soil organ in Boston. Its disappearance was all to the good. Apart from its editorial policy, it had little to offer its readers. At a time when no newspaper in the city made any attempt at completeness, its coverage of domestic news was markedly spotty and slanted, while foreign developments received barely any notice. Without any dramatic or other artistic criticism, its literary publishing was confined to pirated Dickens novels and excerpts from *Uncle Tom's Cabin*.

During the *Commonwealth*'s entire existence of over three and a half years, the tone of its articles was exceedingly offensive. There was no depth of vulgarity and vituperation to which its writers would not descend to pillory the opposition. But it struck a new low for any newspaper this author has ever examined in its story of the death of Caleb Cushing's sister towards the close of the senatorial election. It described the leader of the indomitables as having hurried his sister into the grave and hurrying back to Boston to lead the fight against Sumner, without having observed a proper period of mourning.[27] One can easily see that, had the miscreant been a coalitionist, the Free-Soilers would have tearfully commiserated with the bereaved figure, who, manfully controlling his grief, had obeyed the call to duty.

Howe's dear friend Professor Felton became so outraged at attacks of this sort that he canceled his subscription. Not an abolitionist to begin with, already growing distant from his old associates, he had taken the paper only because he thought Palfrey was to be editor, but when he read its slanderous articles written in a tone of "universal vulgarity, violence and insolence," in particular an attack on Edward Everett, he decided "it was unfit to be seen on the table of a gentleman." [28] Anyone who has examined a file of the paper can

---

[26] The *Commonwealth*, Sept. 21, 1854.

[27] The *Commonwealth*, April 24, 1851.

[28] Felton to Howe, April 2, 1851, Howe Papers, Houghton. Everett naturally was a favorite Free-Soil target. The man who had taught many of them, and had aided others, for example, Howe, had sunken to a low state in their estimation by the

understand his point. Apparently even those devoted to stamping out slavery were unable to stand the paper either. To the historian, the *Commonwealth* is at best a source of limited value, merely as the spokesman of an idea. Any history of the period based on that as its chief source would be completely unreliable.

II

Howe picked his way carefully through the disorderly path of politics in the fifties. More than ever he preached no compromise with principle. Viewing the situation as a private citizen, he found matters in an appalling state.[29] There was no devotion to principle anywhere; men in public life, seeking only the approbation of their constituents, substituted public opinion for conscience.[30] Too few, he said, trusted the maxim, "Do the will of God, that is, do the right, though the heavens threaten to fall and crush you." The evil at the root of the disorder in political life, he felt, was the separation of politics from morals. People had ceased to submit men and programs to religious tests, though they often applied the "sectarian test, but this is no more like true religion, than the crucifix is like Christ." (Nowhere does he explain what this "true religion" is, but from the way he uses it, he apparently means "natural law," a concept dear to the hearts of enlightened nineteenth-century liberals.) Men deficient in this quality he found occupying the most elevated pulpits in the land, from which they preached "not the high law of God, — not the inflexible rules of morality, — not the eternal principles of right, — but merely the lower law of man, — the pliant doctrines of expediency, — and the temporary considerations of profit or loss." [31]

During the election of 1852, following true religion as his guide, he found he could vote for neither of the major party candidates,

---

fifties. The *Commonwealth* pictured him as a weak cringing figure, "abject before the bullies of the slave power," a cold rhetorician incapable of glowing enthusiasm for liberty. *Commonwealth*, March 23 and 25, 1854.

[29] The description of the political background in this section comes from Bean, "Party Transformation in Massachusetts," pp. 120–311.

[30] Howe to Sumner, Aug. 4, 1852, Howe Papers, Houghton.

[31] "The Spirit of the Press," the *Commonwealth*, Jan. 17, 1853.

neither the Whig Winfield Scott, nor the Democrat Franklin Pierce. His course was clear to him,

to go for the abstract right & disregard the consequences. We must teach all parties that there are some men (& they [are] becoming more numerous) who will not be bought & sold & handed over by any conventions.

. . . . Why is it deemed necessary to go with great parties, & to twist principles until they all but break, — why but because there are so few men who will be inflexible! Let me make those few more and all will be right.[32]

He of course supported John P. Hale, the Free Democrat candidate for President.

To none was Howe more severe in applying these standards than to his closest friends. Even Horace Mann could not escape the doctor's wrath when that keeper of the conscience suspected a slight deviation from rectitude. Though Mann, now a Congressman, was at last a Free-Soiler, he suffered an attack so severe as to cause him to swear before Heaven that he had acted according to conscience. He at least called Howe's attention to the serious defect in his character we have long ago seen, namely, an unwillingness to admit that others could honestly differ with him.[33]

But, of course, the most brazen example of expediency and unprincipled political maneuvering which lately had disgraced the political scene was the Free-Soil-Democratic coalition which lasted through 1852, although it had begun to show cracks its first year. In between expressions of revulsion, Howe maintained that the arrangement was at best a shotgun wedding. He urged his party to break away. They had been the "bottle holders" of the Democrats long enough, and he was sure that before long the partners must fight each other. He preferred the Whigs, certain that "when their tyrant and oppressor — the lord & master of their bodies & souls — Black Dan — is dead politically or corporeally — if it happens soon — they will be better allies than the Dem's." [34]

[32] Howe to Sumner, July 2, 1852, Howe Papers, Houghton.
[33] Mann to Howe, Feb. 22, 1850, *New England Quarterly*, XII, 4 (Dec. 1939), 740.
[34] Howe to Sumner, Dec. 12, 1851, Howe Papers, Houghton.

In the meantime things looked black. After Sumner's election and some excitement about fugitive slaves had died down, abolition ceased to hold interest for most people.[35] There was very little in the newspapers about slavery. Not even the *Commonwealth* could drum up concern. Howe, looking about him, saw his beloved Boston, under "Hunker" control, comfortably relax into conservatism. Fervently he hoped for the speedy reaction that he felt was sure to come.[36] His native city had become so distasteful to him that he hated the thought of growing old there. So great was its self-conceit and intolerance, that to him it was truly a pitiful place. For once his optimism deserted him; he thought things would never get any better there. The incoming flood of Irish immigrants, he noted with disgust, were crowding out the Americans. At first he had been indulgent toward them, but now he was in doubt as to the reception they should have:

So long as these poor creatures came to us only fast enough to be leavened by the little virtue there was in us so long our [arms] welcomed them; but if they are to pull us down instead of our pulling them up we may well cry hold off! However — I suppose this evil is only local: as a whole the process may be a good one for humanity; & we have no right to partition off Gods earth, & say here shall be Saxon, & here shall *not* be Celt.[37]

Poor Chev, even the refuge of nativism, in which many abolitionists were beginning to find comfort, was closed to him.

The Whigs in regaining control of the state at the 1852 election dealt a critical blow to the coalition, but the partners still stuck together. To Howe this was the last straw. The Free-Soilers, he cried, were following the lead of the Democrats. His heart bade him make a clean break, declare open war, appeal to the "Conscience Whigs," the core of the party, and "march out of the ranks with a banner of our own." [38] The Hunkers now in power would shortly

[35] See next section on fugitive slaves.
[36] Howe to Sumner, Dec. 16, 1851, Howe Papers, Houghton.
[37] Howe to Mann, May 30, 1852, Howe Papers, Houghton.
[38] Howe to Sumner, Jan. 16, 1853, Howe Papers, Houghton.

show their true colors and would cause so violent a reaction as to make the triumph of antislavery all the more sweet.[39]

But conditions did not get better. The Free-Soilers did not gain strength; if anything they were foundering. A one-idea party can subsist only by agitation and Boston was quiet. There were no fugitive slaves to rescue and Kansas had not yet become an issue. As all the other parties decayed, so did theirs. They had even stopped using their old name, having switched to calling themselves occasionally Free Democrats. It was under that banner that John P. Hale ran for President in 1852, and Henry Wilson for Governor the next year.

Though Howe refrained from running for office, he remained active in party activities. In a letter read to the New York convention of Free Democrats he mirrored the instability of the period. Democracy and slavery, he insisted, were incompatible, yet the Democrats supported the latter. "To talk of a slavery supporting democrat is like talking of an honest thief or a truthful liar." He grieved that of all its former high principles the party of Jefferson retained only its name. It was a Janus-like organization. To the East it appeared the spokesman for the oppressed, but elsewhere it supported a frightful tyranny, in proof of which "three millions of witnesses protest before heaven that it is true." [40]

Whig power, lingering on in Massachusetts throughout 1853, although pretty well nonexistent elsewhere, triumphed again at the fall elections.[41] Howe misinterpreted this to mean that people were concerned only with making money, and conservatives would run rampant, while the Slave Power would exult. It seemed to him that the Free-Soilers were scattered and discouraged, with no fight left. Only the Garrisonians, he complained, were keeping up the fight for human freedom. Progress could not be held up forever. Now that Stephen A. Douglas was about to introduce the Kansas-Nebraska Bill, there was need for a stern prophet to awaken mankind. Howe urged Sumner to take advantage of this oppor-

[39] Howe to Sumner, Jan. 30, 1853, Howe Papers, Houghton.
[40] The *Commonwealth*, Oct. 18, 1853.
[41] Bean, "Party Transformation in Massachusetts," p. 180.

tunity, "I wish to God you felt it to be your time & mission to send a blast through the land." He implored the statesman to send encouragement.

> Do not I beseech, wait for, but *make,* — *seize* an opportunity — now while public sentiment is not formed, . . . do you thunder & lighten over the land. For God's sake & man's sake, disregard all punctilios — all ceremonies, — all considerations of a monetary or a conventional nature, & strike for freedom while it is yet time. "The one time"! — every time is the due time: who strikes early, strikes twice.[42]

Howe was premature. Sumner's time was not yet come. Nor were the antislavery men as down and out as he thought. Beaten though they were in one campaign, they could still rally their forces for another try.

All over the nation during 1854 a new spirit of nativism, hostility to foreigners, in particular Irish Catholics, was abroad. From mysterious beginnings the movement grew rapidly until it became one of the major political groups. Nothing could show more powerfully the fluid nature of American politics than the rise of the American party, popularly referred to as the Know-Nothings. The Free-Soilers too were absorbed into the organization. Sensing the possibility of re-grouping the antislavery front, they flocked eagerly to the new standard. Nowhere was it more eagerly welcomed than in Massachusetts, where abolitionists felt especially bitter toward Boston's immigrant classes. Time and again they had seen their program frustrated by the green arrivals, most recently in 1853, when their proposed constitution suffered rejection.[43] They were convinced that the immigrants by these acts had proven themselves undesirable additions to the population.

Henry Wilson led those among the Free-Soilers who felt there were possibilities in nativism. Though the parties did not merge, it was known that he was collaborating closely with Know-Nothings. In November 1854, they scored a shattering victory in their first try at the polls. The new Governor, the disreputable, unprincipled

[42] Howe to Sumner, Jan. 18, and 25, 1854, Howe Papers, Houghton.
[43] George H. Haynes, "The Causes of Know-Nothing Success in Massachusetts," *American Historical Review,* III, 1 (Oct. 1897), 67–82.

Henry J. Gardner, the Lieutenant-Governor, the entire Senate, and most of the House were of that persuasion. In no other state had Know-Nothingism scored so sweeping a success. At one blow the Democrat and Whig parties were removed from the field of serious consideration. Both Haynes and Bean show as well as can be shown that Know-Nothing support stemmed from the Free-Soilers who moved over into the new party practically in a body.[44]

But there were important hold-outs. Howe and his circle had not fallen for a doctrine as opposed to American ideals as the one that temporarily enthralled its followers. He was not chagrined as were many of his friends, but pleased that "two corrupt old organizations" had been undermined irrevocably. "Chaos has come, & out of the confusion better order will arise." He saw too the increasing development of individuality. The prestige of family, standing, respectability, even character (the last only temporarily) were gone. Yet he could not conceive of the survival of nativism. It had performed a great function in having stirred up politics, but would shortly die. Unable to bring himself to vote for any Free-Soiler who had sold himself "to this selfish narrow & inhumane organization," he had scratched out Wilson's name on his ballot.[45]

Henry Wilson, the adroit opportunist, had hitched himself to Know-Nothingism for what he could get out of it, and he got a senatorship. Following Edward Everett's resignation, the legislature elected him to fill out the term. He now had a broader field for his remarkable talents. Wilson, an erstwhile cobbler of Natick, was one of the most skillful manipulators of policy ever to direct the Bay State's affairs. Without the learning or forensic brilliance of his colleague, Sumner, he was many times the senior senator's superior in the handling of men. Wilson was the politician *par excellence* among the abolitionists. He arranged, he schemed, he plotted, he

[44] Bean estimates that 78 per cent of the Free-Soilers voted Know-Nothing in 1854, "Party Transformation in Massachusetts," p. 243.

[45] Howe to Mann, Nov. 14, 1854, Howe Papers, Houghton. Julia summed up the Howe stand more succinctly when she rhymed:

> "We didn't go vote for the know-nothing Mayor,
> A know-nothing's what we cannot bear."

Richards and Elliott, *Julia Ward Howe*, I, 163.

coalesced, he compromised, and even temporized, much to the grief of Howe and his associates, but he got results.[46] Of course Howe could never fathom Wilson's activities. To him the new senator was a renegade.[47]

Howe detested the party of which Wilson had become the leader, nor would he join the "Know Something" lodges that were beginning to spring up as antidotes to the ignorance holding sway. He would never go blindfolded into anything. "The end does not justify the means in this country at least," he wrote Sumner, "where we can speak & act as we will." [48]

Sumner and Parker were with him in this view. Parker was especially critical of the nativist program. Although his ancestors had arrived in America before 1640, he knew that they were not necessarily better than those who had just arrived. The only test of a man should be his character, and he preferred a *"Higher Law* 'Catholic' to a Lower Law 'Protestant,' and a noble man born in Scotland, England, Ireland to a mean man born on Plymouth Rock." [49]

Most antislavery men felt that way too. They could not remain in a party that denied the principles for which they fought, and kept them from meeting the one problem needing solution. Not even Wilson believed in the Know-Nothings' anti-foreignism. The abolitionists began to draw away. In the summer of 1855 they denounced Know-Nothingism, and later that year joined the new Republican party, which spoke as they liked to hear politicians speak.[50]

III

By mid-decade Boston society had completed its split along partisan lines. People took their politics so seriously that members of one group would no longer consort with those of another. Since

[46] Bean, "Party Transformation in Massachusetts," pp. 269–271.
[47] Howe to Sumner, Feb. 9, 1855, Howe Papers, Houghton.
[48] Howe to Sumner, Feb. 9, 1855, Howe Papers, Houghton.
[49] Parker to James Orton, Feb. 22, 1855, Letterbook 4, p. 280, MHS.
[50] Jeeter Allen Isely, *Horace Greeley and the Republican Party, 1853–1861* (Princeton, 1948), pp. 119–121; Bean, "Party Transformation in Massachusetts," pp. 283–301; Howe to Sumner, July 19, 1855, Howe Papers, Houghton.

the Winthrop-Sumner quarrel of 1846, social polarization had grown apace. The 1848 election was fought so bitterly that Julia reported to sister Annie, "Oh! how the old Whigs do hate us! They will hardly speak to Sumner, or invite him to their homes." [51] Slavery and abolition reached into the most intimate precincts of the heart to snuff out the good will that men felt for each other. The Five of Clubs, falling victim to the passion of the times, divided into two groups, Hillard and Felton in one, and Longfellow, Sumner, and Howe in the other. By 1850 it was just a memory, but the actual break, although imminent, had not yet come. Webster's speech in favor of the Compromise precipitated the final quarrel. Parker denounced the oration and Felton defended it. In the ensuing argument, Sumner sided with Parker.

Forgotten was the affection of many years between "Corny" and "Charlie," with its merry times, dinners, and visits. All was swallowed up in heated newspaper articles and an exchange of recriminatory correspondence in which Howe served as unhappy go-between. After several notes, Sumner wrote Felton that he considered his last communication to him more vindictive than Garrison's worst philippics. Of all the Harvard faculty, he had sided with slavery against freedom.[52] Stung by these charges, Felton insisted to Howe that he had always been a true friend, but that Sumner was too ready with contempt for the intellectual rights of others. Surrounded by flatterers whose constant approval confirmed him in his belief of the bad faith of his opponents, he was pursuing a strange philanthropy that concerned itself about distant problems while "it turns its bitterness and venom in flooding tides upon white neighbors and associates. . . . One by one he is outraging his friends and driving them away," the professor declared, pleading with Howe to open Sumner's eyes.[53]

Felton's appeal was in vain. Howe too had drifted away, although there was no open rupture. Felton did not know that Howe, the most incorrigible of Sumner's "flatterers," had advised Sumner

[51] J. W. Howe to Annie Mailliard, Nov. 13, 1848, Howe Papers, Houghton.
[52] Sumner to Felton, April 9, 1850, Sumner Papers, Houghton.
[53] Felton to Howe, April 11, 1850, Howe Papers, Houghton.

to write the note that had been so painful. No longer did "Chev" think of having Crawford, his sculptor brother-in-law, mold "Corny's" head into little forms of "jolly shaking jellies, & rich ice cream . . . which will shed the oil of joy around," for the Howe daughters to partake of in the hope that they might grow, like him, into the "jolliest, wisest, best children in the world." [54] Alas, Howe acknowledged, Felton's pique was a lesson in how completely most minds are shaped by external pressure. What a pitiful figure he had become, not a law unto himself as Sumner was, "he is not even richly gifted in capacity for the highest & best moral attainments. . . ." Sadly Howe recalled him as he had been. More than ever the quarrel had shown what Sumner meant to Howe. Earlier, he had merely merited and had "the homage of the heart & the affections — for your own overflowed to your friends; but now you have a claim for the approval & admiration of the intellect." [55]

The gulf became wider. In December 1851, Howe realized even more strongly how profoundly distant from each other they had grown when he heard Felton express his opinion on the necessity of obeying law as law. Sumner would never have spoken that way, for "nothing can truly become *law — real* law, that contravenes the eternal principles of right." [56]

Hillard too continued his withdrawal, first noted in 1846. Sumner's old partner had entered politics, but remained a stanch Webster Whig. A man of great talent (Julia felt he had more than his sensational associate),[57] he was upset by all the uproarious developments. At one point he denounced politics, promising never to concern himself with public matters again.[58] In 1865, when as a prominent senator with much patronage at his disposal, Sumner

---

[54] Howe to Sumner, April 26, 1846, Howe Papers, Houghton.

[55] Howe to Sumner, n.d., #1018 (catalogued under 1850), Howe Papers, Houghton.

[56] Howe to Sumner, Dec. 5, 1851, Howe Papers, Houghton. Mann too had a falling out with Felton a few months after Sumner, Sumner to Howe, Sept. 3, 1850, Howe Papers, Houghton. The *Advertiser,* Aug. 24, printed a letter of Felton's denouncing Mann's classical learning and his politics. Other letters appeared Oct. 3 and 4.

[57] J. W. Howe, *Reminiscences,* p. 170.

[58] Howe to Sumner, Dec. 12, 1851, Howe Papers, Houghton.

could virtually appoint judges in Boston, he recalled the pleasure he might have had placing Hillard in so comfortable a post, "if he had not made it impossible." [59]

The sad story of broken friendships and the ostracism that abolitionists began to face long before an anonymous contributor to the *Advertiser* called for it, was characteristic of many in antislavery. The letter-writer merely recognized what had been the situation for several years:

Who is it that forms this pack of Rev. and lay detractors of the good name of the Merchants? Are they, or any of them, men who have achieved any good work for their country or their kind? Are they men who have been conspicuous for their good sense or known for benevolence? Are they not on the contrary those in whose discretion no one would trust and whose philanthropy runs only to incendiarism?

These slanderers seem bent on severing themselves from social contact and friendly intercourse with those whom they so basely calumniate. A decent self respect in those who are thus assailed demands that confidential relations with them should cease. [60]

The *Courier* approved of this program. To the *Commonwealth*'s charge of persecution, it replied that while one can sympathize with the abolitionists in their errors, one did not care to have such men as Sumner, Dana, Jr., and Parker as one's friends. They were untrustworthy practitioners of their professions, who spent so much time on their outside activities that they could not give enough attention to their clients. [61]

Though Howe did not suffer this treatment as did the others, there was still a marked cooling between him and the old guard as shown in his letters. The abolitionists bore up under their punishment as well as they could, but it was painful. They could take the newspaper attacks, but, as Palfrey told Thomas Wentworth Higginson, what really hurt was "the attitude of men who have loved you, and whom you have loved all your life, and who pass you by in

[59] Sumner to Lieber, Feb. 18, 1865, Sumner Papers, Houghton.
[60] *Boston Advertiser*, June 2, 1851.
[61] *Boston Courier*, June 9, 1851.

the streets without speaking to you." [62] When conditions reach such a pass, the ultimate development cannot long be delayed.

IV

Each month, almost each day, increased Howe's bitterness against the South. The Compromise of 1850, with its Fugitive Slave Act, proved to Howe and his friends the servitude of the North to the Slavocracy. Was it possible that the planters would dare to institute legal proceedings to recover their slaves? Abolitionists were determined never to allow the iniquitous law to be enforced. Within a month of its enactment in September 1850, they organized a new Vigilance Committee with Parker as chairman. [63]

They had moved just in time. Within a week of the committee's creation, Howe learned that agents of a master were in town with warrants for the arrest of a fugitive couple, William and Ellen Craft. Mobilizing its machinery, the committee spirited the frightened pair out of the country to England. [64] Several scares later, in February 1851, a slave known simply as "Shadrach" was arrested and taken to court, the first case to have proceeded this far. At noon as the hearing adjourned for lunch, an armed mob rushed in, enveloped the prisoner, and escaped with him into the throng. By nightfall, Shadrach, rescued as it were from a second fiery furnace, was out of the law's reach, safely on the way to Canada. [65] Howe raged at the thought "that a man must fly *from* Massachusetts to the shelter of the red cross of England to save himself from the bloodhounds of slavery." [66]

Howe, as a member of the Vigilance Committee, met mysteriously with his colleagues many times during the next three years. They did not feel as if they were circumventing the rule of law, the principle at the basis of the American social order. The Fugitive

[62] *Reunion of Free Soilers of 1848* (Boston, 1888), p. 25.

[63] John Weiss, *Life and Correspondence of Theodore Parker* (New York, 1864), II, 94–95. There were eventually over 200 members.

[64] Weiss, *Life and Correspondence of Theodore Parker,* II, 96–98; Parker to S. J. May, Nov. 4, 1850, Parker Letterbook 5, p. 149, MHS.

[65] *Boston Advertiser,* Feb. 17, 1851.

[66] Howe to Mann, Feb. 18, 1851, Howe Papers, Houghton.

Slave Act was not a true law since it was not in harmony with the nation's ideals. It was not they who were violating the law, but the Slavocracy.

With the Vigilance Committee ever vigilant, hundreds of slaves passed through the city safely.[67] Only twice did it fail in its duty. The first time was in April 1851, when Thomas Sims was returned to his master. The city was in ferment for a week; the Vigilance Committee was in session constantly, but there was nothing they could do.[68] The shame the abolitionists felt at the rendition of Sims was heightened many times during the rendition of Anthony Burns in May 1854, when casting caution aside, the Reverend Thomas Wentworth Higginson, of Worcester, led a group of followers in an attack on the Court House, where Burns was being held. The rioters were beaten off, but one guard was killed. The power of the Slavocracy was displayed brazenly on the afternoon of June 2 when, surrounded by armed guards, Burns was publicly paraded through the streets to the harbor, where he was placed aboard ship to return to bondage.[69] Howe, standing in the crowd that grim day, "wept for sorrow shame & indignation." All his efforts, the meetings he had planned, the speeches he had delivered, the conferences he had attended, all had been in vain.[70] "Boston & Massachusetts," Samuel May, Jr. despaired, "lie, bound hand & foot, willing slaves, at the foot of the Slave Power, the most cruel & accursed despotism this poor world has ever been oppressed by." [71] Like the prophet of old, abolitionists cried out, "How much longer, O Lord?" [72] Slowly they were learning to act rather than to speak. Higginson had failed the first time he used force, but then he led a small group. The next time the South tried their patience, abolitionists would answer with deeds in addition to words.

[67] No full records were kept, but from hints dropped in letters during these years, the impression is given that a considerable number of fugitives was helped.

[68] *Boston Advertiser,* April 4–15, 1851.

[69] All Boston papers for June 3, 1854 have accounts of the procession.

[70] Howe to Mann, June 18, 1854, Howe Papers, Houghton.

[71] Samuel May, Jr. to Higginson, June 2, 1854, item 20 Burns Collection, BPL.

[72] For a fuller account of fugitive slave cases, see Harold Schwartz, "Fugitive Slave Days in Boston," *New England Quarterly,* XXVII, 2 (June 1954), 191–212.

XIII

Kansas Agitation

As excitement over fugitive slaves died down, a new problem arose
to occupy the public mind in 1854, when Congress passed the
Kansas-Nebraska Act. The brain child of Stephen A. Douglas, the
powerful Illinois Senator, the new measure, full of equivocal provisions, was a guarantee of civil strife. By expressly repealing the
generation-old Missouri Compromise, it threw into jeopardy all the
vast territories north of the sacred line 36°30'. There was no longer
any guarantee that these regions were to be free. Under the doctrine
of "popular sovereignty" the settlers of each territory were to decide
for themselves which labor system was to predominate.

It looked as if slavery were preparing to extend itself north of
the Mason-Dixon line; it might even seek to have itself recognized
in the Free States as well. The North rose solidly to protest.

I

Boston, Cotton Whiggery and all, was overwhelmingly opposed
to the Kansas-Nebraska Bill. It was strange to see the *Advertiser* on
the same side of the fence as the *Commonwealth,* but there it was.
For once in a majority, Howe was one of the guiding spirits who
arranged a protest "Convention of Delegates" at Faneuil Hall for
February 16.[1] In flaming terms, but not fiery enough to please him

[1] Howe to Sumner, Jan. 28, 1854, Howe Papers, Houghton.

so that he refused to attend,[2] the resolutions denounced the proposed change in sectional equilibrium:

Resolved, That this attempt to plant the accursed institution of slavery in the heart of the Continent, and to check the westward advance of civilization, is but another step in the aggressive march of the Slave Power towards the complete and permanent control of the destinies of America.

Resolved, That the territories of the United States are held in trust for the landless, — for the laboring people of this country, and for the refugees from the oppression of the old world; and we therefore protest against legislation which forever shuts out the actual settler from Nebraska, except on condition of sinking him to the level of a slave. . . .

Resolved, That if this new conspiracy against liberty in America shall be consummated, if force is to be the only standard of justice and honor with the South, it can not complain if the fire thus kindled at the North, consuming all compromises which have given shelter to slavery, shall spread into a conflagration which will not be checked until it has swept away slavery itself.[3]

These words were not idle mouthings. There would be no compromise over this issue. With averted face the Free States had given in to the slaveholders' every demand, only to find that each appeasement had whetted their appetites for more. The Compromise of 1850 represented the last concessions the North would make; anything further meant fight.[4] Howe's stand was typical of his section of the country. He urged Sumner to step carefully in debate, to wait "& do what the crisis may require. We want *peace,* — peace, — and a century of it if possible, but we must have progress, — we must remove the impediment in the way to it, & if despots oppose us we must remove them peaceably if we can forcibly if we must." [5] The "True Grandeur of Nations" was not attained by peace at any price.

In March, when the bill passed the Senate, there was no longer

---

[2] Howe to Sumner, Feb. 16, 1854, Howe Papers, Houghton.

[3] The *Commonwealth,* Feb. 17, 1854.

[4] For expression of similar sentiments throughout the North, see Allan Nevins, *Ordeal of the Union* (New York, 1947), II, 125–132.

[5] Howe to Sumner, Feb. 16, 1854, Howe Papers, Houghton.

any doubt that it would get through the House, and receive the signature of the pusillanimous Franklin Pierce.[6] Howe, available for any plan that would beat down the Slave Power, welcomed a scheme of assisted emigration, which Eli Thayer, Representative of Worcester in the General Court, unfolded to a small group on the eleventh.[7] Combining idealism with the profit motive, he proposed the creation of a corporation that, besides arranging for travel accommodations at reduced rates for *bona fide* emigrant bands, would also invest in western lands and engage in business enterprises. Drawing up a petition of incorporation, he saw his bill through the legislature, where it met with little opposition. The Governor signed it April 26.[8] Thus was created the Massachusetts Emigrant Aid Company, ambitiously capitalized at $5,000,000 to ransom Kansas from its abductors. Besides Howe, the indefatigable Thayer had rounded up many of the old Free-Soilers of '48 as incorporators, among them Charles Allen, Stephen C. Phillips, Alexander H. Bullock (later a governor), Henry Wilson (shortly to be senator), Samuel Sewall, Otis Clapp, and Anson Burlingame.[9]

Though Thayer emphasized the commercial aspects of the project, most of his associates were dubious of its profitability. Like Charles Francis Adams, who gave $25,000, they were willing to contribute what money they could (needless to say, few could match him), without expectation of any return.[10] The cause was what mattered. The company immediately began a stock-selling campaign.[11] Operations were hopefully extended to New York and Worcester.[12] On June 7, Howe was appointed to a twenty-man committee to procure subscriptions in Boston, while a special Executive Committee to direct operations in New York was also created.[13]

[6] The *Commonwealth*, March 9, 1854.

[7] Eli Thayer, *The New England Emigrant Aid Company, and Its Influence through the Kansas Contest upon National History* (Worcester, 1887), pp. 13–14.

[8] The *Commonwealth*, April 5, 17, 1854; Thayer, *New England Emigrant Aid Company*, p. 16.

[9] Thayer, *New England Emigrant Aid Company*, pp. 15–16.

[10] Thayer, *New England Emigrant Aid Company*, p. 20.

[11] *Boston Advertiser*, May 15, 1854.

[12] *Boston Advertiser*, June 1, 1854.

[13] *Boston Advertiser*, June 8, 14, and 21, 1854.

Contemporaneous developments should have aided the sale. The final passage during the last week in May of the Kansas-Nebraska Act, which demonstrated the South's political power, and the Burns case immediately following, should have resulted in a great outpouring of money, considering the attitude of the North.[14] However, despite all efforts, the drive did not proceed well. Owing to an unclear charter, prospective stockholders feared full liability. During the summer Thayer attempted to remedy matters by obtaining a new charter in Connecticut. Still the situation remained critical.

In the reorganization, Amos A. Lawrence became the leading figure in the corporation, shouldering the major burden of financial affairs.[15] That such a man as Lawrence could align himself in the movement to make Kansas a Free State is proof of the disordered state of the nation. The son of Amos Lawrence of the textile family, he had been brought up in the traditions of Cotton Whiggery, conservative government based on respect for law and order. Only three years before, he had denounced Sumner's candidacy for senator and had organized a fund to support House Whigs during the election crisis. During the Sims case he had offered his services to the Marshal, but by the time of the Burns case he preferred "to see the court house razed" rather than have the poor fugitive returned.[16] Still a conservative, Lawrence believed in the Union, and favored every legitimate means to oppose the expansion of slavery. He looked on the Emigrant Aid Company only as a patriotic venture, never expecting a return on his money. In fact, he urged persons planning to invest for gain to put their money elsewhere.[17]

[14] The *Commonwealth*, unable to believe that Free State men would be satisfied to remain as "hewers of wood and drawers of water" for the South, called on the people to rise in their wrath and form a new party to combat the bill. "This bill has been forced through Congress by bribery and corruption, against the wishes of the people and in defiance of honor and decency, and there is nothing too base or villainous to be undertaken by the men by whom this work has been done." May 24, 1854.

[15] Thayer, *New England Emigrant Aid Company*, p. 27; *History of the New-England Emigrant Aid Company* (Boston, 1862), p. 6.

[16] William Lawrence, *Life of Amos A. Lawrence* (Boston, 1888), pp. 74–76.

[17] Lawrence, *Life of Amos A. Lawrence*, pp. 80–81.

In July 1854, the company began operations, sending out its first band of settlers on the seventeenth, at an estimated cost per person of half the usual rate.[18] A crowd of well-wishers, who lent a festival atmosphere to the departure, gave three cheers as the train began to move.[19] With new members joining the party steadily, the emigrants' passage across the state resembled a triumphal procession. Under the guidance of Charles H. Branscomb, they made the first Free State settlement in Kansas, at a point thirty-five miles up the Kansas River from where it joins the Missouri. Appropriately enough it was named Lawrence, in honor of the company's treasurer.[20] The type and press for a newspaper to be called the *Herald of Freedom* were also sent out during July. Plans called for it to begin publication in Lawrence in September.[21]

All together, five bands totaling 750 persons emigrated under the company's aegis during the 1854 season. In addition to Lawrence, the sites of Ossawatomie, Pottawatomie, and Topeka were settled. All the emigrants went of their own free will and at their own expense. The company had not solicited them, but once they had decided to go, it organized them into parties, arranged their transportation, and sent along an agent as guide.[22] The settlers were in no way bound to the corporation after reaching Kansas, although its two resident agents, Charles Robinson and Samuel C. Pomeroy, were at their service to solve any problems that might arise. It proved, as had been foreseen, that where these two capable men had chosen to locate sawmills and other utilities, which were built with company funds, the emigrants chose to establish themselves too.[23]

During the winter of 1854–1855, throughout the North, preparations were under way for the new migrating season. The Emigrant Aid Company strengthened its organization too. In February 1855

[18] The *Commonwealth*, July 10, 1854.
[19] The *Commonwealth*, July 19, 1854. John Greenleaf Whittier commemorated the event in the "Kansas Emigrants" which appeared in the *Commonwealth* on the 24th.
[20] *History of the New-England Emigrant Aid Company*, p. 7.
[21] The *Commonwealth*, July 24, 1854.
[22] *History of the New-England Emigrant Aid Company*, pp. 7–8.
[23] *History of the New-England Emigrant Aid Company*, p. 9.

it was rechartered as the New England Emigrant Aid Company
with John Carter Brown of Providence as president, Eli Thayer
one of two vice-presidents, and A. A. Lawrence, treasurer. Howe
remained a director. There were other changes. Capitalization was
cut to $1,000,000.[24] Despite its precarious condition, word had gotten
around that it had the $5,000,000 originally authorized. The South,
feverishly trying to counteract it, was firmly convinced that Northern commercial power was behind the venture.[25]

II

With the new year, conditions in Kansas got out of hand. The
inept Governor, Andrew H. Reeder, proved unable to maintain
order. At the instigation of United States Senator David Atchison
of Missouri, pro-slavery forces, whom the Free Staters promptly
dubbed the "Border Ruffians," roamed the plains at will, threatening Northern settlers. In the fall of 1854 over 1700 of Atchison's
cohorts swarmed into the territory to cast illegal ballots at an election for congressional delegate. During the next year the situation
deteriorated still further. Wilson Shannon, a Slave Stater, succeeded
Reeder, and another election, this time to a constitutional convention, was stolen. Free-State men, their faith in the government lost,
held their own counsels at Topeka. Hitherto peaceful (it was
claimed that during 1854 and 1855 they had gone unarmed), they
began to gather their own military forces.[26] James H. Lane, a wild
unprincipled demagogue, placed himself in command of them. In
December of that year, though bloodshed was narrowly averted
with the peaceable settlement of the so-called "Wakarusa War," it
was apparent that disorder would break out shortly unless a firm
honorable hand took control. Both sides accelerated their preparations.

In Washington ill will between factions proved as great as in
Kansas. As Congress convened, Sumner was struck by the predomi-
nance of bad feelings as shown by the absence of social relationships

---

[24] Charter approved Feb. 21, 1855, to be found in the A. A. Lawrence Papers, XIV,
11, MHS.
[25] Nevins, *Ordeal of the Union*, II, 309–310.
[26] *History of the New-England Emigrant Aid Company*, p. 14.

among senators of opposite parties. "Seward, Wilson and myself are the special mark of disfavor," he wrote. "God willing, something more shall be done to deserve this distinction." [27] Two months later, Douglas introduced a bill authorizing the inhabitants of the territory to organize a state government preparatory to admission to the Union. The debate was on, and "you will hear nothing but Kansas from this time forever —" Sumner told Parker.[28]

Back in Massachusetts, antislavery men, Free-Soilers, and former Cotton Whigs, banded together for concerted action. At a conference in Lawrence's office in 1855, they decided that the foremost need of Kansas settlers was to be supplied with efficient firearms. They voted to raise a fund for the purchase of Sharps rifles, the standard weapon of the day.[29] Agents shortly covered the state, and within a few weeks, the first of a steady stream of firearms began to arrive in Lawrence. Between August 23, 1855 and February 13, 1856, Dr. Samuel Cabot paid over $1050 to Amos A. Lawrence, the debt on that day being $500. By November 20, 1856, contributions reached $5875.61 of which almost $4500 went for rifles, revolvers, ammunition, and bowie knives. Cabot, in later years, estimated that he eventually expended over $11,000 in defense of the Free State cause.[30]

All types among the population contributed. Howe gave at least twenty dollars, the cost of one rifle;[31] one man pledged $20,000 if $10,000 more were raised for 1000 rifles and ten breech loading cannon, while a lady offered Howe $100 and a clergyman the same.[32] One deacon, taking the Sixth Commandment literally, could not allow his money to be used for killing his fellow men, but his conscience allowed him to contribute $25 to buy beef for those

[27] Sumner to Parker, Dec. 14, 1855, Parker Letterbook 10, p. 327, MHS.
[28] Sumner to Parker, Feb. 25, 1856, Parker Letterbook 10, p. 285.
[29] Frank P. Stearns, *The Life and Public Services of George Luther Stearns* (Phil., 1907), p. 105.
[30] Cabot to Lawrence, Oct. 23, 1884, A. A. Lawrence Papers, LVII, 187, MHS. A notebook in the Emigrant Aid Company papers in the MHS indicates the volume of contributions to the fund.
[31] Howe to Sumner, Jan. 26, 1856, Howe Papers, Houghton.
[32] Howe to Sumner, Jan. 7, 1856, Howe Papers, Houghton.

who would carry the rifles. However, he never asked for a voucher to verify the exact disposition of his offering.[33]

By 1856, emigrants to Kansas went fully armed. In April, Parker watched the departure of a hymn-singing company of forty, with "20 copies of *'Sharps Rights of the People'* in their hands of the new & improved edition."[34] For those already in the territory, relief supplies were shipped from the Emigrant Aid Company's offices at 3 Winter Street in downtown Boston. Books were packed in with the rifles in the hope that they would disguise the true contents and explain the great weight of the cases.[35]

III

In the Senate debate on Kansas dragged on, growing daily more bitter. Sumner so far had said nothing, though he told Parker that he was preparing to use "plain words" when he should speak.[36] A few weeks later he promised the "most thorough Phillipic [*sic*] ever uttered in a legislative body."[37] Sumner fulfilled this promise fully. Entitling his long address "The Crime Against Kansas," he loosed the most vulgar diatribe that had been heard up to that time.[38] Deluded by the thought that the mantle of Demosthenes and Cicero in their most inspired moments had descended upon him, he fancied that he was delivering the classic oration of the age, one which would guarantee his fame forever. There can be no denying that this has become his most famous address, but not for the reasons he hoped. He had now been in Congress for five years, and for five years his colleagues had been forced to put up with his insufferable pretensions and sanctimonious idealism. He had become the most hated man among them. Few could bear him, but one lost control. On May 22, as Sumner sat at his desk, Representa-

---

[33] *Reunion of Freesoilers of 1848* (1888), p. 38.

[34] April 2, 1856, Parker's Journal, III, AUA. He was struck by the irony that the rifles were to defend their soil from the American government.

[35] Arthur T. Cabot, to S. A. Green, Sept. 10, 1903, New England Emigrant Aid Company Papers, MHS.

[36] Sumner to Parker, March 26, 1856, Parker Letterbook 10, p. 287, MHS.

[37] Sumner to Parker, May 17, 1856, Parker Letterbook 10, p. 288.

[38] Most readily available in *Works* (Boston, 1874), IV, 137–256.

tive Preston S. Brooks of South Carolina beat him into insensibility with a cane. At last having attained a martyr's crown, after years of conducting himself as one, Sumner lay on the floor of the chamber, a victim of Southern extremism.[39] His blood staining his coat, and trailing along the floor, foreshadowed the coming strife. He played his part to the full.[40]

Howe and all the others of his group were beside themselves with grief. Their champion was at death's door, perhaps to remain an invalid for life, unable to resume his duties even if he should recover. It was almost too much for Howe to bear.

> My heart & soul has [*sic*] been full, — too full for me to find words. What words indeed can one address to you now? . . . .
>
> Had I not been so situated as to be unable to leave my post of duty I should have followed by impulses and gone to Washington — though I could not have done any thing more than manifest my sympathy & affection; it would have been only too easy — too tempting indeed to seek [a] quarrel with the bully who assailed you.
>
> Out of the evil will come good; — great good, & you have not bled in vain.

The attack had convinced Howe that the Union was falling apart and would have to be reconstituted on a sounder basis. It was time for a new Constitution. The North must show the slaveholders that it could get along better without them.[41]

New England had been miraculously brought to Sumner's side. Men politically opposed to him expressed the greatest indignation at the assault. They were now assured that there could be no reasoning with the South. Governor Gardner presided at the Faneuil Hall meeting at which Hillard spoke and served as a vice-president along with Felton.[42] At a private dinner party on possibly

---

[39] *Boston Advertiser*, May 23, 1856 and days following.

[40] The coat came to be regarded almost as if it were a relic of a saint. The way John Brown looked at it, one might think it was never cleaned again. See James Freeman Clarke, *Anti-Slavery Days* (New York, 1884), pp. 153–154.

[41] Howe to Sumner, May 25, 1856, Howe Papers, Houghton.

[42] *Boston Advertiser*, May 26, 1856.

the same day Felton gave the toast, "Charles Sumner — his restoration & re-election." [43]

Edward Everett was one who was not converted. For his refusal to speak at the meeting, the Connecticut Legislature withdrew an earlier invitation it had tendered him to address them.[44]

Within a few days of Sumner's tragedy came harrowing news from Kansas, the Border Ruffian "Sack of Lawrence" during which the Free State Hotel was destroyed and the *Herald of Freedom*'s offices wrecked.[45] Hard upon that came John Brown's retaliatory massacre on the Pottawatomie. There was now open civil war on the plains. The Missouri River from St. Louis up to Fort Leavenworth was closed to Free Staters. Details of Border Ruffian atrocities inundated the East as relatives and friends of the settlers began to receive alarming accounts of daily killings and Indian-style scalpings.

Every little while we are set upon by bands of ruffians, acting under the officers of the General Government [wrote one former resident of Concord to his brother]; towns are sacked and burned, men murdered and property destroyed. Until lately the free State folks have not offered much resistance to these outrages. It was known that bands of these ruffians encamped in the vicinity, where they carried on their trade of horse-stealing and robbery, and murdered a man with whom I was well acquainted; he was riding by near one of these camps, and was shot dead by some of the guard. . . .[46]

In Massachusetts, protests were the order of the day. As Julia put it, "New England spunk seems to be pretty well up." [47] Boston had three meetings in less than two weeks, two about Sumner and one about Kansas.[48]

Howe's spunk too had risen, as high as it could go. The events of the preceding weeks had impressed upon him the necessity of acting more vigorously than he had hitherto. During the gestation

---

[43] Howe to Sumner, May 25, 1856, Howe Papers, Houghton.
[44] J. W. Howe to sisters, probably May 29, 1856, Howe Papers, Houghton.
[45] *Boston Advertiser,* June 2, 1856.
[46] Cyrus Adams to brother, Aug. 24, 1856 (clipping), #659, Higginson Papers, Houghton.
[47] J. W. Howe to Sisters, May 29, 1856, Howe Papers, Houghton.
[48] *Boston Advertiser,* May 24 and 26, and June 4, 1856.

period of the controversy, he had, of course, been worried to the extent of serving as an incorporator and director of the Emigrant Aid Company; he had contributed his own money to the rifle fund, and solicited donations from others; but these were relatively passive efforts. He realized now that lovers of freedom must strain every energy to make Kansas free.

On the night of June 3 he addressed a mass meeting in Faneuil Hall called to discuss means of aiding the settlers beyond what had already been done. The gathering resolved to set up a committee for the relief of the Free Staters by means of clothing and money. He was appointed its chairman. This body became known simply as the "Faneuil Hall Committee." [49] With Howe as its "invigorating spirit," its fund-raising campaign was extraordinarily successful, $10,000 being raised within a month.[50] Persons who had never contributed before gave now to one or another of the funds being collected. Mark Hopkins of Williams College sent his first donation. He had always declined solicitations, but since reading of the sack of Lawrence he realized that "I *must* do something — that every one ought to." [51] Franklin B. Sanborn, just out of Harvard, spent the first half of the summer organizing town committees throughout Middlesex County and raising money. By February he claimed to have collected over $17,000.[52]

But to youthful, exuberant Higginson, an active agent of the Emigrant Aid Company, things did not appear to be moving fast enough. All was sluggishness. The Crimean War was being fought on a smaller scale while the people of New England took things easy. Other sections showed an energy that disgraced his native region. Except for a few like Howe, New England was ill-prepared for the emergency. "The busy give no time & the leisurely no energy & there is no organisation," he complained.[53]

[49] *Boston Advertiser,* June 4, 1856. The Emigrant Aid Company seems to have been closely connected with these activities, since in a circular it urged all towns in the state to organize similar committees, A. A. Lawrence Papers, XIV, 11, MHS.

[50] Samuel Breck to Howe, July 10, 1856, Howe Papers, MHS, speaks about fundraising in Bridgewater.

[51] Hopkins to Lawrence, June 7, 1856, Lawrence Papers, XIV, 6, MHS.

[52] Franklin B. Sanborn, *Recollections of Seventy Years* (Boston, 1909), I, 51–52.

[53] Higginson to Mother, June 26, 1856, #560, Higginson Papers, Houghton.

The direction of this extensive drive had brought Howe close to exhaustion. Still he refused to rest, but conceived the notion of going out to Kansas to survey the situation for himself, and arrange for the disbursal of the funds there.[54] After sending Julia and the children to Newport for the summer, he headed West to "help the cause, — than which, in none, can one die better." [55]

On June 25, another committee was organized, the Massachusetts Kansas Aid Committee, to which Howe also belonged, with George L. Stearns the chairman.[56] Its object was to aid the settlers "directly," that is, supply them with arms. It is difficult for this author to keep the two committees separate, especially since Stearns seems to have been chairman of both eventually. On paper the Faneuil Hall group was a disaster-relief organization, while the State Committee, as it was generally known, was designed to buy guns which were shipped from the Emigrant Aid Company's offices. Since there was so much overlapping of membership, to all intents and purposes they merge into one. There is no need to keep clear distinctions in mind.

IV

About Independence Day, Howe set out from Boston with complete authority and discretion over the disposition of the Faneuil Hall Committee's funds, the treasurer having been directed to hold $10,000 subject to his drafts or those holding drafts from him.[57] His first stop was Buffalo, where on the tenth he attended a convention of state Kansas committees which met under the presidency of Andrew H. Reeder, former governor of the territory. Out of the two-day sessions, besides the usual resolves, came a National Kansas Aid Committee with Eli Thayer as General Agent to superintend the coördination of the independent state groups. Gerrit Smith, the wealthy landowning abolitionist and wholesale reformer of up-state

[54] Howe to Sumner, June 20, 1856, June 26, Howe Papers, Houghton.
[55] Howe to Mann, June 30, 1856, Howe Papers, Houghton.
[56] *Boston Advertiser*, July 4, 1856.
[57] P. T. Jackson to Howe, June 30, 1856, Howe Papers, MHS.

New York, pledged $1500 a month for the duration of the crisis. The Illinois representative on the National Central Committee was a certain "Abram" Lincoln of Springfield.[58]

Howe was occupied for the rest of July in his investigation of Kansas and its immigrants. He traveled in the company of Thaddeus Hyatt, on a similar mission for the New York Tabernacle Committee, Gotham's equivalent of the Faneuil Hall body. The Missouri River being closed from St. Louis up, and the city dangerous for Free State men, the two investigators followed a roundabout route to the frontier.[59] Leaving the railroad at a point eight miles east of Mount Pleasant, Iowa, they resorted to more primitive means of transportation.[60] For ten days they crawled across the plains by means of horseback and cart, "sleeping in said cart or in worse lodgings, among dirty men, on the floor of dirty huts." [61]

At length they reached Mount Tabor, eight miles east of the Missouri, the jumping-off point of the emigrants. At this last outpost of civilization Howe learned of the critical condition of the Free State cause. The whole northern line of Kansas was infested by marauding bands. Even after allowing for customary exaggeration, there was no doubt that robbery and murder were rife on the frontier. Unarmed men could not travel in safety. The Ruffians, having been driven from the southern portion of Kansas, had swarmed up to the north where they lay in wait for emigrants forced to use the only route open. Howe could enter the territory either by joining a large body of armed settlers who could fight their way in, or alone on horseback, running a gauntlet of over one hundred miles to the first Free State settlement. He had neither the time for the first, nor the energy for the second.

Ironically enough, he also learned that the northwestern counties of Missouri had become excited by reports that a large body of

[58] *New York Times*, July 11, 1856. Apparently the telegrapher sent out Lincoln's name incorrectly, since the *Advertiser*, July 12, spelled it that way too.
[59] J. H. Webb to Howe, July 1, 1856, Howe Papers, MHS.
[60] Thaddeus Hyatt to the Tabernacle Committee, Aug. 16, 1856, Hyatt Collection, Kansas State Historical Society, photostat in author's possession.
[61] Howe to Sumner, July 27, 1856, Howe Papers, Houghton.

armed Free Staters were marching through Nebraska. Each side was apprehensive of the other's power.[62]

To Howe and Hyatt, theirs was the cause of yeoman against aristocratic cavalier. At times they spoke as if the English Civil War of the seventeenth century were being refought. Mount Tabor, the Free State base, fulfilled their ideal of a town of "true Cromwellian grit: praying-fighting Christians, with a faith ever ardent & with 'powder' always 'dry.'" [63] It was there that they met the Cromwell of the Free State forces, Colonel or "General" James H. Lane. This Indiana-born adventurer did not impress them. A man of shady reputation, he had gone to Kansas to seek his political fortunes, prepared to fight for either side. He chose the Northern since it offered greater promise to him, although while serving in Congress he had voted for the Kansas-Nebraska bill. By flaunting his military experience gained during the Mexican War, he easily succeeded to the leadership of the Free State forces. Now he stood before the two investigators, a clean-shaven figure, with unkempt hair, a narrow forehead on which "suavity" was the most marked phrenological feature, and deep-set eyes, penetrating and restless. With "Firmness, Self-esteem & Approbativeness" the controlling organ of his "Coronal" and "moderate Cautiousness, united to a basilar in which Secretiveness Acquisitiveness and Destructiveness are moderately developed with large Combativeness," neither Howe nor Hyatt felt any confidence in him.[64]

Lane was guilty of extreme indiscretion in having spoken in Mount Tabor when it was urgent for him to remain incognito. He now wished to speak at Nebraska City, using an assumed name.[65] Since he was already under indictment for treason, his presence among the emigrants would give a marshal's posse a pretext to attack the whole train as a filibustering expedition.[66] Determined to

[62] Letter of July 26, printed in *Boston Advertiser,* August 9, 1856.

[63] Hyatt to Committee, p. 2.

[64] Hyatt to Committee, p. 2; and Wendell Holmes Stephenson, *The Political Career of General James H. Lane,* Kansas State Historical Society, *Publications,* III (Topeka, 1930), frontispiece and p. 51.

[65] Hyatt to Committee, p. 4.

[66] Stephenson, *Lane,* p. 74.

get rid of Lane, Howe made his departure from the camp a condition of granting any funds. It was vital for the settlers to preserve their law-abiding character, Howe explained to Hyatt. They "cannot & ought not to oppose the civil process: in the uncertainty & division of counsels mischief will arise, a conflict be brought, & our friends, whether beaten or victorious will stand wrong before the country."[67]

Hyatt took the ultimatum to Lane at his headquarters in Civil Bend. After a stormy scene the soldier-of-fortune acceded to all demands. Shortly thereafter, he stole over the border secretly to make his way to Lawrence. None could now be endangered by his irresponsible activities. Howe and Hyatt were relieved to be rid of him.[68]

On the twenty-ninth, the train crossed the river to Nebraska City, a settlement "of a half dozen houses just starting into life," situated in the Nebraska Territory between the Missouri and the "Weeping" or "Murmuring Waters."[69] From here the emigrants hoped to take the downboat from Council Bluffs to Leavenworth, where they would debark, and with an escort of federal troops reach Lawrence. However they learned that no boat was expected for almost a week. They decided to go overland. Howe had no faith in the army. It was a mockery to say it had driven the Border Ruffians out of Kansas. Although the officers sympathized with the Free-Soilers, they had played into the hands of the slavocrats.[70] The emigrants would have to trust to God and their own strength, to "hew their own path into the promised land."[71] His rage mounted within him as he thought of the brave pioneers intrepidly toiling cross-country in the summer heat because of the brutality of the Missourians in

[67] Howe to Hyatt, July 30, 1856, Hyatt Collection, Kansas State Historical Society, typescript kindly supplied the author by the Secretary.

[68] Hyatt to Committee, p. 4. Stephenson in his biography of Lane says that he received Howe's demand with tears in his eyes, but for the sake of a free Kansas surrendered his authority. Stephenson makes him out a more worthy figure, *Lane*, p. 75.

[69] Hyatt to Committee, p. 1.

[70] Howe to Sumner, July 31, 1856, Howe Papers, Houghton.

[71] A letter of July 29, printed in the *Boston Advertiser*, Aug. 12, 1856.

blocking the most convenient route. "How long will the North eat dirt & not turn sick," he groaned.[72]

The doctor was impressed with the character of the settlers, whom he found intelligent, sober, and resolute.

There is no whiskey in the camp. There is no noise or confusion, no swearing, no bragging. — More than one-third are people from Wisconsin; all temperance men; many of them pious. They have their prayer meetings, bible classes for children, sabbath services and the like. They give a tone to the whole encampment.[73]

Hyatt, after a night in the field, testified to the primitive conditions prevailing on the banks of the Weeping Waters. Howe, familiar with camp life from the old days, remained in the relative comfort of Nebraska City. For supper the pioneers had boiled rice

made palatable by sugar of a superlative brown, served up on a very dubious looking tin platter & ladled to my fastidious lips by a more than dubious looking iron spoon. A watery fluid in a tin porringer floating a few black cinders served in place of Coffee for such members of the Mess as were gifted with imaginative faculties.[74]

Nine others slept in the same inadequate tent with him during a night of ground-drenching rain. Throughout the storm the sentinels had to guard not against savages, but worse, night surprise by "the bloodthirsty, drunken, boasted, bloated chivalry of the South! and the treachery of an accursed and perjured Administration."[75] Yet those freedom-loving yeomen, who had endured so much and would undergo even more privation, even to facing death in the next few months, did not complain of their lot or show "discontent at the coarseness of their fare. . . . There was but one expressed murmur & this was their great delay in getting in and especially their *want of arms.*"[76] Despite such characters as John Brown and Jim Lane, Howe and Hyatt saw the two parties in black and white

[72] Howe to Sumner, July 31, 1856.
[73] *Boston Advertiser,* Aug. 12, 1856.
[74] Hyatt to the Committee, pp. 4–5.
[75] Hyatt to the Committee, p. 5.
[76] Hyatt to the Committee, p. 6.

terms, the Southerners all bad, drunken rowdies, and the Northern-
ers all good, God-fearing, temperate, and honest.

The two investigators were dissatisfied with the armament of the
emigrants. The Border Ruffians, they were convinced, had all the
latest-model guns, while the clean-cut Wisconsin boys, who never
swore or cursed, had only a few. The Davenport company of twenty-
nine men they reported was equipped with but two rifles, a shotgun and eight or ten bowie knives.

What a soldiery to meet the mounted and armed myrmidons of the
Border & their Government backers! Sheep precipitated into the midst
of wolves! I felt that it were a sin and a shame to be accessory to such
an ignominious defeat! [77]

It was now time for the Easterners to leave. They had examined
conditions on the frontier, Howe had entrusted his $10,000 to worthy
men, and arranged for an agent in Kansas.[78] Just before leaving he
gave the emigrants a last bit of advice. At all costs they were to
hold on to their arms and not yield them under any pretext. If they
should be opposed by United States troops, or men disguised as such,
they were to rest where they were, or retire into a Free State, still
bearing their arms.[79] On August 1 the emissaries began their homeward journey.

Howe reached Boston completely worn out from his exertions of
the past month. While not fully satisfied with the results, he felt
that he had been able to accomplish some good to the Free State
cause by having hamstrung "that adventurer" Lane, and by having
afforded much material aid along with moral support to the emigrants. He regretted that he had been prevented from going to
Sumner, who was recuperating at a resort, but a greater duty called.
He felt that this might be the last mission of its type he would ever
be called upon to make, and he had to do it. Ill as he was, he still
planned to attend a meeting of the National Kansas Aid Committee
at Saratoga at the end of August.[80]

[77] Hyatt to the Committee, pp. 7–8.
[78] Hyatt to the Committee, p. 4.
[79] Draft of letter to agent and leader of the emigrant train, Aug. 1, 1856, Howe
Papers, MHS.
[80] Howe to Sumner, Aug. 23, 1856, Howe Papers, Houghton.

V

With war flaring up after an uneasy lull in July, the news from Kansas remained critical for the rest of the summer. Free State settlers lived in dread of new massacres which might come at any time. E. B. Whitman, the agent Howe had appointed, reported that there were 400 troops in Lawrence to beat off any attacks. The surrounding country had been summoned to assemble for war. He pleaded for money which only the East could supply. "Everybody is busy collecting food and preparing for the contest. An Army cannot be fed or clothed for naught." [81] Pomeroy, the Emigrant Aid Company's agent, also wrote to Howe for funds to outfit mounted companies for service as scouts and advance guards. [82]

News of disaster poured in without letup. Ossawatomie was burned early in September, but Free Staters triumphed at Palmyra. The St. Louis firm of Simmons and Leadbeater, agents of the Faneuil Hall Committee, informed Howe that they were caring for five Leavenworth merchants and their families, who along with all the Free State men of that city had been driven from their homes. All were completely destitute. Desiring revenge above all, most of the men hoped to go to Chicago to join the Free State army being formed there. Provisions worth $5000 awaited the arrival of this force at Nebraska City. [83]

Lawrence was like a city besieged. The women and children were evacuated to Fort Leavenworth. The Reverend Ephraim Nute, who accompanied them, has left a grim description of their harrowing flight through the flaming countryside. Charred ruins of former homes dotted the landscape. Nute estimated that over sixty families had been burned out, and in some cases all the males in a family had been butchered. Their mangled bodies were to be found along the roadside between the two settlements. Though in danger of being shot several times, he had so far managed to escape injury. Nute had seen much of the Ruffians. He had obtained confessions

[81] E. B. Whitman to Howe, Aug. 22, 1856, Howe Papers, MHS.
[82] S. C. Pomeroy to Howe, Sept. 8, 1856, Howe Papers, MHS.
[83] Simmons & Leadbeater to Howe, Sept. 9, 1856, Howe Papers, MHS.

from them to the most craven assaults. "They are a pack of mean, sneaking cowards," he wrote Parker. "One hundred of our men with Lane at their head, or with the report that he was there, would have driven a thousand of them howling into the Missouri." [84]

In Massachusetts men took confused steps to counter Border Ruffian atrocities. Some wanted the Governor to call a special session of the General Court and have them donate a large sum to the Free State party. Parker hoped at least $1,000,000 would be appropriated.[85] Higginson, favoring more drastic measures, felt that the people were ready to resist the power of the federal government. While the majority might shrink from that action, others were ready for it. They had come to see that if Kansas were to be made free, force would have to be used. He for one had no doubt that the issue would be settled by force, not politics. The nation was already in the midst of a revolution without knowing it, just as after Bunker Hill. He had already instructed departing emigrants neither to obey the government nor to disobey, leaving it up to those in charge.[86]

Howe was terribly upset. Alone in Boston while his family vacationed, he saw no one except for the hour or two each day he devoted to Kansas affairs. To keep the settlers from want during the coming winter, he foresaw a hard struggle in which there could be no relaxation. Massachusetts would have to give liberally.[87]

That was the only thing it could do to any advantage, and it did it very well. There were meetings at which collections were taken, Ladies Aid societies packed boxes of clothing, and, of course, individuals sent in checks of varying size. Some attached naïve notes to their donations, like Mrs. George Russell who sent $500 with the

---

[84] Ephraim Nute to Parker, Sept. 14, 1856, Parker Letterbook 9, pp. 317–322, MHS.

[85] Sept. 7, 1856, Parker Journal, III, AUA. Wilson told Parker that Massachusetts had no rights in Kansas. It could vote a charitable gift to suffering countrymen, but not on the grounds of protection. If they attempted the latter they would be following slaveholding doctrine. Wilson to Parker, Dec. 5, 1856, Parker Letterbook 11, p. 152, MHS, discusses the legality of such a grant.

[86] Higginson to James Freeman Clarke, Aug. 17 or 19, 1856, Transcript of letters in Historical Dept. of Iowa in Villard Coll., Columbia University.

[87] Howe to Sumner, Sept. 21, 1856, Howe Papers, Houghton.

injunction, "Do be quite sure that the Border Ruffians do not get it, for it is so disheartening neither to use your money yourself, nor to have it do any good to those for whom you intended it." [88]

VI

The advent of autumn marked the end of the emigration season. Numerically the North had won an overwhelming victory. Its settlers had far outnumbered the Southerners. "The late contest," wrote Howe with some exaggeration, "was mainly between Massachusetts & Missouri; if Missouri had had a larger purse & could have fully provided for the men who were ready to keep the field the result might have been different." [89]

Under a new governor of skill and integrity, John W. Geary, who arrived early in September, Kansas was pacified. Unable to believe one of Franklin Pierce's appointees could be fair, New Englanders distrusted his motives. To Higginson, on the scene, the governor's policy was a conquest of the Free State men just as they had expelled the Missourians.

Geary's intention is to give them peace & bread, at the price of obedience to the laws of the false legislature. He is making a clear path therefore for a contest between the inhabitants & the U. S. troops, first or last. The people are braver than anything I ever dreamed of, & when they once adopt the policy of resistance to the U. S. will do it. . . ." [90]

Higginson was wrong as usual. As the year drew to its close, it became apparent that Geary was a man of his word, really determined to act fairly, and not inimical to the Free State cause. By December land values were higher than ever before. Settlers began to feel new confidence. Whitman spoke of Geary as "opening up . . . finely for our cause. All is hopeful for the future." [91]

Peace continued; hope mounted. The territory was in the midst

[88] James Jamison to Howe, Sept. 9, 1856; E. M. Bruce to Howe, Sept. 16, and Mrs. S. S. Russell to Jamison, Sept. 14, 1856, all in the Howe Papers, MHS.
[89] Howe to Sumner, Sept. 21, 1856, Howe Papers, Houghton.
[90] Higginson to his mother, Sept. 24, 1856, #568, Higginson Papers, Houghton.
[91] E. B. Whitman to Howe, Dec. 3, 1856, Howe Papers, MHS.

of a land boom. "Land! Land! is the cry." [92] Howe himself appears to have invested, since Whitman, who also managed his business affairs for him, spoke of having sold a quarter section at $10 an acre.[93]

A few days before Christmas, Howe urged that the Faneuil Hall Committee should wind up its affairs and announce that Kansas had no further need of charitable contributions. However, he did believe that as an insurance against the revival of strife in the spring, Massachusetts should follow the lead of Vermont and appropriate $100,000 or $200,000 for relief.[94] On the basis of the Free State victory in Kansas, the North should press every advantage over the Slave Power. Magnanimity, he held, could be shown only at the expense of a duty which "bids us act as we should do if some of our mothers or children of our loins were among the four million bondmen." For his own part he would never hold out the olive branch since the Slavocracy "would devour it dove and all, as they have ever been disposed to, if now we waver & hesitate." [95] In April 1857, the National Kansas Committee disbanded because of an almost total cessation of contributions.[96]

VII

In 1857 Howe turned westward again, but, conditions being so much better, his trip was almost as much for pleasure as for business. Julia accompanied him as far as Louisville. En route they stopped off at Yellow Springs, Ohio, to visit the Horace Manns (Mann was now president of Antioch College), who "almost ate us up, so glad were they to see us. . . ." [97] It was now possible to reach Kansas by the most direct method, from St. Louis up the Missouri River to Leavenworth. The struggle in the territory had shifted to the ballot boxes, the Free Staters at Topeka opposing the

[92] Whitman to Howe, Dec. 6, 1856, Howe Papers, MHS.
[93] Whitman to Howe, March 16, 1857, Howe Papers, MHS.
[94] Howe to A. A. Lawrence, Dec. 22, 1856, A. A. Lawrence Papers, XIV, 216, MHS.
[95] Howe to Lawrence, Dec. 23, 1856, A. A. Lawrence Papers, XV, 1.
[96] H. B. Hurd to Howe, April 1, 1857, Howe Papers, MHS.
[97] J. W. Howe to Annie Mailliard, May 26, 1857, Howe Papers, Houghton.

Slave State men at Lecompton. Howe, after leaving money to sustain the members of the Free State "legislature" during the trial, left on May 29 to return home.[98] Unlike the previous year, it was a pleasant journey completely without accident, delay, or failures of communication.[99] At the fall election the Free State cause was completely victorious, the Lecompton Constitution being overwhelmingly rejected.[100]

By 1858 the controversy had quieted down.[101] Howe even thought of the possibilities of organizing a Free State in the western part of Texas, going so far as to inquire about the prospects of emigration from Kansas.[102] Definitely, the worst of the crisis was over. The Massachusetts reformers could turn their attention to a more sensational aspect of antislavery activity.

[98] M. F. Conway to George L. Stearns, May 29, 1857, Howe Papers, MHS.
[99] Howe to Mann, June 25, 1857, Howe Papers, Houghton.
[100] Whitman to Howe, Oct. 22, 1857, Howe Papers, MHS.
[101] Howe to Conway, June 27, 1858, #1154 (catalogued under 1855), Howe Papers, Houghton.
[102] Howe to Conway, Dec. 4, 1858, Howe Papers, MHS.

XIV

The Prelude to Harpers Ferry

Kansas was lost to slavery, but Howe could not be sure. Unable to tell when the Border Ruffians would strike again, he was willing to aid anyone who would fight for freedom. The other Massachusetts reformers felt the same.

One day Howe told Julia of a remarkable man who "seemed to intend to devote his life to the redemption of the colored race from slavery, even as Christ had willingly offered his life for the salvation of mankind." He assured her that she would hear more of him. Several months later she learned that she was to receive this singular person that afternoon. "His name is John Brown," Howe said. At the appointed hour the bell rang. Julia, answering it herself, "beheld a middle-aged, middle-sized man, with hair and beard of amber color, streaked with gray. He looked a Puritan of the Puritans, forceful, concentrated, and self-contained. We had a brief interview. . . . I saw him once again . . . and then heard no more of him for some time." [1]

For all she knew he was just another of the strange characters who drifted in and out of their home. But had she noted his glittering eyes more closely, she would have seen a man possessed. Instead

[1] J. W. Howe, *Reminiscences,* pp. 253–254.

of a "Puritan of the Puritans," Coleridge's Ancient Mariner had come to life.[2]

I

It has always been difficult to see John Brown as he really was, for he is a figure both glamorized and vilified by legend. There is the flavor of the Old Testament about him, as he has come down to us. Driven to deeds of violence with the name of God on his lips, dealing out the Hebrew judgment of an eye for an eye, he saw only atonement through blood for the evils of slavery. Such a spirit could always draw approval from New England Unitarians whose minds, but not their hearts, had overthrown the grim injunctions of Calvinist theology.

Brown, descended from a *Mayflower* passenger, was born in Torrington, Connecticut, in 1800. A rough, motherless existence on the Ohio frontier, where he was taken at the age of five, scanty schooling, entry into the leather business at fifteen, and marriage for the first time at twenty to a "REMARKABLY PLAIN; but neat industrious & economical girl; of excellent character; earnest piety; & good practical common sense," and he was a man ready to make his own way in the world.[3] Devoted to Methodism (a strange type to be called a Puritan), a pillar of the church wherever he lived, he was a model of Christian piety. In his private life, he conducted himself in true patriarchal Biblical fashion, ruling his horde of children with stern and loving hand. But in business matters he was nineteenth-century American. For over three decades, in one state after another, he speculated and planned deals that never quite came off. James C. Malin goes so far as to say that he was dishonest, but Villard feels that his difficulties arose from a congenital restlessness.[4] In his wanderings Brown grew to hate slavery, although it is

---

[2] Almost everyone who has written on Brown, no matter how little, has commented on his eyes. See Sarah Forbes Hughes, *John Murray Forbes* (Boston, 1899), I, 180. Also, Stephen Vincent Benét, *John Brown's Body, Selected Works* (New York, 1942), I, 27.

[3] Oswald Garrison Villard, *John Brown, 1800–1859, A Biography Fifty Years After* (Boston, 1910), Brown's own biographical note, pp. 1–7.

[4] James C. Malin, *John Brown and the Legend of Fifty-Six*, American Philosophical Society, *Memoirs*, XVII (Phil., 1942), 3 and 10.

doubtful that he really made his family take an oath to fight it, or even that he promised to use force to destroy it, as some of his children claimed later.[5]

In 1854 he was an old man, a failure, but the providential opening of Kansas to settlement offered a new field for more deals. Leaving his wife and younger children at the family farm in North Elba, New York, he followed his elder sons westward in October 1855.[6] On the rude frontier where incongruities were the rule, Brown's distinctive personality made a strong impression. His years of hard life had begun to tell. His close-cropped hair streaked with gray, his stooping shoulders that made him appear shorter than his five feet eleven, his measured step and the earnestness of his manner, betokened the patriarch, but his movements retained their resoluteness, his speech its promptness, his sight its keenness, and his eyes their accustomed brightness.[7]

It was on such a man of proven instability and incompetence that Howe and his closest associates depended to safeguard the Free State cause in Kansas, lending him their confidence, moral encouragement, and financial assistance.

II

During the disorder that swept the territory until the arrival of Governor Geary in September 1856, Brown became possibly the most notorious of the Free State guerrillas. His band was the equal of the Border Ruffians in the perpetration of atrocities. Shortly after the sack of Lawrence, the nation was horrified by the news of the vicious murder of five pro-slavery settlers at Dutch Henry's Crossing in the Pottawatomie region. So shocking was the deed that Brown, though willing to take responsibility as instigator, al-

[5] Malin, *John Brown and the Legend of Fifty-Six*, p. 15; Villard, *John Brown*, p. 48. A. A. Lawrence claimed in 1885 that his firm had hired Brown in 1843 to buy wool in the West, but parted with him because he spoke disloyally of the U. S. government. Signed introduction dated Aug. 10, 1885 to a collection of papers relating to John Brown in the MHS.

[6] Villard follows most biographers in saying he had no intention of settling in Kansas, while Malin says he did. Villard, *John Brown*, p. 93; Malin, *John Brown and the Legend of Fifty-Six*, pp. 7–8, and 13–14. There is disagreement on every point.

[7] Villard, *John Brown*, p. 122.

ways denied his presence at the scene. None of his neighbors believed him. Not even Franklin B. Sanborn, his greatest apologist, felt able to support Brown's disclaimer.[8] Most recent scholarship indicates that he directed the entire massacre.[9]

Brown seems to have developed a megalomania which, if not entirely psychotic, was nevertheless irresponsible. He thought of himself as a great military commander who by his exploits in the field would guarantee a Free State victory. In August, while the war was at its height, he organized the "Kansas Regulars" with himself as captain. It was a peculiar group. Thirty-five men, apparently as rabid as he, signed a pledge to follow him in the "maintenance of the rights and liberties of the Free State citizens of Kansas." They promised to "observe and maintain a strict an [sic] thorough military dicipline [sic] at all times" until their terms of service expired.[10] In typical frontier amateur-soldier fashion, theirs was to be a democratically run company with the men electing all the officers, even the highest, from among themselves. All were to share equally in whatever property was captured. Brown had set up a Christian company too. The rules forbade uncivil, ungentlemanly, vulgar, or profane talk. Nevertheless it was primarily a military organization. Brown made it clear that

A disorderly retreat shall not be suffered at any time, and every officer an [sic] private is by this article fully empowered to prevent the same by force if need be, and any attempt at leaving the ground during a fight is hereby declared disorderly, unless the consent or direction of the officer in command have authorized the same.[11]

In the following months Brown prepared himself for his new career. He made a serious study of war, finding "valuable hints" in the life of Lord Wellington.[12]

[8] Franklin B. Sanborn, *Life and Letters of John Brown* (Boston, 1885), p. 263.

[9] Malin takes 700 pages of exemplary historical detective work to prove that. *John Brown and the Legend of Fifty-Six.*

[10] These articles were signed Aug. 22 and in days following. John Brown's Diary, BPL.

[11] "By-Laws of the Free State Regular Volunteers of Kansas Enlisted under the Command of John Brown," John Brown's Diary, BPL.

[12] John Brown's Diary, BPL.

The date at which he began to receive money from the Massachusetts Kansas Aid Committee is uncertain, but it was probably in August or shortly thereafter. In quest of a subsidy he approached E. B. Whitman with the proposal

to serve hereafter in the Free State cause provided my needful expences [*sic*] can be met should that be desired: & to raise a small regular force to serve on the same condition. My own means are so far exhausted that I can no longer continue in the service at present without the means of defraying my expences are furnished me.[13]

His appeal was accepted and he became a regular recipient of the committee's alms.

Early in January 1857, Brown visited Boston, meeting five of his most loyal supporters for the first time. The effect on the committee men of a personal encounter with him was electric. He was appointed their agent to receive and hold their arms and ammunition. In addition, they appropriated $500 to pay his expenses. Stearns paid out $1300 of his own money for Brown to buy 200 revolvers. He also gave him a $7000 letter of credit to provide for the subsistence of his men.[14] On April 11 the committee added another $500 and turned over to him 100 of the Sharps rifles they had stored at Mount Tabor the summer before. These he was to sell for the benefit of Free State men in Kansas. The committee also requested him to keep an account of his doings as far as possible. There is no proof that he ever obeyed either of these orders.[15]

It is surprising that such hard-headed men should have shown such confidence in one intrinsically so unimportant. Yet he had support all over the East, not only in Boston. Howe, for over thirty years a respected and experienced man of affairs, ordinarily made clear judgments of men, but in Brown's case he lost all perspective. In Howe's eyes, Brown was noble and completely admirable. As a

[13] Brown to Whitman, undated, J. F. Clarke Family Papers, #75, Houghton.
[14] Stearns's testimony before the Harpers Ferry Investigation Committee, *Senate Report*, 36 Cong., 1 sess., no. 278, Appendix, p. 227. Brown traveled to other eastern cities and enjoyed a profitable winter, but his major support came from Boston.
[15] Stearns to Brown, April 15, 1857, Howe Papers, MHS; Stearns's testimony before the Harpers Ferry Investigation Committee, Appendix to *Report*, p. 230.

token of his regard he gave him a rifle and two pistols.[16] George L. Stearns was no fool either. The only businessman among them, he had worked his way up from store clerk to the head of an extremely profitable lead-pipe manufacturing concern in Medford.[17] The two ministers, Higginson and Parker, also occupied responsible positions in society where the judgment of men was an important part of their activities.

Of the five, however, Sanborn was most taken with him. From the moment that Brown entered the committee's offices on School Street, Sanborn was his orderly. A young man, only twenty-six, but two years out of Harvard, and already the head of a private school in Concord, he had become so active in the Free State movement that within six months he had progressed from a mere collector of funds to Secretary of the Massachusetts Kansas Aid Committee.[18] He was so bewitched by Brown's dynamic quality that fifty years later he could write that, though

my acquaintance with him continued hardly three years; yet I seem to have known him better, and to have seen him oftener than those who have journeyed beside me in life's path for sixty years. My actual intercourse with him hardly exceeded a month; my correspondence was some two and a half years . . . and that infrequent; yet the momentous events in which he had a share give to that brief intercourse the seeming duration of a lifetime.[19]

It was ever after to be Sanborn's mission to defend his idol from attack. Though it meant involvement in many controversies, from none of which he shrank, he continued to justify the ways of Brown to man.[20]

[16] Brown to Stearns, April 16, 1857, Howe Papers, Houghton.

[17] Frank P. Stearns, *Life and Public Services of George L. Stearns* (Phil., 1907), pp. 13–65. A. A. Lawrence met Brown and gave him some money, but he was not especially prominent in the affairs of the committee.

[18] Franklin B. Sanborn, *Recollections of Seventy Years* (Boston, 1909), I, 51; Sanborn, *Life of Brown*, p. 347.

[19] Sanborn, *Recollections*, I, 84.

[20] A. A. Lawrence's correspondence of the 1880's contains many references to Sanborn's writings on Brown. Higginson's papers in Houghton and the BPL contain more. Sanborn destroyed his own papers after Harpers Ferry, but there are scattered letters in other collections. For a discussion of Howe in these connections, see

The sixth of Brown's chief supporters was Gerrit Smith of New York, the only non-New Englander among them. A wealthy landowner whose resources were at the entire disposal of abolition, he had been involved in diverse reforms for over a quarter of a century. Despite a somewhat neurotic temperament, he was able to manage his estates with the prudence necessary not only to maintain his fortune but to increase it as well.[21]

These were the so-called "Secret Six" by whose efforts Brown was sustained for the rest of his life. They all felt so deeply about the cause of freedom that they were unwilling or unable to realize that Brown was an irresponsible guerrilla leader whose depredations had prevented peaceful settlement in Kansas without having aided the Free State side.[22] Even if his tactics had once been desirable, there was now no further need for them. Kansas was pacified, there was to be no further bloodshed. Instead of throwing their money down the drain, which is essentially what they were doing, the Six would have done well to have invested in projects designed to build up the country. Unfortunately they did not understand the actual condition. They still thought the pattern of the past year would reappear with the arrival of the new immigration season. It is almost as if Brown's gleaming eyes had hypnotized them.

III

Eastern philanthropy was at Brown's disposal as it was to no one else. All his financial needs were taken care of. Gerrit Smith offered him as much land as he wanted at whatever he could afford, since as he told Lawrence, Brown was "a noble man." [23] The committee raised $1000 to meet the price. Late in July 1857, Sanborn, on the authority of Stearns and Lawrence, took the money to Peterboro, New York, to pay to Smith.[24] Money continued to flow to Brown

Henry Richards to Sanborn, May 14, and Sanborn to Richards, May 15, 1908, in the Higginson Papers, #675 and 676, Houghton.

[21] Ralph V. Harlow, *Gerrit Smith, Philanthropist and Reformer* (New York, 1939).

[22] Malin's view, in *John Brown and the Legend of Fifty-Six*, p. 759.

[23] Smith to A. A. Lawrence, May 3, 1857, A. A Lawrence Papers, XV, 133, MHS.

[24] Stearns's testimony before the Harpers Ferry Investigating Committee, Appendix to *Report*, p. 228; Sanborn to R. C. Winthrop, Dec. 4, 1884, undated newspaper clipping in the Higginson Papers, Houghton, item 659.

even though contributions were not as readily received in 1857 as in the previous year. One of Howe's objects in visiting Kansas during the spring was to see him and to turn over additional funds.[25]

Brown, keeping his own counsel, went about his mysterious activities. The Secret Six, hearing from their agent only when he needed money, knew nothing of his plans. Not understanding that they were his instrument and not vice versa, Howe felt it incumbent upon him to advise him. In the mistaken notion that Brown was preparing to meet new Slave State maneuvers in Kansas, he urged him to act with caution, to wait for Border Ruffian moves, "& checkmate them as they are *developed*. Dont [*sic*] attack them but if they attack you 'Give them Tapie,' & Fremont too; you know how to do it."[26] The doctor's admonitions were as the idle wind. His misunderstanding of the situation was abysmal.

During these months Brown had conceived the notion of creating a new military force, the like of which the world had never seen before, one based on immutable principles of "Right." Somewhere in his experience he had acquired a nodding familiarity with doctrines of natural law. His views are of value in indicating how such principles were understood by uneducated groups among the population. He considered characteristics of "Right" to be "good, true, just, honorable, humane, self-sacrificing. . . ." However men might quail before danger and privation,

Right itself cannot alter, though it may shine more beautiful [*sic*] under persecution. Between Right and Wrong, there can be no compromise. [The object of legitimate authority being the benefit of the people] no majority can rightfully sacrafice [*sic*] the freedom and well-being of any one fellow-man or of posterity.

The test of legitimate authority he found in the Right, in the maintenance of which soldiers were not required to be mere "living machines," but responsible, thinking beings.

It is also self-evident that every citizen is in duty bound to sustain Right, even though he thereby neglect some of his private business: he who

---

[25] Howe's testimony before the Harpers Ferry Investigating Committee, Appendix to *Report*, p. 156.

[26] Howe to Brown, Nov. 7, 1857, Howe Papers, MHS.

regards his personal interests as being of more importance to him, than to exercise a watchfulness at all times for the public good, and for the maintenance of Right: fails in a great obligation towards the Commonwealth.[27]

His men were to be of the thinking responsible variety.

Slowly the army of the Lord took shape. In March of 1857, during a visit to New York, Brown hired Hugh Forbes, a native of Great Britain, who liked to call himself "Colonel," to serve as military strategist and drillmaster. A professional soldier who had seen service with Garibaldi in 1848, he claimed to be an authority on tactics. He prepared special manuals for the use of the men, and was in charge of their training while the captain was absent for long periods attending to supplies and funds.[28] Every few weeks the Secret Six received cryptic calls for more money, perhaps $500 or $1000 "for *secret service,* and no *questions asked.* I want the friends of Freedom to 'prove me now herewith.' " [29]

Brown traveled widely incognito. During the first two months of 1858, he stayed with Frederick Douglass in Rochester, New York, where he received his mail as "N. Hawkins." In February he wrote Parker that he had *"nearly* perfected arrangements for carrying out an important measure, in which *the world* has a deep interest, *as well* as Kansas." He needed only $500 to $800 to perfect "BY FAR the most *important* undertaking of my whole life." He hoped he would never again be driven to *harass* his friends as he had.[30] It was difficult to meet this new demand. The effects of the panic of 1857 were still being felt. As Higginson put it, "I am always ready to invest money in treason, but at present have none to invest." [31]

[27] "The Duty of the Soldier" (1857), in Parker Letterbook 9, pp. 281–285; Sanborn dates this as Sept. 11, 1857, *John Brown,* p. 422.

[28] *New York Herald,* Oct. 27, 1859; Jan. 14, 1858, Brown's Diary, BPL.

[29] Brown to Parker, Sept. 11, 1857, Letterbook 9, p. 280, MHS.

[30] Brown to Parker, Feb. 2, 1858, Letterbook 9, p. 285; also Brown to Higginson, same date, Higginson Papers on John Brown in BPL, I, 1. There is an unclear sentence here. He says, "I have written Rev Theodore Parker, George L. Stearns, & FB Sanborn Esqus, on the subject; but do not know as either Mr Stearns, or Mr Sanborn, are abolitionists. I suppose they are." This is strange since he had met them all the year before, and surely must have known where they stood on slavery.

[31] Higginson to "N. Hawkins," Feb. 8, 1858, Higginson Collection of John Brown Papers, I, 2, BPL.

Whether money was forthcoming or not, Brown went ahead with his program. In vague terms, saying only that he expected to "overthrow Slavery in a large part of the country," he gave the Six the impression that he contemplated a slave uprising. They saw nothing wrong in this, since as Sanborn put it, "The Union is Evidently on its last legs and Buchanan is laboring to tear it in pieces — Treason will not be treason much longer, but patriotism." [32]

The captain, deciding that he could raise more money if he told his backers his plans, invited them to a conference at Smith's home in Peterboro. [33] Only Sanborn went. There on February 22, 1858, Brown unfolded his mad scheme to a few supporters. He proposed to attack at some point in the slaveholding territories, east of the Alleghenies. For this he wanted $800. He read them a "Constitution" he had drawn up in Douglass' house in Rochester for the government of any regions he might rescue.

We listened until after midnight [Sanborn says], proposing objections and raising difficulties; but nothing could shake the purpose of the old Puritan. Every difficulty had been foreseen and provided against in some manner; the grand difficulty of all — the manifest hopelessness of undertaking anything so vast with such slender means — was met with the text of Scripture: "If God be for us, who can be against us?"

Brown prevailed over all attempts at dissuasion. At length, the next day, they saw it was futile to fight him. They must "either stand by him or leave him to dash himself alone against the fortress he had determined to assault. To withhold aid would delay, not prevent him." More out of regard for the man than from hope of immediate success, both Smith and Sanborn pledged themselves to raise money for him. [34]

The following week Brown outlined his project in greater detail to his New England supporters in Boston. [35] He planned to penetrate Virginia with a few comrades but to keep utterly clear of all at-

[32] Sanborn to Higginson, Feb. 11, 1858, Higginson John Brown Papers, I, 3.
[33] Brown to Higginson, Feb. 12, 1858, Higginson John Brown Papers, I, 4.
[34] Sanborn, *Recollections,* I, 145–147.
[35] Brown to Higginson, March 4, 1858, Higginson John Brown Papers, I, 7; also Brown to Parker, same date, Letterbook 9, p. 287.

tempts to create a slave insurrection. Willing to let events guide him, he desired to gather the families of fugitive slaves and establish them permanently in the region. Otherwise, he would take them to Canada via the Underground Railway.[36] Higginson, Parker, Sanborn, and Stearns looked to Howe, as the acknowledged military expert among them, for his opinion. Despite the obvious weaknesses of the plan, namely the recrossing of the Potomac in case of emergency, the doctor approved. He had seen Turkish armies defeated in mountain passes by comparatively small numbers. It seemed to him that the same could be done in the Alleghenies.[37] All opposition to the proposal was now overcome. Sanborn later insisted that Brown never mentioned the exact site he had in mind, although he casually asked him what he thought of Harpers Ferry, but in such a way as to arouse no suspicion.[38]

After having gained promises of continued support, Brown left Boston a few days later. Howe, Parker, Stearns, Higginson, and Sanborn were assessed to raise $100 each, the goal being $1000.[39] At a meeting in Howe's office on Bromfield Street a fortnight later, Stearns was named treasurer of the drive.[40] By the end of April, Brown received $410 of $500 pledged in Massachusetts. Not embarrassed by want of means, he was at his headquarters in Canada completing preparations. He expected "to turn his flock loose about the 15th of May." [41]

IV

All these plans were disrupted by the defection of Hugh Forbes, Brown's chief assistant, who broke with him during the fall of 1857. Money appears to have been the cause. In December, Forbes wrote to Sumner for aid, but the senator merely transmitted the appeal to

[36] Thomas Wentworth Higginson, *Cheerful Yesterdays* (Boston, 1900), p. 221. This was written 40 years later. Higginson's memory may have failed him.

[37] Stearns, Life of *George L. Stearns*, p. 164.

[38] Sanborn, *Recollections,* I, 151.

[39] Sanborn to Higginson, March 8, 1858, Higginson John Brown Papers, I, 8, BPL.

[40] Progress of the drive can be traced in Stearns to Higginson, and Sanborn to Higginson, in March and April, Higginson John Brown Papers, I, 9, 10, and 11.

[41] Sanborn to Higginson, April 20, 1858, Higginson John Brown Papers, I, 12.

Howe and Sanborn, both of whom denied any responsibility to him. The enraged soldier denounced the Boston abolitionists for bad faith. In the following months he deluged Howe with frenetic communications. Sumner again interceded for him, but Howe was adamant.[42] Never having met Forbes, Howe could judge him only from his letters, the tone of which indicated the falsity of his charges. The doctor was surprised that Sumner did not see through them. Howe denied any responsibility for whatever agreement Forbes had reached with Brown. Anyhow the terms were not as Forbes claimed. Brown, who had been more than generous, had promised to pay him only when he had money, and had advanced him six months' salary at the outset of their relationship. Though Forbes was supposed to send that to his family, who were destitute in Paris, he had used the money to publish his book on tactics. There was no reason for any of the committee to concern themselves about him. He had proven himself completely unreliable.[43]

Forbes tried a new approach. Late in April he wrote Howe and Sanborn, threatening to sell his secrets to the *New York Herald* unless he were put in charge of the expedition.[44] After notifying Brown of the worst, Howe, Sanborn, and Stearns held a worried meeting on May 2 to discuss this new aspect of affairs. The doctor was alone in his insistence that the plan proceed according to schedule, while the others urged delay for another year.[45] When apprised of the situation, Higginson supported Howe. They had gone so far; they could not go back. Any postponement meant abandonment forever. Forbes must in some way be put down.[46] Meanwhile Brown had written that he would go ahead as long as supplies held out.[47]

Howe was certain that his forthright treatment had forestalled Forbes.[48] But this smugness was a bit premature.

[42] Sumner to Howe, March 25, 1858, Sumner Papers, Houghton.

[43] Howe to Sumner, April 6, 1858, Howe Papers, Houghton.

[44] Sanborn to Higginson, May 1, 1858, Higginson John Brown Papers, I, 13, BPL.

[45] Sanborn to Higginson, May 5, 1858, Higginson John Brown Papers, I, 14.

[46] Higginson (to either Stearns or Howe), May 7, 1858, Higginson John Brown Papers, I, 15.

[47] Sanborn to Higginson, May 11, 1858, Higginson John Brown Papers, I, 17.

[48] Howe to Higginson, May (n.d.), 1858, Higginson John Brown Papers, I, 19.

Thus rebuffed, Forbes began to undermine Brown in Washington. He told Senator Seward everything.[49] Within a few days Howe began to receive alarming reports from the Capitol. Wilson was especially upset, having heard that Brown was planning some unlawful military expedition in which he would use the arms of the Kansas Aid Committee.[50]

Howe flew into one of his tempestuous rages when he learned of these developments. In a blistering letter to Forbes, the only time he ever wrote him, he refused to desert Brown. Still, he disclaimed responsibility for the gallant captain's acts. Brown was one of "scores & hundreds of men" in whom he had confidence, but confidence did not necessarily entail accountability. Neither he nor any of the Secret Six had delegated power to bind them to another person. They and Brown were free to make any agreements they pleased. In contrast to Brown's integrity, there was Forbes, who would have approved of Brown's plan had he been allowed to lead it, but now threatened to betray it. "You are the guardian Sir of your own honor, but I trust that for your children's sake at least, you will never let your passion lead you to a course that might make them blush." In conclusion, Howe promised to aid his family if they were in need, as he would any family, but he would do nothing if abused. He would not even read any letters addressed to him in passionate terms.[51]

Forbes, responding in kind, told him that his "caprice of refusing to read anything distasteful is so like a pouting, spoilt child, that I should not be surprised at your being easily hoodwinked by any one who were to approach you with flattery and a pleasing story." He stated that the doctor's disclaimer of responsibility for Brown's acts was a "cowardly shirking of responsibility" and "simple absurdity." Forbes outlined an alternative plan which had been agreed to earlier. Instead of one sensational armed attack in Virginia, they had decided on a series of slave stampedes along the northern slave frontier, each one to run off about twenty to fifty slaves a month, eventually increasing the number to that many a week. While the

[49] Forbes to Howe, May 6, 1858; published in *New York Herald,* Oct. 27, 1859.
[50] Howe to Wilson, Jan. 23, 1860, Howe Papers, MHS.
[51] Howe to Forbes, May 10, 1858, Howe Papers, MHS.

fugitives remained in the Allegheny Mountains, New England abolitionists were to call a convention to restore intersectional tranquillity and overthrow the pro-slavery administration. Brown, in setting these proposals aside, had committed a breach of confidence which he could not tolerate. Howe would be "worse than insane — you must be depraved — to expect it of me." Brown was dangerous and had to be stopped. As for the New England "humanitarians," they were planning to speculate on the rise of cotton when war commenced. Forbes had learned that Lawrence had promised Brown $7000 in furtherance of this aim.[52] The conclusion of Forbes's letter with its libelous charges convinced Howe that Brown was fortunate to be rid of him.

The events of the past week had shown Howe the necessity of mending fences. He dashed off a note to reassure Wilson that prompt measures would be taken and resolutely followed up to prevent any monstrous perversion of trust "as would be the application of means raised for the defense of Kansas, to a purpose which the subscribers to the fund would disapprove & vehemently condemn." [53] Stearns, for the sake of the record (and luckily for him as later events showed), warned Brown that the rifles were to be used only in Kansas, and nowhere else.[54] This was all subterfuge. It had been arranged to transfer the arms from the committee's hands to Stearns who took them over as "security" for a loan he had "advanced." [55] (It is strange that a man who had donated many thousands of dollars of his own money should now grant loans on security.) Both Howe and Sanborn urged the change so that they could truthfully tell Wilson

the Kansas *Committee* had not countenanced Brown in "any operations outside of Kansas." But [as Sanborn later claimed] Stearns had not only countenanced the use of his rifles by Brown, in Virginia or further west, but had also supplied him with revolvers at his own expense. It was not

---

[52] Forbes to Howe, May 14, 1858, in *New York Herald,* Oct. 27, 1859.

[53] Howe to Wilson, May 15, 1858, copy, Howe Papers, MHS.

[54] Stearns to Howe, May 14, 1858, Howe Papers, MHS; HF Investigating Committee, Appendix to *Report,* p. 177.

[55] Stearns, *Life of George L. Stearns,* p. 171. Stearns's son wrote that he gave the loan in the summer of 1857, but all the evidence indicates it was done at this time.

intended to inform Wilson of the real state of the case; for that would have been betraying confidence towards Stearns and Brown.[56]

In the face of Forbes's disclosure of the plot, Sanborn placed himself firmly against going on. It was madness to continue, he wrote.[57] But Higginson and Howe refused to give up. Considering it disgraceful to have been outmaneuvered by such a person as Forbes, they urged that there was still time to undertake the raid before he could publish the plan more extensively.[58] Their inquiries in New York about him had shown that he was considered more a fool than a knave. He could easily be circumvented.[59]

Within a few days the two holdouts realized the futility of their position, and agreed to postponement. Howe was especially regretful, but felt he had to acquiesce in the majority opinion. At the end of May, having won over Gerrit Smith to their view, the Secret Six bluntly told Brown, who had come to Boston for the meeting, that he would have to wait until the next year. In the meantime he was to return to Kansas; they would keep him supplied with money. The "property" (the Sharps rifles) was to be transferred so as to relieve them of the responsibility. In the future they were not to know his plans. Blaming Wilson's panicky letter for having intimidated his supporters so that they overrated the obstacles, Brown felt betrayed. He knew that Gerrit Smith was a timid man, nor did he feel that Parker and Stearns abounded in courage.[60]

Nothing more was heard from Brown for the rest of that year except that he was in disguise in Kansas, engaged in running off slaves from Missouri to the Free States.[61] Forbes too disappeared from sight, possibly with some Boston money given out of charity, since Howe promised that any man in distress had a claim upon

[56] Sanborn to Henry Richards, May 15, 1908, Higginson Papers, Houghton, item 676. This letter should be used with extreme caution. It is an apologia written in old age by the most rabid of Brown's defenders to Howe's son-in-law.
[57] Sanborn to Higginson, May 18, 1858, Higginson John Brown Papers, I, 22a, BPL.
[58] Higginson to Parker, May 18, 1858, Higginson John Brown Papers, I, 22b, BPL.
[59] Higginson to Brown, May 18, 1858, Higginson John Brown Papers, I, 23b, BPL.
[60] Memo dated June 1, 1858, Higginson John Brown Papers, I, 27, BPL.
[61] Brown to Sanborn, July 20, 1858, Higginson John Brown Papers, I, 31, BPL.

every humane heart. Despite his abusive language they would not cut him off. "Let me know how without hurting his feelings, we can help him," Howe asked.[62] The truth about Forbes was probably as George Wood, a long-time resident of Washington, whom Howe appears to have met, said: Forbes's difficulty was insanity caused by his family's utter destitution and his inability to help them. There was no doubt that Brown had misled the impecunious soldier by representing himself as the agent of eminent men in important eastern cities.[63]

V

Brown was absent from Boston for the next ten months, but his friends continued to work for him. Howe was devoted to the old warrior's cause. He was willing to answer for Brown's honesty of purpose. Certain that there were many persons in the city who would contribute if properly approached, he undertook to tap the wealthy John Murray Forbes, former China-trade merchant turned railroad builder. In effusive terms, skillfully worded so as to avoid Brown's less savory activities, Howe pointed out his valuable services. He was "the stuff of which martyrs are made." [64]

Out in Kansas, Brown was growing impatient. It was now the "next spring" for which he had been told to wait. Early in March he communicated with Howe in an effort to pry more money out of Boston and, of course, to force some action. "To effect a good seasons [sic] work we ought to begin early: & all that I know of to hinder our doing so is the want of a trifling sum for an outfit." [65]

Sporting a bushy white beard, and with a reward of $3250 out for him as a consequence of his past season's work, Brown turned up in Massachusetts at the beginning of May for the usual round of conferences. Howe having arranged for him to visit Forbes, Sanborn took him out to Milton for tea one day to meet likely prospects among the neighbors. Until after midnight he captivated his audi-

---

[62] Howe to George Wood, May 26, 1858, Howe Papers, MHS.
[63] George Wood to Howe, May 19, 1858, Howe Papers, MHS.
[64] Howe to Forbes, Feb. 5, 1859, in Sarah Forbes Hughes, *Letters and Recollections of John Murray Forbes* (Boston, 1899), I, 178.
[65] Brown to Howe, March 1, 1859, Howe Papers, Houghton.

ence with the power of his "personality." [66] However, all he could get from the industrialist was $100 for his "PAST extravagances" and none for his future.[67] John Albion Andrew, who could barely afford it, gave him $25

because I felt ashamed, after I had seen the old man and talked with him and come within the reach of the personal impression . . . that I had never contributed anything directly towards his assistance, as one whom I thought had sacrificed and suffered so much for the cause of freedom and of good order and good government in the Territory of Kansas. He was, if I may be allowed to use that expression, a very magnetic person, and I felt very much impressed by him.[68]

Some were able to extricate themselves from Brown's mesmeric influence. A. A. Lawrence, who had earlier supported him, regained his perspective. He realized now that Brown was a monomaniac, whose activities were harmful. Testily he confided to his journal that Brown appeared to be suffering from a fever, "probably a righteous visitation for [his] fanaticism." [69]

Despite this defection, and the fact that contributions had not come in as freely as in the past, Brown left Boston after three weeks with over $2000.[70] His backers had seen him for the last time.

[66] Sarah Hughes, *Letters of John Murray Forbes,* I, 180–182.
[67] Forbes to ? (probably Howe), May 12, 1859, Howe Papers, MHS.
[68] Andrew's testimony before HF Investigating Comm., Appendix to *Report,* p. 192.
[69] William Lawrence, *Life of A. A. Lawrence,* p. 130.
[70] Sanborn to Higginson, May 30, 1859, Higginson John Brown Papers, I, 46, BPL.

XV

The Aftermath of Harpers Ferry

Although Brown's whereabouts remained unknown to his Boston supporters, fund-raising continued throughout the summer of 1859. Whenever there was any money, whether Howe's $50, or Gerrit Smith's $100, they sent it to one of the addresses he had given them.[1] As Sanborn put it, "Out of the mouths of babes and sucklings come dollars by the hundred, and what is wisdom compared to that? . . . 'tis a virtue posted in numbskulls, to give money freely. . . ."[2]

I

On the secluded Kennedy Farm which he had rented until March 1, 1860, four miles over the Maryland border from Harpers Ferry, old Brown completed his preparations. He laid aside his cares momentarily to perform his duty as the head of a family. From stern Gideon he softened to loving father as he commended his beloved ones to God. In touching terms, but nonetheless practical, he urged his small daughter Annie to live righteously and efficiently. "I want *you first of all* to become: *a sincere humble, earnest, & consistent, Christian:* & then acquire good and *efficient business*

---

[1] Sanborn to Brown, Aug. 30, 1859, HF Investigation, *Report*, p. 68.
[2] Sanborn to Higginson, Oct. 13, 1859, Higginson John Brown Papers, I, 54, BPL.

habits." Sensing the end that awaited him, he urged her to save the letter to remember him by. A few more words of advice, and he was again the military commander.[3]

At length all was in readiness. His little company of eighteen, of whom two were his sons, and five were Negroes, were fully trained and prepared. Early on the morning of Sunday, October 16, 1859, he gave the quiet order, "Men, get on your arms; we will proceed to the Ferry." [4] The rest is history. For two days the small band held the town at bay, before Colonel Robert E. Lee with a contingent of soldiers and marines could force surrender. Brown was taken alive, though seriously wounded. His sons lay dead. His prisoners testified to his bravery, his coolness under fire, and his leniency toward them.[5]

The South, living in deathly fear of a slave uprising, was relieved when none materialized. The Negroes had not joined as Brown had hoped. In fact, the few he had forcibly freed returned to their masters voluntarily. All were amazed at the small numbers involved, but Henry A. Wise, Governor of Virginia, was mortified that nineteen men had found it possible to capture a government arsenal and hold it as long as they had. He would rather have lost both legs at the hips and both arms at the shoulders than that such a disgrace should have fallen on his state.[6]

Immediately on reading of Brown's capture, Howe mobilized an *ad hoc* committee, of Wendell Phillips, Andrew, and Higginson to provide for his defense. He communicated with Montgomery Blair in the hope that this distinguished public figure would serve as counsel, and even approached the disapproving A. A. Lawrence for a contribution, with the plea, "No stone must be left unturned to save his life & the country the disgrace of his execution." [7]

---

[3] Brown to his family, Oct. 1, 1859, Higginson John Brown Papers, I, 33, BPL.
[4] Villard, *John Brown,* p. 426. Full account of the raid to be found from p. 426 to p. 466.
[5] *Boston Advertiser,* Oct. 20, 1859.
[6] *Boston Advertiser,* Oct. 22, 1859.
[7] Howe to Lawrence, Oct. 10, 1859, A. A. Lawrence Papers, XVIII, 287, MHS. The date is the 10th, but this is impossible. It might be the 18th, or the 20th, or thereabouts.

The doctor dispatched a messenger of "pluck & discretion" to follow developments at the scene. Howe was confident that Brown would not compromise himself or those dealing with him. There would be no need to go outside legal bounds to aid the prisoner, "beyond those I ask no man to follow me however far I may be disposed to go myself." [8] There were many hurried conferences in the week between Brown's arrest and the beginning of his trial. Contributions to the defense fund began to arrive.

Brown held firm during the inquisition following his capture. Refusing to implicate any others, he took the entire blame on himself. However, in his pockets, in the arsenal, and at his farm were found his diary, correspondence, as well as other papers, which gave names and addresses. Howe, Sanborn, Higginson, Stearns, and Gerrit Smith were incriminated. More evidence came out the following week when the *New York Herald,* having bought Forbes's papers, published the bitter correspondence of the previous year. [9]

Virginia justice moved fast, some said with indecent haste. Brown was indicted on October 25, only seven days after his capture, even though he was not yet recovered from his wounds and had to attend court in a cot. [10] His trial concluded in less than a week, he was found guilty of treason and murder, and sentenced to hang on December 2. [11] There was little more that could be done for him. Forcible rescue was impossible.

On the day of the sentencing a new committee of Howe, Samuel Sewall, Ralph Waldo Emerson, and Higginson was formed to raise funds for an appeal which never materialized. [12] It was best that the judgment be carried out. As Higginson had realized even before the verdict, Brown's acquittal or rescue would not do half as much good as his execution. [13] "His death will be holy and glorious, — the gallows cannot dishonour him — he will hallow it," Julia foretold. [14]

[8] Howe to Lawrence, Oct. 24, 1859, A. A. Lawrence Papers, XVIII, 301, MHS.
[9] *New York Herald,* Oct. 25, 1859, and days following.
[10] *Boston Advertiser,* Oct. 26 and 28, 1859.
[11] *Boston Advertiser,* Nov. 1 and 3, 1859.
[12] Circular dated Nov. 2, 1859, Higginson John Brown Papers, I, 64, BPL.
[13] Higginson to his Mother, Oct. 27, 1859, Higginson Papers, #646, Houghton.
[14] J. W. Howe to Annie Mailliard, Nov. 6, 1859, Howe Papers, Houghton.

II

Brown awaited his fate stolidly during the month that remained to him. The martyr's crown sat gracefully upon him. He was calm and collected, showing no signs of the insanity that has been charged to him.[15] In Boston the condition was completely reversed. Men whom the world considered perfectly sane lost control of their actions when they were implicated in the raid. Though Brown had been tight-lipped about his backers, those who were captured with him did not exercise similar forbearance at their trials. Disclosures incriminated Howe and others by name. Gerrit Smith actually suffered a mental breakdown so severe that he had to be committed to an asylum for several weeks.[16]

John E. Cook, one of the prisoners, alleged that Howe had given Brown a carbine and two revolvers, which was, of course, true except that he had done this in 1857. His act had no bearing on the events of the past few weeks.[17] Howe became panic-stricken, fearing that he would be summoned to Virginia as a witness, and, once there, imprisoned. The memory of his weeks in the Berlin Prison, with their loneliness, anguish, and despair, rose like specters before him. His lawyer, John A. Andrew, informed him that by a law of August 8, 1846, a witness whose evidence was deemed material could be arrested without the formality of a summons, merely on the warrant of a federal judge, and required to give bond for his appearance at the desired time. Andrew interpreted this to bar habeas corpus, unless a state judge cared to challenge its constitutionality.[18] They were all liable for arrest, and if they were, they could not expect mercy. The situation appeared serious.

[15] See his letter to Higginson, Nov. 6, 1859, typescript in the Howe Papers, Houghton, in which he asks that his wife not come to see him in prison.

[16] *Boston Advertiser,* Nov. 10, 1859.

[17] *Boston Advertiser,* Dec. 3, 1859; typescript of story in *Ashtabula Sentinel,* Dec. 15, 1859, Villard Collection of John Brown Material in Columbia University Library.

[18] Sanborn to Higginson, Nov. 13, 1859, Higginson John Brown Papers, I, 82, BPL. The act says nothing about precluding habeas corpus. *U. S. Statutes at Large,* IX, 29 Cong., 1 sess., chap. 98, sect. 7.

Sanborn, fearing that those subpoenaed might not be able to raise a tumult in Boston, asked Higginson if he would send his parishioners, who had distinguished themselves in the Burns case, "to take Dr Howe or W. Phillips out of the Marshal's hands?" [19] The doctor did not wait to find out. He published a letter in the newspapers in which he disclaimed all knowledge of the raid. He insisted that it was entirely unforeseen and unexpected;

nor [he continued] does all my previous knowledge of John Brown enable me to reconcile it with his characteristic prudence, and his reluctance to shed blood, or excite servile insurrection. It is still to me a mystery and a marvel.

As to the heroic man who planned and led that forlorn hope, my relations with him in former times were such as no man ought to be afraid or ashamed to avow. If ever my testimony to his high qualities can be of use to him or his, it shall be forthcoming at the fitting time and place. But neither this nor any other testimony shall be extorted for unrighteous purposes, if I can help it.

Howe did not covet martyrdom under authority of the law of 1846. He felt that each citizen must protect himself from forcible apprehension. "Upon that hint I shall act; preferring to forego anything rather than the right to free thought and free speech." [20]

Thereupon, having prevailed on Stearns to accompany him, he fled to Canada where he spent the next few weeks gaining converts to the cause of teaching the blind. Howe's strange action requires some explanation. He had been putting in long hours for over two weeks arranging for Brown's defense.[21] When the exhaustion resulting from this exertion is added to the chronic ill-health and mental depression to which he had been subject for some years, it is not surprising that he should have become hysterical.

Higginson was in just as deep, but he refused to run. Howe's notice saddened him. It was the height of baseness to deny complicity with Brown's general scheme so long as they had not been called upon to say anything. Howe gave the impression that he

[19] Sanborn to Higginson, Nov. 13, 1859. Higginson John Brown Papers, I, 82, BPL.

[20] *Boston Advertiser,* Nov. 16, 1859. The letter was dated the 14th.

[21] J. W. Howe to Annie Mailliard, Nov. 6, 1859, Howe Papers, Houghton.

disclaimed all knowledge, not only of the time and place of the attack but of the enterprise itself, and that was not true.[22] On the other hand, Sanborn felt the letter neither imprudent nor base, so long as no one suffered by it. It incriminated no one, nor did it harm old Brown who still had two weeks to live.[23]

Howe, realizing that he had behaved improperly, later explained his motives. The primary object of the letter was to help Brown by showing that he was not the agent or ally of others, but had acted by himself. There was no wish to create a false impression. During the previous spring, he insisted, Brown had not revealed his destination. *"We had no conversation about his future plans.* His appearance at 'Harper's Ferry' was to me not only unexpected, but astonishing. The original plan as I understood it was quite different from this one; & even that I supposed was abandoned." He admitted that he had sent Brown $50, but out of sympathy, not cognizance of his purpose, though even if he had known his object, he might have given him aid and encouragement, such was his confidence in him. "It is true," he confessed, "that I ought to have expected an explosion and onslaught *somewhere;* but the point is, that I did not expect anything like what happened, or anything more than a stampede." [24]

That was Howe's story, and he stuck to it; but his behavior during the spring of 1858, when he and Higginson had urged Brown to proceed with his plans while the others urged postponement, should not be forgotten. It is possible that he did not realize fully what Brown had in mind. Certainly Howe never sanctioned illegal activity. It will be recalled that throughout the Kansas crisis he had insisted that the emigrants were never to resist federal troops. The only aspects of Brown's activities to which he had given unstinting support were those concerned directly with freeing slaves. The other facets of his work, such as stealing the masters' cattle and horses to defray expenses, aroused Howe's strongest condemnation. During Brown's last visit to Boston he had argued the point with

[22] Higginson to Howe, Nov. 15, 1859, Higginson John Brown Papers, I, 89, BPL. This draft was never sent; a shorter letter was substituted.
[23] Sanborn to Higginson, Nov. 17, 1859, Higginson John Brown Papers, I, 97.
[24] Howe to Higginson, Feb. 16, 1860, Higginson John Brown Papers, II, 176.

him in two interviews. Though Brown had spoken with "great correctness and ingenuity," Howe had remained unconvinced of the justice of stealing property even from slave owners. "I would not be held as a party in any way responsible for a plan involving such a consequence," he asserted.[25] Later he wrote Parker it was wicked to break the laws of society without urgent need, although one might do so to free "the meanest slave," only if one had sold all his property for the cause as Brown had.[26] Howe hoped that his flight, however wrong, would at least "draw attention to the infamous act by which southern slaveholders can throw the lasso over northern citizens when they are wanted for wicked purposes." [27]

Sanborn intended to keep working in Concord until summoned, although he swore to resist arrest and would consent to be rescued only by force. Judge Hoar had promised to defy the statute of 1846 in his case, but not an ordinary summons.[28]

III

Certain that God reigned and arranged everything in the best possible manner, John Brown lived out his last days bravely and serenely, reconciled to his fate.[29] Although he believed he was the first of his line since the voyage of the *Mayflower* either to be imprisoned or sentenced to the gallows, he did not consider himself a criminal when he recalled that his grandfather, who died in battle in 1776,

[25] Howe to Higginson, Feb. 16, 1860, Higginson John Brown Papers, II, 176, BPL. Oswald Garrison Villard offers a different interpretation. He insists that Howe knew the plan, but not the place. "Dr. Howe was not the only one who flinched when the exposé took place. His is an unhappy illustration of the fact that the best of men make grave moral mistakes in great crises, when for a moment their lives and their future appear at stake." *The Nation,* LXXXIX (Sept. 30, 1909), 302.

[26] Howe to Parker, Jan. 22, 1860, Howe Papers, Houghton.

[27] Howe to Sumner, Nov. 20, 1859, #1193 (catalogued under 1857), Howe Papers, Houghton.

[28] Sanborn to Higginson, Nov. 19, 1859, Higginson John Brown Papers, I, 101, BPL.

[29] Brown to Heman Humphrey, Nov. 25, 1859, Papers relating to John Brown given by A. A. Lawrence, p. 43, MHS.

might have perished on the scaffold had circumstances been but *very little* different. *The fact* that a man dies under the hand of an executioner (or otherwise) has but little to do with his true character, as I suppose. . . . Whether I have any reason to "be of good cheer" (or not) in view of my end; I can assure you that *I feel so:* & that I am totally *blinded* if I do not realy [*sic*] experience that *strengthening;* & *consolation* you so faithfully implore in my behalf.

He was ready to die. He was almost sixty and had always been in good health. He had never needed much sleep, and so had already had the equivalent of man's "Three Score years, & Ten." "And now when I think how easily I might *be left to spoil* all I have done, or suffered in the cause of freedom: I hardly dare risk another voyage; if I even had the opportunity. . . ." [30] All would be well. God would deliver Israel from the Philistines. Prophetically he saw that his death might be of more value than his life, "quite beyond all human foresight." [31]

With the approach of the fateful day, dread apprehension mounted throughout the country. Rumors flew that there would be an attempted rescue. To prevent such a move 2000 troops were stationed in Charlestown (now Charleston, West Virginia) at the beginning of December. Oblivious of all the excitement, Brown spent his last day with his wife in calm discussion of matter-of-fact problems such as the rearing of the younger children and the property settlement.

At 11:15 A.M. on December 2, he mounted the gallows with apparent firmness. A few moments later the trap was sprung. "A slight grasping of the hands and twitching of the muscles was seen, and then all was quiet," the *Advertiser* reported. The bright eyes were dulled at last, no longer to exert their mystic power. Thirty-five minutes later, his pulse having ceased, his body was cut down.[32]

The execution was commemorated throughout the North with the tolling of bells. Andrew, unable to work, was driven about

---

[30] Brown to Luther Humphrey, Nov. 19, 1859, #76, James Freeman Clarke Family Papers, Houghton.

[31] Brown to Heman Humphrey, Nov. 25, 1859, Lawrence Collection, p. 43.

[32] *Boston Advertiser,* Dec. 3, 1859.

the streets in a carriage.[33] A new martyr entered the American
Pantheon that day, to rank with the heroes who were to die in
the greater struggle that was to begin within a little over a year.

> He had no gift for life, no gift to bring
> Life but his body and a cutting edge,
> But he knew how to die[34]

one of our greatest poets has written. Yes, Brown knew how to
die. It no longer mattered that his work was of no intrinsic significance, that his raids in Kansas did not safeguard it for freedom,
or that his attack at Harpers Ferry did not bring emancipation of
the slaves any closer.[35] Had he never lived, Kansas would have
developed as it has, and the Civil War would have come when it
did. In death he gained atonement and canonization. In the folk-
lore of the nation, his death is an inspiring tale of noble self-sacrifice.
It is not for this author to rewrite popular tales.

IV

Howe returned to Boston a few days after Brown's execution,
uncertain of his reception.[36] When he saw that he was not to be
arrested, he proceeded openly about his business. There was talk
in Congress of appointing a committee to investigate the raid. He
realized that he and his fellow conspirators would be ordered to
appear before it, but he feared they would not be safe in Washington if they told all they knew about practical abolition. He thought
that Virginia extremists might spirit them over the Potomac and
lynch them, or the Virginia authorities might extradite them and
have them indicted as accessories before the fact. As Montgomery
Blair had urged him not to endanger himself, he asked Sumner if
the law could do anything to an abolitionist who had given money
and aided the underground railroad without knowing its plans.[37]

[33] Henry Greenleaf Pearson, *The Life of John A. Andrew* (Boston, 1904), I, 104.
[34] Stephen Vincent Benét, *John Brown's Body, Selected Works* (New York, 1942),
I, 48.
[35] Malin, *John Brown and the Legend of Fifty-Six,* p. 759.
[36] Howe to Sumner, Dec. 6, 1859, #1195 (catalogued under 1857), Howe
Papers, Houghton.
[37] Howe to Sumner, Dec. 13, 1859, Howe Papers, Houghton.

Sumner reassured him that there was nothing to fear in Virginia's menaces. The only question was his complicity with the offenders. If he could deny that, there was nothing more to worry about. His other activities as an abolitionist were not distinctive enough to cause trouble.[38] He was told that he should dismiss Montgomery Blair's advice from his mind. The Senate committee under the chairmanship of James Mason of Virginia, which was appointed in mid-December, was not unfair. Of its five members two were anti-slavery. One of the latter told Sumner that no one not an accomplice had anything to fear.[39]

Though Howe had decided by now to obey a summons, Sanborn and Higginson were adamant in their decisions to refuse.[40] After conferences with Andrew, Howe, Stearns, and Phillips, Sanborn offered to testify in Massachusetts. He had no doubt that Washington was a trap.[41]

On Christmas eve Wilson wrote that Howe, Sanborn, Higginson, Stearns, and Lawrence were to be sent for. They would have to testify or face contempt charges, even if they incriminated themselves. It was perfectly safe; their evidence could not be used against them as bases for future indictments. "The Committee will cast a drag-net over the North and get all they can," he stated. "Mason thinks that they will discover a great plot and implicate several public men in it. I think he will be mistaken in that." [42] The junior senator from Massachusetts was determined that any of his constituents who were summoned had better appear. He made it clear that he would give no assistance to those who disobeyed a congressional subpoena.[43]

Over the Christmas holidays Howe returned to Canada to appear before Parliament on behalf of the education of the blind.[44] He was

[38] Sumner to Howe, Dec. 15, 1859, Sumner Papers, Houghton.

[39] Sumner to Howe, undated, Sumner Papers, Houghton.

[40] Sanborn to Howe, Dec. 19, 1859, Howe Papers, MHS.

[41] Sanborn to Higginson, Dec. 20, 1859, Higginson Collection of John Brown Papers, II, 130, BPL.

[42] Wilson to Higginson, Dec. 24, 1859, Higginson John Brown Papers, II, 135, BPL.

[43] Sanborn to Higginson, Dec. 25, 1859, Higginson John Brown Papers, II, 136, BPL.

[44] *American Traveller,* Dec. 31, 1859, Howe clippings, second box, Perkins School.

not in flight. Much to Sanborn's annoyance the doctor had given his word to go to Washington.[45] It had been a hard decision for him to make, since he had all the "New Englanders superstition about legal forms. A constable's pole is to me an awful emblem of power; & I should bow to a legal process, as the Turk . . . submits . . . to the bowstring." Misgivings about a trap remained strong.

I think I can take care of myself among bullies & rowdies; at least I hope I should have no more fear of violence in Washington than the rest of you; but a Virginia process would be worse to me than a call to fight with all the wild beasts of Ephesus.[46]

Had he not taken as many missteps as he had, all of which he wished to retrace, he would not have thought of obeying a summons, but he felt his position was too weak to defy the committee.[47] He would go and express the admiration and respect he felt for the old hero. It was disgraceful that there was no Republican senator who could protect them.[48] Howe had no illusions about the real object of the investigation. It was just another prostitution of "Senatorial dignity & duty to base purposes." [49] "An extra judicial investigating Committee may be better than a Virginia District Court," he told Wilson, "but it is not American in its origin or character. Akin to the Inquisition, its Chairman may well take a leaf out of the books of an Austrian Minister of Police."[50]

Montgomery Blair informed Andrew of what they should seek to prove. He had followed the senatorial debate which preceded the creation of the committee, and knew what the Southerners were looking for. It would be necessary to show that the rifles captured in Brown's possession had gone originally to Kansas, and that he appropriated them to his own use without the consent of the Stearns committee. With the burden of evidence early in January pointing to the culpability of the Bostonians, they would have to

---

[45] Sanborn to Higginson, Jan. 2, 1860, Higginson John Brown Papers, II, 142, BPL.
[46] Howe to Sumner, Jan. 15, 1860, Howe Papers, Houghton.
[47] Howe to Sumner, Jan. 21, 1860, Howe Papers, Houghton.
[48] Howe to Parker, Jan. 22, 1860, Howe Papers, Houghton.
[49] Howe to Sumner, Jan. 21, 1860, Howe Papers, Houghton.
[50] Howe to Wilson, Jan. 23, 1860, Howe Papers, MHS.

find something to counteract these accusations, since people would not otherwise believe that Brown had deceived them as to the object of the arms. He pointed out that their refusal to appear would strengthen Mason's position.[51] Luckily for their side, Stearns's letter to Brown forbidding him to use the rifles anywhere but in Kansas was found.[52]

Sumner reassured everyone that every effort would be made not to attract attention by the summonses. The marshals, he said, had been ordered to serve their processes as quietly as possible. Witnesses would have ample time to appear. There was no cause for anxiety. "I do not see how there can be a *man-trap,*" he told Andrew. Nothing would please Mason "more than to have Northern witnesses refuse to come, so that he might say he could not get the testimony he wanted." [53]

Howe was originally scheduled to appear in Washington on January 24, but needing more time, he requested a week's delay, which was granted. "I cannot tell you how much relieved I am by the decision to go on," he told Sumner. "I have yielded too much to others. The thought of any evasion was always repugnant to my feelings. . . ." [54] Testifying before the full committee on February 3, he said what might have been expected. He admitted giving Brown his own money and raising more from others, but denied that he knew anything about the raid at Harpers Ferry until he read about it.[55]

Andrew, Stearns, Wilson, and Lawrence also appeared. Sanborn refused, although summoned. He was actually arrested by the marshal, but was rescued by his neighbors.[56] Higginson was never called, but he too would have disobeyed. They were both enraged at Howe's perfidy.[57] The whole affair blew over harmlessly. All

[51] Blair to Andrew, Jan. 6, 1860, Howe Papers, MHS.
[52] Blair to Andrew, Jan. 21, 1860, Howe Papers, MHS.
[53] Sumner to Andrew, Jan. 12, 1860, Sumner Papers, Houghton.
[54] Howe to Sumner, Jan. 26, 1860, Howe Papers, Houghton.
[55] Harpers Ferry Investigation Committee, *Report,* Appendix, pp. 156–179.
[56] Sanborn, *Recollections,* I, 208–218.
[57] Higginson to Sanborn, Feb. 3, 1860, Higginson John Brown Papers, II, 164, BPL. In their old age these two engaged in a rather silly altercation over whether Higginson had written to Gov. Wise asking that he be called. Sanborn said he had. Higgin-

witnesses denied their complicity, leaving the committee to report that there was no proof of a widespread plot.[58]

All sides had been shown up in a bad light. Howe had behaved with surprising cowardice, but one can hardly blame a man for seeking to avoid imprisonment if he can. After all, he had responsibilities to his dependents, a wife and five children. A sixth was born Christmas morning. Sanborn and Higginson behaved with consistent stiff-neckedness. On the other side, Mason and his Southern colleagues showed that they were not interested in determining the true nature of John Brown's raid, since no attempt was ever made to punish the men who refused to testify.[59] All sought to make political capital while the nation crumbled.

son to Oswald Garrison Villard, Oct. 5 and Oct. 23, 1909, Higginson Papers, #652 and 653, Houghton.

[58] Harpers Ferry Investigation, *Report,* p. 18.

[59] The four were John Brown, Jr., Thaddeus Hyatt, James Redpath, and Franklin B. Sanborn, Harpers Ferry Investigation, *Report,* p. 19.

XVI

"He Is Trampling Out the Vintage"

In the years preceding the Civil War, Howe almost lost heart with the abolition movement. Few asserted antislavery with any vigor, he felt. The Republican Party, born so nobly, had bogged down miserably. He feared it would never succeed until it became openly aggressive, and rose over the Native American elements still in it.[1] The party leaders' lack of principle, in particular their eagerness to compromise in order to bring about immediate results, disgusted him. Henry Wilson was the prime example of a political opportunist, a man without "much of the heroic element," who would never win a martyr's crown as Sumner had.[2] Howe predicted an early death for the organization unless it lived up to the program which had given it birth.[3]

As the crisis deepened during 1860, Howe came to expect bloodshed between North and South. The Union was artificial and a

[1] Howe to Sumner, Nov. 6, 1858, Howe Papers, Houghton.
[2] Howe to Sumner, July 27, 1858, Howe Papers, Houghton.
[3] Howe to Conway, Sept. 13, 1859, Howe Papers, MHS. Nor did he consider the Democrats any better. A hypocritical, despotic group, they required for their destruction a complete revolution in national socio-political feelings. Howe looked on Stephen A. Douglas' re-election in 1858 as bad for the cause of freedom, because he considered him the only person who could save the Democracy from destruction. Howe to Sumner, Nov. 6, 1858, Howe Papers, Houghton.

failure. It had started off with moral and political axioms irresistible in their simplicity and beauty only to taper off to the conventional and the temporary. "I do think we are making a Fetish out of this *political* Union, & forgetting that the *real bonds* thereof would remain untouched though the federation were broken up," he wrote early in 1860.[4] He faced secession with equanimity.

I

Now in his late fifties, advancing age had brought debility to Howe. Despite the vigor he had shown in the Kansas crisis and the John Brown affair, he was ill. He had driven himself too hard, and had sustained great shocks, mentally and physically. His little world had begun to crumble. Except for his children, his greatest joy, home was not too pleasant. He and Julia did not get along well. His old friends had also begun to disappear. Sumner was in Washington or abroad most of the time. Mann was in Ohio as President of Antioch College. Parker was ill, and dying of tuberculosis. Death finally carried off both Mann and Parker in 1859 and 1860 respectively.[5]

Complaining of having lost touch with things, Howe felt terribly out of sorts. So great was his depression that in 1858 he actually thought of resigning from Perkins.[6] The next year he prophesied that he would not hold out much longer: "My machinery was very tough but ah the grit that has got in has worn away some of the main springs." [7] He was too old to form new intimacies, he feared,

---

[4] Howe to Sumner, April 5, 1860, Howe Papers, Houghton.

[5] Mann's death in August of 1859 was unexpected. Howe was prostrated by the news, but was determined that a memorial to the great educator should be raised on the most fitting spot in Massachusetts, the State House Yard. There it would provide a balance to the recently unveiled statue of Daniel Webster, which was an eyesore to him. He organized a committee which raised a sum sufficient to erect a statue that was unveiled in 1865. Howe to Sumner, Aug. 20, 1859, Howe Papers, Houghton, gives his reaction to Mann's death. Most of Howe's letters from Sept. 1859 through the spring of 1860 refer to his efforts to get the subscription going.

[6] Howe to Sumner, July 11, 1858, Howe Papers, Houghton. It would not have been difficult for him to resign. He was rather bored with the place, and had anything good turned up he would have left.

[7] Howe to Parker, Aug. 21, 1859, #1191 (catalogued under 1857), Howe Papers, Houghton.

although he had begun to see much of John A. Andrew, "that loveable & most excellent man." [8]

This new friend was really an old acquaintance from Common School Controversy days, when he had aided Sumner's ill-fated campaign to get on the School Committee. Since then their relationship had grown steadily closer. Short and stout, with a mop of tightly curled hair, Andrew looked cherubic. Equally popular with adults and children, he was in his intimate moments every bit as jolly, merry, and delightful as he looked.[9] A native of Maine, a graduate of Bowdoin, and eventually Sumner's neighbor at 4 Court Street, Andrew had gone through life talking, seeming to prefer that activity to anything else. However he ordinarily chattered to a purpose. Reform was indigenous to his soul, and for him "none so stood for the ideal reformer as Sumner and Howe." [10] Since the mid-forties, as a young lawyer just beginning his practice, he had associated himself with them. Later he generally had the job of introducing the resolutions at the frequent Faneuil Hall meetings called to protest everything from the annexation of Texas to Brooks's assault on Sumner. Step by step during these years, Andrew had gone up, gaining the attention of party leaders. Now, during the spring of 1860, one of the major Republican figures, he was being considered for the governorship.[11]

II

It took only a good rousing cause to give Howe a mission, and the desire to live to see its successful conclusion. The Civil War furnished the stimulation he needed. At first Howe did not oppose secession. He preferred letting the Southern states go if they wanted to, since it was best to avoid strife. At any rate there should be no war to preserve the Union as it was, with "cancerous excrescences which shoot out from its southern extremities." If, for

[8] Howe to Sumner, June 19, 1859, Howe Papers, Houghton.
[9] Florence Howe Hall, *Memories Grave and Gay* (New York, 1918), pp. 146–149; Laura E. Richards, *Stepping Westward* (New York, 1931), pp. 61–62.
[10] Henry Greenleaf Pearson, *The Life of John A. Andrew* (Boston, 1904), I, 47.
[11] Pearson, *Life of John A. Andrew*, I, 1-67, for biographical details.

geographic reasons, it were impossible to allow the slave states to exist alone, and if they refused to institute gradual emancipation through an intermediate status of serfdom, "then in God's name, let the strife come now; & if need be, let it be an aroused one."[12] Howe estimated that it would take 20,000 volunteers, or at most 40,000, only sixty days to "plough through the South, & be followed by a blaze of servile war that would utterly & forever root out slaveholding & slaveholders."[13] He thought that perhaps it was just as well if there were bloodshed; it was the only way the South had left open. The problem of slavery would at last be settled, and the United States would fall in step with the rest of the Western world. All over Europe liberalism was in the ascendant. The "reaction is now in favour of our cause & of individualism," he wrote Sumner.

Let the lines be drawn distinctly; — &, with freedom & right on one side, & slavery & wrong on the other, he is an infidel & an Atheist who can doubt the final result.

Oh, God! for a tithe of your power, that I too might take part in this glorious struggle.[14]

Howe rejoiced in the growing antislavery sentiment which he saw rising in the North. How foolish of the South not to discern the signs of the times! Just as grass grows each year beyond the power of man to stop it, so did the abolition movement.[15] The moral nature of man was coming to the front at last. Now ceasing to speak of old age and death, Howe hoped to live to be a citizen of a real republic, one based on the political equality of all men.[16] Man was again proving himself perfectible.

During the "secession winter" of 1860–1861, before the holocaust

[12] Howe to Sumner, Jan. 20, 1861, Howe Papers, Houghton. Two years later he wrote that if Alsace-Lorraine and Normandy should secede from France, and problems such as the navigation of the Seine arose, the nationality of France would have to be maintained. "The parallelism with our case would be obvious," he wrote Sumner, April 26, 1863, Howe Papers, Houghton.

[13] Howe to Conway, Dec. 10, 1860, Howe Papers, Houghton.

[14] Howe to Sumner, Dec. 20, 1860, Howe Papers, Houghton.

[15] Howe to Conway, Dec. 10, 1860, Howe Papers, Houghton.

[16] Howe to Sumner, Dec. 11, 1860, Howe Papers, Houghton.

came which solved all problems, agitation of the slavery problem
became so bitter that even in Boston it was unsafe for a radical
abolitionist like Wendell Phillips to appear on the streets. Howe
served as part of an escort to protect Phillips on his way home
from a meeting on January 19. Antislavery men, having anticipated
an attempt to obstruct the veteran reformer's path, had prepared
for it.

About fifty hard fisted & resolute Germans went ahead [Howe reported to Sumner the next day], & pushed the mob to the right & left.
Then followed some forty or fifty determined anti-slavery yankees
[evidently Howe's section], who arm in arm, & close ranks, preceded &
followed Phillipps [sic]. A hack had been got ready at the back door,
but, to my great joy, it was decided to go boldly out at the front door,
& by Winter & Washington Streets.

There were a few police men; and we had Sheriff Clark, & the generous aid & some efficient men of that kind, upon whom we really depended.

It was a hard struggle down Winter St & through Washington St as
far as the corner of Bedford St. The mob pressed against us, hooting, &
swearing, & clamouring; a few resolute fellows pressing us against the
wall, & evidently longing for a stop, or melee, in which they could get
a lick at Phillips. . . .

The pressure became so great that Howe was pushed against a
wall, and another man smashed a plate glass window. At last Phillips was safely home. The would-be attackers milled about, groaned
and hooted for a while before dispersing.[17]

With a social system that could encourage such disgraceful proceedings, Howe opposed all compromise. There was talk of a "convention" at this time to save the Union. To Howe it was really a
meeting to save slavery, and he hoped the proposal would be
beaten. The "Old Bay State" must break the political chain which
bound her, repressed her instincts, and prevented her at the moment
of crisis from being true to herself and to freedom. The danger
was great that "She is going, like Peter, to deny her master." [18]

[17] Howe to Sumner, Jan. 20, 1861, Howe Papers, Houghton.
[18] Howe to Bird, Jan. 30, 1861, Howe Papers, Houghton.

Carping moralist that he was, nothing Lincoln did impressed him. The Inaugural Address struck him as a pro-slavery document.[19] At a time when every man who loved humanity, freedom, and the right "should be doing something," the administration seemed to be encouraging opponents of law, reason, right, and humanity. Howe's solution was simple. The North was absolute master and able to dictate terms because it was right, and because it had the power to enforce its will. It needed only to pour down volunteers through the Mississippi Valley. The nation might shudder at the thought of a servile insurrection, but it would be false to humanity if it were unwilling to use every means to save the country for freedom, "& to put an end forever to a system which disgraces & degrades & cripples it."[20]

III

Hostilities, when they came, found Howe at Armageddon in the first rank of fighters for the Lord. To Sumner he wrote,

We have entered upon a struggle which ought not to be allowed to end until the Slave power is completely subjugated, & *emancipation made certain*. It seems as if God had opened the way out of the false position in which our country has been placed by tolerating & extending a barbarous & inhuman institution until it was likely to make of us all barbarians & monsters.[21]

In a frenzy of patriotism he offered his services to the government in any capacity except that of spy.[22] He realized that he was too old for the front lines, "Oh for my old days — of health & strength & activity," he cried. Still he had to do something. His first idea was of volunteering as surgeon, but only "if we are to have a *real earnest war;* . . . I have no taste for parade & sham fighting," which is what he considered the shameful surrender of Fort Sumter had been. His mind relived his youthful days in Greece, where both sides had fought on with no thought of surrender so long as they

[19] Howe to Sumner, March 5, 1861, Howe Papers, Houghton.
[20] Howe to Sumner, April 6, 1861, Howe Papers, Houghton.
[21] Howe to Sumner, April 16, 1861, Howe Papers, Houghton.
[22] Howe to Andrew, April 13, 1861, Andrew Papers, MHS.

had arms.[23] To think that Turks could have been more heroic than Americans! The cause of the North was too holy to be disgraced by such cowardly performances. Lincoln was to blame for having ordered a mere show of resistance.

Howe's government service began almost immediately with the outbreak of war when Governor Andrew, through whose foresight the commonwealth's troops were in readiness when Lincoln issued his call for the militia, asked him to inspect the sanitary condition of General Ben Butler's brigade.[24] Arriving in Washington on May 6, he set to work immediately. The next day he communicated to Andrew that there was more need of health officers and washerwomen than of chaplains and nurses. "Soap! soap! soap — I cry but none heed." [25] Otherwise he had no complaints, for Massachusetts had equipped her sons well. The usual soldier grumblings about sleeping on the ground and the poor food served them did not impress one "who had gone through a whole campaign without tent or bed, save a goat's-hair capote." He

did not shudder much at the story that some companies had been caught at a pinch without tents and blankets, and obliged to lie one or two nights on the wet grass. And if he had, perchance, been so sharp set with hunger as to find relish in boiled sorrel and a luxury in raw snails, of course he would not so readily melt as others might, at hearing that some of our men had actually been limited during a day or two, to dry biscuit and raw pork.[26]

No evidence existed of real privation. What little discomfort there was came from confusion. The old campaigner discovered to his amusement such luxuries as oolong tea, crushed white sugar, and ice, all of which would disappear without having been used.[27] The hospital in Washington was adequate, as if it could have been otherwise when Dorothea Dix, "the terror of all mere formalists, idlers, and evil-doers," went there regularly.[28] The only recommendation

---

[23] Howe to Sumner, April 16, 1861, Howe Papers, Houghton.
[24] Andrew to Howe, May 2, 1861, *Mass. House Doc.* 40 (Jan. 14, 1862), 21.
[25] Howe to Andrew, May 7, 1861, Andrew Papers, MHS.
[26] *House Doc.* 40 (Jan. 14, 1862), 23–24.
[27] *House Doc.* 40 (Jan. 14, 1862), 25.
[28] *House Doc.* 40 (Jan. 14, 1862), 29.

Howe made in his final report was the one he always made and enforced in his two institutions, namely, that cleanliness of person and clothing be maintained. Finding the army's regulations in regard to the protection of soldiers from lice unsatisfactory, he urged that men be assigned to do the laundering. They were better adapted for this type of work than women since they could accompany the army into battle, and do all mechanical functions better.[29] Several months later Howe made a similar inspection of the troops near Boston which was published as *A Letter on the Sanitary Condition of the Troops in the Neighborhood of Boston*.[30]

Howe was concerned about the health of the entire army, including non-New Englanders. While still engaged in his work for Andrew, he was one of several prominent citizens who petitioned Simon Cameron, the Secretary of War, to appoint a commission of civilians to investigate the best means of mobilizing public benevolence in aid of the soldiers.[31] The request was granted. By executive order, approved June 13, 1861, Cameron created the United States Sanitary Commission, to

direct its inquiries to the principles and practices connected with the inspection of recruits and enlisted men; the sanitary condition of the volunteers; to the means of preserving and restoring the health, and of securing the general comfort and efficiency of troops; to the proper provision of cooks, nurses, and hospitals; and to other subjects of like nature.

The Commission will frame such rules and regulations, in respect of the objects and modes of its inquiry, as may seem best adapted to the purpose of its constitution, which when approved by the Secretary, will be established as general guides of its investigations and action.

The commission was promised a room in Washington, and free communication with the War Department.[32] Howe was named a member. The Reverend Henry W. Bellows, a New York clergyman,

---

[29] *House Doc.* 40 (Jan. 14, 1862), 31.

[30] (Washington, 1861.)

[31] "An Address to the Secretary of War," May 18, 1861, U. S. Sanitary Commission, *Documents* (New York, 1866), I, *Doc.* 1, p. 2.

[32] USSC *Documents*, I, *Doc.* 2, 6–7.

was announced as president. The most distinguished member besides Howe was Wolcott Gibbs, Professor of Chemistry at Harvard. Frederick Law Olmsted served as General Secretary.[33]

The commission began work at once. Within a few months it had accredited agents in the various army units who sent back during the first year over 400 reports on health conditions and troop mortality. Had it not been for the organization's work, Howe believed that fatalities would have been even greater than they were: sixty-three per 1000 in the Army of the Potomac, 116 per 1000 in the Army of the West, and 162 per 1000 in West Virginia.[34]

The home front was mobilized behind the work of the commission, which wisely decided to decentralize its activities. It opened branch offices in the leading cities of the North, each with its own officers to direct local fund-raising drives and general relief work. Ladies' auxiliaries were also established in all parts of the country. There were eventually over 7000, one even in Great Britain.[35] Prominent laymen, serving as "associate members," rendered valuable assistance. In Boston these included Governor Andrew, John Murray Forbes, Charles Eliot Norton, Josiah Quincy, Oliver Wendell Holmes. George S. Hillard, Edward Everett Hale, and James Russell Lowell.

The auxiliaries were extremely active. The New England chapter, with headquarters at 22 Summer Street, raised vast sums of money. Among their many projects, the ladies maintained a daily attendant on railroad ambulances between New York and Boston to furnish relief to invalid and destitute soldiers in transit.[36] Never had an army been so well-paid, fed, and clad as the Union forces.[37] The generosity of the people was remarkable. In 1862 after only a few

[33] USSC *Documents, Doc.* 4 (June 21, 1861), p. 4.

[34] S. G. Howe, *A Letter to Mrs. ———, and Other Loyal Women* (Boston, 1862), p. 6. These figures are for late 1861.

[35] Charles J. Stillé, *History of the United States Sanitary Commission* (New York, 1868), p. 172; *The Sanitary Commission of the United States Army: A Succinct Narrative of its Works and Purposes* (New York, 1864), p. 269. Broadsides of various types can be found in a box of pamphlets in the Widener Library. They are not otherwise catalogued.

[36] Stillé, *The Sanitary Commission*, p. 269.

[37] S. G. Howe, *Letter to Loyal Women*, p. 12.

months of service, Howe told New Englanders not to send more clothes and food.[38] The men had enough of everything except noble watchwords and inspiriting ideas, such as are worth fighting and dying for.[39] There could never be enough of those.

Howe's duties required him to go to Washington frequently. He occasionally took Julia with him. On one of these trips, during the fall of 1861, she received the inspiration to write her immortal "Battle Hymn of the Republic" which, more than any other production, with the exception of Lincoln's addresses, expressed the spiritual quality of the Northern cause.[40]

While Howe was eager to serve on the commission, and performed his duties conscientiously, he doubted its desirability as a voluntary organization, feeling that the government should have taken all proper sanitary measures without the necessity of outside aid.[41] He objected to all volunteer relief as likely to exert an influence unfavorable to the development of proper accountability of the army's medical officers.[42] It was vital not to allow the commission to become merely an eleemosynary institution, or almoner of public gifts, he told Bellows.[43]

IV

Howe's major interest was the promotion of emancipation, and the study of its resultant problems. From the earliest days of the war he held frequent conferences at his office with his friends on ways to force government action. On November 8, 1861, the group appointed a committee "to dream up a plan for an Emancipation League," which was finally organized January 27, 1862, with Samuel Sewall, one of the most active members of the old Vigilance Committee, as president, Howe as one of the vice-presidents, Stearns as

---

[38] Howe, *Letter to Loyal Women*, p. 9.

[39] Howe, *Letter to Loyal Women*, p. 14.

[40] J. W. Howe, *Reminiscences*, pp. 269–276. Told also in Florence Howe Hall, *The Story of the Battle Hymn of the Republic* (New York, 1916).

[41] Howe to Andrew, Nov. 27, 1861, Andrew Papers, MHS.

[42] "An Account of the Executive Organization of the Sanitary Commission," USSC *Documents*, I, *Doc.* 60 (1862), 96.

[43] Howe to Bellows, Sept. 12, 1862, Bellows Papers, MHS.

treasurer, and Francis W. Bird one of the executive committee. The league conducted a vigorous program, gathering information on Negroes, circulating documents, and sending out lecturers. "Meetings for debates upon questions relating to the War & Slavery were held during the Winter & Spring, & annual meetings until Emancipation became an accomplished fact," Bird recalled later.[44]

When Lincoln, in September 1862, announced that he would issue an emancipation proclamation at the beginning of 1863, Howe was unimpressed. Never having regarded the President as anything more than a good-willed incompetent, he thought the statement lacked *"persistent* earnestness." He urged his associates to push the matter with all force, to present a wealth of fact on the condition of freedmen elsewhere. "Everything now depends upon the people *backing* up the President & insisting upon his coming to the scratch on the first [of] January," he wrote.[45] The administration, he felt, could show its sincerity by making preparation for the political birth of millions through the establishment of an "Emancipation Bureau." He wrote Salmon P. Chase, Secretary of the Treasury, whom he had met during the fifties, that such action from the White House "is not only due to the people most interested, but it will have potent moral effect South as well as North." [46]

The league continued to campaign for an Emancipation Bureau after the proclamation went into force. In a petition to the United States Senate, it pleaded that if the freedmen were turned loose

[44] Francis W. Bird to Julia Ward Howe, June 14, 1876, Howe Papers, Houghton.

[45] Howe to Bird, Sept. 17, 1862, Howe Papers, Houghton. Throughout the war, Howe grumbled about the administration's policies. He was annoyed because Lincoln did not free the slaves behind Union lines. Instead he kept them as political hostages, to sell to advantage later. The President was a "greater slave-holder than the King of Dahomey," he wrote. [Howe to Sumner, Jan. 21, 1862, *ibid.*] Later in 1862, he realized that Lincoln wished to free the slaves, but was a procrastinator who "puts off, & puts off, the evil day of effort; & stands shivering with his hand on the string of the shower bath." Nor was Congress any better. It had "a few earnest & disinterested patriots, but they could be carried off in an omnibus; & if, after their departure, some Guy Fawkes could successfully explode his mines, there would be no great loss to this world, though doubtless a sudden increase of the population of Hades." [Howe to Bird, March 5, 1862, Personal Miscellany, Library of Congress.]

[46] Howe to Chase, Nov. 19, 1862, Chase Papers, Library of Congress.

without protection, they would fall easy victim to unscrupulous and prejudiced persons.

The negro's claim at the hands of this nation is [the petition said], simply, justice. The freedmen have a right to fair play — to a fair trial of the experiment of their capacity for self-support and progress. Such an experiment has never yet failed; if it fails in our hands we shall be held responsible to God and to posterity for the failure.[47]

Sumner, now one of the most prominent of senators, applied what pressure he could in the right places.

V

Thanks to the urging of Howe and other like-minded individuals in other parts of the country, Secretary of War Edwin M. Stanton authorized the American Freedmen's Inquiry Commission on March 16, 1863. The three-man board was to investigate the condition of emancipated Negroes and to recommend measures to place them in a position of self-support. Besides Howe, the members were Robert Dale Owen, of Indiana, the son of the noted Utopian socialist, who was the best-known of them all to the public, and Colonel James McKaye of New York.[48]

Having been allowed to write its own orders, the commission opened an office during April on Second Avenue and East Ninth Street, New York City.[49] At their initial meeting, the members agreed to divide up the work of preparing a preliminary report, each to investigate a separate area in the South.[50] Howe's high hopes for the commission, namely that it would prove a model of efficiency and economy, vanished inside of a week with the appearance of his characteristic disapproval of his colleagues. McKaye was ade-

---

[47] "Memorial of the Emancipation League," Senate Misc. Doc., 37 Cong., 3 sess., no. 10 (Jan. 12, 1863), 2. The petition itself was dated Dec. 12, 1862.

[48] War of the Rebellion: A Compilation of the Official Records of the Union and Confederate Armies (Washington, 1899), Series III, vol. III, 73.

[49] Owen and McKaye to Howe, March 19, 1863, American Freedmen's Inquiry Commission Papers, Houghton.

[50] Howe to Sumner, April 26, 1863, Howe Papers, Houghton.

quate, but Owen struck him as being "the very slowest work horse that ever I happened to be harnessed in with." [51]

Early in June, Howe made an inspection tour of the military areas in Virginia, which showed him that the problem was more complex than he had thought. In the course of the war, many Negroes had been uprooted, either through flight or by capture of their homes, and they were left dependent on Union forces. Howe was angered at the treatment they received. The Army, he observed, had missed a great opportunity for spreading good will. Even worse, the soldiers, having despoiled the refugees of whatever they had brought with them, exploited them at low wages that were never paid. [52]

Owen and McKaye, who had visited other areas farther south, made similar discoveries. The trio, combining their views in a *Preliminary Report* to Stanton, retained their optimism. Despite the prevalence of injustice, investigation had shown that under proper supervision the Negroes could quickly become useful to the war effort. They were temperate, cheerful, and uncomplaining as laborers when treated with consideration; their vices stemmed from their former condition. Thieving could not be a crime in the eyes of persons who had no understanding of property rights, nor could family ties be sacred to those who had little understanding of the significance of formal marriage. [53] The *Report* recommended that Negro villages be set up at a distance from the military camps and guarded by the freedmen. It did not urge that refugees be compelled to undergo marriage ceremonies, although a judicious superintendent could, by careful explanation, induce them to do so. Those refusing to marry should be forbidden cohabitation, and the men required to support their dependents. [54]

Howe's touch is seen in the suggestion that the freedmen be armed, for in a war being fought for emancipation, those being

---

[51] Howe to Sumner, May 3, 1863, Howe Papers, Houghton.
[52] Howe to Sumner, June 11, 1863, Howe Papers, Houghton.
[53] *Preliminary Report Touching the Condition and Management of Emancipated Refugees; made to the Secretary of War, June 30, 1863* (New York, 1863), pp. 3–5.
[54] *Preliminary Report*, p. 6.

benefited should fight for their rights if they were to merit them.[55] The commission estimated that about 200,000 Negroes could be used as actual combat soldiers, while many thousands more could be used as laborers.[56]

The *Report* outlined the machinery for the care of refugees which was to be independent of the ordinary military organization. Three geographic departments were to be set up with a superintendent in each and the necessary subsidiary officers to supervise the ex-slaves' preparation for freedom. The creation of a school system was of utmost importance. If private philanthropy should prove wanting, then the government would have to pay the teachers.[57] The freedmen were to be trained so that they might early and quickly learn to shift for themselves. They were not to be kept in camps longer than necessary, since such life was especially demoralizing to women and children. While private employment was preferable to government work, those employed by the government were to be paid regular wages rather than rations, even though they might earn less that way. Freedom meant "WAGES FOR WORK" so far as Howe was concerned.[58]

On his own, Howe urged the immediate establishment of a Bureau of Emancipation, and offered to draft instructions to its officers.[59] Far in advance of his time, Howe was completely radical in his proposed treatment of Negroes. Wishing to ignore all color lines,

[55] *Preliminary Report,* p. 38. At the start of the war, he suggested that the slaves be emancipated immediately, and Negro troops used. He discussed with Governor Andrew the possibility of organizing a band of fifty to one hundred Negro refugees in Canada to land near the Great Dismal or Green Swamp and rouse up the thousands of fugitives in those areas to make sallies and onslaughts against the neighboring plantations. [Howe to Andrew, Aug. 17, 1861, Andrew Papers, MHS.] John Murray Forbes felt it was too extreme a suggestion. A Negro insurrection, he held, would unify the South and divide the North. [Forbes to Howe, Aug. 21, 1861, in Sarah Forbes Hughes, *John Murray Forbes,* I, 239–240.] Nothing came of the proposal.

[56] *Preliminary Report,* pp. 15–16.

[57] *Preliminary Report,* p. 30.

[58] *Preliminary Report,* pp. 22–26; Howe to Sumner, June 11, 1863, Howe Papers, Houghton.

[59] Draft of a "Supplementary Report to the Secretary of War," undated, American Freedmen's Inquiry Commission Papers, Houghton.

and opposed even to the creation of separate regiments, he wanted to view and treat the matter as a blind man would.

I want to sink the differences of race [he wrote Andrew turning down a place on a commission to inquire into the use of Negro troops]; & treat the blacks exactly as I would whites in their condition. I do not believe in black colonies, or black regiments. It is only in this way that we can leave free and unobstructed course to that natural law by which the weaker & poorer race is to be absorbed & by the stronger & better one to the improvement of humanity, & the glory of God.[60]

VI

The commission's examination having indicated the vast amount of work yet to be done, the members now settled down to several months of intense labor. During the summer of 1863 each went his separate way. Howe journeyed to Canada to discover how Negroes had fared on their own. Accompanied by J. M. W. Yerrinton, the commission's secretary and reporter, he traversed Canada West three times, visiting all the large towns with considerable Negro populations. He estimated that between 30,000 to 40,000 exiles had found refuge in Ontario since 1800,[61] and that on the whole they had been able to support themselves and to accumulate property.[62] With freedom and equality before the law, they were sober, industrious, thrifty, and moral, definitely worthy citizens. Of course they were imitative, but he felt that they copied only the most desirable features of their white neighbors.[63]

Howe did not prepare his report immediately on returning home. A proper treatment of the Negro problem required a consideration of political, physiological, and ethnological principles, in which fields he felt incompetent. Needing information about Negroes in the United States, where climatic conditions were different, he began the preparation of a questionnaire to send to all officials who had dealings with freedmen.[64] In the course of this work, he turned

[60] Howe to Andrew, undated (1863), Andrew Papers, MHS.
[61] S. G. Howe, *The Refugees from Slavery in Canada West* (Boston, 1864), p. 15.
[62] Howe, *Refugees from Slavery in Canada West*, p. 59.
[63] Howe, *Refugees from Slavery in Canada West*, pp. 101–104.
[64] The Emancipation League had also sent out questionnaires.

to Louis Agassiz for advice on the possibilities of Negro survival in a white-dominated society.[65]

The distinguished naturalist replied that the Negroes should be granted their freedom. True, he thought, they were inferior intellectually to whites and should not have full citizenship privileges; still with proper restraints, they could provide for themselves.[66]

Agassiz' remarks greatly influenced Howe, although he could not accept all of the Harvard professor's teachings. Howe favored granting not only entire freedom, equal rights and privileges, but open competition for social distinctions. Slavery had created the moral deformities that existed. Freedom would restore harmony.[67]

VII

A few days later, the commission's questionnaire, a forty-two part document, went off to officials on both sides of the Mason-Dixon line. In addition to questions on vital statistics, inquiry was made as to the ability of freedmen to support themselves, their regard for family ties, and how they compared with whites in economic pursuits. Within a few days, replies began to come in. These first answers, and those that came in later weeks, indicated that Negroes, if given proper training, could become self-supporting. A St. Louis respondent wrote that "they are considered as a whole fit to take their place in Society with a fair prospect of self-support & progress." A certain Captain C. B. Wilder at Fortress Monroe paid high tribute to the Negro as a soldier. He recommended that confiscated lands be sold them. "The negro character, has been most grossly and wilfully misrepresented. . . . ," he said. "The pretence that if emancipated, they would turn robbers and cut their masters' throats, that they would not work, and that they were cowards and would not fight, all prove false." [68]

From others came disclosures that many of the freedmen bore

---

[65] Howe to Agassiz, Aug. 3, 1863, Agassiz Papers, Houghton.

[66] Agassiz' responses are contained in four letters to Howe, August 9–10–11–15, 1863, transcripts in Agassiz Papers.

[67] Howe to Agassiz, Aug. 18, 1863, Agassiz Papers.

[68] Wilder to Comm., Aug. 26, 1863, American Freedmen's Inquiry Commission Papers, Houghton.

marks of violent usage.[69] One "Superintendent of Contrabands" reported that he had found more men disqualified for military service because of abuse than all other causes, not even omitting age. Their treatment at the hands of the Union Army was not much better. Many accounts of troop bestiality are to be found scattered among the replies to the questionnaire.[70]

At least one person who had contact with the freedmen went against the trend in feeling that they were undesirable citizens. Major James M. Pomeroy, commander of the Ninth Kansas Volunteers stationed in Oklahoma, declared,

> They are the most worthless vagabonds I ever saw or heard of. Their relations with their masters . . . have made them among the *sharpest* . . . of any slaves I have seen. . . . But they are worthless, with few exceptions, in the ratio of their intelligence, which they employ chiefly in devising means to shirk work. . . .[71]

Howe prepared a second questionnaire which he sent out to clergymen, physicians, and prominent persons in Northern cities. It consisted of only thirteen questions, mostly on vital statistics. The answers were so contradictory that the results were inconclusive. From Brooklyn came information that Negroes were as industrious and self-supporting as whites of their economic class, and were in fact more cleanly.[72] On the other hand, Pittsfield officials reported that Negroes resident in that city were not generally industrious, but sought charity in greater proportion than whites, and were otherwise undesirable. They were also more susceptible to disease; mulattoes, the second generation of whom had especially poor health, being in particular subject to tuberculosis. Had it not been

[69] Rev. C. Severance Fiske to Comm., Aug. 31, 1863, American Freedmen's Inquiry Commission Papers, Houghton.

[70] For example, C. P. Day to S. S. Jocelyn, Aug. 11, 1863, American Freedmen's Inquiry Commission Papers, Houghton, apparently a personal letter forwarded to the commission, and Rev. C. Severance Fiske of Memphis to Comm., Aug. 31, 1863, American Freedmen's Inquiry Commission Papers, Houghton.

[71] Pomeroy to Kermott, Sept. 3, 1863, American Freedmen's Inquiry Commission Papers, Houghton.

[72] J. H. Hobart Burge to Howe, Jan. 8, 1864, American Freedmen's Inquiry Commission Papers, Houghton.

for immigration replenishing them, they would have died out.[73] No reliable information about insanity among the Negroes was received. Directors of mental institutions felt though that they were less liable to mental disorder.[74]

VIII

During the fall of 1863 the commissioners toured the Western departments of war, but not the South.[75] By December, back in New York, they were ready to begin the final phase of their work. Howe was ashamed of their incompetence. He felt that they should have visited the West Indies, but they had wasted their appropriation and now they had no money left. In addition, he had been ill and unable to devote his full time, while McKaye was poorly adapted for the work. However, he considered that the greatest cause of inefficiency was Owen, whom he charged with spending too much time writing political pamphlets. "We deserve castigation," he mournfully conceded. Howe felt so conscience-stricken that he was willing to work for three months without compensation. He and McKaye offered to pay Owen's expenses too, but the Hoosier declined, feeling it was dishonorable.[76] Howe regretted that he had not resigned as soon as he realized that the commission would not come up to his idea of duty. Had it been possible for him to return his salary without offending his colleagues, he would have done so.[77]

The three held consultations among themselves on the type of machinery to be set up for the protection of the freedmen. In the border states Howe felt there was no necessity for anything beyond safeguarding the Negroes' legal rights, while in the cotton and sugar

[73] Returned questionnaire, American Freedmen's Inquiry Commission Papers, Houghton.

[74] G. N. Worthington to Howe, Aug. 24, 1863, American Freedmen's Inquiry Commission Papers, Houghton.

[75] They were apparently occupied in this throughout October and November, since there is a letter of Howe to Otis Norcross (Nov. 22, 1863, Norcross Papers, MHS), written from Louisville. See also Richard William Leopold, *Robert Dale Owen* (Cambridge, 1940), pp. 360–361.

[76] Howe to Sumner, Dec. 18, 1863, #1367 (catalogued under 1869), Howe Papers, Houghton.

[77] Howe to Sumner, Feb. 3, 1864, Howe Papers, Houghton.

regions there would have to be military occupation. Though there would undoubtedly be suffering, and there ought to be suffering "as the legitimate & inevitable consequences of slavery," there should be no system of apprenticeship or gradual emancipation substituted to ease the transition to freedom. Such makeshifts would only create more misery. Fearing that anything less than complete unqualified emancipation would be only a disguised system of servitude, he and Owen, but not McKaye, were agreed upon recommending laissez-faire, except in those regions where Negroes would need protection. "Treat poor blacks as we would poor whites," he told Sumner, and there would be no trouble.[78] Give to Negroes the ancient privilege of starving if they preferred not to work, and use no coercion. Though Negroes were "a poor breed physically," he felt they could learn quickly enough to take care of themselves; just make sure that their former masters were forbidden to arrest them for vagrancy.[79]

Howe began preparing his long-delayed report on his Canadian trip of the previous summer, and finished it by the end of January 1864, only to find to his annoyance that Stanton refused to publish it.[80] He decided to pay for it himself. Appearing early in February, the *Refugees from Slavery in Canada West* was a simple recital of what Howe had seen. The results of Agassiz' teachings, however, are evident in his conclusion that Negroes would disappear from Northern climates.[81] The book stated that despite inferiority, Negroes were men as honest and virtuous as one could find, which is all that mattered. It was unfair to say they shirked hard work, since all men try to shift their share of heavy labor to other shoulders, and one should never blame anyone else for trying to do the same.[82]

[78] Howe to Sumner, Dec. 19, 1863, Howe Papers, Houghton.

[79] Howe to Sumner, Jan. 8, 1864, Howe Papers, Houghton.

[80] It is not clear from Howe's papers why Stanton refused, but Howe never seems to have liked him anyhow. McKaye's study, *The Mastership and Its Fruits* (New York, 1864), met with a similar response, and was also privately printed. It was an account of the Lower Mississippi Valley.

[81] S. G. Howe, *Refugees from Slavery in Canada West*, pp. 35–36.

[82] Howe, *Refugees from Slavery in Canada West*, pp. 55-56.

IX

The writing of the commission's final report was the only thing
that remained to be done. The main burden of this task fell to
Owen. In February he finally settled down to it, laboring so in-
cessantly for the next three months that all of Howe's dissatisfaction
with him vanished.[83] By mid-May it was ready. Howe considered
it valuable. Owen had produced a masterly indictment of the white
race for its treatment of the Negroes. The end result of three centuries of slavery in America, the *Report* found, was to debase the
"usurpers" (that is, masters), as well as their victims, and to throw
the nation into the goriest civil war ever fought among men.[84]

If a calm review of this terrible episode in modern history brings no
conviction that the crime which we are now expiating in blood must be
atoned for, as crime can only be, by practical repentance — by thrusting
out from among us the Wrong of the Age — argument will be unavailing. . . .

But all signs indicated the nation had attained this realization.[85]

It was time for humanitarians to consider one of the highest
duties of Christian civilization, measures to implement emancipation.[86] Howe's examination in Canada having proven that the
Negro race had great possibilities of improvement, the commission
looked forward to a time when there would be no distinction made
as to civil or political rights because of color.[87] The freedmen were
to be given all aid necessary to bring them up to a level of equality
with whites, but such assistance was to be temporary. The sooner
they stood alone, the better.

The essential is that we secure to them the means of making their
own way; that we give them . . . a "fair chance." If, like whites, they

[83] Howe to Sumner, May 15, 1864, Howe Papers, Houghton.

[84] "Report of the Secretary of War, communicating in compliance with a resolution
of the 26th of May, a copy of the preliminary report, and also of the final report of
the American Freedmen's Inquiry Commission," *Sen. Exec. Doc.*, 38 Cong., 1 sess.,
no. 53, 25–72.

[85] "Report of the Secretary of War," *Sen. Exec. Doc.*, 38 Cong., 1 sess., no. 53, 72.

[86] "Report of the Secretary of War," 98.

[87] "Report of the Secretary of War," 99.

are to be self-supporting, then, like whites, they ought to have those rights, civil and political, without which they are but laboring as a man labors with hands bound.[88]

Howe's government work was now ended. He had done what he could to gain for helpless persons their due, but his work was mostly in vain. The *Report* was quietly shelved and no notice of it was taken.

The war's close found Howe still looking ahead. He wished the rebellious states, once they were subdued, brought back into the Union as quickly as possible, and the scars of ill-will healed. A few days after Lee's surrender, there was a meeting in Howe's office to consider the expediency of creating an organization to represent the most advanced sentiment of the country on questions of reconstruction and the recognition of political organizations to represent the former Confederacy.[89] This problem however was to be handled by other, although not more skillful, hands.

[88] "Report of the Secretary of War," 110.
[89] Howe to A. A. Lawrence, April 17, 1865, A. A. Lawrence Papers, XXVIII, 7, MHS.

XVII

Postwar Campaigns

The price America paid for its indulgence of slavery cannot be reckoned merely by the frightful number of lives lost during the war, nor in property values destroyed. Among the casualties which can never be tabulated was social reform, the progress of which was delayed a generation because of the more pressing concern with abolition. Those who might have given their attention to the problems of the helpless and the needy were too busy to notice. An entire generation which might have found succor was forced to endure its suffering unaided. When, after Lee's surrender, humanitarians were able to give their attention to problems of peace, they faced a situation aggravated by years of neglect.

I

Howe found himself adrift in 1865. After two decades of strife the snake of slavery was killed, not scotched, and he could rest. Certainly he was old enough to retire, but so long as the doctor drew a breath he never sought repose. He had always to be active, but the fields he chose in his later years, he had worked before. The problems of an industrial society never entered his consciousness. Kindly as he was to the weak in mind and body, his conception of charity did not embrace able-bodied mill workers adrift in a strange world. Laborers were not slaves; in his opinion they could take care of themselves.

Economically Howe was a Jeffersonian, as he had been all his life. He followed the doctrines of a simpler world which thought that if everyone paid attention to his own business, and behaved honorably, there would be no trouble. But above all, men must be free of governmental helps or hindrances. During the fifties when a ten-hour law was under discussion in Massachusetts, Howe came out against it unequivocally. Besides feeling that commerce and trade should be entirely free, and that it was bad policy to enact any but absolutely necessary laws, he feared that the legislature by taking the people under guardianship would emasculate their ability to protect themselves.

Besides [he told Mann], — such a law would seem to favour the notion that labourers *ought* to work 10 hrs daily, — whereas in reality they ought not, in a good state of society, to work more than 6 to 8. The man who has worked hard bodily 10 hours, is incapacitated for working mentally with full appetency & vigour.

Operatives ought not to be obliged to labour more than 6 to 8 hours; but in the present state of society legislation to that effect would be folly & madness; you cannot legislate rightly about it — therefore I would not at all.[1]

By 1865 he understood that dissatisfaction among laboring classes was somewhat justified and that eventually something would have to be done, but nowhere did he propose to champion their cause. Certain realities of life had become evident to him, however, namely that capital, hedged about with privileges and exemptions, sanctified such terms as "law" and "propriety," creating a façade of respectability behind which it hid, oblivious of the suffering it had created. Should such a state of affairs continue, he foresaw an eruption.

I am an ultra in this one thing, to wit, the belief that society never will, & never ought to rest upon solid & peaceful foundation so long as the labours & drudgery of the world is thrown actively upon one class, while another class is entirely exempt from it. There is radical injustice

[1] Howe to Mann, Oct. 21, 1852, Howe Papers, Houghton. Horace Mann once characterized himself in terms that apply to Howe, as a "conservative reformer." By that he meant he sought "the removal of vile & rotten parts from the structure of society, just as fast as salutary & sound ones can be prepared to take their places." Mann to Parker, May 27, 1847, Mann Papers, MHS.

in it; & injustice in society is like a rotten timber in the foundations of a house. If by the inevitable consequences of our present commercial system there must come to be a working class as such, & bound to work or die, — it will be the most dangerous class that ever existed in a great country. Let the rich take heed in time; for our people will ask questions about the rights of property, which will be hard to be answered; & they will not be bamboozled by any superstitions, religious or social. Property must make continual concessions, if it would claim more respect & power than inheres in it by natural right; & among these must be a sliding scale of taxation proportionate to income. There may be an apparent invasion of right . . . but no such invasion of natural right as the labouring classes are often obliged to submit to.[2]

Here was Howe's chance to shake the nation, and strike out on a new path, but he never did. He was no forerunner of Populism or of Bull Moose Progressivism. Untouched by newer currents of nineteenth-century thought, the venerable humanitarian still sounded like an advanced Philosophe whose ideas would have been anathema to the ministers of Louis XVI. Man was a dignified being whose self-respect must be maintained.[3] Howe remained incorrigibly an "optimist in the extremest sense," believing that God had endowed humanity with inherent elements which necessitated upward growth. All that was needed for mankind's development was freedom and favoring social conditions. Nothing could be done without the improvement of material conditions. "Men must be fed & warmed," he wrote Bellows, "& clothed & made comfortable; & must have time & occasion for mental exercise, before they can be refined, & made religious in the highest sense of religion; which is loving one another."[4] Too many persons, he told the German Republicans after the failure of the Revolution of 1848, had not faith enough in humanity at a time when "to doubt is to be damned," and a blasphemy of God. The disillusioned intellectuals "shake their heads," he wrote Sumner, "and call me *red,* very *red;* perhaps they think me green."[5] Possibly he was the latter. Neither

[2] Howe to Sumner, Feb. 10, 1865, Howe Papers, Houghton.

[3] Howe to Parker, July 5, 1850, Howe Papers, Houghton, shows his disapproval of the use of footmen in England.

[4] Howe to Henry W. Bellows, March 18, 1866, Bellows Papers, MHS.

[5] Howe to Sumner, Sept. 26, 1850, Howe Papers, Houghton.

the doctrines of Karl Marx to justify revolt, nor that other perversion of doctrine, Social Darwinism, used at times to justify the status quo, could ever appeal to him.

II

For almost twenty years Howe had neglected his work at Perkins. He had turned up occasionally in South Boston during lulls in the fight against slavery, but it would have been better if he had resigned in the mid-forties, as he seriously thought of doing when he began to stray into alien fields.[6]

Even without him, the school thrived, continuing along the paths he had marked out. Its history during this period is one of steady growth in attainment, reputation, and endowment. Private benefactions added so much to its resources that Howe was able to announce that Perkins stood ready to admit practically all students free.[7] The institution gained new prestige by winning the printing award at the London Exhibition in 1851, the jurors declaring that Boston type provided the best books yet devised for the blind. They hoped to see the American system adopted in England.[8]

Everything seemed to be going well, but basically Howe was dissatisfied. Experience had shown him that he had based his work on an improper theory. Manfully he confessed his errors, hoping to remedy them. One of his most serious miscalculations lay in having overrated the capacities of the blind. Ignorance at the outset of his labors had led him to expect too much from his students. By the late forties he realized that the "blind, as a class, are inferior to other persons in mental power and ability."[9] It was true that

[6] In fact during these years he made several attempts to resign. In 1849 he told the trustees to begin thinking of finding a successor. Francis Lieber was under consideration for a time, but nothing came of it. [Sumner to Lieber, July 17, 1849, Sumner Papers, Houghton.] Howe again thought of resigning in 1858, during a period of physical exhaustion and mental depression. [Howe to Sumner, July 11, 1858, Howe Papers, Houghton.] During the Civil War the Trustees accepted his resignation conditionally. J. T. Sargent and later Edward Jarvis fulfilled his duties until he was again available. [*32d Report* (1864), p. 4.]

[7] *17th Report* (1849), p. 6.

[8] *Reports by the Juries on the Subjects in the Thirty Classes into which the Exhibition was Divided* (London, 1852), p. 417; *21st Report* (1853), 4, pp. 33–38.

[9] *16th Report* (1848), pp. 31–32, 34.

Perkins had some superior students; probably it always would have, but a much larger proportion of children would average decidedly lower in physical and mental vigor than those in the common schools.[10] Correspondence with his colleagues confirmed these conclusions.[11] The blind could not hope to compete with normal persons in as many fields as he had hoped. In the professions they could qualify as church organists and music teachers, but not much else.[12]

In keeping with his deepened understanding, Howe in his later years wished to reorganize Perkins on an entirely new plan. Haunted by the thought that he had created an asylum instead of a school, he feared that the institution, with its barrack-like atmosphere, would lead to as many maladjustments among the children as he sought to remove. He knew now that it was undesirable to keep the handicapped of any class congregated in close relationship for too long a period. While it was necessary at the beginning of their training to give them confidence by showing them that others in the same predicament had mastered their difficulty, after a while it was imperative that they go among normal persons, adjust to a normal world, and not develop a separate class feeling. He favored boarding the students out, and having them come to Perkins every day as if they were ordinary children attending a common school. In 1849 he had proposed this to the Trustees, but was voted down.[13] Still he refused to dismiss the matter. For over twenty years he cherished this idea, and in the odd moments he could snatch from abolition he spread the gospel of diffusion. The ideal to be striven for was a normal existence among normal persons.

He was able to put into practice part of his program through his insistence that the mature blind workers connected with Perkins' Workshop Department reside around the town rather than to-

---

[10] *16th Report*, p. 36. He considered that the infusion of the Celtic element had lowered the average intellectual standard, *25th Report* (1857), p. 7.

[11] *16th Report*, p. 40.

[12] *16th Report*, p. 7. Unfortunately Howe does not say whether the curriculum was changed to meet these new realities. However, music has always been the largest department at Perkins.

[13] *36th Report* (1868), p. 27.

gether. Celibate communities, he held, thwart and stunt the natural growth of human affection. They produce such deformities that even with all their industry and attainments one cannot prevent them from being prolific of evil. Though the blind would be exposed to ignorance and vulgarity in an ordinary neighborhood, it was better to endure these than the learning of monks and the refinement of nuns, so long as "natural feelings and affections" were developed.[14]

So strongly was he opposed to institutionalization that he even opposed the creation of reform schools. In 1854 when the organization of such a school for girls was under consideration, he issued a characteristic blast against it. He stated that the worst thing possible for wayward young women was to be congregated. Penal institutions can never reform. "It is hard work to make straight a single crooked stick — harder yet, a bundle of them *if taken together,*" he wrote William Appleton.[15] Most persons, born without any strong tendency to either virtue or vice, are creatures of circumstance, and grow up to be virtuous or vicious according to the outward influences exerted upon them.

Furthermore, a strong practical objection existed to the plan. There would be no way of avoiding the publicity of a large establishment. The girls, becoming known as belonging to a vicious class, would get the character of such, and the label would stick through life.[16]

For problem children he advocated not separation as he did for adult convicts, but dispersion. In this particular case he urged that the girls be widely distributed throughout the state, under the immediate care of selected families, in order to take advantage of a law of human nature, "which has not, to my knowledge, ever had definite consideration in schemes of reform." [17] Thousands of persons in Massachusetts could furnish worthy examples to young

[14] *18th Report* (1850), p. 26.
[15] S. G. Howe, *A Letter to J. H. Wilkins, H. B. Rogers & F. B. Fay, Commissioners of Massachusetts for the State Reform School for Girls* (Boston, 1854), p. 17.
[16] Howe, *A Letter to the Commissioners of the State Reform School for Girls*, p. 21.
[17] Howe, *A Letter to J. H. Wilkins, et al.*, p. 12.

people, and their homes would exercise a salutary effect on them.

The actual institution needed to be only a small building where the students would be received and from which they would be assigned.[18] As a beginning he suggested that one hundred girls might be boarded around the state, with twelve more added each month. The superintendent would be responsible only for the general result, not the daily doings of his charges. He would place them in suitable families who would give them instruction in needlework and regular housework, and send them to school during the winter.[19] Howe was certain that this training would produce more good than the strict discipline of a large reform school. His urgings were fruitless. With neither time nor energy to press his program during the fifties, the school was set up over his objections.[20]

As he aged, Howe mellowed considerably in his attitude toward the enforcement of discipline. He realized now that there was no fast line between a "good" and a "bad" boy or girl; it was just that some needed more help than others. The world was too quick to categorize, he told Mann.

Ah! this imaginary line between the righteous and sinners! Of how much uncharitableness and wrong is it the origin.

Beware . . . of denying to any youth the chances of o'er-wetting the devil, and getting the top of his own head uppermost again, by fixing upon him the character of immorality. . . . You may destroy souls. This I know, I could not myself have passed your ordeal [Mann planned to withhold degrees from young men of immoral character] when I graduated; I should have been obliged to play the hypocrite, or been denied a degree; been dismissed, that is, with a very black mark, and perhaps become in consequence the very thing I was mistaken for, a very bad man, whereas now I am only an ordinarily bad one, and strive to do some good to offset the bad. . . .[21]

Howe learned his trade slowly, but the time was coming when he would show how well he knew it.

[18] Howe, *A Letter to J. H. Wilkins, et al.,* p. 16.
[19] Howe, *A Letter to J. H. Wilkins, et al.,* pp. 27–28.
[20] Howe to Andrew, Feb. 26, 1861, Andrew Papers, MHS.
[21] Howe to Mann, Aug. 4, 1857, *New England Quarterly,* XVI, 3 (Sept. 1943), 495–496.

III

With the end of the war, Howe returned to education and organized charities full-time. He began seriously to fulfill responsibilities that had been enlarged, Governor Andrew having appointed him Chairman of the newly created Board of State Charities in 1863, in addition to his other posts. Designed to coördinate the commonwealth's eleemosynary institutions, the Board was a body of great influence.[22] The Boston reformer had let his powers lie dormant during 1864, having been busy with war work, but now free to return to his customary pursuits, he began the preparation of the Board's second annual report. Issued in January 1866, it was one of the most comprehensive studies of dependency and charity made up to that time.[23]

Again Howe insisted on the relationship of heredity and environment in the creation of a person's character. Unquestionably, heredity was more influential; the records of the school for mental defectives showed that most of the children came from "inferior stock." Still environment had to be considered. Children who grew up in socially blighted communities could not help but absorb criminal ways.[24]

Nevertheless, Howe thought that all social evils could be remedied. Just as careful breeding had improved cattle, temperate living would improve human stock. Mankind's own natural correctives would restore the harmony of natural laws within a few generations, without enforced abstinence from marriage, or other repression of natural instincts.[25] Foremost among the measures of social reform was the improvement of the material conditions and daily habits of persons who were susceptible to sinking into the criminal class. Good homes, temperance, limitations of hours and work, and street cleanliness were some of Howe's practical recommendations.[26]

[22] "First Annual Report of the Board of State Charities," *Mass. Pub. Doc.* 19 (Jan. 1865), pp. iii–v.

[23] *Mass. Pub. Doc.* 19 (Jan. 1866).

[24] *Mass. Pub. Doc.* 19, pp. xxviii, xxxiii–xxxv.

[25] *Mass. Pub. Doc.* 19, pp. xxxi–xxxii.

[26] *Mass. Pub. Doc.* 19, p. xxvii.

Just as the feeble-minded and lunatics could not be held responsible for their condition, many paupers and criminals were likewise blameless for their condition, and like mental defectives, could be improved by proper treatment.[27] The greatest economy was to spend freely to fight evil. Paupers had to be taken from their environment and placed among industrious persons where they would learn habits of steady work; adolescents with criminal propensities had to be taken from reform schools and placed in decent homes. Old-fashioned almshouses and prisons should be used only as a last resort for habitual paupers and hardened criminals.[28]

IV

So long as Howe wrote in general terms, there was no trouble, but when he became specific and named names and institutions, he roused the fury of those he had impugned. In the later sections of his report he took up the matter of education of the deaf, a problem he had carried in the back of his head for over a quarter-century. He had long been dissatisfied with the provision made for this class of unfortunates. Since the early twenties Massachusetts had sent its deaf children to the American Asylum at Hartford for the Education and Instruction of the Deaf and Dumb. This school, enjoying a large Congressional land grant, was able to educate deaf-mutes more cheaply than any other. Howe became familiar with its work originally through his interest in Julia Brace; but the more he learned of it, the more dissatisfied he became with its methods. The Asylum taught its students only pantomime signs, while Howe favored dactylology, finger language, which he taught to the deaf-blind under his care. Thinly veiled jeers at the Asylum's work, particularly its failure to do anything with Julia Brace, began to appear in the reports of the Perkins Institution. Howe longed for a chance to try his hand with the education of the deaf. During his term in the Massachusetts House of Representatives in 1843, he was chairman of the Committee on Public Charitable Institutions which conducted an annual investigation of the Asylum.

[27] *Mass. Pub. Doc.* 19, pp. xxxviii-xxxix.
[28] *Mass. Pub. Doc.* 19, p. lxxxiii.

In the committee report he urged that Massachusetts set up its own school, one that would admit students at a younger age than the Asylum, and presumably would teach them finger language. Under his direction a bill was passed to allow Perkins to conduct the experiment of teaching deaf children too young to study at Hartford.[29]

Several months later Howe and Mann, during their respective wedding trips, investigated numerous schools for the deaf in Germany, which had advanced beyond mere dactylology to the point of actually teaching mutes to speak. Completely won over to the new method, the Americans determined to bring about its acceptance at home. Mann, arriving first, gave the matter such publicity that the Asylum dispatched its principal, Lewis Weld, to Europe to study the process.[30] On his return in December 1844, he recommended that articulation be taught on an experimental basis. Instruction began in March 1845.[31] After a year the directors expressed their pleasure at the result, but somewhere during the next few years the Asylum ceased its experiment, and reverted to its former program.[32] Howe and Mann were enraged. They charged that the conservative school had not given articulation a fair trial. As was typical with them, they questioned the good faith of the Hartford teachers. Howe went so far as to say that sectarian feelings were involved, since the innovators were Unitarians and their opponents were orthodox. Try as they might, the champions of the new method were unable to have a school chartered in Massachusetts since it was cheaper to send children to Hartford.[33]

Though the controversy died down, Howe never forgot it. Through the years, as he attended to other affairs, the matter of articulation remained in his consciousness. He continued to gather

[29] *Mass. House Doc.* 66 (Feb. 1843); *Boston Advertiser*, March 2, 1843. Not much was ever done under its provisions. Howe had only two students, both of whom had lost their hearing after they had learned to speak. *Volta Review*, XIII, 7 (Dec. 1911), 420–422.

[30] *Boston Advertiser*, July 3, 1844; *Twenty-eighth Report of the Directors of the American Asylum, at Hartford, for the Education and Instruction of the Deaf and Dumb* (Hartford, 1844), pp. 43–44.

[31] *29th Report* (1845), pp. 8, 121; *Boston Advertiser*, March 3, 1845.

[32] *30th Report* (1846), p. 12.

[33] Howe to ?, April 21, 1875, Howe Papers, Houghton.

information from authorities on the education of the deaf in America and Europe.[34] When he was ready to take the matter up again, his facts would be irrefutable.

Mann was dead by 1865, but Howe, unable to forget the abuse heaped upon his friend and cherishing his memory, determined now to reopen the issue in the Board's second report and beat down the Asylum. Tearing the mask from the respected institution, which to his mind was a backward aggregation of entrenched interest, Howe reached new heights of bitterness even for him.[35] Every practice he disapproved of, he found in favor at Hartford. The school was too large; it perpetuated the feeling of separateness among its inmates by failing to bring them into harmonious relationship with the world; all this in addition to teaching them improperly.[36] Persons subjected to such a program would never be self-reliant; they would never be familiar with a normal family life, since even their own parents could have no hand in their upbringing.[37] The Bay State urgently needed a school embodying all the latest advances. He recommended that an unpaid commission for the education of the deaf be appointed to contract with any responsible society or group who would undertake instruction.[38]

In the pamphlet war which followed the publication of this report, the Asylum and its friends strongly resisted Howe's aspersions. Among the most highly placed of the defenders was the Honorable Lewis J. Dudley of the Governor's Council, whose daughter was an Asylum alumna. Dudley insisted that since Howe had shown such ignorance of his task, he be dismissed from all his posts.[39] The Reverend Collins Stone, principal of the American

---

[34] See, for example, two letters to Harvey Prindle Peet of the Institution for the Deaf and Dumb in New York, Jan. 17, 1847 and March 28, 1853, both in the Howe Papers, Houghton. It is possible that other letters have been lost. Howe's hand can be seen in the *Commonwealth*'s publication of an account of an American's visit to a deaf school in France where the children were taught to speak, June 15, 1853.

[35] Howe to ?, April 21, 1875, Howe Papers, Houghton.

[36] "Second Annual Report," pp. liv–lvi.

[37] "Second Annual Report," pp. lx–lxi.

[38] "Second Annual Report," pp. lviii–lix.

[39] Howe to ?, April 21, 1875. See also *Remarks on the Theories of Dr. Samuel G. Howe, Respecting the Education of Deaf Mutes, as Set forth in the Second Report of the Board of State Charities, by a Native of Massachusetts* (Boston, 1866).

Asylum, struck back in his annual report. Articulation, he insisted, was a tedious and exhausting method which brought forth only unsatisfactory and transient results. It would retard the children's accumulation of knowledge several years, since while they were studying speech, they could not learn much else.[40]

Howe, in high dudgeon, considered Stone's strictures unjust to the Board as well as disrespectful to himself. He accused the Asylum of always having repelled suggestions of change as if it were impertinent for anyone to say anything.[41] Howe admitted that he had made mistakes in the past, but that was no ground for the principal's charge of inconsistency. Nothing would ever be righted if one were afraid to break publicly with one's old views. When he had organized Perkins, he continued, there were no schools to serve as models. He had copied existing establishments such as the Asylum. In less than twenty years, however, having realized his errors, he had recommended an entirely different plan to a group from another state who had asked his advice.[42] The success of the Workshop Department at Perkins, where the workers had to live out, proved that he was right. As for educational method, in each recommendation he had made which the Asylum had accepted, he had been justified.[43] The Asylum had committed a serious error by not emphasizing dactylology. Its graduates could not spell as well as Laura Bridgman. Nothing but constant practice had given her the skill she used to communicate with the world, while at Hartford the students never used words among themselves.[44]

The next year Howe again urged the creation of a school in Massachusetts.[45] More contemptuous of his antagonists than ever, he knew that it was only a matter of time before he attained his goal. Each day brought further proof of the truth of his stand. Miss Harriet Rogers, the sister of one of Laura's early teachers, opened a private school at Chelmsford in June 1866 at which she taught

[40] *50th Report* (1866), pp. 16–39.
[41] S. G. Howe, *Remarks in Defence of the Second Report* (Boston, 1866), p. 15. Howe was too harsh on Stone.
[42] Howe, *Remarks in Defence of the Second Report*, pp. 24, 25.
[43] Howe, *Remarks in Defence of the Second Report*, p. 36.
[44] Howe, *Remarks in Defence of the Second Report*, p. 32.
[45] *Mass. Pub. Doc.* 17 (Jan. 1867), pp. lxiii–lxxiii.

articulation successfully, while out in Northampton, John Clarke expressed willingness to endow a duly chartered academy. Friends conferred with Governor Alexander H. Bullock, who in his message of January 1867 recommended it to the legislature.[46]

Both Howe and Franklin B. Sanborn, now a colleague on the Board of State Charities, appeared before the joint legislative committee in a series of hearings during January and February. The venom of twenty-five years poured forth from Howe's soul, and a rare vintage it was, as he pilloried the American Asylum in the presence of its alumni, staff, and students.[47] The forces of reform overwhelmed the Asylum and its friends. A bill was favorably reported. Passed and approved June 1, 1867, the law chartered a new school for the education of the deaf in Massachusetts, but did not prevent parents from sending their children to Hartford if they preferred.[48] Upon the organization of the corporation in July, Clarke presented it with $50,000, and in his honor the school, which began operation in October, was named the Clarke Institution for Deaf Mutes.[49]

Howe took great satisfaction in the opening of the institution he had fought to establish. But for the interference of the Asylum, he wrote, it would have been created at least fifteen years earlier.[50] Its success equaled Howe's hopes for it. Even Dudley came around. He enrolled his daughter there and was so pleased with the result that he eventually became one of the trustees.[51]

V

Though Howe, immersed as ever in charitable work, appeared to be the Howe of old, there had been a profound change in his in-

---

[46] "Address of His Excellency Alexander H. Bullock to the Two Branches of the Legislature of Massachusetts," *Mass. Sen. Doc.* 1 (Jan. 4, 1867).

[47] *Mass. Sen. Doc.* 265 (May 1867), Appendix. This is a volume of 236 pages. See in particular Howe's interchange with Stone, pp. 176–179. Also *Boston Advertiser,* Jan. 25, Feb. 1 and 8, 1867.

[48] *Mass. Acts and Resolves* (1867), chap. 334.

[49] *First Annual Report of the Clarke Institution for Deaf Mutes at Northampton Mass. for the Year 1867* (Springfield, 1868), pp. 4–8.

[50] "Fifth Report of the Board of State Charities," *Mass. Pub. Doc.* 17 (1868), p. lxxxv.

[51] Howe to ?, April 21, 1875, Howe Papers, Houghton.

terests. He no longer cared for the type of work that had brought him world fame, and to which he had devoted his best years. Even as he fought for the creation of the Clarke Institution, he preferred doing something else. As in 1841, while the Western world rang with praise for his teaching of Laura Bridgman, he had sought to become Secretary to the American legation in Spain, now again he desired to enter the diplomatic service, this time as Minister to Greece. He was old, tired, and ill. A shift, he said, would be like "a new lease of life." In vain Sumner cautioned him against changing his occupation at his advanced age, but Howe was adamant. Pathetically he implored the powerful Senator, now chairman of the Foreign Relations Committee, to use his influence for him.[52] This was the first time Howe ever asked a favor for himself from Sumner. Even Julia was pressed into service. Early in May 1866 she went to Washington to see President Johnson.[53] Her efforts were wasted. At the end of the month Howe learned that Johnson would not nominate him.[54]

The disappointed aspirant tried to bear up, but it was hard. There would have been no difficulty at all had he realized from the start the futility of his quest. Even apart from the fact that he was the closest friend of one of the President's leading tormentors whom nothing but removal from office would satisfy, he had no right to expect favor from an administration whose policies he had promised never to approve.[55] Unfortunately Howe's yearning was so great that he blinded himself to the realities of the situation. Too late he realized his fatuousness. "Had either the Pres. or the Minister been persons of delicacy or generosity," he noted morosely, he would have been informed "kindly but decidedly that there would be no use in

[52] Howe to Sumner, March 23, April 22, April 27, 1866, Howe Papers, Houghton.
[53] Richards and Elliott, *Julia Ward Howe,* I, 246.
[54] Howe to Sumner, May 31, 1866, Howe Papers, Houghton.
[55] Howe to Sumner, April 28, 1866, Howe Papers, Houghton. Howe followed Johnson's impeachment eagerly. During the trial he wrote daily letters to Wilson and Sumner. Rev. H. A. Dunham, "Recollections of Dr. Howe's Office Boy," taken down by Claudia Potter. This is in the Perkins School. It disgusted him to hear people rejoice over Johnson's acquittal, or, as he preferred to call it, "escape." What was needed was "another 'come out' movement as that of the Conscience Whigs." Howe to Sumner, May 18, 1868, Howe Papers, Houghton.

pressing the matter. That they lack delicacy & generosity is their misfortune." He realized there was no use brooding over Johnson's spitefulness; "& now, for work in other fields, while my little of life remains." [56]

VI

A new opportunity to get busy came to Howe just as he despaired the worst. During the summer of 1866 the island of Crete, left under Turkish domination when the Greek mainland was freed, rose in revolt. In November the Cretan Central Committee in Athens appealed to their American champion.[57] Four decades fell away when he received the call. He was young again. Calling his friends together at his office, Howe quickly arranged for a public meeting which was held on January 7, 1867, at Bumstead Hall. Strikingly youthful for all his sixty-five years, the veteran Phil-hellene delivered a fighting speech. The scene was reminiscent of old abolitionist meetings. Former Governor Andrew, in one of his last public appearances before his premature death later in the year, introduced the resolutions; Wendell Phillips shared the speakers' platform, and the audience made Howe chairman of a relief committee.[58] Amos A. Lawrence donated his services in his old capacity as treasurer.[59] The team that had beaten the Slavocracy was now reactivated. The Turks had better look to their laurels.

Within a fortnight Howe had arranged for the organization of a similar committee in New York.[60] Contributions began pouring in, from Gerrit Smith's $500 down.[61] Lawrence offered a cache of "peacemakers," 400 breechloaders, originally worth $13,000, but for which he had paid only $3000. Howe, considering these the most important aid the revolutionists could get, assured the donor, "I

---

[56] Howe to Sumner, June 5, 1866, Howe Papers, Houghton.
[57] *Boston Journal,* Dec. 24, 1866. Scrapbook on the Cretan Insurrection, Perkins.
[58] *Boston Advertiser,* Jan. 8, 1867.
[59] Howe to Lawrence, Jan. 7, 1867, Cretan Letterbook, Howe Papers, Perkins; Howe to Lawrence, Jan. 8, 1867, Lawrence Papers, XXX, 22, MHS.
[60] *New York Tribune,* Jan. 21, 1867.
[61] Smith to Howe, Jan. 11, 1867, Cretan Letterbook, Perkins.

shall do my best to put your *alms* into the right hands, and do not doubt that good reports thereof will be heard." [62]

Rejuvenated by this new crusade, Howe's old hatred for the Turks returned as virulently as ever.

I feel by instinct that we are on the eve of the most important struggle that has taken place for a long time; & that the mutterings which we have from Thessaly & Epirus are only the preludes of a storm which will rage with fury next year.

I should like to see the tail of the last Bashaw streaming northward as he sails over [*sic*] Southwards over the Hellespont.[63]

Strong words, but the fiery old Philhellene would have done it himself, had he been able to. He decided to go to Greece to direct the distribution of relief among the 12,000 refugees clustered on the mainland. The New York and London organizations appointed him their almoner as well.[64] Howe was now the agent of three groups.

Setting sail on March 13, with his wife and only two of his daughters, Julia Romana and Laura, he missed the last stages of the battle for the creation of the Clarke Institution. In Liverpool less than a fortnight later, he held a meeting with the local committee on the evening of his arrival. Despite his eagerness Howe did not hurry to Greece, but made the trip across the Continent in leisurely stages.[65] Not until after Easter, which was spent in Rome

[62] Howe to Lawrence, Feb. 20, 1867, XXX, 57; March 1, XXX, 74 1/2, A. A. Lawrence Papers, MHS. The figures are from a note Lawrence added, probably when he pasted these communications into his letterbook, or possibly when they were presented to the MHS. However, Lawrence to Howe, Feb. 23, 1867, Cretan Letterbook, Perkins, speaks of others owning them: 3 unpaid notes amounting to $200. Lawrence offered to meet half the charge if Howe would raise the other half. It is unclear just what these guns were. It is possible that they were old Civil War rifles stored in the Cambridge arsenal.

[63] Howe to Sumner, Jan. 27, 1867, Howe Papers, Houghton.

[64] Estimated number of refugees from Finlay to Howe, Feb. 16, 1867, Howe Papers, Houghton. New York turned over $12,000, Tuckerman to Howe, Feb. 11, 1867, Cretan Letterbook, Perkins. Howe to Andrew, Feb. 19, 1867, Andrew Papers, MHS. Lawrence announced total contributions as $16,120.30. *Boston Advertiser*, March 12, 1867.

[65] "Notebook of the Journey to Greece, 1867," Howe Papers, Houghton, lists the schools and prisons he visited.

with Julia's sister Louisa, did he push on to Athens, arriving there on May 9, to be received with all the honor befitting his attainments and his present mission.[66] One of the pleasantest moments of his first day was his meeting with George Finlay, whom he saw again after long years of correspondence.

Setting to work immediately, he ascertained conditions for himself among the refugees, who, having been unable to bring money or property with them, and unable to find employment on the mainland, were in a wretched plight.[67] Enforced idleness Howe considered as most damaging to self-respect. Work relief was the only way of giving alms, as it had beeen in 1828. With the assistance of missionaries he put the Cretan women to work on a bag-making project, while the children were cared for in nurseries.[68] Meanwhile he arranged to have provisions smuggled into Crete under the noses of the Turks.[69]

Upon the arrival of a box of clothing from America the Minister of Marine allowed him the use of a creaky old tug, long since declared unseaworthy, for its distribution. In this gallant bark he visited Aegina where he had the satisfaction of seeing that the mole he had constructed almost forty years before was still giving good service.

Grateful to us it was [he wrote], landing upon this broad, substantial mole, to find assembled upon it the populace of Egina, many of whom were witnesses of its structure, and all of whom regarded it as a monument of the generosity and of the practical beneficence of the American people.[70]

But on rigidly blockaded Crete there was nothing he could do except continue smuggling. While the Great Powers enforced a policy of nonintervention, the legions of Omer Pasha were gradually overcoming the revolutionists. Starvation was rife throughout

---

[66] Howe to Rodocanakis, May 10, 1867, First Letterbook of the Greek journey, Howe Papers, Houghton. Howe to Henry Marion Howe, June 8, 1867, Howe Papers.
[67] S. G. Howe, *The Cretan Refugees and Their American Helpers* (Boston, 1868), p. 12.
[68] Howe, *The Cretan Refugees*, pp. 18–19.
[69] Howe, *The Cretan Refugees*, p. 29.
[70] Howe, *The Cretan Refugees*, pp. 39–40.

the island after the government confiscated the crops.[71] Though forbidden to land on Crete, Howe went anyway, even though it meant prison if he were captured. At Rethimon on the north shore, he learned tales of new atrocities, to all of which stories he gave full credence. He considered the Turks capable of any barbarity imaginable and probably a few unimaginable. Omer Pasha, he later declared, had converted the island into a vast prison, in which he tortured the inhabitants to gain submission. His men, ordered to scorch the earth, had left nothing alive.[72]

Back in Athens by July 12, Howe spent the remainder of the month on the mainland finishing up his work. What he had seen had saddened him. He knew that there was no hope for the rebels. Turkish pressure was becoming unbearable, and men could not fight on empty stomachs.[73]

At the end of July when the heat became too intense for him, he left his beloved Greece, never to return. Before his departure he made arrangements with Finlay and others to care for the refugees with the money remaining. Fatiguing and disquieting though his task had been, still his sojourn had not been unpleasant. In his journeys around the country he had visited the old scenes, in particular the site of his colony on the Isthmus of Corinth, which he was pleased to learn had flourished for many years before disappearing during a period of civil wars.[74] Above all, it had been good to see Finlay again. Poor old Finlay was beginning to feel his age. Two years Howe's senior he was ready for the fireside, while the Chevalier, spry as ever, had climbed the Acropolis almost daily.[75]

Others of the Howe family had enjoyed the trip too. Twenty-three-year-old Julia Romana, her father's loyal secretary and untiring assistant, had become attracted to a young Greek collegian, Michael

---

[71] C. M. Stillman to Howe, June 24, 1867, Cretan Letterbook, Perkins. Stillman was American Consul in Crete.

[72] Third and Fourth Letterbooks of Greek journey, Howe Papers, Houghton; *Boston Advertiser,* Aug. 9 and 10, 1867. Howe wrote a series of letters to the *Advertiser* during his trip abroad.

[73] Howe to Warren, July, 1867, Fourth Letterbook.

[74] Fifth Letterbook.

[75] Howe to Sanborn, Aug. 28, 1867, Fifth Letterbook.

Anagnostopoulos, who had offered his services to the relief committee free of charge. Having made himself invaluable to both
father and daughter, he was to follow them home shortly. It was
certain that he would marry Julia.

VII

The Howes spent the rest of the summer traveling in Western
Europe, imbibing culture. The girls were old enough now to appreciate what they saw. Their father, though, unable to take a complete holiday ever, mixed in some business as usual with his pleasure, visiting as many prisons, schools, asylums, and reformatories
as he could. His only regret was that he could not inspect enough
of them. Switzerland was a delight in his eyes. The canny nation
of hotel keepers did everything properly, especially in education.
Their schools for the deaf, he declared on his return, were the best
in the world.[76] He rejoiced to see that the claims of his opponents
in the articulation controversy, that the deaf could not learn to
speak French because of the homophonies of the language, were
being disproved. With his own ears he heard the children at the
Yverdon school intone Gallic syllables intelligibly. The Geneva
institution, where he examined an advanced class, was just as successful in its work. There could no longer be any question of the
eventual triumph of the method at home.

In Bavaria, Howe found a school that agreed with him so completely about teaching only articulation, and nothing else, that it
favored sending its students to a regular trade school after they had
learned to speak.[77] It was good to see that some schools in Europe
knew what to do, thought Howe.

Late in September he observed the Gheel Insane Asylum in
Belgium, an institution run completely to his satisfaction. Extending
over an area of a hundred square miles, there were no bars, cells, or
guards. Lunatics were boarded with private families, among whom
they lived in close relationship. Once given tasks to perform around

---

[76] *Boston Advertiser*, Oct. 10, 1867. Letter from Yverdon dated Aug. 24.

[77] Notebook of Journey to Greece, Aug. 21, 1867, Howe Papers, Houghton. Howe
to Sanborn, Aug. 28, 1867, Fifth Letterbook.

the house, they were harmless. Unchained, they wandered freely in perfect safety. Howe noted that even raving maniacs were left alone. One woman, who shrieked at him, became so pacified within a few minutes when left alone that she was allowed to fondle small children.[78] How much better this was than the marble-halled monstrosities of America with their benevolent cruelty!

Boston looked good to the travelers on their arrival home late in October. The reunited family had much to tell each other, what with scenes in Europe, and all the Parisian finery the girls had brought back with them. On the other hand, Maud had shot up during the summer, and was now quite a young lady. Her parents exchanged significant glances when they saw her for the first time in several months.[79]

Howe's feelings about his trip abroad were mixed. Although he had gained new insights into the treatment of the handicapped, the fact remained that his mission had failed. The Cretan revolt had been suppressed, and once again the hapless islanders lay prostrate under the oppressor. Still, he refused to give up the fight. Throughout the fall and winter, and on into the spring, he continued agitation. In April 1868, Julia conducted a fair for the benefit of Crete which raised several thousand dollars.[80] At the same time, Howe began the sporadic publication of a newspaper, *The Cretan,* in the hope that he could rouse interest for the unhappy people.[81]

VIII

Howe returned to his work at Perkins determined to make a clean break with the past. What he had seen in European asylums (he could not consider most of them as schools), with their segregation and consequent intensification of the inmates' psychological

[78] Fourth Letterbook, Sept. 25, 1867. *Boston Advertiser,* Nov. 2 (supplement), Nov. 15, Nov. 28 (supplement), Dec. 3, and Dec. 13, 1867.

[79] Maud Howe Elliott, *Three Generations* (Boston, 1923), p. 79.

[80] J. W. Howe, *Reminiscences,* p. 320.

[81] The first issue appeared in April 1868. Eight issues were published at irregular intervals, the last bearing the date June 1869. To the end, Howe rattled the saber, certain that Christianity would triumph over Moslem barbarity. His letters also show how determined he was to continue the struggle. See Howe to Sumner, April 10 and July 14, 1868, Howe Papers, Houghton.

disorders, pushed him at last into taking the fateful step he had delayed for almost twenty years.[82] After many meetings he gained the trustees' consent to reorganize the school on a more intimate basis.[83] Although he was still unable to make Perkins a purely day school by boarding the children in normal families, he sought to create something approximating that in the cottage system, which enabled a group of children to live together in a family-like environment under the supervision of an adult who would stay with them always.[84]

During the next two years he put through the herculean task of remaking an institution which had flourished for over a generation in its original form. Howe worked hard at his problems, determined to have all the material arrangements of grounds and building for carrying on the establishment upon his principles. Perkins would become the first school of its type to be organized on a sound theory.[85] Fearing only that he might not live to see his program brought to fruition, he regretted that he had delayed so long.[86]

At first the board had considered a move to the country, as South Boston was losing its desirable characteristics. Formerly a quiet, salubrious suburb distant from the city's heart, the mud flats had by the late sixties been drained, streets cut through, and the neighborhood rapidly settled. Teeming South Boston had come into being. However, the expense of such a move was too great. The institution was to remain where it was for another forty years.

With assistance from public and private sources, four cottages and a new schoolhouse, all for the girls, were built.[87] (The boys continued to live in the main building until the transfer to Watertown in 1912, when cottages for all were at last provided.) In the new regime Howe decreed strict separation of the sexes. Since in

---

[82] *36th Report* (1868), pp. 21–28.

[83] *39th Report* (1871), p. 5.

[84] *36th Report* (1868), pp. 27–28.

[85] Howe to Sumner, March 23, 1868?, Howe Papers, Houghton.

[86] *36th Report* (1868), p. 29.

[87] The state appropriated $95,000 and a fund-raising drive produced another $25,000. *39th Report* (1871), p. 6.

many cases blindness was shown to be hereditary, he considered it desirable to hinder the development of intimacy among the older students, although he recognized its practical impossibility.

Howe did not consider his innovation the final word. Still feeling that it was best for the blind to attend the common schools, he was certain that it was feasible in more cases than was at first apparent.

Depend upon it [he wrote], one of the future reforms in the education of the blind will be to send blind children to the common schools, to be taught with common children in all those branches not absolutely requiring visible illustration, as spelling, pronunciation, grammar, arithmetic, vocal music and the like. We shall avail ourselves of the special institutions less, and the common schools more.[88]

Except for his advocacy of the cottage system, Howe fell behind in his later years in other aspects of his profession. His prize-winning method of printing which had pervaded the field, and of which he was understandably proud, was rendered obsolete by the work of a brilliant young newcomer, William B. Wait. Wait, since 1863 the director of the New York Institution for the Blind, had quickly become displeased with raised lettering. An examination of several of the nation's schools for the blind showed that only 34 per cent of their students could learn to read any line type with facility, 31 per cent moderately, while 35 per cent were completely unable to read.[89] At the same time a test at a school in Missouri showed that 65 per cent of the pupils there had learned to read a system of points with facility and 35 per cent had learned moderately well.

In 1868 Wait introduced his own alphabet of thirty modified phonetic and five-word and part-word signs, which proved to be more legible than others, while requiring a third less space.[90] This "New York point," as it came to be known, quickly established its superiority over all other systems of printing, although the Perkins

---

[88] "Letter to the Second Convention of the American Instructors of the Blind," *40th Report* (1872), p. 26.

[89] *Thirty-Second Annual Report of the Managers of the New-York Institute for the Blind to the Legislature of the State, for the Year 1867* (New York, 1868), p. 21.

[90] *Thirty-Second Report of the Managers*, p. 33.

Institution held out against it until several years after Howe's death.[91]

It is hardly a sign of failure for an old man to be supplanted by one of the coming generation. The law of the prize ring holds true in other fields as well; the old and tired champion, with mind jaded by the campaigns of many years, must give way to the young and fresh contender in the prime of life. Howe had built upon the achievements of Valentin Haüy in his youth, as now Wait built upon Howe's. In his day the director of the Perkins Institution had been undisputed ruler of his field, his successes unequaled by any of his contemporaries. The wonder is not so much that he was eventually surpassed, but that it took thirty-six years before anyone could rival him. Few in any profession can point to so long a pre-eminence.

IX

Despite all his attainments, Howe was dissatisfied. Frequently melancholy, he mourned the fate that had made him a teacher of the blind. He felt that he had wasted his life, although he acknowledged that he had done some good. Now he was old, and there was nothing to look forward to. Only his sense of duty and the necessity for employment kept him working. In reality, he wrote Sumner, "the Lord did not make me for a philanthropist. . . ."[92] If he was not that, it is difficult to say quite what he was, but the fact that Howe was always available for political activities and journalistic enterprises shows what he probably wished he could have become. Still there was one last fling awaiting him, one last rejuvenation before the curtain came down.

[91] 95th Report of the Perkins Institution (1926), pp. 28–30.

[92] Howe to Sumner, March 23, 1868 (?), Howe Papers, Houghton. If this were the only letter that contained such defeatist statements, it might be discounted as merely temporary exhaustion, but from the mid-fifties on these sentiments appear with greater frequency. Even as early as the mid-forties he began complaining of his life running its course without his having accomplished enough. "Howe is in a nervous morbid state. He has no enjoyment in social intercourse, being painfully conscious of the passing of time, as if life were slipping from under his feet. At the Asylum a bell rings every quarter of an hour as a constant memento mori; and wherever he goes he hears this melancholy bell." Oct. 29, 1845, Henry Wadsworth Longfellow Journal, Houghton.

XVIII

Santo Domingo and Samana Bay

After 1869 Howe felt his career on the larger stage of national affairs was over. The new administration refused his bid for the Greek mission, even though Sumner, temporarily in favor at the White House, pleaded with the Secretary of State, his old friend Hamilton Fish, for the appointment.[1] Occupied with his regular duties at home, Howe feared he would never fulfill the "higher mission" of his life; he would never do the good he had been designed for; he would never overthrow Mohammedan tyranny and restore pristine Christianity to the Levant.[2]

May God grant that by some means or other republicanism political & religious freedom may be more ably & openly represented from the loved land of my birth to the land of my early love — than they have yet been: & let history be able to write that a land not born when Phocion died, was the first to begin paying off the debt of gratitude which the world owes to Greece.[3]

Suddenly in 1871, he was back in the vortex of politics.

[1] Sumner to Howe, March 28, 1869, Sumner Papers, Houghton.
[2] Maud Howe Elliott testifies to the drive with which her father discharged his duties as chairman of the Board of State Charities. See her *Three Generations*, pp. 82–83.
[3] Howe to Sumner, April 2, 1869, Howe Papers, Houghton.

I

General Ulysses Simpson Grant was President. Had he realized his own inadequacy, he would have remained in private life, the honored defender of the Republic, but here his customary modesty deserted him. There was one last prize his grateful countrymen could give him, and he accepted it as his due. Ignorant of statecraft, but full of grandiose ideas, he now ruled a nation too busy making money to exercise proper vigilance over its officials. Debauchery reigned triumphant while virtue fled into the hearts of a few men. In most departments the situation was soon a scandal, but the conduct of foreign relations was relatively pure, mainly through the efforts of Hamilton Fish, a man of great talents and deep integrity.[4] Still even there one finds blots.

One of the most disgraceful aspects of this administration was Grant's attempt to annex Santo Domingo. For many years, dating back to Pierce's time, there had been a series of plots to gain control of this wretched, revolution-ridden land.[5] Occupying the eastern two-thirds of the island which Columbus christened Hispaniola, Santo Domingo exhibited all the political immaturity characteristic of Latin America. A nation of barely 200,000 people, it had never had a stable government since its achievement of independence from Haiti in 1844. Revolutions succeeded each other with rapidity until 1861 when Spain reoccupied its former colony. Upon Spanish withdrawal four years later, the situation reverted to its previous state.

While many Dominicans favored Yankee control in the hope that it would bring order, pacification of a country for the sake of its inhabitants could hardly attract the hardy breed of empire builders. Santo Domingo seemed to offer great opportunities for ruthless exploitation. The soil was fertile, and geological surveys had indicated great mineral wealth, the island of Alta Vela being especially

---

[4] Fish's integrity is unquestioned by all scholars who have investigated his career. See Allan Nevins, *Hamilton Fish* (New York, 1936), pp. 115–123, for his feelings on taking up his duties.

[5] For the interest of the government in Santo Domingo, see "Report of the Secretary of State in Regard to San [sic] Domingo," *Sen. Exec. Doc.*, 41 Cong., 3 sess., no. 17 (Jan. 16, 1871).

rich in guano, a fertilizer much used at the time. The country was desirable also for its strategic value. Samana Bay, on the north shore, was a superb site for a naval base, necessary for the defense of the inter-oceanic canal Americans knew they would build some day. It was this possibility that had attracted Seward during his tenure in the State Department.[6]

Although a sizable syndicate of financiers and bankers were involved, two disreputable adventurers, "General" William L. Cazneau and "Colonel" Joseph Warren Fabens, led the plot. Both natives of Massachusetts, they had gained their military titles in Texas, where they also proved apt pupils of the land speculators.[7] As an agent of the State Department, Cazneau became interested in Santo Domingo during the fifties.[8] In 1859 Fabens joined him there. During the succeeding years, while hatching a series of wild-cat schemes that fleeced any number of honest investors, they entrenched themselves in the Caribbean land.[9] By the late sixties, possessed of great concessions which would have given them control of at least one-tenth of the country's territory, they prepared to put through their most ambitious coup, annexation.

There appeared to be little opposition among the natives. President Buenaventura Baez was amenable if the United States assumed his government's inflated debts. In and out of office several times in the preceding twenty years, and at the moment fighting two generals, José Maria Cabral and Gregorio Luperon, Baez was nearing the end of his tether. He saw his only chance to save himself was in annexation. Most of the money America was to pay would have ended up in his pockets, leaving him the dominant figure in the

[6] For a discussion of earlier schemes see Charles Callan Tansill, *The United States and Santo Domingo, 1798–1873* (Baltimore, 1938), pp. 1–337; for the history of the country during this period, see Sumner Welles, *Naboth's Vineyard* (New York, 1928), I, 142–358.

[7] Their earlier careers are summarized in Nevins, *Fish,* pp. 252–257, and Tansill, *United States and Santo Domingo,* pp. 343–344.

[8] Cazneau to Cass, Dec. 30, 1859, Special Missions, American Hemisphere, II; Dept. of State Records, National Archives.

[9] See, for example, the *Report of the American West India Company* (June 1, 1865) for the details of one of their plots. This is available in the New York Public Library.

nation's politics. (He may have expected to become senator after admission as a state, although there is a possibility that he planned to live in Paris.) The articulate classes, the small upper crust of Creoles, wanted big power protection also. No one asked the depressed white and Negro peasantry what they thought, but their opinion had never been solicited before anyhow, and this was hardly the time to begin.

With Grant's inauguration the hucksters saw their chance. Skillfully they made their preparations, finding spokesmen in such key Congressional figures as Nathaniel P. Banks and Ben Butler. Knowing of Fish's hostility to the plan, Fabens and Cazneau approached the President through his aides. Grant fell in with the scheme, and thought it would be popular with the people. He sent down his private secretary, Orville E. Babcock, on an "inspection trip" during the summer of 1869. The envoy returned in September with an outline of a treaty. Grant was now determined to put through a formal pact.

Although originally opposed to the project because he realized its true character, Fish went along with it. More than anything else, he needed a free hand in his work. The settlement of the Alabama Claims was pending, and it would require great tact to avoid war. There was also the matter of the Cuban insurrection which had strained relations with Spain. The Secretary had to give in on Santo Domingo or resign, and considering the Chief Executive's taste in appointments, he shuddered to think who his successor might be.

Under Fish's direction two treaties were prepared. The first called for the annexation of Santo Domingo on American assumption of its debts for $1,500,000. In case this were rejected, the other treaty was for the lease of Samana Bay at a rental of $150,000 annually for fifty years, with the right of annexation for $2,000,000 at any time during that period.[10] Upon the signing of these agreements late in November, American naval forces were ordered to protect the Baez government from attack. Haiti was warned to respect the

[10] Texts of the treaties may be found in *Sen. Exec. Doc.*, 41 Cong., 3 sess., no. 17 (Jan. 16, 1871), 98–102.

integrity of Santo Domingo's borders. Early in December the Stars and Stripes was raised over Samana Bay.

Submitted to the Senate in January 1870, both agreements were emphatically rejected by the tie vote of 28–28 after a session-long wrangle.[11] The sordid story of the negotiations and the private advantages some had gained was publicized. The administration suffered a humiliating defeat for which it blamed Sumner, although he had been only one of the opposition leaders. Carl Schurz, the former German still devoted to the principles of Forty-eight, had also fought ratification, as had Thomas F. Bayard of Delaware and Justin S. Morrill of Vermont. Only one scapegoat was needed, however, and since the Massachusetts Senator had been most prominent as well as most outspoken in his distinctive manner, he was singled out in contemporary newspapers. Most historians have followed the original error.

Grant, finding the taste of defeat as unpleasant as it was unwonted, refused to let the matter die. In his annual message to Congress, December 1870, he recommended that a commission be appointed to negotiate a new treaty.[12] Senator Oliver P. Morton of Indiana introduced a resolution authorizing such a body merely to investigate Santo Domingo.[13] His motion said nothing about a treaty. A titanic struggle ensued in Congress.[14] Sumner, implacable when he had a cause, considered himself to be fighting for a people threatened with a new kind of slavery. It was Kansas all over again (although the speech he delivered was entitled "Naboth's Vineyard"), and the same pressures were exerted against him "as in the olden time." The Santo Domingo business was of "heartless cruelty," he wrote Howe.[15] Never in his life had he felt himself more right than now as the Senate chamber resounded to his denunciations. "How could I do otherwise," he asked, ". . . without

[11] *Journal of the Executive Proceedings of the Senate of the United States of America* (Washington, 1901), XVII, June 30, 1870, 500–508.

[12] James D. Richardson, *A Compilation of the Messages and Papers of the Presidents* (Washington, 1898), VII, 100.

[13] *Congressional Globe,* 41 Cong., 3 sess., 53, 61.

[14] *New York Tribune,* Jan. 10, 1871, p. 1, has an account of the excitement prevailing in Washington during the debate.

[15] Sumner to Howe, Dec. 30, 1870, Sumner Papers, Houghton.

abandoning all those sentiments under which I have acted." [16] The
veteran statesman was magnificent, but the resolution as amended
by the House finally passed the Senate on January 11, 1871. Grant
signed it the next day.[17]

The measure authorized the President to appoint a three-man
commission to travel to Santo Domingo for a close examination of
the country. They were to go where they pleased, look at what they
wished, and stay as long as they liked; and on the way back, stop
off at Haiti for consultations with that government as well. The
whole matter was to be completely aired.

As the resolution neared the end of its travels through Congress,
Grant began to think of the appointments. Wishing to create a
commission of distinguished men, respected for their probity and
intellect, he chose Ben Wade, the former Radical Senator from
Ohio, Andrew D. White, the young President of Cornell University,
and a certain Bishop Simpson of Louisiana.[18] At the last moment,
however, Simpson declined, and Grant hastily appointed Samuel
Gridley Howe, who accepted.[19]

II

Howe's entry on the scene was as surprising as it was sudden.
Like all citizens interested in daily affairs, he had followed the steps
leading to the joint resolution. It seemed to him that there had
been "jobbery & trickery" in the whole thing. In a vague way he
favored the projected annexation, since he considered it a "sort of
national duty to extend the benefit of our political institutions by
peaceful means over the W. I islands. . . ." [20] However, he had
taken no part in the public discussion. About the tenth of January,
he was in Worcester for a meeting of the board of the lunatic
asylum. As he stood in the station waiting for a train home, he was
approached by a man who suggested he volunteer for membership

[16] Sumner to Edward L. Pierce, Dec. 30, 1870, Sumner Papers, Houghton.

[17] *Congressional Globe,* pp. 416, 431, 479.

[18] Grant to White, Jan. 10, 1871, Grant Letterbook, Lib. of Cong.

[19] Babcock to Fish, Jan. 14, 1871, Fish Papers, Lib. of Cong.

[20] "Memorandum on the Commission to Sto Domingo, expenses &c, beginning
Jan. 10,71," p. 1. Howe Papers, Perkins.

on the commission.[21] The doctor laughed off this suggestion. The following day this same individual asked his consent to telegraph the White House urging his nomination. Howe told him to do as he chose, and dismissed the matter from his thoughts.

On Friday 13 — at 3 P.M. Burt[?] sought me out at the Mass General Hospital [Howe was a director of this also] & showed me a telegram from U.S. Grant to the effect that if S.G.H. would accept the place of Commissioner I should report myself at New York on Monday.[22]

"S.G.H" notified the President of his willingness, and on the night of January 16 he arrived at the commission's quarters in the Astor House where the envoys were hectically concluding preparations for their departure the next day.[23]

Howe and Grant had never met before. In fact they did not meet until after the commission's return. All Grant knew of him was that he was Sumner's lifelong friend.[24] Undoubtedly Fish exerted his influence in the matter. As one of Sumner's closest associates he knew of their relationship, and that the Senator would have faith in anything Howe said. The three appointments were well received, the naming of Howe especially favorably.[25] Fish felt that a trio of such distinction would disarm criticism and inspire confidence in the administration's motives.[26]

On the seventeenth, the steam frigate U.S.S. *Tennessee* sailed out of New York bound for Samana Bay. Besides the commissioners there were on board such prominent figures as Frederick Douglass in the capacity of assistant secretary, and General Franz Sigel whose services were much desired because of his integrity. A corps of

[21] "Memorandum on the Commission to Sto Domingo," Howe Papers, Perkins. The date cannot be determined exactly. The name is illegible in the manuscript. It might be Burt or Burton. Someone named Allan A. Burton was secretary to the commission.
[22] "Memorandum on the Commission to Sto Domingo," Howe Papers, Perkins, p. 2.
[23] Babcock to Fish, Jan. 14, Jan. 16, and Jan. 17, 1871, Fish Papers.
[24] *New York Tribune*, Jan. 17, 1871, p. 1.
[25] *New York Tribune*, Jan. 14, 1871, p. 1.
[26] Fish to Bancroft, Jan. 16, 1871, Letterbook II, 843; Fish to Washburne, Jan. 17, *ibid.*, 848, Fish Papers.

scientists, interpreters, and clerks, in addition to ten newspaper correspondents, brought the total passenger list up to thirty-two. The first day out the commission held its first meeting, at which Wade was chosen president.[27] Their orders were explicit: they were to visit Santo Domingo, ascertain the sentiments of the people, and examine the country. They were to be completely free in everything they did. Except for their expenses, they were to receive no compensation for their services, they learned on opening the sealed instructions Fish gave them before they left.[28]

The envoys insisted they were open-minded and without any strong views on annexation. Wade was known to favor it, but he was said to be willing to change if the evidence should warrant it.[29] White's feelings were completely unknown. A man of scholarly pursuits, he improved his time aboard ship by prodigious reading in the commission's hastily assembled library of Dominigiana.

> Dr. Howe [continued the *New York Tribune* correspondent], is wholly unbiased, and the country may rest assured that he will make such a report as his investigations shall warrant regardless of friendships or party fealty. A Commission was never organized possessing more honest determination to do their whole duty than this.[30]

The passengers were a lively company, one of the most sophisticated that could have been gathered together at that time among Americans. Wade, still straightforward, rough, and unpolished, vigorous in old age, as befitted a Buckeye politician, spoke of the

---

[27] Jan. 18, 1871, Journal of the Santo Domingo Commission, National Archives. This was also printed in their official "Report," *Sen. Exec. Doc.,* 42 Cong., 1 sess., no. 9 (April 5, 1871). The records of the commission are in 3 volumes in the National Archives. The first contains the journal and correspondence, in addition to statements in Spanish from settlements and military posts attesting to their desire for annexation. Volume 2 contains testimony of witnesses and separate reports on the resources of the country made by its investigators. Volume 3 consists of material in Spanish made available by the Dominican government. All that is needful is in the published "Report."

[28] Instructions to the Santo Domingo Commission, Jan. 14, 1871, Special Missions, American Hemisphere, II, Dept. of State Records, National Archives.

[29] Considering Wade's record in the Senate, one wonders if any amount of evidence could convince him to change his mind once his opinions were set.

[30] *New York Tribune,* Feb. 21, 1871, p. 1; Andrew D. White, *Autobiography* (New York, 1905), I, 489, has characterizations of Wade and Howe.

old days in the Senate. Howe "full of humor," recalled his youth in Greece so entertainingly as to "repay the suffering from the stormy coast of Hatteras." Sigel told about the war, and Douglass reminisced about his years as a slave. Even the ship's captain joined in the story-telling. Yes, a voyage to the Caribbean, especially when undertaken at government expense, was a perfect way to avoid the rigors of the northern winter.

Seven days out of New York, Samana Bay was sighted. On anchoring, messengers were dispatched to the capital, Santo Domingo City, announcing the arrival of the Americans. No time was lost in fitting out three separate parties to explore the region. Howe set about drawing up a plan of inquiry.[31] Shaken by the stormy voyage, the ship's company hurried ashore, eager to observe their future compatriots at close range. Disappointment greeted them. Despite the euphony of the name Santa Barbara de Samana, they found a miserable settlement of about eighty or ninety bamboo huts roofed over with cocoa leaves, which provided living quarters for perhaps 250 or 300 natives, most of whom crowded down to the wharf to gape at the strangely dressed visitors. A plaza, two churches, one Catholic and the other Methodist (used by a group of American Negroes who had lived there for over forty years), and a jail completed the roster of public buildings. This was what most of the sightseers thought was to become a major coaling base for the United States Navy.[32]

Howe's plan was ready the next day. It was similar to that of the old Freedmen's Inquiry Commission. He proposed that they determine the population and ratio of the races, their physical condition, way of life, status of the family, religion, and education. In addition they were to collect the views of the people on their short-lived union with Spain during the sixties, and their opinion of a federation with Haiti. While on the subject, he suggested they might also seek to discover how far the desire for annexation to a

[31] Sto. Domingo Commission Journal, Jan. 23, 1871; *New York Tribune*, Feb. 22, 1871, p. 2. Newspapers were a month late in their stories owing to poor communications. There was no telegraph service to Santo Domingo. Because no news was received for so long a time, the *Tennessee* was feared lost in a storm off Hatteras.
[32] *New York Tribune*, Feb. 21, 1871, p. 1.

foreign power arose from their fear of subjugation by Haiti.[33]

The investigators spent about a week at the Bay getting the feel of the country and starting their surveys. Dogged by the reporters, they traveled throughout the peninsula, but only Howe rode a bull, the universal beast of burden. He offered a sight

worth the trip to behold. The Doctor is the tallest gentleman, except for Fred. Douglass perhaps, in the party, and the bulls are very low. Curling up his feet and legs to keep them from the ground, guiding the bull with one hand by a rope attached to a ring through the animal's nose, and applying the whip with the other, the Doctor's picture, with his linen coat streaming in the air and his broad-brimmed hat covering his magnificent head, was novel and instructive.[34]

No one could ever deny Howe's venturesome spirit.

To Yankee eyes the inhabitants were an "uncommonly lazy set of vagabonds," albeit good-humored and fairly intelligent. The women took care of what little work needed to be done while the men lounged about the shops sucking oranges and looking at strangers. There was, however, a gang of male laborers finishing off the Methodist church.[35] Data collected throughout the region pointed to unanimity in favor of annexation, the Negroes being enthusiastic for it, and the whites, whom Howe called "Spaniards," desiring it quietly. Testimony was unequivocal on the hatred all Dominicans bore toward Haiti. Scientific expeditions returning to the coast from the interior reported the same thing. The constant warfare, with its resultant insecurity, had brought about economic chaos. Depredations were incessant, and with the courts unable to operate efficiently, there was no redress from robbers. Should the United States refuse to take the country, Howe felt the people would offer themselves to any other power that would protect them.[36]

[33] Commission Journal, Jan. 24, 1871.
[34] New York Tribune, Feb. 21, 1871, p. 8.
[35] Howe, "Memorandum on Santo Domingo," p. 8.
[36] New York Tribune, Feb. 21, 1871, p. 8; Howe, "Memorandum," p. 29; Commission to Fish, Feb. 14, 1871, Commission Records, I; Commission Journal, Jan. 26, 1871.

Their preliminary work concluded, the envoys sailed for Santo Domingo City, the first settlement to be established in the Western Hemisphere, which they reached on the morning of February 2, after an overnight sail around the eastern bulge of the island. At noon President Baez and his ministers received the trio.[37] Smooth, polished, and affable, the gaudily attired Baez played his part to perfection. He was a light mulatto, aware of his handsome appearance and he took advantage of it. His North American guests succumbed to his blandishments. Instead of Sumner's "political jockey," Howe found "a cultivated and distinguished gentleman and patriot" in the full vigor of manhood, "simple and courteous in manners," considerably cultured, familiar with European countries and languages, respected and beloved by his neighbors. White, only slightly less enthusiastic, deemed him a patriot of the highest order.[38]

Briefly Baez outlined his situation. Haiti was at the root of his government's troubles, supplying Cabral with arms and officers. Santo Domingo, he charged, faced not a civil war but a foreign invasion. He offered ample evidence to substantiate his claims.[39] This was all Wade needed to know; he was ready to back Baez with American arms if necessary. Howe was more cautious. Though he had no doubt of Haiti's imperialist desires, he felt American interference would be not only unconstitutional, but wrong. "I am naturally fond of a scrimmage you know," he wrote his wife, "& if there is one 'may I be there to see'; — but I will not be party to any unlawful act." While the present government was the lawful one, it might not be the next day. Anyhow, he feared Baez might

[37] Commission Journal, Feb. 2, 1871.
[38] S. G. Howe, *Letters on the Proposed Annexation of Santo Domingo in Answer to Certain Charges in the Newspapers* (Boston, 1871), pp. 14–15; White, *Autobiography*, I, 490. Sumner's characterization of Baez is to be seen in the *Congressional Globe*, 41 Cong., 3 sess. (Dec. 21, 1870), p. 227.
[39] *New York Tribune*, Feb. 21, 1871, p. 8. That there was an agreement among Luperon, Cabral, and the Haitian government of Nissage Saget is shown by Sumner Welles, *Naboth's Vineyard*, I, 361–362. See also Harold T. Pinkett, "Efforts to Annex Santo Domingo to the United States," *Journal of Negro History*, XXVI (Jan. 1941), 25.

seek to involve the commission in some actual aggression against Cabral or Haiti.[40]

The doctor tried to guard himself against being misled by the Dominican government. He knew it was an absolute machine which would not hesitate to force the people into admitting they favored annexation but within a short while he was convinced that there was no need for Baez to force public opinion. Conditions were so bad that the people cried out for union with the States.[41] One look at the dilapidated capital would have shown that to anyone. Crumbling shells of once splendid buildings stood everywhere, memorials of an ancient time when the city was the seat of Charles V's New World empire. Now it was just a stagnant town on the edge of encroaching wilderness, so weakly defended that a small force of lightly armed men could have taken the city, were it not protected by the American Navy. The harbor garrison was so poorly supplied that it was unable to answer the *Tennessee's* courtesy salute until it had borrowed powder from the ship.[42]

While fourteen expeditions fanned out to all corners of the country, the commissioners spent almost three weeks in the capital conducting their examination. Baez supplied them with the result of a plebiscite on annexation which showed an overwhelmingly favorable sentiment.[43] This poll was, of course, a travesty of democratic procedures, but there was no way for the Americans to determine that.[44] Day after day they sat, listening to civil servants and army officers (all Baez men) tell of their desire for union. Among the many deputations was the Senate of the republic, which suggested that Santo Domingo be admitted as a territory in which status it would remain for eight or ten years. By then they felt the people

[40] Howe to Julia Ward Howe, Feb. 6, 1871, Santo Domingo Letterbook, Howe Papers, Houghton.

[41] Howe, "My Experiences in Santo Domingo," pp. 1–4, Howe Papers, Perkins. This was written in 1874 to Dr. Blackwell; the covering letter is dated Sept. 6.

[42] *New York Tribune,* Feb. 21, 1871, p. 8.

[43] These figures and reports were transcribed and given to the commission who dutifully included them in their official documents. They make a tidy volume.

[44] Welles, *Naboth's Vineyard,* I, 385–387, describes the voting and the fate of those known to oppose annexation.

should have enough training in democratic self-government and could become a state.[45]

Greatest credence was given to "Professor" William M. Gabb of Philadelphia, director of the Dominican geological survey. Ostensibly engaged in valuable work for the nation, but in reality seeking out the best lands for the Fabens-Cazneau syndicate's exploitation, he stated flatly that 98 to 99 per cent of the people favored annexation.[46] Gabb worked on the commissioners with great skill. Repeatedly he gave them "the same old story about the value of the country, resources, opinions of the people, absurdity of Cabral etc. *ad infinitum*" until he felt relieved to get back to field work. So convincingly did he speak that they came to trust his opinions over those of their own geologists. His reports on the mineral wealth of the country, which had been very guardedly written in anticipation of such an occasion, indicated vast resources. He was certain that the commissioners would endorse his findings, even though the commission geologist had reservations as to the island's riches.[47]

In the face of overwhelmingly favorable evidence the commission was won over. Though White was noncommittal, he was considered safe. Wade, without any reservations at all, declared publicly that the devil must have gotten into "Brother Sumner" to make him oppose annexation.[48] Howe, equally enthusiastic, announced the devotion of his energies to bringing Santo Domingo into the Union.

It seemed to me as a rare and golden opportunity for extending and fortifying our own political and social institutions: for the growth of our commerce: and especially for diverting the vast stream of wealth collected by slaveholders from continuing to go to the support of despotic

[45] Howe, "Memorandum on Santo Domingo," pp. 21–22; Commission Journal, Feb. 8, 1871.
[46] Commission Records, II, 145.
[47] Gabb to Fabens, Feb. 11, 1871, quoted in Tansill, *U. S. and Santo Domingo,* p. 437, fn. 100.
[48] Tansill, *U. S. and Santo Domingo,* p. 437, fn. 100.

and aristocratic institutions of Europe: and for turning and using it to the ends of abolishing slavery in Cuba, Porto Rico and Brazil, &c.[49]

Howe liked the island; its balmy climate was a tonic for his neuralgia from which he suffered terribly during the cold Boston winter. Imagine being able to ride horseback and swim in the ocean during February! Enjoying his mission, he let his intellectual interests have full rein in visits to hospitals, schools, and prisons. Above all, he studied the life and thought of a people the like of whom he had never encountered before.

The voodoo of the jungle was never far from the thought of this folk. Christianity, despite three centuries of sway, was at best an admixture which modified their inherent paganism. Among the lower classes Howe was shocked to learn that small value was placed on a child's life. Deceased infants were considered little angels who intercede in heaven for those left behind; it was impious to make an effort to save them. On rare occasions peasants took a dead baby, dressed it, put an iron through its back, hung it up, and worshiped it. However this was more common in Haiti.[50]

Social distinctions dating from colonial days he found still in existence.[51] Although the government tried to conceal the presence of a caste spirit, Howe knew that color lines were strongly drawn, and that among the upper classes intermarriage even with mulattoes was unfavorably regarded. Baez declined to give a state ball; he could not invite Negroes, yet did not dare exclude them.

Morally the country was checkered. Illegitimacy was frequent. There were so many charges on licenses, in addition to the priests' fees, that many omitted taking the marital vow. The status of marriage was consequently somewhat ambiguous, being respected in some places and disregarded in others.[52] Santo Domingo would have added a distinctive design to the American social pattern.

Everyone connected with the commission considered annexation

---

[49] Howe, "Experiences in Santo Domingo," p. 5.
[50] Howe, "Memorandum on Santo Domingo," p. 71.
[51] For a discussion of colonial social distinctions, see Welles, *Naboth's Vineyard*, I, 6.
[52] Howe, "Memorandum on Santo Domingo," p. 61.

a certainty. The majority thought it desirable, but some unofficial observers, namely, H. J. Ramsdell of the *New York Tribune,* felt otherwise. Able to see more things for himself than Wade, Howe, or White, since he was not besieged by Baez's crew of lackeys dinning selected information into his ears, he roamed the city at will. Clearly he saw that the citizens desired annexation, but he wondered whether the country was worth taking. Sumner, he feared, had been right. Baez was a "political jockey" and not much else. When not fawning over the Americans, he manipulated them and his countrymen at will. With his gaily colored clothing, he even looked the part. Though a bachelor, he had many children. In a land so poverty-stricken that it could not pay its chief executive a regular salary, he lived in luxury while his soldiers starved. His power was absolute and he ruled like a royal despot. There was no free speech; all over the city were posted proclamations forbidding the discussion of politics. If one asked about Cabral, people walked away. Ramsdell had no doubt that Baez would get most of the $1,500,000 purchase money, as he and his family were all in high office and were all owed back salaries. Indications were that the public debt approached $3,000,000, twice the official figure, although the Finance Minister would not state exactly what it was. In fact he could not really tell. There was probably no way of knowing, nor could anyone determine how much land was public domain.[53] The whole venture was an attempt to sell the United States a load of goods with a false bill of lading.

The commission remained for a week longer in Santo Domingo City after finishing its work, because of indecision for which Howe and White were mainly responsible. The doctor wasted a few days in a side trip to Seybo which accomplished nothing. Upon his return White left to lead an expedition to Puerto Plata across the island, although a regular party had already been there. Howe and Wade thereupon went to Azua, a town on Ocoa Bay in the western part of the country, the former going overland, and the latter by sea. White was to join them at Port-au-Prince in Haiti.[54]

[53] *New York Tribune,* March 17, 1871, pp. 1–2.
[54] *New York Tribune,* March 17, 1871, p. 1; Commission Journal, Feb. 14.

Emissaries from Cabral appeared at Azua with a message from the general who wished to see the Americans. Baez was faithless and false, he charged; a majority of the people opposed annexation.[55] There was nothing else for the two commissioners to do but send back a reply expressing willingness to hear from him further.[56]

What Howe saw at this stopover enraged him against Haiti. Haitian prisoners of war, proof of Baez's claims of foreign invasion, were presented before him. The activities of these new "border ruffians" were an "outrage of humanity & should be treated accordingly."[57] In this frame of mind, after bidding Baez a cordial farewell, he and Wade boarded the *Tennessee* for the short trip to Port-au-Prince, landing there March 2.

Howe, who hated the confinement of a ship, rushed ashore. Within a few hours he learned that the Haitian government had sent more arms to the front in the last week. Cabral was indeed only its tool, perhaps even its prisoner. The moralistic New Englander knew now where the guilt for the war lay, and it would go hard with them.

From the sea, the capital of the Negro republic looked attractive. At close range it was another story. As Howe walked around, he was shocked by its condition. Foul odors and garbage were everywhere. He spent the night in the town, but returned to the ship the next morning in a raging temper. It had been impossible for him to sleep. Until midnight, a group of natives clustered in the street, below his window, had kept him awake with their singing, yelling, drinking, and fighting. After they retired the mosquitoes drove him wild. He swore that they would "desert friends and kindred to come to him, and he could only keep them off by smoking bad cigars which made him sick." Toward morning just as he had dozed off, the crowing, barking, and braying of the local animals drove him frantically from his bed.[58]

The doctor's disappointment was shared by all his associates.

---

[55] Cabral to Commission, Feb. 25, 1871, Commission Journal.
[56] *New York Tribune,* March 17, 1871, p. 1.
[57] Howe, "Memorandum on Santo Domingo," pp. 84–87.
[58] Howe, "Memorandum on Santo Domingo," p. 92; *New York Tribune,* March 17, 1871, p. 2.

There could be no firmer friends of the Negroes than Howe and
Wade, nor those who believed more strongly in their latent ability
for self-government than Frederick Douglass, himself part Negro,
but they all sorrowfully acknowledged that the experiment was a
failure. The regime possessed none of the elements making for
success, strength, and stability. Three revolutions in the preceding
five years had destroyed all semblances of public safety. One got
the impression that the army consisted of major generals only.
Mulattoes dominated the conduct of public affairs and sought absolute sway. The population, sunk in ignorance and lacking in
energy and intelligence, subsisted on a low level of civilization not
far from barbarism. The administration did not encourage education; there was not a school outside the principal town.[59] Prices
were so inflated that a pound of tea cost $1000.[60] The reaction of the
people to these miserable conditions was a universal desire to get
rich and move to Paris where they thought prejudice against color
did not exist. One of the commission staff who had been in the
country thirty years before found no improvement. This was tan-
tamount to saying the people had retrogressed.[61]

The day after their arrival, President Nissage Saget and his cabinet received the unwelcome visitors. Obviously suspicious of American intentions, the Haitians were formal, stiff, and cold. Anxious
to conciliate them, Wade delivered a short address, with Howe as
interpreter, assuring them of the peaceful desires of his country.
The proposed annexation was not designed as a threat against
Haiti. In his response Saget maintained the friendly feelings of his
government towards its great northern neighbor.[62]

Stuck in Port-au-Prince for a few days longer until White's arrival, Howe had an opportunity to learn more of the disordered
state of the country. Several times more populous than Santo

---

[59] Howe must have accepted this on faith, or on the basis of some evidence since
it does not appear that he ever left Port-au-Prince.

[60] The *Tribune* correspondent does not say in whose money.

[61] Howe, "Memorandum on Santo Domingo," pp. 94–96; *New York Tribune,*
March 17, p. 2.

[62] *New York Tribune,* March 17, p. 2. Howe "Memorandum on Santo Domingo,"
p. 93.

Domingo, although little more than half its neighbor's size, Haiti was a tyranny of caste. Mulattoes, he was told, lived in fear that the full-blooded Negroes would rise and murder them. Unhappily he was forced into the conviction he had feared to face, that the Negroes of the West Indies if left to themselves would revert to barbarism, as indeed those of the interior already had. The answer to the Negro problem, and he felt that this applied to the freedmen in the United States as well, was not a great Negro confederacy, but constant contact with a highly developed civilization. As he had known since his work on the Freedmen's Inquiry Commission and his correspondence with Agassiz in 1863, Negroes were an imitative race; least of all men could they progress under segregation or isolation.[63] Cabral communicated again with the Americans but they were no longer interested in what he had to say. They had incontrovertible evidence that he was a tool of the Haitian government, not a Dominican patriot.

Before leaving the island, the commissioners began the preparation of their report in order to have it ready by the time they reached Washington. It was to be favorable. Howe, to whom fell the task of writing up the physical, moral, and mental condition of the Dominicans, as well as their views on annexation, was so enthusiastic and so touched by their suffering that he declared he would spend the rest of his life in assisting them to achieve a higher civilization.[64] After a short stop for coaling at Kingston, Jamaica, the *Tennessee* continued its homeward voyage. At sea between Cuba and Florida preliminary drafts were read and considered. In order to save time, the trio debarked at Charleston, proceeding by rail to Washington where they arrived on March 27.[65] Howe was Sumner's guest during the week it took to polish up the report.

While the returned envoys worked, the debate on Santo Domingo, which had begun in Congress over a week before, roared on after

[63] Howe, *Letters on Santo Domingo*, pp. 12–13.

[64] *New York Tribune*, March 17, 1871, p. 2. The draft of Howe's report is in Perkins.

[65] Commission Journal, March 11–26, 1871; *New York Tribune*, March 28, 1871, p. 1.

reaching its peak in one of Sumner's diatribes, this one of only three and a half hours' duration, on the twenty-seventh. Scathingly the recently deposed chairman of the Senate Foreign Relations Committee, smarting under his humiliation, pilloried the administration for making war without the authority of Congress. He said that the use of the Navy to protect Baez meant that the United States had sided with one of the factions in the Dominican civil war, and this was illegal. American power was being used to support a usurper who sought to sell his country. The means being employed to take the island were indefensible, even apart from the desirability of the move.[66] Administration forces put up a bold front (Roscoe Conkling of New York attempted to distract attention from the address by talking in a loud voice to Hannibal Hamlin of Maine), but it was known that for the sake of reuniting the Republican Party the White House would not press the matter. Overwrought debate continued until the end of March. The actual report could be only an anticlimax.

At length, early in April, it was finished. The President, in transmitting the document to the Senate, insisted that the commission's findings had sustained all his claims. He considered that his motives were completely vindicated.[67] While there was no recommendation about annexation, journalistic prophecies of unqualified approval were fulfilled.[68] With Grant satisfied, and Sumner removed from all opportunity to commit further mischief in the conduct of foreign affairs, party leaders moved to bind up Republican rifts. The report was laid on the table, and the special session ended on April 20, with no further action taken.[89] The problem of Santo Domingo was settled for everyone but Samuel Gridley Howe.

[66] *New York Tribune,* March 28, 1871, pp. 1–3.
[67] *New York Tribune,* April 6, p. 1; "Report of the Commission of Inquiry to Santo Domingo," *Sen. Exec. Doc.,* 42 Cong., 1 sess., no. 9 (April 5, 1871), p. 1.
[68] "Report of the Commission of Inquiry to Santo Domingo," *Sen. Exec. Doc.,* p. 34.
[69] *New York Tribune,* April 21, 1871, p. 1.

III

Howe returned to Boston shortly after the commission disbanded.[70] When he was converted to a cause it made no difference whether what he favored appeared alive or dead. For twenty-five years he had nourished thoughts about articulation until suddenly the matter became a live issue. Santo Domingo would be resuscitated at the proper time, of that there was no doubt. Throughout the spring and summer of 1871, annexation was never far from his thoughts. In answer to attacks on the report which came from such scattered sources as James Redpath, the erstwhile abolitionist journalist, and "Many Dominicans," he wrote a series of letters to newspapers, and urged his former colleagues on the commission to do likewise.[71] At the same time, he continued to encourage Grant's hopes.[72] During the fall of the year it seemed to him as if the people were softening in their views and might yet be won over.[73] Meanwhile he continued discussions with Fabens who had a new plan.[74]

The more Howe thought about the defeat of the President's policy, the more angry he became at the opposition. Not even Sumner was spared his ire. Intimate confidants for over thirty years, they had rejoiced and sorrowed together, with never a cross word between them.[75] But now a cloud came over their relationship. Sumner who could do no wrong had committed a profound error, and Howe would not forgive him. There was a strained correspondence between them beginning in the spring of 1871 and continuing

[70] Sumner made another attempt to gain him the Greek mission and was again rebuffed. Apparently Fish had no faith in Howe's diplomatic abilities.

[71] S. G. Howe, *Letters on Santo Domingo* (Boston, 1871). Redpath had earlier served as Haitian consul in Philadelphia, at which time he wrote *A Guide to Hayti* (Boston, 1860). "Many Dominicans" produced *A Brief Refutal of the Report of the St. [sic] Domingo Commissioners* (New York, 1871); Howe to White, June 5, 1871, White Papers, Cornell.

[72] Howe to Grant, June 4 and 27, 1871, Misc. Mss., NYHS.

[73] Howe to General ?, Nov. 10, 1871, Misc. Mss., NYHS.

[74] Howe to Col. [Fabens], Feb. 3, 1872, Misc. Mss., NYHS.

[75] See, for example, Howe's letters of consolation at the time of Sumner's separation from his wife; Dec. 21, 1867, Dec. 31, 1867, and Feb. 4, 1868, G. B. Pierce Papers, Houghton.

on into the next year, but they never came to a rupture. Howe, separating the Sumner he loved from the statesman, attacked only the latter. During Grant's reëlection campaign of 1872, he found the Senator's fulminations insupportable.

I have been slowly & painfully led to the sad conclusion that Charles Sumner has become morally insane [Howe wrote White].

The great moral influence over the public which he has gained by a noble & brilliant career, he is now wielding to gratify personal hate & envy. God help him; for he knows not what he does.

Much as I love him, I deem it a duty now to guard the public by all my feeble powers, against the evil which this once great & good man is now doing, in his blind phrenzy. . . .

He has deceived & misled the public. He has vilified & abused innocent men. He has retarded the abolition of Slavery in Cuba & Porto Rico. He has imperilled the acquisition of territory by the U.S. which would be of vast advantage to the country; to commerce; & to the progress of freedom & humanity. . . .

The commissioners have great reason for speaking now; & while helping to break Mr Sumners power for evil, may do something for the real good of the Dominicans, or the Haytians & the people of the U. States.[76]

In vain Sumner defended himself. His sense of duty was completely enlisted against Howe's pet project, and there was no way out. In his opinion, Howe was the unwitting tool of unscrupulous persons. Annexation was a crime, instigated primarily by a pro-slavery rebel, Cazneau, and his accomplice Fabens. "It is the case of Ahab & Naboth . . . ," he wrote. The program Howe favored sent a sword to the island rather than peace. If the administration were sincere, it would have aided both Haiti and Santo Domingo to get back on their feet, but "in this there is nothing to gratify the *imperatorial* nature of the Psent." Three million dollars had been wasted in the effort to take over the country during the past two years that might have been used for education. His New England conscience was agonized to think of such means being diverted from a good purpose and employed to keep a nation in distress. "I

[76] Howe to White, Aug. 8, 1872, White Papers, Cornell.

hope you will pardon this freedom," he pleaded. "So do I feel this difference, that, when this question began, could I have foreseen that you were to rush into it so intensely, I should have been tempted to resign my seat in the Senate." [77]

In his younger years Sumner would never have begged in this way. A quarter-century earlier he had broken with Winthrop and others for far less, but in his old age the dean of the Senate was a pathetic figure. Ill and lonely, the veteran spokesman of "Right" and "morality in politics" faced the twilight of his career a broken man. The years had not been kind to him. Rejected and humiliated, outside the councils of the party he had helped to found, most of his influence had been shorn from him by a vengeful Chief Executive. Deprived of domestic felicity he had reached an age when a man ordinarily rejoices in pleasures of the home, the weddings of children and the birth of grandchildren. Howe was partaking of these joys now, but Sumner never would. His brief marriage had ended tragically, and he lived alone in the magnificent home he had built to house his bride. Only his youngest sister, of all his family, was still alive, but she lived in San Francisco.

His loneliness, gnawing at him, drove him at times to pitiable frenzies, no matter who might see them. He sought to cling to the few friends he had left. The controversy had already cost him the regard of Hamilton Fish, and now the dearest of them all appeared to be drifting from him. Even Julia had spoken scornfully of him.[78] Except for Longfellow, there were few to whom he felt he could turn for comfort.

After twenty years in public life Sumner had learned nothing. Still unable to understand the necessity of compromise, he wore his devotion to duty like a halo. "Nothing can be settled which is not right" was the motto he chose to be inscribed on a bust which was to be unveiled in his honor.[79] At times he acted as if he no longer lived in this world but worked only for the future. In that distant time his calumniators would get their due. "When I am gone," he

[77] Sumner to Howe, Aug. 3, 1871; Sumner to Pierce, same date, Sumner Papers, Houghton.

[78] Sumner to Pierce, May 12, 1871, Sumner Papers, Houghton.

[79] Sumner to Pierce, Dec. 21, 1869, Sumner Papers, Houghton.

wrote Howe, "the wild beasts will doubtless prey upon me. It will be for my friends to say what truth & justice require. I know the integrity of my life in all things, & I am sure that there are persons who will hereafter regret what they say now." [80] His speeches were his children, his life. As a connected series, he was certain they would illuminate his career and justify him. Determined to make them a valuable historical source, he taxed his energies in his last years to prepare a revised edition of his *Works*.[81]

IV

So devoted was Howe to Santo Domingo that he would do anything to further its cause, even to partaking in what honorable men would consider a swindle. He thought it was honest; nothing else mattered. Sometime during 1871 he was won over to a new scheme of exploitation of the hapless Dominican people. Fabens and his associates, namely Spofford, Tileston and Company, the same crew who had backed earlier efforts, conceived a plan of leasing Samana Bay and developing the area on their own. The naïve humanitarian fell in eagerly with the scheme. Knowing perfectly well that they wished to use him as a front, he at first refused the use of his name, although he promised to aid them all he could, as he would any project which would lead to the eventual absorption of Santo Domingo into the United States.[82]

At the syndicate's behest he went to the island with Fabens to negotiate an agreement.[83] Julia and Maud went along. After long discussions with Baez, they came to terms about the leasing of the bay to a private company of American citizens. As a sop to Howe,

[80] Sumner to Howe, Sept. 2, 1872, Howe Papers, Houghton. This was of course a rebuke to Howe.

[81] Sumner to Howe, Dec. 7, 1868, Sumner Papers, Houghton; Sumner to Howe, Sept. 18, 1873, Howe Papers, Houghton.

[82] Howe, "My Experiences in Santo Domingo," p. 6.

[83] Howe, "My Experiences in Santo Domingo." This is very strange. When he wrote these reminiscences in 1874 (possibly as part of an autobiography about which he said nothing), he claimed to have gone there in 1865, although from other sources it is apparent that he did not leave the country that year. One is reluctant to say that he dissimulated so as to make the venture seem more honorable. What probably happened is that in the fuzziness of old age he confused dates, despite the fact that he was remarkably vigorous for a man of his years.

the understanding, which became known as the "Howe Convention," contained provisions for the betterment of the native population, the company being required to establish and foster public schools.[84] With a definite commitment from the government, the company's organization proceeded apace upon the return of the negotiators in April 1872. Howe consented to become a director of the new corporation and to take $20,000 worth of its stock, half to be paid for in cash, and the rest to be charged on the books. At an annual salary of $5000 for two years he was to perform what services he could without his having to leave Boston, the arrangement to continue at his option. He was also allowed to dispose of half of his interest to a friend, and he did.[85]

The preliminary work completed, the Samana Bay Company was chartered December 25, 1872, at a capitalization of $800,000.[86] Shortly after this, it concluded a formal contract with the impoverished Dominican government for the lease of Samana Bay and the surrounding area.[87] In return for a rental of $150,000 a year, the same as the United States had agreed to pay for a naval base, the New York syndicate received eminent domain throughout the peninsula, with power to open a free port. Great tracts of public land were included in the deal. In addition, the company received a virtual monopoly over internal improvements in all parts of Santo Domingo, the government assuring it preference over all other bidders in grants for the operation of railroads and telegraph lines, and the building of common roads.[88] In return, the company promised to use its best efforts with Washington to secure a treaty of reciprocity by which products of both countries were to be traded duty-free through Samana Bay. Howe's ideas of improving the popu-

---

[84] Howe, "My Experiences in Santo Domingo," p. 7.

[85] Howe, "My Experiences in Santo Domingo," pp. 8–9. Since Howe sold half his stock presumably at par, he risked nothing in the venture but his good name.

[86] Samana Bay Co. to Hamilton Fish, May 11, 1874, Howe Papers, Perkins. Christmas is a peculiar date for a charter to be issued, but that is the one given.

[87] Howe called this a treaty, but since treaties can be concluded only between sovereign governments, or at least more or less so, one must call this a contract.

[88] Welles, *Naboth's Vineyard*, I, 406–407.

lation were quietly dropped.[89] The Americans paid their rent promptly on January 1, 1873, and received full rights to their fief in mid-April after a plebiscite (undoubtedly one of Baez's fixed polls) showed the people in favor of the arrangement 20,117 to 19.[90]

The mad scramble was on. Speculators, sensing a sure thing, soon moved in. Twenty men risked $20,000 each, so strong was their faith. All investors expected their stock to be worth twenty-five times its purchase price and indeed, some found takers at that inflated figure. But these were merely the "inflation days," then came the "insane days," as Howe put it, when "men went mad over the dreams of vast gain." Money was squandered prodigally on fabulous salaries, traveling expenses, and bonuses to officials who accomplished nothing.[91]

The tangled finances of the Dominican Republic now came to plague the company. In severe financial straits during 1869, Baez had sought to float a loan in London, but no reputable firm would deal with him. Forced to treat with anyone who would accept his business, he turned to Edward Hertzberg Hartmont, a notorious swindler who had fled to Great Britain to escape a prison sentence in Belgium. Hartmont, appointed Dominican Consul-General, negotiated a bond issue with Peter Lawson & Company. Although authorized to raise only £420,000, of which £100,000 was to be commission, leaving £320,000 for Baez, the syndicate printed up £757,000 worth at 6 per cent interest, which they sold at a discount of one-third, leaving the poor betrayed Dominican peasantry pledged to pay for the larger sum.[92] Hartmont turned over £50,000 to Baez and kept the remaining £480,000 for himself. In 1870 the Dominican government repudiated the loan.

Now, in 1872, a demand arose that the Samana Bay Company

---

[89] Howe, "My Experiences in Santo Domingo," p. 11; Fabens to Howe, Jan. 24, 1874, Howe Papers, Perkins.

[90] Samana Bay Co. to Fish, May 11, 1874, Howe Papers, Perkins. Welles gives the figure in favor as 20,496, *Naboth's Vineyard,* I, 408.

[91] Howe, "My Experiences in Santo Domingo," pp. 11–12.

[92] "Special Report from the Select Committee on Loans to Foreign States," *Parliamentary Sessional Papers,* XI (1875), 137–141.

redeem the entire bond issue to bolster its credit. Howe knew that some of his associates were in on the plot, but he never realized the full extent of their chicanery. Spofford, Tileston and Company, who operated the only line to Santo Domingo, the ship *Tybee,* and were the backers of the Samana Bay Company, were also Lawson's American correspondents, while Fabens had for years been Spofford's agent in Santo Domingo as well as Hartmont's Washington representative.[93] Dutifully the company sent a commission to London to buy up Baez's fictitious obligations.

Howe opposed the swindle, but he was alone in a den of wolves. Innocent of devious business ways, he had difficulty in understanding what was going on, but his instincts told him the whole thing was a fraud. Too late he learned that he had been duped, that he had been needed as the respectable front behind whom scoundrels could hide. His first inclination was to resign his directorship and denounce the venture; certainly "a mere regard to my own reputation would have made me do so," he admitted later. But he stayed. Craftily, the hucksters who used him talked him out of his resolve as they dangled the possibility of his $10,000 equity becoming worth $100,000. Only a Sumner or a Schurz could have resisted such tempting bait. Howe yielded to their blandishments. "I am human," he humbly acknowledged afterward when there was no other way of explaining his one genuflection to Mammon.[94]

It is not to be wondered, in view of its mismanagement, that the company's financial condition grew critical during the summer of 1873.[95] The doctor saw in this an opportunity to seize control from the speculators and put it under the guidance of honest men. Cupidity had not been his only motive in retaining his connection with the enterprise. He saw it primarily as the opening wedge in a new annexation attempt which would further the cause of freedom and spread American commercial and political institutions in

[93] Tansill, *United States and Santo Domingo,* pp. 349–350.

[94] Howe, "My Experiences in Santo Domingo," pp. 14–16.

[95] Sumner again tried to have Howe sent to Greece, but Fish was more opposed than ever; Sumner to Howe, Sept. 18, 1873, Howe Papers, Houghton; Nevins, *Hamilton Fish,* p. 656.

the West Indies. In his moments of enthusiasm he saw a historical movement reborn on a grand scale. The great East India Company which had spread British power in Asia had found its spiritual descendant in an office at 29 Broadway in downtown New York. Even after the failure of the venture, he refused to admit that his hopes had been unjustified.[96]

The men of good-will (if there were any connected with the company) failed to take over however. Howe still remained dissatisfied, and but for the harm to Santo Domingo's cause would have withdrawn his name.[97] At any rate, the directors finally made an effort to realize some money from their investment. Early in October, Howe and Fabens, acting as special commissioners for the company, negotiated successfully with the Navy for the lease of Samana Bay as an American base. There appeared to be hope of making something out of the sorry mess after all.[98] Publicly Howe professed pleasure at the turn of events. Company dissensions were about over, and its managers through careful operation would create real value from their franchise. Ultimate success depended on the maintenance of peace. The presence of the American flag would not only guarantee such peace, but make the island a place of refuge for the oppressed of other lands, help the liberal party in Haiti, and extinguish slavery in Cuba.[99]

Then the bubble burst. As Ramsdell of the *Tribune* had foreseen, the various Dominican factions repudiated all their leaders to coalesce behind General Ignacio Maria Gonzalez.[100] Hitherto he had been a colorless government official content to remain in the provinces, but late in November he proclaimed the revolution. Success met the insurgents' arms. Decisively defeated in a few

---

[96] Howe to Bird, Sept. 1, 1873, Howe Papers, Houghton; "My Experiences in Santo Domingo," p. 10.

[97] Howe to Fabens, Jan. 25, 1874, Howe Papers, Perkins.

[98] Samana Bay Co. to Fish, May 11, 1874, Howe Papers, Perkins.

[99] *New York Independent,* Nov. 27, 1873, p. 1477.

[100] Ramsdell had written that, if annexation were defeated, the Dominicans would reject all their leaders including Baez, Cabral, and Luperon in favor of entirely new men who would bring peace. *New York Tribune,* March 17, 1871, p. 2.

weeks, Baez resigned his office on January 2, 1874, and fled the country.[101] Gonzalez became provisional President.

Having risen against the former government because it had alienated a portion of the national territory, the new leaders looked with jaundiced eye on the concession to the Americans. In February the Dominicans issued a peremptory demand for their rent. The company, still in sore financial straits, offered Gonzalez a smaller cash payment along with a share of the profit, but to no avail. In this critical situation the directors turned to Howe once more, appealing to him to return to the Caribbean country at the head of a three-man commission to seek a compromise. Disgusted with the venture, the tired old man at first refused, but giving ear to his doctor who recommended a warm climate, he reconsidered. Julia went with him.

Howe realized the futility of leaving without at least a token sum of between $20,000 to $30,000 to offer the junta, but there was nothing in the treasury.[102] A prompt but frigid reception greeted the forlorn band, now no longer backed by Uncle Sam and/or his gold. There could be no question that times had changed. Gonzalez was firm. He wanted money, $150,000 worth, and if he did not get it, he would annul the contract. Howe offered his own note for $5000, but the tyro statesman was not to be placated.

With the approval of the populace, Gonzalez promulgated his decree canceling the rights of the Samana Bay Company. Noisily the people celebrated the restoration of sovereignty over all parts of the national domain. Howe was convinced that nonpayment was a mere pretext; that the European powers and their commercial agents had instigated the whole thing in order to prevent American hegemony, and all that it meant, over the surrounding islands.[103]

There was a sad gathering at Samana Bay a few days later when the company's flag was furled. Howe read a formal protest, after

---

[101] Welles, *Naboth's Vineyard*, I, 410. Baez apparently fled to the United States for a short while since Howe invited him for a visit. Howe to Fabens, Jan. 25, 1874, Howe Papers, Perkins.

[102] Howe to Spofford, April 6, 1874, Howe Papers, Perkins.

[103] Samana Bay Co. to Fish, May 11, 1874; Howe, "My Experiences in Santo Domingo," pp. 20–39.

which he made a little speech to the employees who formed in a circle around him. "The old Crusader never appeared nobler or better than on this occasion," wrote Julia, "when his beautiful chivalry stood in the greatest contrast to the barbarism and ingratitude which dictated this act. My mind was full of cursing rather than blessing."[104] The plot to exploit Santo Domingo had failed, but for once the only losers were speculators and bankers rather than the public. Probably in that fact alone lies its uniqueness.

Howe and Julia remained alone at the Bay after the departure of their compatriots. Far from the chill winds of early spring, they lived an idyllic existence, he drinking in the sun and air, swimming and riding, while she studied her books and preached to the Negro congregation who listened in awe. At length, it became apparent that the contract was not to be restored. The peaceful couple, who meant no harm, could stay no longer. It was a sad parting. They had grown to love the country, and the failure of their hopes for its improvement saddened them. Howe knew that he would never return.[105]

After a last dinner at the White House, and a discussion of Dominican problems with Grant, with whom he had maintained cordial relations since their first meeting three years before (despite the administration's refusal to send him to Greece), Howe returned to Boston from what proved to be his last mission on June 10, 1874.

Howe's crusading days were over. He was seventy-two and he felt it. Illness, some of it dating from his Greek days, racked his frame. Only with great effort could he do his work. Gradually he had been resigning his myriad posts, although he retained Perkins. With the aid of his son-in-law, Michael Anagnos, he spent the summer preparing his famous "Forty-third Report," in which he summarized his achievements at the institution.

It is regrettable that his last crusade should have been the shady affair it was. None realized that more fully than he did now.

Parts of it are like a romance. Parts read like the hopes and fears of the adventures of the pioneers of the East India Companies. Parts recall

[104] Richards and Elliott, *Julia Ward Howe*, I, 337.
[105] Richards and Elliott, *Julia Ward Howe*, I, 338.

the South Sea Bubble, and parts the Spanish pursuit of Eldorado in Mexico and Peru; parts the French Buccaneers, while parts were enacted by lovers of chivalrous and dangerous adventure [how many besides Howe fitted into this category?], imitators of the noble Quixot[e] whose high aim ever was to redress wrongs, put down evil doers, and lift up the fallen and oppressed.[106]

The best one can say of Howe's part was that he meant well, but that he strayed far beyond his depth in trying to match wits with the wolves of Wall Street.

V

Howe the revolutionist, Howe the teacher, Howe the journalist, Howe the abolitionist, and Howe the patriot, in all of these he attained great distinction; but as Howe the empire-builder and adviser of presidents, he was a wretched dupe and miserable failure. In a period characterized by resurgent imperialism, when the leading nations of Europe led in the looting of the world's backward areas, he had sought to bring enlightenment and the "American Way of Life" (which he thought meant democracy, liberty, and social justice) to an "unprogressive" society. In reality he partook in a scheme as unrestrained and ruthless as one could find.

That it failed, that America refused to annex Santo Domingo or back up the claims of the Samana Bay Company, is only partially a tribute to the good sense and fairness of such men as Sumner and Schurz who opposed it openly, and of Fish who refused to press it. The true reason lay in the fact that America was too busy developing its industries and building up its unsettled regions to care about opportunities on a steamy, insect-ridden island. The absorption of Santo Domingo would have brought a serious race problem in addition to the one the United States already had. Santo Domingo, so far as Americans were concerned, was not worth taking.

---

[106] Howe, "My Experiences in Santo Domingo," p. 67.

XIX

Husband and Father

In 1868 Howe received an honorary LL.D. from his alma mater, Brown University, in recognition of his humanitarian accomplishments.[1] His achievements were common knowledge; his fame was widespread; his position in the hearts of men seemed secure. Nothing was stranger to his children than that their mother should eclipse him. In the home his vibrant personality had dominated and cowered them all.[2] As in everything else, there too he sought to be undisputed leader.

I

Too restless to inhabit any quarters for too long a time, Howe kept his family on the move. The first of many homes was the "Doctor's Wing" of the Perkins Institution to which he brought his wife and baby on their return from Europe in September 1844. To gain more privacy as the family increased, a few years later he bought a small estate near Perkins. A quaint house, estimated to be over two centuries old, stood there. He repaired the building, added a wing, and landscaped the grounds. Julia was so excited at the thought of moving into her own home that, as she entered it for the first time, she cried out involuntarily, "This is green peace!"[3]

[1] Alexis Caswell to Howe, Nov. 23, 1868, #79, Howe Papers, Houghton.
[2] Maud Howe Elliott, *This Was My Newport* (Cambridge, 1944), p. 64.
[3] J. W. Howe, *Reminiscences*, p. 151. It is impossible to say where the house was. On the basis of an examination of old maps and pictures, one researcher has con-

The name stuck. Green Peace was always their favorite dwelling, where they spent some of their happiest years. During the fifties, sixties, and seventies the family for greater convenience lived in town, generally on Beacon Hill, while Green Peace was leased out, but the institution was always ready to receive them when for various reasons Howe found it expedient to reside there. Their summer estate was at Lawton's Valley and later Oak Glen, both of them near Newport, Rhode Island. Wherever they were, their home was a magnet for distinguished visitors, from penniless political refugees in America, who knew of his sympathy for revolutionists, to leading literary figures such as Arthur Hugh Clough.[4] Even old Orestes Brownson, the passions of the Common School Controversy of a quarter century earlier forgiven, was a guest at his dinner table.[5] It was always one of the high points of any stay in Boston to visit the home of the famous philanthropist and his charming wife.

II

Six children were born to Howe and Julia: Julia Romana, 1844, Florence, 1846, Henry Marion, 1848, Laura Elizabeth, 1850, Maud, 1854, and Samuel Gridley, Junior, 1859. (Practically a member of the family was cousin Francis Marion Crawford, Louisa's son, who was sent to America from his native Italy for his education.) They were an insufferably precocious crew who would have overshadowed any parents but the ones they had. Julia Romana, better known as "Dudekins," wrote plays and stories before she was ten, rather striking creations in which her father sometimes had to take a part, perhaps as one of the three bears.[6] Florence, who was named after Florence Nightingale, a good friend of her parents, invented dances which she performed in the parlor. As Lady Macbeth with a dagger

cluded it was probably at the present junction of G and East Fifth Streets in South Boston, Allan J. Doherty to Laura E. Richards, Dec. 26, 1936, Howe Papers, Houghton.

[4] J. W. Howe, *Reminiscences;* Florence Howe Hall, *Memories Grave and Gay;* Laura E. Richards, *Stepping Westward* (New York, 1931); and Maud Elliott, *Three Generations* (Boston, 1923), *passim.*

[5] Howe to Mrs. Mary Eliot Parkman, Jan. 22, 186? Marvin Papers, Houghton.

[6] Florence Hall, *Memories Grave and Gay,* p. 34.

in her hand, she "crept and rushed and pranced and swooped about in a most terrifying manner. . . . A sofa-pillow played the part of Duncan, and had a very hard time of it." No less tragic was her "Julius Caesar" dance in which all taking part had a grand time stabbing right and left with sticks of kindling wood.[7]

As the only son for many years, Henry Marion, so christened in memory of Julia's two dead brothers, occupied a special place in the family's affections. When he was born, March 2, 1848, his overjoyed father wrote in the family Bible, *"Dieu donné!"* Then, with his mind full of the revolutions sweeping Europe at the time, he added, *"Liberté, Egalité, Fraternité!"* [8] A true son of his father, Harry was "by nature a Very Imp." Not two years old when he began to pull the tails of all the little dogs he met, the love of mischief was rooted in him by inheritance.[9] It is not likely that he needed much inspiration from his father who loved to regale all of the children with his juvenile reminiscences. Howe generally concluded each recital with the confession that he was a very naughty boy, "and Harry must never do such things. (But Harry did!)" [10]

Two years younger, Laura Elizabeth, named in honor of Perkins' most famous alumna, was Harry's natural playmate and usually his victim. Since relatives, teachers, and cats fell afoul of his wiles, one can imagine what his little sister, who always trailed him, must have put up with.[11]

Maud (Julia liked the name) was the youngest daughter, and possibly the most beautiful of them all. At her birth Parker begged to be allowed to adopt her. After all, he reasoned, the Howes had four other children, while he had none. He would name her Theodora and make her his heir.[12] Parker's childlessness was one of the sorrows of his life. Frequently he catechized his wife:

[7] Laura E. Richards, *When I Was Your Age* (Boston, 1894), pp. 15–22.

[8] Richards and Elliott, *Julia Ward Howe*, I, 130–131.

[9] Richards, *When I Was Your Age*, p. 36; Richards, *Stepping Westward*, pp. 19–20, for more of his stunts.

[10] Richards, *When I Was Your Age*, p. 91.

[11] Richards, *When I Was Your Age*, pp. 39–40.

[12] Elliott, *Three Generations*, p. 6. Laura Richards says the name would have been Thyrza, *Stepping Westward*, p. 23.

Question. What are you?
Answer. A bear.
Question. What must this bear do to be saved?
Answer. Have pups.[13]

But it was not to be, there never were any "pups," and Howe, much as he felt for Parker's disappointment, would never give up one of his children.

The family treasures were a source of wonder to the children. The tall hat tree that stood in the hall wherever they lived was one of the most prominent features of the household. On its topmost peg was Lord Byron's helmet, a souvenir picked up by Howe in Greece at an auction. It was Laura's plaything since it fit only her.[14] The little American girl was proud to know that she had a head like a great poet's. Not quite so pleasurable was another relic, the brain of Theodore Parker, sent to Howe by the physicians who attended the clergyman at his death in Florence. An object of horror to the recipient and the entire household, it languished on the top shelf of a cupboard.[15] Then there was Julia's Chickering grand piano. How the children loved to gather around it to sing songs in different languages while their mother accompanied them. The most striking acquisition in later years was a carriage ordered by Jefferson Davis, but not finished until after the war began. Dubbed the "Jefferson Davis," it served as the Howe coach for many years.[16]

The children were occasionally oppressed by the sense of greatness that surrounded them. "We could not fail to notice that our parents were above the average," wrote Maud. "Everybody told us so; almost every word of theirs proved it." The effect on her at least was depressing. She felt she had no individuality. Everywhere she went she was known only as the daughter of either Dr. Howe or Mrs. Howe. Nothing she did seemed worthwhile because she

---

[13] Elliott, *Three Generations*, p. 5.
[14] Maud Elliott, *Lord Byron's Helmet* (Boston, 1927), p. 27; Richards, *Stepping Westward*, p. 7.
[15] Richards, *Stepping Westward*, p. 18.
[16] Hall, *Memories Grave and Gay*, p. 140.

knew she would never "match up" to them. "Was I never to get out of the shadow of these two monumental persons, who . . . had brought me into the world?" she wondered on occasion. She tried to make her own friends and strike out on her own, only to find that she owed these friendships to the fact that "I was the daughter of S.G.H. and J.W.H." [17] Nevertheless, Maud, like the rest of her sisters, loved her father. He was like a god to them.

III

All of Howe's warmth, kindness, and gentleness went out to his children. Firm, harsh, and unbending with evil-doers, he softened on contact with the innocence and charm of childhood. His four daughters and two sons were his chief delight in a world that would have been unbearable without them. Separation from them made him ill.[18] When he fled to Canada in December 1859, he took their pictures with him. Placing the photographs on a table near his bed, they were the last thing he saw at night, the first on arising.[19] He romped with them, acted in their plays, and kept them entranced with tales of his boyhood and of his years in Greece. When they complained of the food as in the best of homes, his ready question was how would they like to eat toasted wasps as he used to when he was a soldier.[20] Tone deaf though he was (none could guess what tune he was torturing until he shouted out "Oh — Su-san-na!"), he would even sing with them.[21] The parties he arranged for them were always gay. His sympathy and understanding for children was so great, Longfellow noted, that he managed such matters admirably.[22]

Howe's experience as the head of two educational institutions had shown him that many women who never expected to earn

[17] Elliott, *This Was My Newport*, p. 64.

[18] Howe to Sumner, Sept. 26, 1850, Howe Papers, Houghton.

[19] F. W. Bird, "Remarks," in *Memoir of Dr. Samuel Gridley Howe* (Boston, 1876), p. 97. Parker reminisced in 1859 of a time ten years before when Howe, after accompanying him to Portland, Maine, felt so anxious about his daughters that he rushed back to Boston, Aug. 8, 1859, Journal, IV, AUA.

[20] Elliott, *Lord Byron's Helmet*, p. 28; Richards, *Samuel Gridley Howe*, pp. 16–17.

[21] Richards, *When I Was Your Age*, pp. 91–92.

[22] Samuel Longfellow, *Henry Wadsworth Longfellow*, II, 238.

their own living are often obliged to do so. Hence when his daughters grew up he insisted that they be taught to support themselves. Consequently Florence and Maud learned bookkeeping. The former kept the books of the Idiot School for some years, and the latter took care of the family accounts.[23] Julia Romana taught Latin, French, and German at Perkins.[24]

The doting father's efforts to have his girls become skilled in the domestic arts failed. His crew of intellectuals could never learn to duplicate the excellent jams and jellies his nieces, the daughters of his elder brother Joseph (known familiarly as Hpesoj, the "H" silent as in hour), made. As Maud explained it, "The children of eagles are eaglets; eagle parents cannot hope to raise a brood of doves!" [25] He should have found consolation in the fact that his daughters could write better than their stodgy cousins on Ashburton Place.

Should anything happen to one of his children, Howe felt that he would not survive.[26] Tragedy struck the Howe family in May 1863, when Samuel Gridley, Junior, the last and dearest of them all, died. Born on Christmas morning, 1859, just after Howe's return from Canada, he was the true "Samuel South Boston . . . a hale hearty fellow, hailing from Cuba." [27] A beautiful baby, he comforted Howe during his few moments away from war work, and was the companion of Julia during her husband's long absences.[28] The child's death crushed them both. They felt "baptised into a new order of suffering" which made earth a place "sown with tears, with the beauty and the glory gone out of it." They discovered that those who had lost children "can never be like those who have not." [29] They never forgot Sammy or ceased to mourn him.

Possibly grief underlay the intensity of Howe's work on the American Freedmen's Inquiry Commission, which was just getting

---

[23] Hall, *Memories Grave and Gay*, p. 176; Elliott, *Three Generations*, p. 88.
[24] Hall, *Memories Grave and Gay*, p. 178.
[25] Elliott, *Three Generations*, p. 37.
[26] Howe to Annie Mailliard, Aug. 19, 18??, #819, Howe Papers, Houghton.
[27] Howe to Parker, Jan. 22, 1860, Howe Papers, Houghton.
[28] Richards and Elliott, *Julia Ward Howe*, I, 178.
[29] J. W. Howe to Annie Mailliard, May 22, 1863, Howe Papers, Houghton.

under way. In the succeeding months he visited Virginia, assisted in the preparation of the *Preliminary Report,* and spent the summer in Canada gathering material for his *Refugees from Slavery in Canada West.*

IV

It was much more difficult to be the wife of Samuel Gridley Howe than to be one of his children, as Julia Ward found out. "Life with a Comet-Apostle was not always easy," their daughters have written, succinctly understating the issue.[30] Chev had brought his bride to a strange city where he introduced her to a strange way of life. Adjustment presented its difficulties. From the wealth and luxury of her New York home to the cold drabness of South Boston and the depressing atmosphere of institutional living was about as great a break as could have come to her.

Although her heart remained in the practice and study of music, art, and poetry, she now had to become a housewife, and learn to perform the household tasks of cleaning, cooking, and raising babies. Notwithstanding her sketchy knowledge of the culinary arts, she settled down to the problem of preparing the elaborate dinners her husband desired for the frequent meetings of the Five of Clubs.[31] She tried hard, but she never became much of a cook.

Things might have been easier had Howe understood her problems, but that was beyond him. Blind children and mental defectives needed education, slaves had to be freed, prisoners regenerated, and Sumner elected to the Senate. These were people who needed help. Julia was young and strong, perfectly capable of taking care of herself. It never occurred to him that babies, especially when born at twenty-month intervals to a society belle, present crushing problems too. Julia was left alone with two infant daughters, and no one to turn to for help. "I used to sit with one upon each knee, and cry in very helplessness when they cried," she wrote during the early days of her motherhood, when she still had only two children.[32] Where was Howe? Julia knew:

[30] Richards and Elliott, *Julia Ward Howe,* I, 150.
[31] Richards and Elliott, *Julia Ward Howe,* I, 110.
[32] J. W. Howe to Louisa Crawford, Nov. 31 [*sic*], 1847, Howe Papers, Houghton.

Rero rero riddlety rad,
This morning my baby caught sight of her Dad,
Quoth she, "Oh Daddy, where have you been?"
"With Mann and Sumner a-putting down sin!" [33]

As Julia became accustomed to Boston and her new life, she began to feel better. As the children grew older, and she had more free time, she even assisted her husband in his work during his tenure on the *Commonwealth*. She began to go out more to the theaters and concert halls, in particular the splendid *Howard Athenaeum* which opened in October 1846, and the Music Hall, 1852. She also resumed her writing. In 1853, her first book, *Passion Flowers,* appeared, meeting with great success. Although published anonymously, its authorship was no secret.

V

The difference in ages between Howe and Julia grew more marked as he aged. When he was in his sixties, declining in bodily strength, she was only in her forties, still in the prime of life, and vigorous. The children had grown beyond the stage where they needed constant care. After the death of her son, Julia had much time to herself. She stepped up the pace of her literary activity in the year following the funeral, writing out lectures on ethics, the duality of character, and a series on religion, which she began to deliver before small groups.[34] Now it was she who was away from home. Howe, becoming more irascible with the years, objected to her outside activities. Such behavior on the part of a woman seemed improper to him. Nevertheless, he had to admit defeat. In his last years, he was no longer surprised by anything she did, even when she began agitating for woman suffrage.

Surely women have the right of suffrage [he told Finlay]; and will obtain it soon: but zeal in pursuit of it, does not justify neglect of domestic relations and occupation; nor attempts to abolish those differ-

---

[33] Richards and Elliott, *Julia Ward Howe,* I, 121.

[34] J. W. Howe Diary, May 27, 1864, quoted in Richards and Elliott, *Julia Ward Howe,* I, 199.

ences in our political and social sphere and duties, which spring out of difference in the very organization of the sexes.[35]

Howe was a reformer, not a revolutionist; the "modern woman" was too much for him.

VI

Chev was getting on. With one exception, the children were married, and he was now a grandfather. Only Maud lived at home. The venerable Dr. Howe looked leonine, his copious hair now streaked with gray hung long and shaggy; his beard, which he no longer dyed, was completely white and much bushier than it had been. Where the skin showed through, one saw a face lined and wrinkled. The weaknesses of old age attacked him. To his recurrent malaria were now added rheumatism, neuralgia, and heart "affection" as well. In acute discomfort much of the time, he wished now to live only long enough to see his youngest daughter married.[36]

At the age of seventy-one, he at last began to curtail his activities. In September 1873, he submitted his resignation from the Chairmanship of the Board of State Charities which the Board accepted October 15, 1874.[37] Sanborn succeeded him as Chairman although Howe retained his membership on the Board. He was also absent from Perkins much of the time, leaving the actual administration in the hands of his son-in-law, Michael Anagnos, who proved himself a worthy successor.

As the winter climate of Boston was too severe, Howe eagerly accepted the opportunity to spend the cold months in Santo Domingo as the representative of the Samana Bay Company. Julia accompanied him. Used to his whims and passions, she found him pathetic in these days of declining strength. Perched in an eyrie overlooking the bay, they lived a pleasant life in the pursuit of

[35] Howe to Finlay (transcript), Aug. 13, 1874, Howe Papers, Houghton.
[36] Howe to Sumner, Sept. 7, 1873, Howe Papers, Houghton.
[37] Howe to Sanborn, Sept. 25, 1873, Howe Papers, Houghton, Board of State Charities, *Eleventh Report, 1874, Mass. Pub. Doc. #17* (Jan. 1875), p. lxxxi.

their own activities. His health improved remarkably, to the point where he rode daily.[38] Still, he missed his home:

Dear old Boston! I long to see you again as soon as the rugged winter which meets & throttles you like an enemy is gone. And I trust I shall enter your streets & walk over the stumps of the Paddock elms, before the middle of March; & dine with the boys every Saturday afternoon.[39]

He returned in May to a world grown suddenly cold. Sumner was dead. The news, reaching him at Samana Bay, filled him with sorrow.[40] He was now the "last leaf" on the bough. For years he had watched the "circle of light & warmth" grow "less & less" as the "light of old friendships" went out almost every day. In America there had been Horace Mann, Theodore Parker, and Charles Sumner. In Greece there had been George Finlay with whom he had corresponded for almost a half century. These were men "whose esteem & warm friendship to have enjoyed, give a value & charm to my life; the last twenty five years of which would, without some such comfort & without the love of children, have been an utter blank." [41]

His illness returning to him almost immediately on his return, he suffered constantly throughout the succeeding summer as he worked on his "forty-third Report," in which he summarized his work at Perkins. Recognizing the symptoms of his end, he bided his time. There was still fight left in him though. He felt Sumner had been wrong about the annexation of Santo Domingo, and much as he hated to detract from the great statesman's achievements, he said so publicly. Bird rebuked him for this unkindness to the dead man's memory.

Alas! Alas! Alas! That before the sod is green over dear Sumner's grave *you* should speak of *him* as "blinded by passion & prejudice" — of him who, if ever mortal man did, kept his soul swept & garnished.

[38] J. W. Howe to Annie Mailliard, April 8, 1874, Howe Papers, Houghton.

[39] Howe to Bird, April 9, 1874, Howe Papers, Houghton. He probably meant May. Edward Waldo Emerson, *The Early Years of the Saturday Club* (Boston, 1918), has scattered references to Howe.

[40] Howe to Bird, April 9, 1874, Howe Papers, Houghton.

[41] Howe to Sumner, Sept. 7, 1873, Howe Papers, Houghton.

I have never told you & I now almost swear I never will how dearly he loved you, & how tenderly he moaned over the change in your feelings towards him.[42]

Howe was humbled. He too regretted their difference of opinion, although Bird was wrong in saying it had brought any change in feeling. More clearly than ever, he now appreciated the purity of Sumner's motives in everything he did.

Would I were worthy of the affection which he accorded to me during so many years of an intimacy as great as between brothers; & greater than between ordinary brothers.

Ah! the times when we walked or drove daily together; spent our evenings together; & finally retiring to our chambers, with a door open between them, talked & communed about matters, great or small, until one dropped asleep with the music of the others voice subsiding from audible words, into the music of dreams! Dear Charlie! the hope of renewed youthful intercourse, makes immortality all the more desirable; although by no immortal spirit can chaster purer, nobler, sentiment be expressed, than were expressed by thy mortal lips! Never an impure word, never a selfish wish; never a dishonest purpose.[43]

VII

Howe lingered on, growing weaker and more irritable. At times, he was not himself. He was so weak during the summer of 1875 that he needed almost constant attention. Julia cared for him much of the time.

Howe presided at Sunday dinner for the last time on January 2, 1876. Two days later came his final attack. He lay senseless the next day, with neither speech nor recognition from him, his eyes open and sightless. The family remained in constant attendance. All hope was gone.

On the morning of the ninth, Laura Bridgman came to his bedside to kiss him farewell. The family maintained its death watch. About noon, Julia went to her room to prepare herself for the arrival of the Reverend James Freeman Clarke. A few moments

[42] Bird to Howe, Aug. 1, 1874, Howe Papers, Houghton.
[43] Howe to Bird, Aug. 12, 1874, Howe Papers, Houghton.

later, Mrs. McDonald, the matron of Perkins, summoned her urgently. "I came & found the breathing changed to gasping, very gentle & not painful to witness. Maud fell into Hysterics & faintings, — the rest all quiet." It was about 12:20 P.M.

The last of the circle was gone. Its central figure, he was the most worldly of the lot. Although exceeded in general learning by Sumner, in abstract thought by Parker, and in educational theory by Mann, Howe knew more of society, and understood people, and the ways of man, better than any of them. Without their quirks of character and their narrowness, he did nevertheless have his own flaws. He could be harsh and unfair to his opponents, and he was; but in most matters he was kind, considerate, selfless in devotion to right, truth, duty, and justice. His only serious intellectual failing was his inability to realize that not all his fellow men, infinitely perfectible though he thought them, were as willing as he and his friends to concern themselves over the problems of those weak, helpless souls who could not help themselves.

Julia understood all that now when, a month after his splendid funeral, there was a great memorial meeting in the Boston Music Hall. Governor Alexander H. Rice presided and many leading figures spoke.[44] Julia understood all now:

I have had my share of a very high and noble companionship, alas! profiting so little by its' [sic] manifold opportunities of good. . . . I sit at my desk with the beloved books, dictionaries & papers about me. I ask, what have I done? He, my dear one, built up such noble undertakings. In this Community, those who understand the public work, find traces of him everywhere. Unfortunates of nearly every class bless his aid, his watchful benevolence. . . . Oh happiest of men, to have left such a record.[45]

Progress had been Howe's watchword, and because he had believed in it, and fought for it, mankind had progressed. "Oh happiest of men," indeed, to have made the world a better place.

[44] The proceedings of the memorial meeting, held Feb. 8, 1876, are to be found in Julia Ward Howe, *Memoir of Dr. Samuel Gridley Howe* (Boston, 1876).
[45] J. W. Howe to "Lizzie," Feb. 15, 1876, Howe Papers, Houghton.

Note on the Manuscript Sources

This work is based mainly on contemporary materials: letters, newspapers, addresses, and magazine articles. Fortunately Howe and his associates were articulate men who preserved the letters they wrote and received, and signed their names to what they published.

Howe's manuscripts are to be found in four different collections in three libraries. The letters and journals of his years in Greece are in the Houghton Library of Harvard University. While most of the journals are in Howe's own hand, those of the later years are available only in typescript. The author does not know where the originals are, and has never sought them.

The majority of Howe's letters are in the Howe family papers, also in Houghton. This is a vast collection of several thousand items, containing letters by and to most of the members of the family. They range in date from the 1820's to mid-twentieth century and are still being added to. Unfortunately, there is one serious gap in the collection, Howe's correspondence during the 1830's. During these years Howe was extremely active professionally and socially. Were letters available, we would very likely have answers to many questions concerning his social life about which we can only conjecture now, such as the engagement to Marian Marshall that Elizabeth Peabody reported.

The collection of Howe papers at the Massachusetts Historical Society contains material relating to Kansas affairs during the 1850's, and other scattered items.

Surprisingly enough, the Perkins School at Watertown has custody of Howe's letters about his activities in Crete, Santo Domingo, and the Samana Bay Company.

The manuscripts of other persons do much to clarify Howe's work in various fields. The Laura Bridgman Papers, also at Perkins, are especially valuable for the insights they offer into his work as teacher. This collection includes the extant thirteen journals of her teachers, her own journals, and much of her correspondence, in addition to scrapbooks of newspaper clippings. Laura's own handwriting is at times rather difficult to read, but worth the effort. Her journals are fascinating; only less so are those of her teachers.

The papers of Howe's friends are also valuable, since they contain many letters by Howe, as well as references to him in many others. The collection of Thomas Wentworth Higginson's papers at Houghton, while concerned primarily with Higginson's literary activities, also contains a good deal about his abolitionist work. Horace Mann's letters and journal at the Massachusetts Historical Society are indispensable for anyone doing work on the Common School Controversy, as well as abolition. The letterbooks of Theodore Parker, also at the Massachusetts Historical Society, are uncatalogued, but if one goes through them page by page, much valuable material on a variety of subjects will be found. The same is true of Parker's journal, deposited at the library of the American Unitarian Association in Boston. The volumes are of the greatest significance for an understanding of his mind. Unfortunately, in spots they are illegible, or at best decipherable only after great effort. They should be published by some hardy editor with good eyesight, and a public-spirited publisher who can stand the financial strain.

Also at Houghton are the papers of Charles Sumner, for thirty-five years Howe's closest friend and confidant; Sumner's papers are extremely important. While most of Howe's letters were torn from their places in the letterbooks and returned to the family on the Senator's death, some still remain, as well as many of Sumner's letters in answer to Howe's. The two collections taken together constitute a correspondence which bridges the most active years of each man, and offers insight into the development of their characters.

Other manuscripts offer important bits on more limited aspects of Howe's work. The Louis Agassiz papers in Houghton contain the correspondence between Agassiz and Howe during the summer of 1863 on the future of the Negro in America. The questionnaires prepared by the American Freedmen's Inquiry Commission, along with responses received, are available at Houghton in a collection presented by Howe.

John Brown's Diary at the Boston Public Library, and material about Brown compiled by Thomas Wentworth Higginson, also at Boston, contain much useful material, as does a collection relating to Brown presented to the Massachusetts Historical Society by Amos A. Lawrence. The Columbia University Library also possesses materials on Brown, presented by Oswald Garrison Villard, which are mostly transcripts of papers in other libraries from Boston to Kansas.

The papers of John Albion Andrew, Richard Henry Dana, Jr., Edward Everett, Amos A. Lawrence, The New England Emigrant Aid Company, and Robert C. Winthrop, all at the Massachusetts Historical Society, have interesting bits concerning Howe's abolitionist activities.

The James Freeman Clarke Family Papers, and the papers of Dorothea Lynde Dix at Houghton, also contain much useful information.

OTHER MATERIAL

Persons interested in pursuing any subject further can find a complete listing of printed materials either by consulting the bibliography of my doctoral dissertation on deposit in Widener, or by examining the references in the text which are rather complete.

Index

Harvard Historical Studies

(Early titles now out of print are omitted.)

Genesis of Napoleonic Imperialism. 1938.

42. *Ernst Christian Helmreich.* The Diplomacy of the Balkan Wars, 1912–1913. 1938.

43. *Albert Henry Imlah.* Lord Ellenborough: A Biography of Edward Law, Earl of Ellenborough, Governor-General of India. 1939.

44. *Vincent Mary Scramuzza.* The Emperor Claudius. 1940.

45. *Richard William Leopold.* Robert Dale Owen. 1940.

46. *Gerald Sandford Graham.* Sea Power and British North America, 1783–1820. 1941.

47. *William Farr Church.* Constitutional Thought in Sixteenth-Century France. 1941.

48. *Jack H. Hexter.* The Reign of King Pym. 1941.

49. *George Hoover Rupp.* A Wavering Friendship: Russia and Austria, 1876–1878. 1941.

51. *Frank Edgar Bailey.* British Policy and the Turkish Reform Movement. 1942.

52. *John Black Sirich.* The Revolutionary Committees in the Departments of France. 1943.

53. *Henry Frederick Schwarz.* The Imperial Privy Council in the Seventeenth Century. 1943.

54. *Aaron Ignatius Abell.* Urban Impact on American Protestantism. 1943.

55. *Holden Furber.* John Company at Work. 1948.

56. *Walter Howe.* The Mining Guild of New Spain and Its Tribunal General. 1949.

57. *John Howes Gleason.* The Genesis of Russophobia in Great Britain. 1950.

58. *Charles Coulston Gillispie.* Genesis and Geology: A Study in the Relations of Scientific Thought, Natural Theology, and Social Opinion in Great Britain, 1790–1850. 1951.

59. *Richard Humphrey.* Georges Sorel, Prophet without Honor: A Study in Anti-intellectualism. 1951.

60. *Robert G(eorge) L(eeson) Waite.* Vanguard of Nazism: The Free Corps Movement in Postwar Germany 1918–1923. 1952.

61. *Nicholas V(alentine) Riasanovsky.* Russia and the West in the Teaching of the Slavophiles. 1952.

62. *John King Fairbank.* The Opening of the Treaty Ports: Trade and Diplomacy on the China Coast 1842–1854. Vol. I, text. 1953.

63. *John King Fairbank.* The Opening of the Treaty Ports . . . Vol. II, reference material. 1953.

64. *Franklin L. Ford.* Robe and Sword: The Regrouping of the French Aristocracy after Louis XIV. 1953.

65. *Carl E. Schorske.* German Social Democracy, 1905–1917. The Development of the Great Schism. 1955.

66. *Wallace Evan Davies.* Patriotism on Parade: The Story of Veterans' and Hereditary Organizations in America, 1783–1900. 1955.

DATE DUE

DEC 2 '64			
NOV 27 '65			